FEDERAL CORPORATE TAXATION

SIXTH EDITION

By

HOWARD E. ABRAMS
Professor of Law
Emory University

and

RICHARD L. DOERNBERG
K. H. Gyr Professor of Law
Emory University

FOUNDATION PRESS

WEST

© 1987, 1990, 1995, 1998, 2002 FOUNDATION PRESS
© 2008 By FOUNDATION PRESS
   395 Hudson Street
   New York, NY 10014
   Phone Toll Free 1–877–888–1330
   Fax (212) 367–6799
   foundation–press.com
Printed in the United States of America

ISBN 978–1–58778–995–3

TEXT IS PRINTED ON 10% POST CONSUMER RECYCLED PAPER

PREFACE

This book is aimed at students taking a course in corporate taxation. We hope it will serve to aid and to enrich students' understanding of what is unquestionably dense and difficult statutory material. Because the focus of the book is on corporation taxation, little attention is paid to those topics normally covered in an individual tax course. Accordingly, the tax consequences of day-to-day corporate operations (e.g., what constitutes income, what is deductible under § 162, depreciation methods) are not emphasized.

As the tax system in general and the corporate tax provisions specifically reach greater heights (or depths) of complexity, it becomes more important than ever to understand the framework of the system – the big picture. Failure to do so will condemn a student to a purgatory of isolated rules, seemingly unconnected to one another. Even with a framework, the intricacies can be overwhelming. This book is purposely noncomprehensive: it is not a treatise. Our goal is to find and contemplate the forest rather than each tree. On the other hand, if we avoid all the trees, we would not know much about the forest.

We have tried to look at corporate tax through a variety of perspectives. Where appropriate, historical and economic analyses are offered. But much of what follows is a search for an internal logic and consistency in the corporate tax system itself: given the goals of a corporate tax structure, how do the rules implement those goals. The internal logic, or lack thereof, is what many students find appealing about the study of tax. In order to keep the book manageable in length, there are places where we can do no more than introduce intriguing ideas tangential to the subject at hand.

This book takes a "cradle-to-grave" approach to corporate taxation. We believe that this presentation is easiest for students. We also have no doubt that other approaches are equally worthwhile. With that in mind, we have tried to make each chapter stand alone so that the chapters can be read out of order. For example, Chapter 1 dealing with some policy questions will perhaps make more sense if it is read at the end of the book. Chapter 2 considers the formation or birth of a corporation – § 351 and related provisions. Chapter 3 then looks at a collection of issues relating to the operation of a corporation once formed. Matters such as tax rates, the minimum tax, capital structure and the corporation as an entity are discussed. Chapters 4 through 7 deal with nonliquidating distributions: dividends, redemptions, stock dividends, and preferred stock bailouts.

In Chapter 8, liquidation of a corporation is the subject. Chapters 9 through 11 focus on corporate acquisitions. Chapter 9 addresses taxable acquisitions, while Chapter 10 considers tax-free reorganizations. In Chapter 11, the carryover of tax attributes in both taxable and nontaxable corporate acquisitions is explored. The final two chapters are concerned with subjects that are covered in some basis corporate tax courses but not in others. Chapter 12 explains the corporate penalty provisions while Chapter 13 dissects the intricacies of subchapter S.

While this is not a casebook, leading cases are discussed and cited where they are helpful to the discussion. Throughout the book, we have liberally cited to the Code and regulations. We believe that it is the ability to read and understand the Code that will make the study of corporate taxation a joyous occasion. Indeed, it is probably wise to show your ambidextrous talent by reading this book simultaneously with the Code.

In short, we hope that this primer will help students solve or at least understand some of the wondrous mysteries of corporate taxation. Many of you were hooked on tax by your individual tax course. We hope to sink the hook deeper.

We wish to thank the students of Emory Law School for their helpful suggestions. We also wish to thank three of our colleagues at Deloitte & Touche, LLP: Mr. Larry Axelrod for his assistance with affiliated corporations, Mr. Michael Lux for his assistance on the Chapter covering S corporations, and Mr. Fred T. Witt for his help on bankruptcy reorganizations. Finally, we wish to thank Professor Bernie Wolfman of the Harvard Law School whose contributions to the teaching of corporate tax are pervasive. Of course, the errors are ours alone.

This book is current through October 1, 2007.

HOWARD E. ABRAMS
RICHARD L. DOERNBERG

Emory University
October 2007

iv

TABLE OF CONTENTS

*

FEDERAL CORPORATE TAXATION

*

CHAPTER 1. THE CORPORATE DOUBLE TAX

1.01 Introduction and History. We have had a corporate income tax continuously since 1909, longer than we have had a personal income tax. Prior to enactment of the sixteenth amendment, the Supreme Court upheld the 1909 corporate tax as a valid excise tax imposed on businesses exercising the privilege of operating in corporate form.[1] With the passage of the sixteenth amendment, the constitutional foundation of the corporate income tax is secure whether characterized as an excise tax or as an income tax.

The basic premise underlying subchapter C[2] is that a corporation should be a taxpayer distinct from its shareholders. From this premise follows the central feature of corporate taxation: the double tax on corporate profits. The first tax on corporate profits is imposed at the corporate level when profits are earned by a corporation. The second tax is imposed at the shareholder level when these profits are distributed by the corporation to its shareholders. Because the distributing corporation is not entitled to deduct amounts distributed as dividends, the over-all effect of this system of taxation is to impose a double tax on distributed corporate profits.

One of the early issues faced by the courts under the corporate income tax was the proper treatment to a corporation distributing appreciated property as a dividend. Despite the government's argument that the corporation ought to recognize gain on the distribution as if the property had been sold, the Supreme Court held that no gain or loss could be recognized at the corporate-level. This rule, known as the *General Utilities* doctrine,[3] opened the door to avoidance of the corporate-level tax by causing corporations to distribute

---

1. *Flint v. Stone Tracy Co.*, 220 U.S. 107 (1911). In *Pollock v. Farmers' Loan & Trust Co.*, 158 U.S. 601 (1895), the Supreme Court invalidated the first federal personal income tax as a direct tax requiring apportionment under article 1, clause 9 of the Constitution. As part of that early decision the Court also invalidated a corporate income tax too intertwined with the personal income tax to stand on its own.

2. The Internal Revenue Code is divided into a number of "subtitles," each subtitle into "chapters," each chapter into "subchapters," and each subchapter into "parts." Thus, the study of the code is something like the study of living organisms, with species replaced by parts, genus replaced by subchapters, etc. Most of the rules of corporate taxation are in sections 301 through 386, those sections comprising subchapter C (corporate distributions and adjustments) of Chapter 1 (normal taxes and surtaxes) of subtitle A (income taxes).

3. See Section 4.04 *infra*.

appreciated assets in anticipation of sale. The *General Utilities* doctrine and the congressional attempts to circumscribe its potential for abuse influenced much of the development of subchapter C.

Several tax acts chipped away at the *General Utilities* doctrine, with its substantial repeal made part of the Tax Reform Act of 1986. Much of subchapter C has changed as a result, including not only the taxation of distributions but also the taxation of asset sales prior to liquidating distributions and the taxation of purchases of stock of one corporation by a second corporation. Critics of the *General Utilities* doctrine long argued that its repeal would simplify the Code. In theory they probably are right, but you will have to decide for yourself whether the congressional treatment of the repeal brought simplicity or new complexity.

Historically, distributed corporate profits were taxed as ordinary income to the shareholders. However, gain from the sale of corporate stock always has been treated as capital gain. Because the increase in value of corporate stock often reflects corporate profits that have not been distributed,[4] a shareholder wishing to obtain his share of the corporation's profits while avoiding ordinary income would be forced to sell his stock prior to declaration by the corporation of a dividend. In fact, in many circumstances the shareholder could sell his stock back to the issuing corporation and still qualify for capital gains treatment.[5] This relative favoritism of undistributed corporate profits taxed as capital gain as compared with distributed profits taxed as ordinary income has motivated many a taxpayer to avoid dividends in favor of other, less direct ways of obtaining corporate earnings.

You may be surprised to discover that you already know many of the rules governing the taxation of corporations. Like other taxpayers, corporations are subject to § 61 for determining their gross income. Thus, rents, royalties and interest are taxable to corporations just as to non-corporate taxpayers, as are gains from the sale or exchange of property. Similarly, corporations may deduct their ordinary and necessary business expenses under § 162, their interest payments under § 163, and their losses under § 165. The concern of subchapter C—and the concern of this book—is not on the various rules applicable to corporate and non-corporate taxpayers alike but rather on those rules applicable uniquely to corporations and their shareholders. For the most part, these rules deal with the transactions between a corporation and its shareholders.

---

4. Stock appreciation can result from market revaluation of the corporation's future prospects, from realized but undistributed corporate profits, and from unrealized appreciation in corporate assets.

5. See Chapter 5 *infra*.

1.02   Revenue Effects. The corporate tax raises substantial revenue, in round figures about $229 billion per year,[6] or a little more than 27 percent of the revenue raised by the individual income tax. Relatively few corporate returns are filed, though, with individual returns numbering about 132 million per year as compared with about 5.5 million corporate returns. The highest corporate tax rate is 35 percent.[7]

There is a second sense in which we have more than one corporate income tax, for there is the regular income tax and the alternative minimum tax. Discussed more fully elsewhere,[8] the alternative minimum tax ensures that profitable companies pay some federal tax even if they structure their investments to exploit every tax incentive in the Code. While not a substantial revenue raiser, the alternative minimum tax may respond to a widespread concern that wealthy taxpayers and large corporations are able to avoid paying their fair share of the federal tax burden.

1.03   The Incidence of the Corporate Tax. Because the corporate tax raises, both absolutely and relatively, a substantial amount of revenue, it is reasonable to ask who ends up paying the corporate income tax. By "paying the tax" we do not mean "tendering payment to the taxing authority" but rather who bears the economic burden of the tax, who is worse off by reason of that particular tax having to be paid.

To see the difference between the nominal payor of a tax and the party bearing the burden of the tax, consider the sales tax imposed under state law on most purchases of tangible goods. Suppose a hot dog vendor at an amusement park sells hot dogs for $1.00 apiece and charges no sales tax. One day, the vendor is told that he must remit four cents per dog to the state. If he changes his sign to read: "Hot Dogs: $1.00, tax included," and if you buy one dog, who ends up paying the tax?

Phrased differently, have you paid $0.96 for the hot dog plus $0.04 in tax, or did you pay $1.00 for the hot dog and the vendor paid the tax? The way to begin to answer this question is by asking

---

6.   These figures are for taxable years ending in 2004. Data on the number of returns filed, the amount of taxes paid, and a host of other tax-related information is publicly available from the Internal Revenue Service on its web page (www.irs.gov) and is published in the Statistics of Income Bulletin.

7.   § 11(b)(1)(D) (ignoring the surtax in the final flush language of § 11(b)(1)); *see* Section 3.01 *infra*.

8.   See Section 3.01 *infra*.

another: if no sales tax had been imposed, how much would you have paid for the hot dog? If the answer is $1.00, you have not paid the tax because, *tax or no tax,* you would be out the full $1.00.[9] Rather, it seems to be the vendor who has paid the tax because, *but for the tax,* he would have the full $1.00 to keep.

On the other hand, suppose the vendor changes his sign to read: "Hot Dogs: $1.00, plus tax." If you now purchase a hot dog, it is you and not the vendor who bears the burden of the tax because it is you who is worse off because of the tax.[10]

Return to the first example in which the price of the hot dog is $1.00 including tax, and assume that you paid no part of the tax. Does that imply that the full burden of the tax landed squarely on the shoulders of the vendor? Not necessarily. It may be that the vendor cut the pay to his employee slightly to offset the tax. In that case, the tax is borne by the employee. Or he might have told his supplier that he would change mustard brands because of the tax, and the supplier agreed to a price reduction to keep the vendor's business. In this case it is the supplier who has effectively paid the tax.

Where a tax ultimately lands is referred to as the "incidence" of the tax. As the above example demonstrates, the incidence of a tax may be hard to discover and is dependent on the business relations among large numbers of people. In the example, it is dependent on the price customers are willing to pay for hot dogs, on the wages that the vendor's employee is willing to accept, on the profit margins of the vendor and his supplier, and probably on a variety of other items such as the effect of the tax on the cotton candy distributor and other competitors of the hot dog vendor. Indeed, because the soft drink vendor may suffer if fewer hot dogs are sold, some of the burden of the tax may, indirectly, be felt by vendors not in competition with the one on whom the tax nominally is laid.

In general, the incidence of a tax nominally paid by one person will be divided in some proportion between the nominal payor and the persons with whom he deals.[11] In particular, the incidence of the tax need not (and usually will not) fall on any one person but

---

9. Assuming that the vendor has not changed the size of the hot dog, reduced the number of available condiments, limited the availability of napkins, or in any other way reduced the value of his product.

10. Perhaps the most likely response by the vendor to the tax is to change the price of his dogs to 99 cents plus tax, in which case only part of the tax is shifted to consumers.

11. See J. Pechman, Who Paid the Taxes, 1966–85, at 24–31 (1985); Harberger, *The Incidence of the Corporation Income Tax,* 70 J.Pol. Econ. 215 (1962).

may be shared in seemingly arbitrary ways. The customer might in effect bear one cent of the tax, the vendor one-half of one cent, and the remainder by the mustard supplier. Or the incidence might be entirely different depending on the ways in which the various economic actors in this little play adjust their relationships to account for the tax.[12]

Where is the incidence of the corporate tax? One thing that can be said without qualification is that *no* part of the corporate tax is borne by corporations: corporations do not bear taxes, only people do. A corporation is simply a nexus of contracts between individuals—shareholders, creditors, suppliers, customers, employees, etc. To be sure, it may be that the corporation's treasury is depleted because of a certain tax, and for that reason the equity owners of the corporation may be worse off by reason of the tax. In such a case, the incidence of the tax is on the corporation's stockholders, not on the corporation. On the other hand, it could be that a tax nominally paid by the corporation is shifted from the equity owners to the corporation's employees or suppliers. If so, we say that the tax has been shifted "backward." Conversely, the corporation may raise its price to cover the tax, in which case we say that the tax has been shifted "forward" to the corporation's customers.[13]

Can we determine empirically how the corporate tax is shifted around? The answer, as of now, is no—the task is simply beyond our means. Studies have been conducted and have suggested where the incidence might lie, but unfortunately these studies often conflict and even the best can only suggest possible answers.[14] It may be that someday the economists will have a good answer to this question, but that day is not yet here.

In trying to determine the incidence of the corporate tax, it is helpful to break down the problem into two smaller problems. First, who bears a tax immediately after it is imposed and before most individuals and companies can modify their behavior to account for the tax? That is, who bears the tax *in the short run*? Second, who bears the tax after sufficient time has passed to allow

---

12. Economists use the term "elasticity" to describe the extent to which a change in price or other factor affects economic behavior. With the proper definitions, the concept of "elasticity" can be quantified in such a way that predictions can be made regarding, for example, the incidence of a tax.

13. More accurately, raising the price of its product will not shift the tax fully forward unless the quantity of goods sold by the corporation does not change despite the price increase. Since quantity demanded usually falls as price rises, the price increase will fail to fully offset the tax, leaving some of it to be borne by the corporation's investors or shifted backward to its employees.

14. See generally J. Pechman, Federal Tax Policy 135–40 (4th ed. 1983); Klein, *The Incidence of the Corporation Income Tax: A Lawyer's View of a Problem in Economics*, 1965 Wis.L.Rev. 576.

for adjustments to the tax; that is, who bears the tax *in the long run?*

It may seem as if only the long run is relevant to the corporate tax because the corporate tax has been around a long time. Although it is true that we have had some corporate tax since 1909, we have had the current form of that tax only a short while: the corporate tax, like the individual tax, is changed by Congress almost annually in ways great and small.[15]

The various changes that Congress makes affect the incidence of the corporate tax. The short run effects of these changes can be substantial, substantial enough at times to warrant special *transition rules* intended to mitigate the costs of adjusting to the tax changes.[16] To frame the appropriate transition rules, one must predict short-run effects of legislation.

The short-run effect of increasing the corporate income tax should be to reduce the wealth of equity owners of corporations. If corporations are engaging in activities that maximize their profitability prior to the tax increase, the effect of the increase will be to lower the corporations' profits. Those holding residual interests in the corporations should be the first to suffer as a result.

Over the long-run, corporations will change their behavior in ways that minimize the effect of the tax increase on corporate profitability. Investors also will change their behavior, investing in corporations that best adapt to the new economic climate or investing in non-corporate enterprises. As investment capital is redeployed away from the corporate sector, average returns from corporate and non-corporate investments should tend to equalize. Thus, the burden of the corporate tax may be shifted to all investment capital, corporate and non-corporate alike.

Under some circumstances, investors may reduce the aggregate amount invested in all business enterprises, with a concomitant increase in personal consumption. Thus, the corporate tax may have a negative impact on the aggregate amount of savings in this country. Because of the variety of these possible long-run responses, estimation of long-run effects is considerably more complex than

---

15. See Doernberg & McChesney, *On the Accelerating Rate and Decreasing Durability of Tax Reform,* 71 Minn. L.Rev. 913 (1987).

16. See generally Graetz, *Legal Transitions: The Case for Retroactivity in Income Tax Revision,* 126 U.Pa. L.Rev. 47 (1977); Shachar, *From Income* to Consumption: Criteria for Rules of Transition,* 97 Harv.L.Rev. 1581 (1984); Abrams, *Rethinking Tax Transitions: A Reply to Dr. Shachar,* 98 Harv.L.Rev. 1809 (1985); Kaplow, *An Economic Analysis of Legal Transitions,* 99 Harv. L.Rev. 509 (1986).

estimation of the short-run effects. All we can know for sure is that people—not corporations—pay the corporate income tax.

1.04 Integrating the Corporate and Individual Income Taxes. Having seen that no one knows—and probably cannot know—which taxpayers actually bear the corporate income tax, what can we say about the legitimacy of the tax itself? It is of course within congressional power to levy a corporate tax, but does it make sense to do so?

The federal income tax primarily raises revenue—revenue used to pay for the federal government's various expenditures. The incidence of the income taxes accordingly determines in large measure the way in which the cost of government is divided. Reasonable people can differ over how that cost should be allocated.[17] Some argue that the cost of government should be spread among taxpayers in proportion to income, taxing all economic receipts at a single, flat rate. Others argue that taxpayers with substantial disposable income have a greater ability to pay and so should be taxed more heavily; that is, they argue in favor of a highly progressive income tax.

Can the corporate income tax satisfy anyone's notion of fairness? It may be that the corporate income tax is borne by the very wealthy, thereby satisfying at least those in favor of a "soak the rich" philosophy of taxation. It also could be that it falls primarily on consumers of corporate goods—that is, it falls on everyone—and so is reasonably consistent with flat rate taxation. The problem is, of course, that no one knows for sure and so no one can be satisfied.

Additional arguments can and have been raised against the corporate income tax. As we shall see, the tax encourages corporations to raise capital as debt rather than equity, arguably causing undue loan defaults and corporate bankruptcies. Also, to the extent that the corporate tax is not shifted forward or backward, it is borne by shareholders of profitable corporations, disproportionately by shareholders of the most profitable ones. If so, it will have the unfortunate effect of making inefficient producers competitive with their more efficient rivals to the detriment of consumers generally.

Why does Congress not eschew corporate taxation entirely, taxing only individuals?[18] Congress can levy the individual income tax using flat rates, progressive rates, or any other way it desires.[19]

---

17. Reasonable people can differ over the ideal level of government expenditure. But this analysis applies for any level of government expenditure.

18. See generally Joshua Mishkin, *The State of Integration in a Partial Integration State*, 59 Tax Law. 1047 (2006).

19. Of course, if the corporate tax is

By using an increased individual income tax in lieu of a corporate tax, the tax burden can be targeted more accurately. Does this suggest that the corporate tax is a low-cost tax from the legislator's perspective: revenue can be raised without particular taxpayers knowing—and complaining—that they are paying the tax?

If Congress wanted to eliminate the corporate income tax, what should it do? The answer, it turns out, is more difficult than first meets the eye, at least if the individual income tax rates are progressive. Suppose for example that Congress repealed the corporate income tax, making all corporations completely tax-exempt.

Taxpayer B wants to invest $100 in a taxable bond paying 8 percent per year for 20 years. If B purchases this bond directly, he will receive $8.00 of income for 20 years. If B is in the 28 percent bracket, his after-tax annual return will be 5.76 percent. Assuming that B can reinvest his after-tax returns in some other investment paying 8 percent per year, B will have $306.50 after 20 years.

On the other hand, suppose that B invests $100 in a corporation, and the corporation then purchases the bond. Assuming that the corporation receives $8.00 per year on the bond, and assuming also that the corporation can reinvest the bond interest in some other investment paying 8 percent per year, the corporation will have $466.10 after 20 years.[20] If that amount is distributed to B, he then will be taxed on a gain of $366.10, producing a tax liability of $102.51.[21] After paying his federal income taxes, B will be left with a total of $363.59.

How is it that B ends up with substantially more ($363.59 compared to $306.50) by causing the corporation to make the investment? By using the corporation, B has avoided the periodic imposition of tax on the bond interest, instead paying a tax only when that interest income is removed from corporate solution. In this example, B has managed to defer taxes on year one's interest for 19 years, on year two's interest for 18 years, etc. The total value of that deferral for B ends up worth $57.09, or more than half the amount of B's original investment.

As this example shows, simply abolishing the corporate-level income tax without making additional changes to the individual income tax offers deferral advantages to taxpayers willing to earn profits in corporate solution. Indeed, given the basis rule of § 1014

eliminated, the individual income tax (or some other tax) must be increased to raise the same aggregate revenue.

20. Of that amount, $366.10 will be interest and $100.00 will be B's initial principal.

21. B's stock basis equals $100 so that his gain under § 1001(a) will be $366.10. At a tax rate of 28%, B's tax liability is $102.51.

(which provides a fair market value basis for property, including stock, passing through the estate of a decedent), a taxpayer who invests in corporate form and holds the stock until death will avoid all taxation of gain earned by the corporation. To eliminate these deferral possibilities, corporate profits must be taxed annually.

To tax corporate profits annually without imposing a double tax, one might impose only a corporate-level tax on corporate profits. That is, the corporate-level tax would be retained but the shareholder-level tax on distributed corporate profits would be eliminated. Done in this manner, the corporate-level tax serves as a withholding tax on the income of the shareholders. This corporate income tax, coupled with the elimination of the shareholder income tax on distributed profits, seemingly would eliminate the double tax without creating deferral opportunities.

For example, suppose that X Corp. is wholly owned by individual B. If X has profits of $100 and those profits are taxed immediately to X at B's tax rate, the tax imposed on X is a complete substitute for an immediate tax on B. Thus, if B's tax rate is 28 percent, X will pay $28 in taxes and will have $72 to distribute. If that entire amount is distributed tax-free to B, it is just as if B were distributed the full $100 and then B were taxed on that amount.

While coupling a corporate-level tax with tax-free receipt of dividends by shareholder will at times eliminate the double tax, under some circumstances the double tax will remain. Consider the case of X Corp. formed by individual B with cash of $100. The incorporation is tax-free to both X and B,[22] and B takes a basis in the X Corp. stock of $100.

Assume that X invests the $100 in some asset that appreciates during the first year to $150. Assuming that X retains the asset, no tax will yet be due because unrealized gains are not taxable to corporations just as they are not taxable to individuals. B's stock should now be worth $150 because it represents the entire ownership of a corporation with assets of $150.

What if B now sells his stock for $150? B will have a taxable gain under § 1001 equal to the excess of the amount realized, or $150, over B's adjusted basis in his stock, or $100. Thus, B is taxed on the sale on the appreciation of the asset held by X. Of course, if X now sells its asset for fair market value of $150, X also will recognize a gain of $50. Thus, both individual B and X Corp. end up

---

22. See §§ 351(a) (shareholder's taxation), 1032 (corporation's taxation) and 358 (shareholder's basis in stock received). See generally Chapter 2 *infra*.

taxed on the appreciation of corporate assets. The double tax remains![23]

What went wrong was that we eliminated the double tax on *distributed* corporate profits but left intact the shareholder-level tax on *undistributed* profits, a tax incurred whenever a shareholder sells appreciated stock. If we are to eliminate all vestiges of the shareholder-level tax, we must provide not only that dividends can be received tax-free but also that gains from the sale or exchange of stock will be ignored.

Will this change eliminate the double tax without creating new problems? To see that it does not, we need to step back at bit and view the problem from a broader perspective. Ignoring for the moment all problems of valuation, the corporate tax could be eliminated by requiring shareholders to include corporate profits on their individual returns as earned at the corporate level whether distributed or not.

Suppose that this complete integration of the corporate and individual taxes were enacted when all income was subject to a flat tax, say of 28 percent. Consider the case of X Corp. having 3 equal shareholders. If X has $300,000 of taxable income, each shareholder would report $100,000 of tax on his individual return, increasing his tax liability by $28,000.

As we have seen, the government could obtain the same revenue without imputing the corporation's profits to its shareholders by simply taxing the corporation itself at the shareholders' rate. Thus, the corporation would pay a tax of $84,000, precisely equal to the sum paid by all three shareholders under the imputation scheme. Of course, the shareholders would pay no further taxes when the profits were distributed because they were already taxed (implicitly) when the profits were earned. A corporate-level tax operates as a proxy for a shareholder-level tax so long as the corporation's tax rate equals that of the shareholders.

Unfortunately, there is no single-level shareholder tax rate. If we tax corporate profits at the highest individual rate, then we are implicitly over-taxing those shareholders whose individual incomes (including their share of corporate profits) would put them in some lower bracket. In particular, corporations owned fully or in part by

---

23. This problem would be avoided if the gain recognized by B increased X's adjusted basis in its assets. Compare § 743(b) applying such an approach to partnerships and the sale of partnership interests. The basis adjustment provided by § 743(b) is elective in the partnership setting, and when elected it introduces substantial complexities into the partnership's tax computations (such as recomputing depreciation schedules).

tax-exempt organizations will be dramatically over-taxed, because the proper corporate-level tax allocable to such shareholders is zero.

If we tax corporations at some lower rate, then we offer a windfall to corporations (and through them to their investors) having shareholders in the highest bracket. In other words, complete integration of the corporate and individual income taxes cannot be achieved in a system having multiple tax brackets without imputing corporate profits to shareholders.

Is such imputation feasible? Possibly—it is done in the context of subchapter S corporations and in the context of partnerships, even as to partnerships with hundreds of partners.[24] However, except as to the simplest partnerships in which every partner has a fixed share of all items of income and loss, allocating the partnership tax items among partners having varying interests in the partnership (as common and preferred shareholders have varying interests in their corporation) is very complicated.[25]

Alternatively, we might tax shareholders on the annual change in value of their shares. This approach taxes shareholders on their share of corporate profits and on their share of unrealized appreciation in corporate assets, since both recognized profits and unrealized asset appreciation should increase share value.

Consider the case of corporations traded over a major securities exchange. We could require each shareholder to value his stock at the beginning and at the end of the year. The difference between those two values, plus all amounts distributed to the shareholder during the year as dividends, constitutes the shareholder's allocable portion of the corporation's profits and unrealized appreciation.

Unfortunately, for many corporations this system cannot be easily implemented. There is no active market for the stock of most closely-held corporations, eliminating annual valuation as a serious possibility. In addition, annual taxation of stock value changes effectively repeals the realization doctrine for corporate securities. Unless a move were made to eliminate the realization doctrine generally, eliminating it only with respect to stocks raises troubling questions of tax equity as the financial markets respond to such a dramatic change.

In recognition of these and other difficulties,[26] some tax theoreticians have argued in favor of *dividend relief* rather than complete

---

24. Several European nations including Germany, France and the United Kingdom employ imputation systems where shareholders receive a tax credit for taxes paid at the corporate level.

25. For an idea of this complexity, see Regs. § 1.704–1(b).

26. Another problem that must be faced in trying to integrate the individual and corporate income taxes is that the character of corporate-level income and

integration. Under this proposal, a corporate tax is imposed but with a deduction provided for dividend distributions. The effect is to tax undistributed corporate profits at the corporate rate while taxing distributed profits at the shareholders' tax rates.

The charts that follow compare both complete integration and dividend relief with the classical, double tax system. The comparison assumes that $1,000 is invested in a corporation for 10 years, and that the corporation earns 10% per year on its capital. In Chart 1–1, it is assumed that the corporate profits are retained by the corporation for the entire 10 years and then distributed in complete liquidation of the corporation. In Chart 1–2, it is assumed that the profits are distributed annually and that the shareholder earns 10 percent on his reinvested dividends. Chart 1–3 repeats the comparison of Chart 1–2 with debt replacing equity as the shareholder's investment under the classical, double tax system. In all cases it is assumed that the corporate tax rate is 35 percent, that the individual tax rate is 35 percent on ordinary income and 15% on capital gains and dividends, and that the corporation liquidates after 10 years.[27]

Chart 1–1

Full Retention

	After-Tax Return to Shareholder [28]	Annual Return
No Taxes Imposed	$1,594	10.0%
Complete Integration	877	6.5%
Dividend Relief	746	5.7%
Classical Double Tax	746	5.7%

deductions must be preserved. This issue includes the distinction between ordinary income and capital gains but expands well beyond it. For a partial list of the items posing this characterization problem, see §§ 702(a) (partnerships), 1366(b) (S corporations).

27. We additionally assume that both the corporation and the shareholder can invest arbitrarily small amounts at a return of 10% per year.

28. As of the end of year 10, excluding the initial investment of $1,000.

Chart 1–2
Full Distribution With Equity

	After-Tax Return to Shareholder	Annual Return
No Taxes Imposed	$1,594	10.0%
Complete Integration	877	6.5%
Dividend Relief	877	6.5%
Classical Double Tax	746	5.7%

Chart 1–3
Full Distribution With Debt

	After-Tax Return to Shareholder	Annual Return
No Taxes Imposed	$1,594	10.0%
Complete Integration	877	6.5%
Dividend Relief	877	6.5%
Classical Double Tax	877	6.5%

What can we learn from these charts? First and not surprisingly, under a system of complete integration, the taxpayer's after-tax return equals his pre-tax return of 10 percent less his taxes of 35 percent.[29] Thus, he is taxed just as if the investment had been made individually and not through his corporation.

Dividend relief produces the same result as complete integration only when the corporation distributes its profits annually.[30] This result makes sense because dividend relief system taxes the shareholders on distributed corporate profits and taxes the corporation on undistributed profits. Accordingly, if there are no undistributed corporate profits, dividend relief eliminates the corporate tax as fully as does complete integration.

Chart 1–3 emphasizes that the corporate interest deduction under current law goes a long way in the direction of dividend relief. Because interest payments are deductible to the corporation while dividend distributions are not, corporations can reduce their tax liability by raising debt capital in preference to equity capital. In many instances the Commissioner has asserted that corporate investments labeled debt by the corporation and its investors should be treated as equity. This issue, the debt/equity issue, is explored more fully in Chapter 3.

29. See the second line of each Chart.

30. Compare lines two and three of Chart 1–1 with lines two and three of Chart 1–2.

The relationship between the classical double tax with full retention and the classical double tax with full distribution (line 4 in Charts 1–1 and 1–2) is complex, involving the corporate tax rate on ordinary income, the individual tax rate on ordinary income, and the individual tax rate on capital gain. When all corporate profits are retained until final liquidation, the investment's annual return of 10% is taxed each year at the corporate rate of 35% and then in year ten at the individual capital gain rate of 15% because the corporate profits are then distributed to the shareholder in complete liquidation of the corporate venture. Thus, the corporation will have $1877.14 after 10 years,[31] and that amount will be distributed to the shareholder, producing a taxable gain of $877.14.[32] This yields a tax liability of $131.57,[33] leaving the shareholder with an after-tax profit of $745.57.

If the corporation distributes its after-tax profits annually, the shareholder will receive $65.00 from the corporation each year, and that dividend distribution will be subject to the shareholder's individual tax rate of 15%, leaving only $55.25 for the shareholder to spend or invest. We assume that the shareholder invests everything he receives from the corporation in some noncorporate vehicle paying 10% per year, so the shareholder will receive an after-tax return from this noncorporate investment of 6.5% per year, that being the investment's return of 10% less the shareholder's individual tax rate of 39%. Thus, after 10 years the shareholder will have received 10 dividends in the amount of $55.25 each as well as compounded interest on those reinvested dividends. While the profits earned in corporate solution are subjected each year to an immediate double tax amounting to 45.20%,[34] the compounded earnings on the dividends are taxed only at the individual tax rate of 35%.[35] Accordingly, the shareholder's total tax burden will be somewhere between 45.20% and 35%, and in fact it turns out to be 43%. In other words, because the shareholder's investment over the 10 years is partially made in corporate form and partially made individually, the return on the shareholder's initial investment is determined by a blending of the tax burden imposed on corporate investments and the tax burden imposed on noncorporate invest-

---

31. The corporation has an after-tax return on its investments of 6.5%, and $1000 compounded at 6.5% for 10 years equals $1877.14.

32. The amount distributed to the shareholder will by $1,877.14, and the shareholder's adjusted basis in the stock surrendered equals $1,000, leaving a taxable gain of $877.14.

33. The taxable gain of $877.14 is taxed at the capital gain rate of 15%, yielding a tax liability of $131.57.

34. The corporate tax burden of 35% coupled with an individual tax burden of 15% produces a total tax burden of 45.20%.

35. Note that the highest nominal individual tax rate currently is 39.1%.

ment. Given the assumptions underlying Chart 1–2, that blended rate is 43%.

Let us reconsider the classical double tax system with full retention of profits as compared with full distribution of profits, but this time we will assume that the individual tax rate on ordinary income and the individual tax rate on capital gains equals the corporate tax rate of 35%. Under this new assumption, we get the following results:

Chart 1–4
Classical Corporate Double Tax

	After-Tax Return to Shareholder	Annual Return
Full Retention	570	4.6%
Full Distribution With Equity	570	4.6%

Chart 1–4 may seem counter-intuitive: annual distributions trigger the shareholder-level tax each year while corporate retention postpones that tax until liquidation. Why is there no benefit from this tax deferral?

If a corporation earns $65 after taxes and distributes it as a dividend, a shareholder-level tax will be imposed on that $65. If the corporation reinvests the $65 instead of distributing it, the corporation will have $69.23 to distribute one year later. If the $69.23 is then distributed, the shareholder-level tax will have been postponed but its eventual imposition will be on a greater amount. So long as the annual corporate tax rate equals the annual individual tax rate and the tax rate on dividend distributions equals the tax rate on liquidating (i.e., capital gain) distributions, two effects will cancel one another out.[36]

Historically, the tax rate imposed on dividend distributions was significantly higher than the rate imposed on long-term capital gain. When that was true, there was a significant bias in favor of corporate retention of earnings to avoid the high rate of tax imposed on dividend distributions. Alternatively, taxpayer mechanisms were created (sometimes successful, sometimes not) to bail-out corporate earnings as capital gain. As we will see, much of the complexity in Subchapter C arose from congressional attempts to distinguish proper capital gain distributions from inappropriate bail-outs. With the tax rate on most dividend distributions now set equal to the rate applicable to long-term capital gain, that struggle (though not all of the complexity) has disappeared.

---

36. See generally Warren, *The Timing of Taxes*, 39 Nat'l Tax J. 499 (1986).

Not too many years ago, the corporate tax rate exceeded the individual tax rate, and the maximum individual rate imposed on capital gains as well as on dividend distributions equaled the maximum individual (ordinary) tax rate of 28%. In Chart 1–5, we reconsider the facts of Chart 1–4 but assume that the corporate tax rate is 34% while the individual tax rate imposed on ordinary income and capital gains is 28%.[37] Making these assumptions, we get:

Chart 1–5
Classical Corporate Double Tax

	After-Tax Return to Shareholder	Annual Return
Full Retention	644	5.1%
Full Distribution With Equity	663	5.2%

Now, the shareholder is slightly better off with annual distributions. We have seen that the discounted-value of the shareholder-level tax is the same whether corporate profits are distributed annually or at the end. The total tax paid on the earnings, of course, is determined by both the shareholder-level tax and by the corporate-level tax. If annual profits are distributed, the shareholder will invest them and be taxed on their growth at the individual tax rate of 28 percent. On the other hand, if the corporation retains its profits, it will invest them and be taxed on the growth at its tax rate of 34 percent.

The slight preference appearing in Charts 1–5 for annual distributions as compared with full retention reflects the slightly higher tax rate applicable to corporate reinvested profits as compared with shareholder reinvested profits.[38] When the individual and corporate tax rates are equal, the shareholder is indifferent between annual distributions and complete corporate retention of profits. When individual rates are higher than corporate rates, there is an incentive for corporations to accumulate profits rather than to distribute them.

37. These rates were enacted by the Tax Reform Act of 1986 and lasted about one year.

38. If the difference between the corporate and individual tax rates were greater, then the incentive to distribute profits annually also would be greater. See generally Warren, *The Relation and Integration of the Individual and Corporate Income Taxes*, 94 Harv.L.Rev. 717 (1981).

CHAPTER 2. FORMING A CORPORATION

2.01 Introduction. Generally, when a taxpayer exchanges property for other property, gain or loss realized on the exchange must be recognized under § 1001. For example, if T exchanges a piece of undeveloped real estate with a basis of $5,000 and a fair market value of $20,000 for a boat with a fair market value of $20,000, T must recognize a $15,000 gain. It is as though T sold the land for $20,000 and used the money to purchase the boat.

The wisdom of recognition may be weakened if the exchange does not substantially alter the nature of T's investment. Under our tax system, the mere appreciation of T's land from its $5,000 cost to its current $20,000 fair market value is not a taxable event. Suppose T continues as an owner of undeveloped real estate by exchanging the real estate for other undeveloped real estate. While T has a $15,000 realized gain, §§ 1001(c) and 1031 may provide that the gain need not be recognized since the property is exchanged for property of like-kind.[1] If the gain is not recognized, § 1031(d) provides T with a basis of $5,000 in the property received, thereby preserving the unrecognized gain for any later disposition.

Section 1031 embodies the congressional mandate that taxation of an exchange is inappropriate where a taxpayer has a sufficient continuity of investment before and after the exchange. Suppose instead of exchanging the land for other land, T exchanges the land for all of the stock of newly created X Corp. Although § 1031 does not apply to the transaction,[2] T has a stronger continuity than in the case where real estate is exchanged for real estate. Here, T continues to own the same real estate, albeit indirectly through his 100 percent ownership in X Corp. which owns the real estate.

Since 1921, Congress has provided that this kind of property for stock exchange should not be a taxable event. However, it has never been the case that all transfers of property to a corporation are free of taxes. For example, a taxpayer who transfers appreciated property to a corporation in which he owns no stock in exchange for

---

1. Among other requirements under § 1031, the property exchanged and received must be held for use in a trade or business or for investment.

2. Section 1031(a)(2)(B).

17

cash no longer has a continuity of ownership in the property transferred and will be taxed on the gain.

The essence of § 351 and related provisions is to ascertain whether a transferor has a sufficiently continuous relationship with the property transferred to a corporation to justify nonrecognition treatment or whether the transferor has severed the relationship with the transferred property, thereby justifying recognition.

2.02   Section 351: The Basics. Section 351 is not an elective provision. If by its terms it applies, then a taxpayer must defer recognition of gain or loss. Section 351 mandates nonrecognition only if the taxpayer-transferor: (1) transfers property to a corporation; (2) receives stock in exchange; and (along with other transferors, if any), (3) is in control of the corporation immediately after the transaction. Note that § 351 can apply both to the formation of new corporations and to transfers to existing corporations (sometimes referred to as "midstream" transfers).

Each of the three major requirements of § 351 is intended to ensure a continuity of investment. The "property" requirement precludes a taxpayer who exchanges services for stock from enjoying nonrecognition. § 351(d)(1). Stock received for services performed is taxable upon receipt. Congress is unwilling to tender nonrecognition where a taxpayer turns human capital into corporate capital—the change in form of investment is too great.

The "stock" requirement is intended to ensure that what the transferor receives carries with it sufficient continuity in the property transferred. Suppose T and three other joint owners of appreciated real estate transfer the property to newly-formed X Corp. T receives cash while the other transferors receive X Corp. stock. For T, nonrecognition is unavailable since T merely sold the property. If T had received stock along with the other transferors, § 351 would have provided nonrecognition for T who would have continued to enjoy the financial benefits of ownership of the property indirectly through ownership in X Corp. If T received some cash and some stock for the property, realized gain would have been recognized to the extent of the cash received since T has sold a portion of his interest in the land.

What happens if T transfers the property in exchange for an X Corp. financial instrument which carries less continuity than stock but more continuity than cash? If T receives a debt instrument in exchange for T's property, the transaction falls in the middle of a spectrum between a sale for cash and a transfer for stock. Some debt instruments have characteristics that provide continuity similar to stock. For example, a forty-year bond may link the transferor to the property transferred in much the same way as the receipt of stock. Indeed, for financially disabled corporations, debt ownership may provide greater ownership rights than stock ownership. On the other hand, if T were to receive a three-year debt instrument bearing appropriate interest in exchange for the transfer of property, it is as if T sold the property on the installment method.

Section 351 used to distinguish between long-term debts (securities) and short-term debts (notes), providing nonrecognition treatment for receipt of the former and sales treatment for receipt of the latter. This distinction proved troublesome as the line between securities and notes was not easily drawn, and so Congress drew a sharper line, providing that only the receipt of stock would qualify a transferor for nonrecognition treatment. Unfortunately, astute tax planners could blur even this line by creating financial instruments nominally equity but lacking any significant long-term relationship to the corporation, and so Congress responded in § 361(g) by defining a class of "nonqualified preferred stock" that is for some purposes treated as stock and for others as less than debt.

The third requirement—"control"—also implements the continuity concept. The mere fact that T exchanges property for stock does not guarantee that T will possess a sufficient continuity in the property transferred. Suppose that T and the other transferors transfer their jointly owned real estate to IBM Corp. in exchange for IBM stock. T's relationship to the real estate is far more attenuated than if the transferors had transferred the property to a newly formed, closely held corporation. These transfers to IBM will be treated as though the transferors had sold the property to IBM and had used the proceeds to purchase IBM stock.

Section 351 refers to the control test in § 368(c) which requires that the transferors own at least 80 percent of the total combined voting power of all classes of stock entitled to vote and at least 80 percent of the total number of shares of all other classes of stock. Like many provisions in the corporate tax area, the 80 percent requirement offers a bright line test whereby Congress is willing to substitute a degree of certainty for a painstaking factual analysis of what constitutes control in each situation. Notwithstanding this intent, it is often difficult to determine what constitutes "the transaction." For example, if two transfers are made to X Corp. within six months, are the 80 percent tests applied after each transfer or are the two transfers combined and the 80 percent tests applied only once?

Consider one final point on the basics of § 351. Suppose a dozen independent business people transfer their separate and unrelated businesses to a newly-formed corporation, each receiving stock equal in value to the assets exchanged. Notice that the nature of each business person's economic interest has changed dramatically, but § 351 makes no requirement of a continuity of economic interest. Diversification achieved through § 351 is not prohibited.[3]

2.03　A Section 351 Roadmap. Upon the transfer of property to a corporation, the tax treatment of both the transferor(s) and transferee-corporation are important. Sections 351 and 357 determine whether gain or loss realized on the exchange is taxable to the transferor(s). The basis taken by the transferor(s) in the stock, securities or other property received from X Corp. is determined in accordance with § 358.[4] With adjustments, the basis of the property transferred becomes the basis of the property received.

Section 1032 provides nonrecognition for the transferee-corporation issuing stock in exchange for money or other property. The transferee-corporation determines its basis in the property received under § 362. With adjustments, the transferee-corporation carries over the transferor's basis, although the transferree-corporation's basis in contributed property generally cannot exceed the fair market value of the property at the time of the contribution, § 362(c). Section 1223(2) requires "tacking" in determining the holding period of property received from the transferor(s).

To illustrate how these provisions work, suppose B owns a building with a basis of $25,000 and a fair market value of $70,000. C owns undeveloped real estate with a basis of $50,000 and a fair market value of $30,000. Together they form X Corp. in exchange for their assets. B and C each receives X Corp. stock worth $70,000 and $30,000, respectively. On the exchange, § 351 prevents B and C from recognizing gain and loss. One "price" of B's nonrecognition is the transfer of his $25,000 basis in the building to the stock received. § 358(a). The realized but unrecognized $45,000 gain on the building may be recognized when, and if, B sells the stock. One "consolation" C gets for the nonrecognition of her loss is the transfer of her $50,000 basis in the real estate to the stock. The $20,000 loss that went unrecognized upon formation of X Corp. may be recognized when, and if, C sells her stock. (Note that B and C could just as well be corporations rather than individuals.)

On a sale or exchange of their stock, B and C must "tack" the holding period of their assets (if they are capital assets or § 1231

---

3. But see § 351(e)(1) which addresses so-called swap funds. Investors holding undiversified appreciated securities cannot take advantage of § 351 to diversify by forming holding companies with other similarly situated investors.

4. Section 1223(1) requires "tacking" in determining the holding period of stock, securities or other property received on the transfer.

assets at the time of the exchange) on to the holding period of their stock. § 1223(1). For example, if the total period of time during which B held his capital asset and stock is greater than one year, the sale of stock will produce long-term capital gain or loss, assuming the stock is a capital asset in the hands of C.

X Corp., which exchanges its stock for the assets of B and C, receives nonrecognition treatment under § 1032. The basis of each asset in the hands of B and C becomes X Corp.'s basis, resulting in a $25,000 basis in the building and a $50,000 in the undeveloped real estate. § 362(a). Upon a sale or exchange of the assets X Corp. must tack on the holding period of the transferors whether or not the assets were capital in the hands of the transferors. § 1223(2).

Note that if B sells his stock immediately after receipt for $70,000, he will recognize a $45,000 gain, and if X Corp. sells the building for $70,000, it will recognize a $45,000 gain.[5] This double gain is the thrust of the corporate tax system. At its heart, the corporate income tax is aimed at post-incorporation earnings or gain from the sale or exchange of assets with post-incorporation appreciation. As discussed above, the system envisions a corporate level tax, followed by a shareholder level tax upon distribution. Why should there be a potential double tax on pre-incorporation appreciation?

Could Congress avoid this double tax by giving B, the transferor, a step up in basis? If B received a $70,000 basis in the stock received, B could cash in on the building's appreciation with no immediate tax consequences by selling the stock for $70,000. At some point in the future if X Corp. sold the building for $70,000, the tax on the pre-incorporation appreciation would be paid by X Corp. In short, B could convert the asset to cash without tax consequences.[6]

Suppose instead that X Corp. took the building with a basis of $70,000 while B acquired a $25,000 basis in the X Corp. stock received. Now if X Corp. sells the property, it could convert the $45,000 of unrealized appreciation into cash without recognizing gain. At some point in the future, if B sells the X Corp. stock, the pre-incorporation gain may be recognized.

Both of these approaches may suffer from the problem of deferral. While both approaches preserve a single tax on the preincorporation appreciation, by strategic selling it is likely that

5. Similarly, if X Corp. sells the asset and distributes the proceeds, there will be a double tax. See the discussion of § 301 in Chapter 4 *infra*.

6. Presumably, the price paid for B's stock would to some degree reflect the potential tax to X Corp. from its sale of the building.

either the shareholder or the corporation could turn that appreciation into cash without any immediate tax consequences. Could Congress design a system whereby gain is recognized on whichever is sold first—the stock or the building—with a step up in basis for the asset not sold?

A double tax on pre-incorporation appreciation may not be overly troublesome because the shareholder can avoid the double tax by a pre-incorporation sale of the appreciated asset. Note, however, that Congress has determined that allowing a double loss *is* overly troublesome: the basis rules now ensure that the incorporation of loss assets will produce only a single loss, usually at the shareholder level. Why is the possibility of a doubling of loss more problematic than a doubling of gain? Recall that it is the taxpayer who chooses to incorporate assets, so while the basis rules are in a sense a one-way street, it is the taxpayer who elects whether or not to drive.

An additional problem with giving the corporation a fair market value basis in contributed assets is that there is no easy way to determine the proper value of such assets: the transaction does not provide a valuation, and the parties do not have incentives to get the value right. While this is not an insurmountable hurdle (we generally tax parties who exchange one property for another even though such an exchange does not provide a market valuation and each of the parties has an incentive to minimize the reported value), it does provide another, practical reason why Congress might want to give the corporation a carry-over basis in contributed assets.[7]

With the basics of § 351 in mind, consider the three major requirements of nonrecognition treatment: property must be transferred, stock must be received and the transferor(s) must satisfy the 80 percent control requirements.

2.04 "Property" Requirement. This requirement covers not only fee interests in property but other equity interests as well. Money qualifies as property for the purposes of § 351.[8]

Section 351 was never intended to permit transferors of services to receive their compensation in the form of stock without recognition of income. § 351(d)(1). This restriction applies to stock received for past, present or future services. At first glance it may seem as though this restriction is intended to prevent conversion of ordinary income from services into capital gains when the services-

---

7. *But see* § 362(d)-(e) (requiring valuation of property contributed to a corporation under § 351).

8. See Rev. Rul. 69–357, 1969–1 C.B. 101.

transferor sells the stock received. But one need not transfer a capital asset in order to satisfy the property requirement of § 351. For example, the transferor of appreciated inventory who receives stock in a § 351 transaction might be able to sell the stock and report a capital gain, and if the property is not inventory in the hands of the corporation, it, too, might get capital gain treatment upon a sale.

Another possible explanation for the property requirement is that the philosophy of § 351 does not countenance nonrecognition for a change in form from human to financial capital. Yet, suppose a cash basis transferor holds accounts receivable after performing services for a third party prior to incorporation. Will a transfer of receivables satisfy the property requirement of § 351? In *Hempt Bros., Inc. v. United States*,[9] the court ruled that accounts receivable did constitute property for purposes of § 351.[10]

Suppose a transferor agrees to perform services for the transferee and transfers that promise in exchange for stock. Alternatively, suppose that the transferor has already performed services for the corporation for which he receives an account receivable. The transferor then exchanges the account receivable for stock of the corporation.[11] Will any of these transactions allow a transferor to sidestep the property requirement of § 351? Transactions like these are likely to meet with skepticism by the Service which may recharacterize the supposed property transfer as a transfer of services.[12]

Nowhere is the line between services and property fuzzier than in cases involving intellectual property. It is clear that patents, patent applications, trademarks, tradenames and goodwill consti-

---

9. 490 F.2d 1172 (3d Cir.1974). See also *United States v. Frazell*, 335 F.2d 487 (5th Cir.1964). There the taxpayer, a geologist, investigated certain oil and gas properties to be acquired by a joint venture. Before any interest in the joint venture was transferred to him, a corporation was formed and part of the stock was given to the taxpayer. It was not clear whether the taxpayer acquired an interest in the joint venture which was then exchanged for stock or whether he acquired stock directly in exchange for services performed. The court found that either the taxpayer was taxable on transferring services for an interest in the joint venture or he was taxable on transferring services in exchange for stock in the corporation. See also *Mark IV Pictures, Inc. v. Commissioner*, 969 F.2d 669 (8th Cir.1992), for a collection of cases on the property vs. services issue.

10. Consider the assignment of income implications at Section 2.08(b) *infra*.

11. Similar transactions might include the promise to perform services for another transferor which is then exchanged for stock or the actual performance of services for another shareholder in exchange for an account receivable which is then exchanged for stock.

12. See, e.g., *James v. Commissioner*, 53 T.C. 63 (1969) (contract promising to perform services not property for purpose of § 351).

tute property under § 351. Less clear is the status of "know-how." That umbrella term encompasses inventions, unpatented or unpatentable secret processes or secret formulae and technical information and skills. In Revenue Ruling 64–56,[13] the Service ruled that property includes "secret information as to a device, process, formula etc., in the general nature of a patentable invention," but that the status of other "know-how" would be determined on a case-by case basis. The Service's focus on a nexus to a "patentable invention" may be out of step with judicial decisions emphasizing secrecy and the right of the holder to protect against unauthorized disclosure.[14]

What if a taxpayer transfers property to a corporation in a transaction otherwise described in section 351 but the property is encumbered by a liability equal to or in excess of the value of the contributed property? If the corporation assumes the liability, then arguably there has been no transfer of property in exchange for stock because no net value has been transferred to the corporation. Proposed regulations now adopt this analysis. *See* Prop. Reg. § 1.351–1(a)(1)(iii) (proposed March 10, 2005).

2.05　What Constitutes a "Transfer". Section 351 requires that property be "transferred" to a corporation. Ordinarily, the "transfer" requirement is straightforward. However, in the case of certain intangibles, the transfer requirement can pose a problem. Suppose the owner of a patent or trademark grants a license to a corporation for the right to exploit the property and receives stock in exchange. The owner might have assigned the property outright, but instead preferred to retain certain controls over its utilization and the right to recover the property in the event of the transferee's bankruptcy or misappropriation. For example, the transferor may want to retain a veto over any sublicensing agreements or the right to terminate the license if the transferee fails to utilize the property rights effectively.

The Service has taken the position that in order to qualify under § 351, the transfer must amount to a sale or exchange within the meaning of § 1222.[15] However, in *E. I. Du Pont de Nemours & Co. v. United States*,[16] the court held that the sale or exchange requirement of § 1222 is not embodied in § 351. Accordingly, a nonexclusive, royalty-free license exchanged for stock was a

13. 1964–1 C.B. (Part 1) 133. See also Rev. Rul. 71–564, 1971–2 C.B. 179.

14. See, e.g., *Commercial Solvents Corp. v. Commissioner*, 42 T.C. 455 (1964).

15. See, e.g., Rev. Rul. 69–156, 1969–1 C.B. 101; Rev. Rul. 71–564, 1971–2 C.B. 179.

16. 471 F.2d 1211 (Ct.Cl.1973).

"transfer" within the meaning of § 351 because the license was irrevocable and perpetual.

The transfer requirement is inextricably related to the property requirement. If too many strings are retained by the transferor, the Service may well argue that there has been no transfer and that if there was a transfer, the bundle of licensed rights does not amount to property for purposes of § 351.

2.06 "Stock" Requirement. Before exploring what constitutes stock, one should inquire why it matters. Section 351(a) provides nonrecognition on an exchange only if it is *solely* for stock of the transferee corporation. Note that long-term debt instruments issued by the transferee corporation do not qualify under § 351. An equity interest in a corporation embodies a sufficient continuity of investment in the property transferred. And yet, § 351(b) informs us that "solely" does not mean solely. If a transaction would be governed by § 351(a) but for the receipt of nonqualifying property ("boot") in addition to stock, § 351 will still govern the transaction.[17] Consider now how the boot will be taxable.

(a) Boot. Section 351(b) requires a transferor receiving boot to recognize any realized gain on the transaction to the extent of the money or fair market value of any nonqualifying property received. For example, suppose T transfers an asset with a basis of $5,000 and a fair market value of $20,000 to X Corp. in exchange for $15,000 of X Corp. stock and $5,000 of cash in a transaction that would otherwise qualify under § 351. T is taxed on the $15,000 gain to the extent of the $5,000 boot received. Note that T would prefer to treat the cash as a return of T's original $5,000 investment in the property, but § 351(b) requires recognition of gain before basis can be recovered.

The character of any gain recognized—capital gain or ordinary income—is determined by focusing on the nature of the property transferred. In the example above, if T transfers inventory, the $5,000 gain will be ordinary; if T transfers investment real estate, the gain will be capital; if T transfers machinery used in a trade or business, the gain will be subject to § 1231, which normally will produce a capital gain. Suppose, though, that T had taken deprecia-

---

17. The term "boot" presumably originates from the fact that the transferor receives stock and other property "to boot." Where does the expression "to boot" come from? Under Anglo–Saxon law, a freeman who injured another would redeem himself with the king by paying the "wite," or fine. Having avoided execution, he would then be required to pay an additional amount, the "bot," as compensation to the injured party. The "bot" was thus further payment, and "to boot" came to mean "in addition" or "additionally." See F. Pollock & F. Maitland, The History of English Law 45 (2d ed. 1968).

tion deductions with respect to the machinery, but that the property had not, in fact, depreciated in value. The $5,000 gain T must recognize under § 351(b) may be ordinary income if the depreciation is subject to recapture under §§ 1245 or 1250. In the absence of boot, a transferor does not recognize recapture on a § 351 transaction. §§ 1245(b)(3) and 1250(d)(3).

In the example above, suppose T transfers property with a basis of $25,000 and a fair market value of $20,000 in exchange for $15,000 of X Corp. stock and $5,000 of cash. The boot is not taxable since there is no realized gain on the transaction. § 351(b)(2). Instead, the $5,000 is treated as a return of T's original investment in the property.

(b) Assumption of liabilities. If a transferee-corporation assumes or takes subject to a liability of the transferor, the effect on the transferor may be the same as the receipt of boot. Suppose T transfers an asset with a basis of $40,000 and a fair market value of $50,000 to X Corp. in exchange for X Corp. stock worth $40,000 and X Corp.'s assumption of T's $10,000 liability secured by the property. Following the transaction, T holds $40,000 of X Corp. stock as well as the $10,000 in cash that T borrowed and can now keep with no obligation to repay.[18] X Corp., in exchange for the property received from T, has distributed $40,000 of its stock and, by assuming the liability, is obligated to pay $10,000 to T's lender. Economically the entire transaction is equivalent to X Corp. distributing $40,000 in stock and $10,000 of cash in exchange for the property.[19]

Viewed in this manner, the assumption of a liability by the transferee-corporation should be a taxable event to the transferor to the extent of realized gain. In *United States v. Hendler*,[20] the Supreme Court held that an assumption of the transferor's indebtedness constituted boot under somewhat parallel reorganization provisions. Having won the battle, Treasury soon realized it might lose the war. One consequence of boot treatment for a transferor is that the transferee-corporation is entitled to increase its basis in the property received under § 362(a), thereby increasing depreciation deductions and decreasing gain (or increasing loss) on the eventual sale of the property. While the statute of limitations may

18. For tax purposes, T is deemed to be relieved of the obligation even if T remains secondarily liable on the note. § 357(d)(1)(A).

19. The fact that X Corp. is obligated to pay the lender in the first scenario and has actually made a $10,000 distribution in the second scenario is irrele-

vant economically and for tax purposes if the loan bears a market rate of interest. Indeed, to make the comparison identical, assume that X Corp. pays off the loan following the § 351 transaction.

20. 303 U.S. 564 (1938).

have run on many pre-*Hendler* transferors of encumbered property, the transferee-corporations were eager to utilize any basis increase.[21]

Congress responded to Treasury's fears by enacting § 357(a) which provides that the assumption of a liability (or taking subject to a mortgage) by a transferee does not constitute money or other property and does not preclude nonrecognition under § 351. The enactment of § 357(a) creates an inconsistency between the economically identical transactions considered above. Where X Corp. assumes T's $10,000 liability, §§ 357(a) and 351 give T full nonrecognition. As will become clearer in the basis discussion, the $10,000 that T obtained from the lender and can keep without an obligation to repay is considered to be a return of T's basis. On the other hand, where T receives $10,000 as boot from X Corp., a $10,000 gain must be recognized under § 351(b). Thus, there is a "gain first" rule for boot and a "basis first" rule for liabilities assumed.

Under § 357(b), the inconsistency is removed where, taking into consideration the nature of the liability and circumstances surrounding its assumption by the transferee, the principal purpose of the taxpayer with respect to the assumption is to avoid Federal income tax or is not a bona fide business purpose. Under these circumstances, the assumption is treated as money or other property received for purposes of § 351.

To understand the reach of § 357(b), assume in the example above that the liability assumed by X Corp. was incurred by T immediately before the § 351 transaction. Moreover, T used the money for personal purposes. Under these facts, the $10,000 assumption must be treated as boot by T and recognized in full. In general, liabilities incurred in the normal course of business such as mortgages placed on business property, trade obligations, and business bank loans should escape the reach of § 357(b). But note that if the tax-avoidance motive exists with respect to *any* assumed liability, *all* liabilities are treated as boot.[22] This harsh and seemingly unwarranted treatment may have discouraged courts from finding the necessary tax avoidance motive.

Courts may also have eschewed § 357(b) since § 357(c) offers a less draconian way of treating at least some of the assumed liabilities as boot. Because § 357(a) employs a "basis first" rule, it makes

---

21. See the mitigation provisions of §§ 1311–1314 which now might prevent the Treasury from such a one-sided fate. Note that the *Hendler* "problem" was a one-time event due to the statute of limitations. In general, taxing a shareholder on transferred liabilities while giving the corporation a stepped up basis causes no problems for the Treasury and indeed would accelerate the collection of revenues.

22. Regs. § 1.357–1(c).

sense that where the assumption exceeds the transferor's basis, the excess is considered gain. Section 357(c) treats such excess as a gain from the sale or exchange of the underlying property.[23]

In the example above, suppose that T received $35,000 of X Corp. stock and that X Corp. assumed T's $15,000 mortgage. Suppose further that T had a $10,000 basis in the asset. Assuming § 357(b) is inapplicable,[24] § 357(c) treats the first $10,000 of assumed liabilities as a return of basis and the next $5,000 as gain recognized from the sale or exchange of the underlying asset. Recall that if § 357(b) applied or if X Corp. had distributed $15,000 as part of the § 351 transaction, the full $15,000 would have been taxable to T. Section 357(c) allows a transferor to aggregate the "total of the adjusted basis" of all assets transferred before determining whether gain must be recognized.[25] The theory seems to be that a transferor has cashed in his gain only to the extent he has recovered all of his capital. Therefore, if T contributed additional cash or property with an aggregate basis of $15,000, T would not recognize gain on the transfer because the total of the adjusted bases of all property transferred would not be exceeded by the liabilities assumed by X Corp.

Section 357(c) applies even when the transferor remains legally responsible for the liabilities "assumed" by the corporate transferee (*e.g.*, a recourse liability where the transferor remains secondarily).[26] However, if it is expected that the transferor will ultimately satisfy the liability, then the liability is not considered to be "assumed" for purposes of § 357(c). For purposes of § 357(c), even a nonrecourse liability can be "assumed."[27] However, if the nonrecourse liability that encumbers transferred property also encumbers other property and it is expected that the transferor rather than the transferee will satisfy part or all of the liability, then the amount of the liability "assumed" for purposes of § 357(c) cannot exceed the fair market value of the property transferred.

If encumbered property is transferred to a corporation and the encumbrance is *not* treated as "assumed" by the corporation under § 357(d), it still might be the case that the corporation pays off

---

23. Section 357(c) applies even where the transferor remains personally liable on the liabilities assumed by the transferee-corporation. § 357(d)(1)(A). See *Smith v. Commissioner,* 84 T.C. 889 (1985). This result is consistent with the treatment of the transferor when the transferee satisfies the liability. There will be no gain to the transferor even though *Old Colony Trust Co. v. Commissioner,* 279 U.S. 716 (1929), might suggest there should be if another person discharges a personal liability of the transferor.

24. Under § 357(c)(2)(A), § 357(b) takes precedence over § 357(c) where the two conflict.

25. Regs. § 1.357–2(b).

26. § 357(d)(1).

27. § 357(d)(1)(B).

some or all of the encumbrance to increase its equity in the property. While the statute does not directly speak to the tax consequences of such a payment, it seems clear that the transaction ought to be taxed as a deemed distribution from the corporation to the shareholder followed by a payment by the shareholder to the creditor. As discussed in Chapter 4, such a deemed distribution often will result in dividend income to the shareholder without any increase in the shareholder's stock basis. In such circumstances, gain recognition under § 357(b) or (c)(1) ultimately might prove more favorable than deferring the gain by avoiding a corporate "assumption" of the encumbrance.

Suppose individual B owns Blackacre with adjusted basis and fair market value of $1,000. If B wishes to purchase Whiteacre for debt, B might offer both Blackacre and Whiteacre as security for the loan. Thus, for example, B might acquire Whiteacre for nothing down while signing a nonrecourse note for $1,000 secured by both properties.

If B now contributes both properties to a newly-formed corporation in exchange for stock, B will not recognize gain or loss on the transaction and will take a $1,000 in the stock received. But if B transfers each parcel to a separate newly-formed corporation, arguably B will take the stock of each corporation with a $0 basis: because the liability encumbers each asset, it reduces B's stock basis in each § 351 transaction. Yet, this plainly is counting the liability twice. B can avoid this double counting by agreeing with one of the corporations that it will not be liable for satisfaction of the debt. See § 357(d)(2)(A).

Recall that a corporation's basis in contributed property is carried-over from the contributing shareholder, increased by the amount of any gain recognized by the shareholder on the contribution. § 362(a). What if the gain nominally recognized by the contributing shareholder goes untaxed, perhaps because the contributing shareholder is not subject to US taxation? For example, suppose that in a § 351 transaction, T transfers property with a basis of $100 and a fair market value of $500, encumbered by a $900 liability that is also secured by other assets that the transferor holds. If the transferor can avoid reporting the § 357(c) gain on the transfer, in the absence of a corrective rule the transferee-corporation would take a basis of $900 in an asset with a fair market value of $500. This could create artificially high depreciation deductions or an artificial loss if the corporation sold the transferred assets. In accordance with § 357(d)(2), the amount "assumed" for purposes of § 357(c) is limited to $500, thereby limiting the transferee to a $500 basis in the assets.[28]

The treatment of assumed liabilities takes another twist where the liabilities assumed would give rise to a deduction had the transferor paid them. Consider T, a cash-basis taxpayer, who holds a $5,000 account payable and an account receivable with a $0 basis and a $20,000 fair market value. As part of a group of transferors, T exchanges his account receivable for $15,000 of X Corp. stock and X Corp.'s assumption of the account payable in a transaction governed by § 351.

Recall that the general rule of § 357(a) treats the assumption as nontaxable, but § 357(c) contains an exception to the extent the liability exceeds the basis of the assets transferred. However, § 357(c)(3) contains an exception to the exception where the liability assumed exceeds the basis of the assets transferred but would be deductible if paid by the transferor.[29]

In the example above, it is as though X Corp. borrowed $5,000 from T's creditor obligating itself for repayment and distributed the $5,000 along with $15,000 of X Corp. stock in exchange for T's $20,000 account receivable. T then uses the $5,000 distributed to discharge T's obligation to the creditor. Viewed in this manner, T would recognize the $5,000 gain because of the boot under § 351(b) as ordinary income and would have an offsetting $5,000 deduction for the deemed payment of the account payable under § 162. Section 357(c)(3) achieves this result by not characterizing deductible liabilities as liabilities for purposes of § 357(c)(1). In the example, there would be no $5,000 liability and, accordingly, no liability in excess of basis.[30]

For purposes of consistency, one would expect that X Corp. not get a deduction when in fact it paid T's creditor. As to X Corp., the repayment is akin to repayment of loan principal. Notwithstanding, in Rev. Rul. 80–198,[31] the Service ruled that the transferee-corpora-

---

28. See § 362 discussed below.

29. Even prior to the enactment of § 357(c)(3), courts achieved the same results through some creative reasoning. See, e.g., *Bongiovanni v. Commissioner*, 470 F.2d 921 (2d Cir.1972) (account payable not a liability for purposes of § 357); *Thatcher v. Commissioner*, 533 F.2d 1114 (9th Cir.1976) (constructive deduction permitted under § 357(c)); *Focht v. Commissioner*, 68 T.C. 223 (1977) (following *Bongiovanni*).

30. Note that if the underlying property is a capital asset, the "wash" treat-

ment of § 357(c)(3) may deny the transferor the benefit of the preferential tax rate given net capital gains under § 1(h). If the transferee-corporation had distributed boot instead of assuming the account payable, the transferor would have recognized a capital gain on the boot and would have an ordinary deduction for the deemed payment to the creditor.

31. 1980–2 C.B. 113; see also Rev. Rul. 95–74, 1995–2 C.B 75.

tion can take the deduction. While it might be easy to dismiss this result as another manifestation of the corporate double tax system, there is no apparent reason why a pre-incorporation account payable ought to be deducted twice—once implicitly by the transferor and once explicitly by the transferee.

Suppose T who conducts a business as a sole proprietor holds assets with a combined basis of $40,000 and a fair market value of $100,000. The assets are subject to a $55,000 mortgage for a nondeductible debt which was incurred for business reasons. If T transfers the assets to newly-formed X Corp. in a transaction qualifying under § 351, T will recognize a $15,000 gain in accordance with § 357(c). If in addition to the other assets transferred, T were to transfer $15,000 of cash to X Corp. then T would not recognize gain under § 357(c) because the liabilities transferred do not exceed the total of adjusted basis of the property transferred.

Suppose instead that T transfers "a promise" to pay $15,000 in five years, such promise memorialized in a debt instrument bearing appropriate interest. If T is treated as having a $15,000 basis in his own note, then no gain will be recognized under § 357(c). In *Peracchi v. Commissioner*,[32] the court ruled that a transferor's basis in his own note was equal to the face value. Accordingly, the transferor did not recognize gain under § 357(c).[33]

Historically, contingent liabilities transferred as part of an incorporation transaction were simply ignored, much like the transfer of deductible liabilities are ignored pursuant to the explicit dictates of §§ 357(c)(3) and 358(d)(2). A series of famous tax shelters were based around these rules, and while the details varied they had in common the use of section 351 and its associated basis provisions to create stock with an adjusted basis far in excess of value, stock which when sold would produce an immediate capital loss.

Consider the following. X Corp. forms SubCo by transferring unimproved real estate having adjusted basis of $100 million but

---

32.　143 F.3d 487 (9th Cir.1998).

33.　See also *Lessinger v. Commissioner*, 872 F.2d 519 (2d Cir.1989) where the Second Circuit reached the same conclusion (*i.e.*, no gain under § 357(c)) but on different grounds. The court did not hold that T had a $15,000 basis in the note. Rather, it held that the basis concept did not apply to T's own liability. The court reasoned that § 357(c) should not be recognized where a taxpayer transfers assets subject to a liability in excess of basis if at the same time the transferor promises to eliminate this excess by contributing cash to the corporation in the future. Instead, it is appropriate to look at the basis of the assets in the hands of the transferee-corporation for purposes of determining gain under § 357(c). Because a transferee-corporation normally should take a basis in the debt instrument equal to the fair market value of the instrument ($15,000 in the example above), no gain is recognized to the transferor.

subject to environmental clean-up obligations of approximately the same amount. Thus, the stock of SubCo received by X Corp. has little or no value. However, if the environmental clean-up costs are ignored either because they are too contingent to be taken into account or because they would be deductible by X Corp. when paid, X Corp. will take a basis in the SubCo stock of $100 million unreduced by the liability. If the SubCo stock is then sold by X Corp., X Corp. will be entitled to claim an immediate capital loss of the full $100 million less the little it receives for the stock.[34]

In response to these types of transactions, Congress enacted § 358(h). Section 358(h) reduces a taxpayer's basis in stock received in a § 351 transaction by the amount of any liability assumed by the corporation on the transaction to the extent the liability did not already reduce stock basis under § 358(d)(1). Thus, this rule speaks directly to liabilities that otherwise would be ignored because they are too contingent to be taken into account or because they are deductible and so do not reduce basis by reason of § 358(d)(2). Note, however, that the § 358(h) will not reduce basis below the value of the stock received in the transaction. In addition, in an attempt to limit § 358(h) to artificial, abusive transactions, § 358(h) does not apply to the incorporation of the assets of a trade or business or to the incorporation of "substantially all of the assets" associated with the liability. § 358(h)(2). This last limitation presumably will apply when a taxpayer incorporates either the loan proceeds or the assets purchased with the loan proceeds.

(c) The definition of "stock". Keeping in mind the treatment of nonqualifying property—boot—in a § 351 exchange, consider the delicate question of what constitutes qualifying or nonqualifying property. The term "stock" is defined neither in the Code nor in the Regulations. It is clear that the term "stock" includes common and preferred stock, whether voting or nonvoting. It is also clear that for purposes of § 351 stock does not include stock rights, options, warrants or other rights to purchase stock at a fixed price.[35] Perhaps these potential equity investments do not currently evidence a sufficient continuity of investment to justify nonrecognition under § 351. But what if a transferor satisfies the control requirement under § 368(c) without considering any stock rights, etc. Why then should these instruments be treated in the same manner as cash or other boot?

34. See, e.g., *Coltec v. United States*, 454 F.3d 1340 (Fed.Cir.2006).

35. Regs. § 1.351–1(a)(1). This regulation may have originated from *Helver-ing v. Southwest Consolidated Corp.*, 315 U.S. 194 (1942), holding that warrants were not voting stock within the meaning of a reorganization provision.

Courts have been more lenient towards contingent stock than stock rights. Suppose a transferor transfers property to X Corp. in exchange for stock and a certificate for additional shares to be issued later, contingent on valuation of the transferor's property. The Tax Court in *Hamrick v. Commissioner*,[36] distinguished contingent stock from stock rights, etc. on the grounds that with the former no additional payment is required from the transferor. This distinction seems unconvincing. For purposes of the stock continuity requirement, the focus should be on the nature of what is *received.* Whether additional payments by a shareholder are required seems irrelevant.

Under § 351(g), certain "nonqualified preferred stock" is treated as boot if received in a § 351 transaction along with stock other than nonqualified stock. Note that while nonqualified preferred stock may constitute boot in some cases, it still counts towards the control test under § 351. For example, suppose that three equal transferors contribute property to a newly-formed corporation in exchange for all of its stock. A and B each get common stock and C gets nonqualified preferred stock. Section 351 applies to the transaction even though C receives solely nonqualified preferred stock. In this example, C will be taxed on the difference between the fair market value of the preferred stock and the adjusted basis in the property transferred in accordance with § 1001. If the difference produces a loss, C can recognize the loss in accordance with §§ 165 and 267 if applicable. If C receives any stock other than nonqualified stock along with the nonqualified stock, then the nonqualified stock is treated as boot for purposes of § 351(b) (which would prevent C from recognizing any loss on the transfer).

Such nonqualified preferred stock must first be "preferred stock" within the meaning of § 351(g)(3)(A) and then must be nonqualified as specified in § 351(g)(2)(A), subject to the limitations in § 351(g)(2)(B)–(C). In general, such nonqualified preferred stock is subject to a redemption right or obligation within 20 years or has an dividend rate that references interest rates or an equivalent index.

A corporation's common stock represents a residual interest in the entity, which means that the holders of the common stock are paid last but in a potentially unlimited amount. A corporation's bonds and debentures, on the other hand, represent an investment that is both preferred and limited: debt holders are preferred in the sense that they are paid before equity holders, and their interests

---

36. 43 T.C. 21 (1964). See also *Carlberg v. United States,* 281 F.2d 507 (8th Cir.1960).

are limited in the sense that they receive only a specified interest rate (albeit one that may vary over time) and a fixed return of their principal regardless of the success of the venture. Thus, common shareholders take a large risk (because they are paid last) for a bigger potential gain (because their return is unlimited).

For purposes of § 351(g), stock is "preferred" only if it is both preferred *and* limited. § 351(g)(3)(A). Further, stock is not "preferred" in this sense if it can share in future growth of the corporation by being converted into some other class of stock. Thus, taxpayers wishing to avoid application of § 351(g) should be able to do so by using a class of stock that either is not preferred (i.e., does not stand ahead of common stock as to the payment of dividends or upon liquidation) or is not limited (i.e., that participates to some significant extent in the growth of the company). This definition of "preferred" is much more restrictive than that used in the context of §§ 305 and 306.[37]

Even if stock is both preferred and limited, it is not "disqualified" preferred stock unless it contains a feature described in § 351(g)(2). If the preferred stock must be redeemed, it is disqualified. § 351(g)(2)(A)(ii). If redemption is not mandatory but merely optional, the test is more complex. If the holder of the preferred stock can demand redemption, the stock is disqualified, § 351(g)(2)(A)(i), but if it is the corporation that can insist on redemption, then the stock is disqualified only if (as of the issue date), it is more likely than not that the redemption will occur, § 351(g)(2)(A)(iii). However, these redemption provisions are relevant only if they can be exercised within 20 years of issuance of the stock and the redemption is not subject to a contingency which makes the likelihood of redemption remote. § 351(g)(2)(B). In addition, special provision is made for redemptions related to death, disability, or change of employment status. § 351(g)(2)(C).

Finally, preferred stock is disqualified if the dividend rate on the stock varies with interest rates, commodity prices, or similar measures. Such preferred stock, by paying a periodic payment tied to interest rates or some similar measure and offering no share in the growth of the corporate venture, is considerably closer to straight debt than to common stock on the debt/equity spectrum.

(d) Debt instruments. Under current law, if a transferor exchanges property for a combination of stock and debt instruments in a § 351 transaction, the debt instruments will constitute nonqualifying property under § 351(b). However, the fair market value of the debt instruments is not immediately taxable as boot to the

---

37. See Chapters 6–7 *infra.*

transferor. Under § 453, the transferor may be able to report gain on the debt instrument under the installment method.[38] However, note that under § 453(a)(2)(B), gain from inventory property exchanged for a note must be recognized immediately. Under § 453(d) a transferor may elect out of installment reporting. A transferor will make this election if, for example, there is an expiring loss deduction that will offset the gain.

For example, suppose T transfers an appreciated asset with a basis of $10,000 and a fair market value of $40,000 to X Corp. in a § 351 transaction. In exchange, T receives $20,000 of X Corp. stock and a seven-year debt instrument bearing appropriate interest with a fair market value of $20,000. As discussed in more detail below, T's basis in the assets transferred will be allocated to the stock received so that T's basis in the debt instrument is $0. When the debt instrument is satisfied by X Corp., T will recognize a $20,000 gain. The character of that gain is determined by the character of the assets transferred in the § 351 transaction. If the assets transferred are subject to some depreciation recapture, T must recognize that ordinary income in the year of the § 351 transaction even though no cash is received at the time of the § 351 transaction.[39]

Preferred stock having a dividend rate that varies with interest rates or some similar index is treated not as stock in a § 351 transaction but rather as boot, § 351(g)(2)(A)(iv), presumably because such preferred stock too closely resembles debt. However, no statutory provision permits a transferor who receives such disqualified preferred stock to use installment reporting to defer recognition of gain. Thus, such debt-like stock is actually taxed more harshly than actual corporate debt.

(e) Transferor's basis. Recall that § 351 does not forgive the gain (or take away the loss) realized by a transferor—it is a nonrecognition provision. Rather, the basis provision of § 358 operates to preserve the unrecognized gain (or loss). The basis of property reflects its tax history or genealogy. Suppose T transfers property to X Corp. with a basis of $12,000 and a fair market value of $20,000 in exchange for $20,000 of X Corp. stock in a § 351 transaction. Section 358 gives T a basis of $12,000 in the stock received, thereby preserving the realized but unrecognized $8,000 gain in the event T sells the stock.

Suppose instead that T receives $15,000 of X Corp. common stock and $5,000 of X Corp. preferred stock. T must still preserve the realized but unrecognized $8,000 gain. Section 358 accom-

---

38.   Prop. Regs. § 1.453–1(f)(3)(ii).   **39.**   § 453(i).

plishes this by allocating T's original basis between the common stock and the preferred stock in accordance with fair market values. Thus, T would hold common stock with a basis of $9,000 and preferred stock with a basis of $3,000.[40]

In light of the way that basis is allocated, there may be incentives for a transferor to try to designate which assets were transferred for which stock instruments in an effort to manipulate basis or holding period. Suppose that T has two assets each worth $1,000, one with a basis of $1,500 and one with a basis of $100. In a transaction that qualifies under § 351 T exchanges the assets for $1,000 of common stock and $1,000 of preferred stock. If T knows that he will be selling the preferred stock shortly after the exchange, T would prefer to designate the asset with a $1,500 basis as the one exchanged for the preferred stock. In Rev.Rul. 85–164,[41] the Service indicated that the aggregate basis of the assets transferred has to be allocated between the common stock and preferred stock received in proportion to the fair market values of those stock instruments. In the example, the common and preferred stock would each have a basis of $800.

Now suppose in exchange for his property with a basis of $12,000 and a fair market value of $20,000 T receives $14,000 of X Corp. stock and $6,000 of boot (either cash or nonqualifying property with a fair market value of $6,000). On the § 351 exchange T must recognize $6,000 of his $8,000 realized gain. § 351(b). T's stock basis under § 358 reflects T's recognition. Starting with T's original $12,000 basis, § 358 requires the transferor to subtract any cash (or the fair market value of any property) received and then to add any gain recognized on the § 351 transaction. The effect of § 358 is that starting with T's original basis, boot received has a claim on that basis up to its fair market value. § 358(a)(2). Any remaining basis is allocated to the qualifying property—the stock or securities—after it is adjusted upwards to reflect gain already recognized. In the example above, T starts with a basis of $12,000, subtracts the $6,000 of boot received and adds the $6,000 of gain recognized on the § 351 exchange. As a result, T holds his $14,000 of X Corp. stock with a basis of $12,000, thereby preserving the realized but unrecognized $2,000 of gain. The $6,000 of original basis reserved for the boot becomes the basis of the boot.[42]

---

40. Regs. § 1.358–2(b).

41. 1985–2 C.B. 117.

42. At first glance it may appear that the requirement in § 358 that the fair market value of boot be subtracted and the gain added will always cause a "wash." But suppose in the example that T received $9,000 of stock and $11,000 of boot. Under § 358, T's basis in the stock is $12,000 minus the $11,000 of boot received plus the $8,000 gain recognized. Not surprisingly, T, whose realized gain was fully recognized

With this exploration of boot in mind, consider the situation where T transfers property with a basis of $12,000 and a fair market value of $20,000 in exchange for stock of X Corp. worth $15,000 and a $5,000 debt instrument. T's basis in the stock is equal to $12,000 (his basis in the property) minus $5,000 (the fair market value of the boot) plus $5,000 (the gain recognized).[43]

Accordingly, T holds stock with a fair market value of $15,000 and a basis of $12,000, thereby preserving $3,000 of the realized but unrecognized $8,000 gain. The remaining $5,000 gain will be preserved by giving the $5,000 debt instrument a basis of $0—the difference between T's original $12,000 basis and the amount allocated to the qualifying property.[44] Normally nonqualifying property is given a basis equal to fair market value because the property is taxable on receipt. Debt instruments are not taxable on receipt and, therefore, are allocated any basis left over after determining the basis of the qualifying property under § 358(a).

To this point, the basis treatment of stock, debt instruments and other boot have been explored. Now consider the basis implications inherent in the assumption by the transferee of the transferor's liability. Suppose T transfers property with a basis of $12,000 and a fair market value of $20,000 to X Corp. in exchange for $14,000 of X Corp. stock and X Corp.'s assumption of T's $6,000 bona fide nondeductible liability. Under § 357(a) T does not recognize any gain on the § 351 exchange; the assumption by X Corp. is not treated as boot but is treated as a return of basis. Section 358 carries out Congress' approach by treating the assumption as cash received for purposes of calculating basis. § 358(d)(1). T's basis in the $14,000 of stock would equal his basis in the property of $12,000 minus the liability assumed of $6,000 plus zero gain recognized, or a basis of $6,000. The $6,000 preserves the $8,000 realized but unrecognized gain and reflects the fact that T recovered the other $6,000 of his original basis when he was relieved of his debt obligation without tax consequences.

If in exchange for the property transferred, T receives $5,000 of X Corp. stock and X Corp.'s assumption of T's $15,000 bona fide nondeductible liability. T recognizes a $3,000 gain under § 357(c). T's basis in the $5,000 of X Corp. stock received reflects the $3,000 gain recognized and preserves the remaining $5,000 gain that was realized but not recognized on the § 351 exchange. Under § 358,

on the § 351 exchange, takes a $9,000 basis in stock with a fair market value of $9,000.

43. Notice that basis is increased by the $5,000 of boot even though the gain

on the note won't be recognized until payment is made. Prop. Reg. § 1.453–1(f)(3)(ii).

44. Prop. Regs. § 1.453–1(f)(3)(ii).

T's basis equals the basis of the assets transferred ($12,000) minus the deemed cash received ($15,000) plus the gain recognized ($3,000). The $0 basis in the $5,000 of X Corp. stock preserves the realized but unrecognized $5,000 gain until T sells the stock.

Now suppose that T transfers property with a basis of $6,000 and a fair market value of $20,000 in exchange for X Corp. stock with a fair market value of $12,000 and X Corp.'s assumption of T's $8,000 bona fide deductible liability. Recall that although the assumed liability exceeds T's basis, § 357(c)(3) relieves T of taxation on the § 351 transfer by, in effect, allowing T to offset the deemed receipt of boot with the deemed deduction T would have enjoyed by paying the deductible liability. Because the deemed boot distribution to T is not a return of basis (but rather is taxable and then offset by the deemed deduction), § 358(d)(2) does not treat the assumption of a deductible liability as cash received for purposes of the basis calculation. T's basis in the $12,000 of X Corp. stock is $6,000, reflecting the $6,000 of potential net gain that T would have had to recognize in his original property.[45]

Suppose, in a transaction qualifying under § 351, that T transfers property with a basis and fair market value of $20,000 in exchange for X Corp. stock with a fair market value of $1,000 and X Corp.'s assumption of T's $19,000 deductible expense (*e.g.,* a liability for deferred compensation or environmental remediation) for which T will remain liable. At first glance, it appears that under § 357(c)(3) T has no gain on the transfer and that T receives stock with a basis of $20,000 and a fair market value of $1,000. § 358(d)(2). If this were the case, T could sell the stock and report a loss of $19,000 and might also be able to take a $19,000 deduction under § 162 if T pays the liability. However, § 358(h) requires T to reduce the basis of the stock by the amount of the deductible liability that does not reduce basis under § 358(d)(1). In the example, the T's basis in the X Corp. would be $20,000 minus $19,000 or $1,000. That is, T cannot create a loss on the X Corp. stock by having X Corp. assume the liability. However, § 351(h) does not apply (and so the transferor's stock basis is not reduced) if the trade or business or substantially all of the assets with which the liability is associated is transferred to X Corp.

(f) Treatment of the transferee. A transferee-corporation might start out with nothing, print up stock certificates and issue those certificates in exchange for a transferor's property. In the absence of a nonrecognition provision, it is well established that the ex-

---

45. T had a $14,000 potential gain, but would have had an $8,000 deduction   if the deductible liability were paid.

change of appreciated property for other property will be a recognition event.[46] Is there any reason to treat a transferee-corporation differently? If a corporation is truly a separate entity from its shareholders for tax purposes, then in the absence of a nonrecognition provision gain should be recognized on the issuance of stock.

But a corporation is not independent of its shareholders, nor should it be so treated. Prior to a corporation's formation, its stock has no intrinsic value: the value of the stock is a function of what the corporation receives for it. For example, suppose a corporation exchanges its stock for $10,000 of cash. Taxing the corporation on the $10,000 received makes no sense. There is nothing to tax. No asset has increased in value, no services have been performed, no productive activity of any kind has taken place.

Section 1032 provides that a corporation does not recognize gain or loss on the receipt of property (including cash) in exchange for stock.[47] In the context of a § 351 transaction, in some respects § 1032 is the corporate-level counterpart to § 351, although the corresponding basis provisions are dissimilar.[48] Section 358 essentially gives a transferor a substituted basis in the property received, thereby preserving the unrecognized gain. Section 362(a) does not mandate the same treatment for the transferee-corporation. If it did, the transferee-corporation would presumably take a $0 basis in the transferred assets.

Instead, the basis provision of § 362(a) helps to prevent the use of a transferee-corporation as a vehicle for turning appreciated property of a transferor into cash without recognition of gain. Suppose T owned an asset with a basis of $7,000 and a fair market value of $30,000. If T converted the asset to cash, there would be a $23,000 gain. Suppose instead that T transferred the asset to X Corp. in exchange for $30,000 of X Corp. stock in a § 351 transaction.

46. See, e.g., *United States v. Davis,* 370 U.S. 65 (1962) (exchange of appreciated securities for release of wife's dower rights was considered a recognition event).

47. While § 1032 shields the corporation from recognition of gain (or loss) on an exchange of stock for property, Regs. § 1.1032–1(a) offers the same protection when stock is issued for services. Not only is gain not recognized, but a transferee-corporation issuing stock for services can take a deduction equal to the fair market value of the stock if payment in cash would be an ordinary and necessary business expense. Rev. Rul. 62–217, 1962–2 C.B. 59, modified by Rev.Rul. 74–503, 1974–2 C.B. 117.

Section 1032 does not govern a transferee-corporation's issuance of securities in exchange for property, but the mere borrowing of money is not a taxable event under our federal income tax system.

48. Note though that § 1032 applies even if § 351 does not. For example, if a taxpayer sells property to a corporation in exchange for its stock in a transaction not governed by § 351, § 1032 still gives nonrecognition treatment to the corporation.

Section 362(a) provides that the transferor's basis in the transferred property carries over to the transferee. If the transferee corporation receives several properties, the corporation's basis in each is carried over from the transferor.[49] In the example above, X Corp. would take a $7,000 basis and would recognize a $23,000 gain on the sale of the property.

The rule of § 362(a) is limited, however, to ensure that a contribution of property under § 351 cannot create a built-in loss to the corporate transferee. There are two statutory limitations on using § 351 to create a built-in corporate loss, § 362(e)(1) and § 362(e)(2). The first, § 362(e)(1), generally applies to an inbound cross-border incorporation of loss property; that is, to the transfer to a domestic corporation by a person or foreign corporation not subject to US taxation. Such an attempt to import a loss into the US taxing regime will fail because § 362(e)(1) limits the domestic corporation's basis in such property to fair market value. Note that this provision operates on a property-by-property basis so that the importation of built-in gain property cannot be used to offset the importation of built-in loss property.

Under the second provision limiting the creating of corporate built-in losses, § 362(e)(2), a corporation cannot take an aggregate basis in contributed property in excess of the aggregate fair market value of such property. Thus, if multiple assets are contributed in a single transaction, there can be built-in losses in some of the properties so long as they are offset by built-in gains in others. Note that this provision applies to all § 351 transactions including those in which the transferor is subject to US taxation. The statute provides that the limitation of § 362(e)(2) applies only after the limitation of § 362(e)(1).[50]

Consider the following example. Individual T contributes properties P, Q and R to newly-formed X Corp. in exchange for stock of X. At the time of the contribution, asset P has a adjusted basis of $100 and a fair market value of $60, asset Q has an adjusted basis of $200 and a fair market value of $180, and asset Z has an adjusted basis of $120 and a fair market value of $150. Under the general rule of § 362(a), T would take a stock basis of $420.

---

49. See *P.A. Birren & Son v. Commissioner*, 116 F.2d 718 (7th Cir.1940).

50. To see why the ordering of §§ 362(e)(1) and (2) is important, consider the incorporation of three assets: asset X with value of $100 and adjusted basis of $80, asset Y (described in § 362(e)(1)(B)) having value of $50 with adjusted basis of $70, and asset Z (not described in § 362(e)(1)(B)) having value of $50 with adjusted basis of $70. Because § 361(e)(1) is applied first, there will be no reduction to the carryover basis of asset Z; if § 362(e)(2) had been applied first, the corporation would take a basis of only $40 in asset Z (see § 362(e)(2)(B)).

However, because of the limitation in § 362(d)(2), T's stock basis is limited to the fair market value of the properties contributed; that is, to $390. Under § 362(d)(2)(B), the basis limitation is applied to the contributed properties with built-in losses in proportion to those losses so that X Corp. will take a basis in asset P of $80, in asset Q of 190, and in asset R of $120. T's basis in the stock received equals carry-over of $420 under § 358(a).

The basis limitation in § 362(e)(2) ensures that a section 351 transaction cannot be used to double losses. There is, as noted earlier, no similar rule limiting the doubling of built-in gains. When the limitation of § 362(e)(2) is triggered, the built-in loss will be continued in the contributing shareholder's stock but will not be carried over into the contributed property in the hands of the corporation. However, if the transferor shareholder and the transferee corporation agree, that rule can be flipped so that the limitation imposed by § 362(e)(2) will be applied to the transferor shareholder's stock basis rather than to the transferee corporation's asset basis. § 362(e)(2)(C). In the example above, that means that X Corp. will take a carry-over basis in each of the asset but T will take a basis of only $390 in the stock received.

Note that because of section 362(e)(2), the value of assets contributed to a corporation always must be valued. Given that administrative burden, should § 362(a) be amended to give the corporation a fair market value basis in all cases and not only when the property has, in the aggregate, a built-in loss? Recall the discussion above (and in Section 2.03) suggesting that such a rule would allow a corporate contribution to be used as a mechanism for effecting a tax-free disposition of appreciated property.

Suppose Parent Corp. owns all the outstanding shares of Sub Corp. If individual E is an employee of Sub Corp., E might wish to have some proprietary interest in the venture yet Parent Corp. might be unwilling to give E a direct interest in Sub Corp. Accordingly, Parent Corp. might transfer some of its own stock to E as part of E's compensation. Since E does not work directly for Parent Corp., how should this transaction be taxed?

Under Regs. § 1.83–6(d), this transaction is treated as if Parent Corp. contributed its own stock to Sub Corp. and then that stock was retransferred to E. The first step of this two-step transaction is taxed as a contribution of capital by Parent Corp. to Sub Corp. As a result, the transaction is tax-free to both corporations, and under § 362(a) Sub Corp. takes a carryover basis in the Parent Corp. stock treated as contributed to its capital. But what is that carryover basis?

Under Regs. § 1.1032–3, Sub Corp. takes a fair market value basis in the contributed Parent Corp. stock, just as if cash was contributed by Parent Corp. and then Sub Corp. used this cash to purchase the Parent Corp. stock. The regulations adopt this circular cash approach only when the stock of Parent Corp. (or a stock option of Parent) is transferred by Sub Corp. in a taxable transaction *immediately after* receiving it. Thus, because Sub Corp. is treated as transferring the Parent Corp. stock to E immediately after receiving it, Sub Corp. recognizes no gain or loss on the second step of the transaction.[51] If, though, such stock had actually been contributed by Parent Corp. to Sub Corp. and then transferred from Sub Corp. to E after some delay, it is the Service's position that Sub Corp. would have a zero basis in that stock and so Sub Corp. would recognize gain on the transfer to E. See, e.g., Rev. Rul. 74–503, 1974–2 C.B. 117.

To the extent that the transferor recognizes any gain on the § 351 transaction because of the receipt of boot, the transferee-corporation's basis is increased.[52] For example, suppose that a transferor transfers property with a basis of $7,000 and a fair market value of $30,000 to a corporation in a § 351 transaction. Suppose further that the property is subject to a $60,000 nonrecourse liability that exceeds the value of the transferred asset.[53] At first glance it appears that the basis of the transferred property in the hands of the corporation would be $60,000—the transferor's $7,000 basis increased by the $53,000 gain recognized under § 357(c). That would give the corporation a basis in excess of the fair market value of the property. That might not be such a bad result if the transferor is taxable on a $53,000 gain, but suppose that the transferor is not taxable on the exchange either because it is a nonresident of the United States or is otherwise tax-exempt on the transfer. Now there is the potential for an inflated basis by the corporation with no prior gain to the transferor.

Congress reacted to this perceived abuse by enacting §§ 357(d) and 362(d). Section 357(d) essentially limits the gain recognized by any transferor to the amount of the liability that the transferee really incurs. In the case of a nonrecourse liability, that amount is

---

51.　Assuming that payment to E for services rendered is an ordinary and necessary expenditure if made by Sub Corp., the transfer of Parent Corp. stock to E will give rise to a deduction to Sub Corp.

52.　See Rev. Rul. 68–55, 1968–1 C.B. 140 (transferor's gain on transfer of multiple assets in a § 351 transaction must be allocated to transferee's basis in a pro rata fashion).

53.　This might be the case where the liability is secured not only by the asset transferred but by other assets as well that were not transferred.

limited to the fair market value of the transferred property.[54] This limitation is bolstered by § 362(d)(1) which limits a transferee's basis to fair market value when it assumes a liability.[55]

If a transferor receives debt instruments in a § 351 transaction, no gain is recognized by the transferor until the debt instruments are satisfied. Should the transferee-corporation increase its basis in the property received by the amount of gain *to be* recognized by the transferor? Prop. Regs. § 1.453–1(f)(3)(ii) allows the transferee to increase basis as the transferor recognizes gain.

Suppose as part of a § 351 transaction, X Corp. distributes both stock and a piece of appreciated real estate to its shareholders. The shareholders will be taxable on the boot received to the extent of any realized gain on the transfer of property to the corporation. In addition, X Corp. will be taxable on the distribution of the appreciated real estate as if the property had been sold to the shareholders. § 351(f). However, if X Corp. distributes real estate with a basis in excess of fair market value, X Corp. may not recognize the loss.[56]

2.07 "Control" Requirement. Section 351(a) incorporates the control requirement of § 368(c) in order to ensure that a transferor possesses a sufficient continuity of investment in his original property. If T transfers a piece of appreciated property to IBM in exchange for IBM stock, nonrecognition may be inappropriate since T's interest in his original property is almost nonexistent. T has effectively diversified his original investment. On the other hand, if T and two others transfer equal amounts of property to a newly-formed corporation in exchange for its stock, although T has diversified his investment somewhat, nonrecognition treatment may be intuitively defensible. How to draw the line between sufficient and insufficient continuity is the problem. Congress might have left the solution to the courts on a case-by-case basis. Instead, Congress opted to trade the costs and uncertainties of such subjective evaluation for the greater certainty but also greater arbitrariness of a bright line test.

---

54. In the case of a nonrecourse liability in excess of the fair market value, the transferee would walk away from the property if confronted with a payment obligation.

55. Any assumption of a nonrecourse liability is proportionate to the fair market value of the transferred property compared to all property encumbered by the liability. In the example above, if $120,000 of property were secured by the $60,000 liability, then the transferee's basis would equal $22,000—the transferor's $7,000 basis increased by a proportionate amount of the nonrecourse loan ($60,000 loan x $30,000 transferred property/$120,000 total encumbered property).

56. See the discussion of § 311 at Section 8.02 *infra*.

Section 368(c) sets out two 80 percent tests for purposes of determining control. The transferors of property are in control of the transferee if, immediately after the transfer, they own at least 80 percent of the total combined voting power of all classes of stock entitled to vote and 80 percent of all other classes of stock.[57]

The right to vote is one feature of some stock instruments. Other features include dividend rights and preferences and liquidation rights and preferences. All of these features are reflected in the fair market value of the stock. If the vote is important, then all other things being equal, a share of voting stock will have a greater fair market value than a share of nonvoting stock. Why, then, should there be multiple 80 percent tests?

Note that the 80 percent tests are somewhat arbitrary in at least two respects. First, consider the 80 percent figure itself? Why not 67 percent or 85 percent? Also, 80 percent tests applied to a group of transferors does not guarantee continuity for any one transferor. The transferor not entitled to nonrecognition on transferring property to IBM in exchange for its stock because of his attenuated interest in the original property may nevertheless qualify under § 351 if the transferors as a group satisfy § 368(c). Thus, if 1,000 transferors form a corporation and each receives the same amount of stock for the same amount of property transferred, § 351 is available even though each shareholder holds a .1 percent interest in the corporation.[58]

Why should the tax consequences of one transferor depend on how much stock is received by other transferors? Perhaps the transferor should be required to attain some minimum percentage of the transferee-corporation's stock—say, 10 percent—in order to qualify under § 351 rather than focusing on a group of transferors. With this approach, it might make sense to attribute ownership of the stock of a related party (e.g., a parent) to a transferor in order to satisfy the percentage ownership test.[59] Apparently Congress decided that for purposes of evaluating control, the transferors as a

---

57. Suppose after a purported § 351 transaction, the transferors own 95 percent of the voting stock, 75 percent of the class A nonvoting preferred stock and 95 percent of the class B nonvoting preferred stock, for an overall 88 percent interest in the total preferred stock and a 91 percent interest by fair market value of all of the stock. Do the transferors have control? In Rev.Rul. 59–259, 1959–2 C.B. 115, the Service ruled that while classes of voting stock can be combined in applying the 80 percent test, *each* class of nonvoting stock must satisfy the 80 percent test.

58. The one area where Congress has recognized the potential of broad diversification under § 351 is where a group of transferors each owning stock get together and form an investment company receiving shares of that company for their shares of stock. Section 351(e)(1) denies the nonrecognition of § 351 to this attempted diversification.

59. See Section 5.02 *infra* for a discussion of the § 318 attribution rules.

group would be considered related and that 80 percent control is the minimum percentage. But note that pre-existing stock owned by related taxpayers who were not transferors will not be counted for purposes of the 80 percent tests.

Recall that certain "disqualified" preferred stock is taxed as boot rather than as stock. § 351(g)(2). However, for determining "control" under § 368(c), even disqualified preferred stock counts as stock. Thus, this disqualified preferred stock is something of a chameleon, looking like stock for purposes of control but like boot for purposes of recognition of gain.

(a) The "Control" Group. Deciding who is in the control group causes a great deal of uncertainty. Recall that under § 351 the transferors must *be* in control after the exchange; they need not acquire control in the exchange itself. Suppose that X Corp. was formed several years ago by B and C with B receiving 60 percent and C 40 percent of the X Corp. stock. B now transfers sufficient additional property to give him 20 percentage points more of X Corp. stock—B now holds 80 percent and C 20 percent. Even though B has increased his stock interest by only 20 percentage points, the transferor is in control of X Corp. after the transaction within the meaning of §§ 351 and 368(c).

Now suppose that D transfers enough property to X Corp. to give her 50 percent of the X Corp. stock outstanding.[60] By herself, D would not satisfy the control requirement and would not qualify for nonrecognition. Aware that transferors need not *acquire* 80 percent control, D induces B to purchase one additional share of X Corp. stock—to act as an accommodation transferor. Are D and B together transferors who control at least 80 percent (actually 90 percent plus one share) of the outstanding X Corp. stock? Regs. § 1.351–1(a)(1)(ii) takes the position that stock issued for property "which is of relatively small value" compared with stock already owned shall not be considered as issued for property if the primary purpose is to qualify the exchange for other persons.[61] In the example above, B would not be considered a transferor of *property* and D could not rely on B's stock ownership for purposes of § 351. D would recognize any gain (or loss) on the exchange.

In Rev. Proc. 77–37,[62] the Service stated that for purposes of obtaining an advanced ruling, property will not be considered "of relatively small value" if it equals at least 10% of the value of stock

---

60. B's interest is reduced to 40 percent and C's to 10 percent.

61. See also *Kamborian v. Commissioner,* 56 T.C. 847 (1971), aff'd, 469 F.2d 219 (1st Cir.1972) (upholding the regulation).

62. 1977–2 C.B. 568.

or securities already owned by the transferor. In the example above, if B contributes enough property to bring his interest up to 44%, he would seem to be on safe ground.[63]

A related situation involving an accommodation transferor arises in the context of stock received for services performed. Suppose B and C form X Corp. with B contributing property with a basis of $10,000 and a fair market value of $40,000 and C contributing $40,000 of services. Not only will C be taxable on the fair market value of the stock received for his services, B will not qualify under § 351 since the transferors of *property* do not satisfy the control requirement of § 368(c) (B holds only a 50 percent interest).[64]

Does C become a transferor of property by contributing to X Corp. enough cash to purchase one share of X Corp. stock as part of the attempted § 351 transaction? The Service's position is that the amount of the property contribution must equal or exceed 10 percent of the value of the stock or securities received for services performed.[65] Note that if C, a transferor of services, does contribute enough property to be considered a transferor of property, C will still be taxable on the fair market value of the stock received for the services performed. However, B may now qualify for nonrecognition under § 351 since the transferors of property satisfy the control requirement under § 368(c).[66]

(b) "Immediately After". To this point, the focus has been on who should be included in the "control" group. A related question has also generated its share of uncertainty—when should the 80 percent tests under § 368(c) be applied? Section 351 requires that the transferors of property be in control of the transferee-corporation "immediately after the exchange." This aspect of the control requirement arises in two contexts—where a transferor disposes of stock received shortly after the purported § 351 exchange and where the transferee-corporation issues additional stock shortly after a purported § 351 transaction.

Suppose B and C form X Corp. by each contributing appreciated property ($10,000 basis and $40,000 fair market value) in exchange for X Corp. stock in an attempted § 351 transaction.

---

63. Remember that Rev. Proc. 77–37 only represents the Service's ruling position; it does not mean the Service will challenge all transactions failing its standards or that such challenges, if made, will hold up in court.

64. See *James v. Commissioner*, 53 T.C. 63 (1969).

65. See Rev. Proc. 77–37, 1977–2 C.B. 568.

66. If a transferor of services and property qualifies as a transferor of property, *all* of that transferor's stock can be counted for purposes of the 80 percent tests—not just the stock received for property transferred.

Shortly after the exchange, B sells her stock to D for $40,000 and reports a $30,000 long-term capital gain. The issue raised by this transaction is the applicability of § 351. Did B and C have control immediately after the exchange? But why does that even matter since B reports a $30,000 gain on the sale—the same gain she would have reported if § 351 had not been applicable? It is true that B recognizes the $30,000 gain but the timing of that recognition may differ depending on whether B should have recognized the gain on the initial transfer or on the subsequent sale.[67]

Perhaps more importantly, the availability of nonrecognition to C depends on the control requirement. If B and C are deemed not to be in control, then C must recognize his $30,000 realized gain on the exchange.[68] Moreover, whether B and C satisfy the control requirement will determine X Corp.'s basis. If § 351 applies, X Corp. takes a carryover basis in each asset of $10,000 for purposes of depreciation or eventual sale. If instead § 351 is not available, then X Corp. will take a cost basis of $40,000 in each asset pursuant to § 1012.[69]

Similarly, suppose that B and C make their transfers to X Corp., but that shortly after the transaction, X Corp. issues additional stock (enough stock to constitute a ⅓ equity interest) to D for services performed. In any case, D will be taxable on the fair market value of stock received as compensation, but the fate of B and C will depend upon how D's transaction is treated. If it is deemed to be separate, then B and C will satisfy the control requirement. On the other hand, if D's transaction is combined with that of B and C, then B and C will fail the control requirement and must recognize any gain on the exchange with X Corp.

Having set out the stakes, focus now on the resolution of the problem. In deciding whether to combine multiple transactions (e.g., an exchange followed by a sale or an exchange followed by a second exchange), courts have articulated a variety of "tests." Perhaps the most widely used test is the "mutual interdepen-

---

67. If § 351 does not apply B would have recognized the entire $30,000 gain on the transfer and would have taken a cost basis under § 1012, thereby recognizing no further gain on the sale. If § 351 applies, installment reporting would be available on the sale.

68. Note that if the exchange with X Corp. and the purported sale are combined for tax purposes, § 351 will be unavailable since C will end up with 50 percent of the X Corp. stock and D is not a transferor of property to X Corp. If D had purchased stock directly from X

Corp. while C contributed property, the exchange would qualify under § 351. X Corp. could then have purchased the property from B. Throughout subchapter C it is often the case that choosing the correct form is paramount. But see Regs. § 1.368–1(e)(i) (disposition of stock to persons not related to issuing corporation after a reorganization does not break continuity of interest).

69. See *Intermountain Lumber Co. v. Commissioner,* 65 T.C. 1025 (1976).

dence"[70] test set out in *American Bantam Car Co. v. Commissioner*:[71] "Were the steps so interdependent that the legal relations created by one transaction would have been fruitless without a completion of the series?" In that case, the court determined that transferors who received common stock for their manufacturing assets qualified under § 351 even though five days later the transferors agreed to pay more than 20 percent of their common stock to underwriters for their services in selling the corporation's preferred stock to investors. The court found that the loss of control was not an integral part of the § 351 transaction.

Certainly, the absence of a preexisting binding commitment was helpful to the taxpayer in *American Bantam Car*. If there is a binding agreement, transactions will be stepped together; if there is not a binding agreement, transactions may be stepped together.[72] Aside from the presence or absence of a binding agreement, the amount of time between the transactions is probably the most important aspect—in general, the closer the transactions are in time, the more likely they will be combined.[73]

The Service has recognized that not all post-incorporation transfers of stock run afoul of the goals underlying § 351. In Rev. Rul. 2003–51,[74] the Service explained that a pre-arranged transfer of stock in a second § 351 transaction will not preclude satisfaction of the control requirement of a prior § 351 transaction because the tax-free transfer of stock, being a mere change in form of ownership, "is not necessarily inconsistent with the purposes of section 351." A similar conclusion was reached in Rev. Rul. 84–111[75] in which a partnership converted to corporate form by transferring its assets to a corporation and then distributing the stock received in complete liquidation of the partnership.

In noncommercial settings, it seems less likely that a purported § 351 exchange followed by the transferor's gift will be stepped together to deny § 351 treatment to the transferor. If B and C form X Corp. in exchange for X Corp. stock, and B makes a gift of her

---

70. One wonders what "non-mutual interdependence" might be.

71. 11 T.C. 397 (1948), aff'd per curiam, 177 F.2d 513 (3d Cir.1949).

72. See *McDonald's Restaurants of Ill., Inc. v. Commissioner*, 688 F.2d 520 (7th Cir.1982).

73. But compare *Commissioner v. Ashland Oil & Refining Co.*, 99 F.2d 588 (6th Cir.1938) (steps that were six years apart were integrated) with *Henricksen*

v. Braicks, 137 F.2d 632 (9th Cir.1943) (steps that were one-half hour apart were treated separately). In the special statutory rule of § 351(c), corporate transferors can distribute the stock received in a § 351 transaction to their shareholders without violating the control requirement.

74. 2003–1 C.B. 938.

75. 1984–2 C.B. 88.

stock to her daughter shortly after the exchange § 351 treatment will probably be available.[76]

2.08 The Relationship of Section 351 to Other Provisions and Legal Doctrines. Having focused on the components of § 351, it is now appropriate to step back in order to view the nonrecognition provision in the broader context. The alternative to nonrecognition is recognition in accordance with § 1001(c). While under most circumstances nonrecognition is a superior alternative for most taxpayers, that is not always the case. For example, a transferor might have a realized loss that he would like to recognize or a transferor with net operating losses might be willing to recognize gain in order to secure a higher basis for the transferee-corporation.

While § 351 nominally is not an elective provision, the provision contains enough requirements to offer taxpayers the flexibility to avoid nonrecognition treatment when desirable. For example, a transferor with property whose basis exceeds its fair market value might attempt to divorce his transfer from those of other transferors seeking nonrecognition. If successful, the nonrecognition-seeking transferors will control the corporation after their exchange thereby qualifying under § 351 while the loss-seeking transferor will fail the control test after his exchange thereby recognizing his loss.

The ability to sell property to oneself or to a related party in order to recognize a loss is circumscribed by § 267. The purpose of this provision is to prevent taxpayers from recognizing built-in losses while retaining control over the property through a related party. An individual is considered related to a corporation only if more than 50 percent in value of the corporation is owned by the individual. Thus, the opportunity to recognize a loss while still maintaining some control is available to taxpayers in the § 351 context.

(a) Section 351 vs. Sale. Often the owner of appreciated real estate slated for development would prefer to recognize the gain while the property is investment property rather than waiting until it is converted to property held for sale to customers. By so doing, an owner may be able to lock in some of the gain at favorable capital gains rates instead of recognizing all of the gain at ordinary income rates. Section 267 does not preclude a taxpayer from recog-

---

76. Compare *Wilgard Realty Co. v. Commissioner,* 127 F.2d 514 (2d Cir. 1942) (§ 351 applicable since no obligation to make gift) with *Fahs v. Flori-* *da Machine & Foundry Co.,* 168 F.2d 957 (5th Cir.1948) (direct issuance of shares to donee precluded § 351).

nizing gain on a transfer to a controlled corporation. Even when there is no capital gains preference, because of the restrictions on deducting capital losses, there still may be an advantage in generating capital gain rather than ordinary income since capital losses can be deducted to the extent of capital gain.[77]

Suppose B owns investment real estate with a basis of $100,000 and a fair market value of $300,000. B intends to develop and subdivide the property into single family dwellings that will have an aggregate fair market value of $600,000 upon completion.[78] If B undertakes the development and then sells the property, there will be $500,000 of ordinary income. B would prefer to recognize $200,000 of the gain as capital gain, but current law does not permit such bifurcation.

Suppose that B transfers the undeveloped real estate to X Corp., a previously formed corporation wholly owned by B. In exchange B receives five-year notes bearing appropriate interest with a fair market value of $300,000. B would like to treat the transaction as a sale, reporting $200,000 of capital gain on the installment method as the notes are paid off. X Corp., the purchaser, would take a $300,000 cost basis under § 1012 and following development and sale would report $300,000 of ordinary income. The economic effect of a sale to a wholly owned corporation is as if B had sold the property to himself. But for tax purposes, the treatment is quite different.

Section 1239 in some circumstances recharacterizes what would otherwise be capital gain as ordinary income on a sale between related parties. However, the application of § 1239 is restricted to property that would be subject to depreciation in the hands of the purchaser. Here, since the transferee-corporation would hold the purchased property as inventory, the transferor would escape recharacterization of any recognized gain.

Under these circumstances, it is likely that the Service would recharacterize the transaction. It might argue that the financial instruments received by the transferor constitute stock in the corporation. Particularly if the corporation is thinly capitalized, the Service might argue that the transferor's likelihood of payment is inextricably tied to the performance of the transferee and that therefore there is sufficient continuity to bring the transfer within § 351. Under this recharacterization, the transferee would take the transferor's basis under § 362. Alternatively, the Service might argue that the financial instruments received by the transferor

---

77. § 1211.

78. For purposes of the example, ignore the costs of development.

should be ignored because payment is so speculative. Under this rationale, the transfer of property would be treated as a nontaxable contribution to capital, and the transferee would take the transferor's basis under § 362(a).

In *Burr Oaks Corp. v. Commissioner*,[79] three individuals transferred land to a controlled corporation, receiving in exchange three notes bearing interest of 6 percent, due in two years. Each note had a face amount of $110,000. The taxpayer claimed that the transaction was a sale, but both the Tax Court and the Court of Appeals ruled that the transaction was a contribution to the corporation in exchange for preferred stock. Since the corporation was capitalized with only $4,500, the purported debt was more than 80 times that amount. The courts found that the payment of the transferors was dependent on an undercapitalized corporation with uncertain prospects. The promise of payment hinged on the success of the corporation. The finding that the transaction was not a sale meant that the taxpayer took a carryover basis under § 362 rather than a cost basis under § 1012.[80]

When an attempted sale is recharacterized by the Service as a contribution to capital, what are the consequences to the transferor and the corporate transferee? When a shareholder makes a contribution to capital, the shareholder recognizes no gain or loss, and must increase his or her stock basis by the basis of the property contributed. Treas. Regs. § 1.118–1. Under § 118, the corporation recognizes no gain or loss and receives a carryover basis in the property. § 362(a). When the corporation makes payments on the "notes," the purported interest may be a dividend that may be ordinary income to the shareholder. See § 301. Retiring the "debt" may create ordinary income due to a failed redemption. See Chapter 5 *infra*.

(b) Assignment of Income. The same respect granted to a corporation as a separate judicial entity that may allow a transferor to report gain on a sale to a wholly-owned corporation causes problems in the judicially developed assignment of income area. Recall that if a transferor transfers an account receivable to a corporation in exchange for stock, no gain will be recognized if the requirements of § 351 are met. The transferee-corporation will take the transferor's basis in the accounts receivable. § 362. The conclusion that an account receivable is property so that § 351 can apply does not determine who will be taxed when the account receivable is paid off.

---

79. 365 F.2d 24 (7th Cir.1966).

80. See also *Aqualane Shores, Inc. v. Commissioner*, 269 F.2d 116 (5th Cir. 1959).

In *Lucas v. Earl*,[81] where Mr. Earl attempted to shift his income from future services to his spouse, the Supreme Court held that the assignment of future services income was an ineffective means to shift income to the assignee for federal tax purposes. The Supreme Court in *Helvering v. Eubank*[82] extended the rationale of *Lucas v. Earl* to previously earned income. There, a taxpayer assigned the right to receive insurance commissions which he had earned from work in previous years. In *Commissioner v. P.G. Lake, Inc.*[83] involving an exchange rather than a gratuitous transfer, the taxpayer assigned an oil payment right to a creditor to discharge a debt. Viewing the oil payment right as a right to receive future income, the Supreme Court held that the consideration received by the taxpayer was taxable as ordinary rather than capital income since it was a substitute for future ordinary income.

Taking these cases together, one might conclude that a transferor should be taxed on the ordinary income when the account receivable is paid off. In many ways, a § 351 transfer is treated as a gratuitous transfer since gain normally is not recognized and the transferee-corporation carries over the transferor's basis. If so, *Lucas v. Earl* and *Eubank* suggest that the transferor ought to be taxed on collection. If viewed as a nongratuitous transfer, the transaction might be governed by *P.G. Lake*. Nevertheless, in *Hempt Bros., Inc. v. United States*,[84] the court held that Congress intended for § 351 to facilitate the incorporation of ongoing businesses and that to apply assignment of income principles would frustrate such incorporations.

It is worthwhile to note that favoring § 351 over the assignment of income doctrine does not necessarily mean a shifting of income. Indeed, the fact that the transferor and the transferee-corporation both take the basis that the transferor has in the receivables[85] preserves the possibility of a double tax—a tax on the transferee-corporation when the receivables are paid off *and* a tax on the transferor if and when his stock is sold or a tax on the transferor upon distribution of the receivable proceeds. Conversely, when a taxpayer transfers deductible accounts payables to a corporation as part of a § 351 transaction, the Service has permitted the transferee-corporation to deduct the payables[86] even though the effect of §§ 357(c)(3) and 358(d)(2) is to give the transferor-shareholder an equivalent deduction.[87]

---

81. 281 U.S. 111 (1930).

82. 311 U.S. 122 (1940).

83. 356 U.S. 260 (1958).

84. 490 F.2d 1172 (3d Cir.1974).

85. Section 358 (transferor) and § 362 (transferee-corporation).

86. Rev. Rul. 95–74, 1995–2 C.B. 36.

87. See p. 30–31 *supra*.

(c) Business Purpose. Before concluding that § 351 is all powerful, overriding entrenched judicial doctrines, note that in *Hempt Bros.*, the transferors were incorporating an ongoing business for an uncontested business purpose. Where § 351 is employed for a nonbusiness purpose, the nonrecognition provision will often be ignored or give way to other principles. In general, neither the Service nor the courts consider tax avoidance standing alone or as a major motivation for the transaction as a "business purpose." The ubiquitous "business purpose" doctrine rears its head in a variety of contexts. For example, a transferor who forms a corporation under § 351 solely for the purpose of collecting the transferor's accounts receivable will be taxed when the transferee-corporation collects the payment.[88] Similarly the formation of a corporation solely for the purpose of qualifying a subsequent exchange of stock for nonrecognition under the reorganization provisions will be disregarded where a direct exchange of assets for stock would have been a taxable event. If a transferor transfers appreciated property to a corporation which then sells the property and distributes the proceeds, the purported § 351 transfer may not apply and the transferor may be treated as having sold the property directly.[89]

(d) Tax Benefit Rule. The tax benefit rule creates another tension between the nonrecognition principles of § 351 and judicially developed conservation of income principles. Under that rule, a taxpayer who derives a tax benefit (e.g., a deduction) in one year must recover that deduction in income in a subsequent year if some event inconsistent with the earlier deduction (e.g., a recovery of the deducted item) occurs. Suppose that B, an accrual basis transferor, holds $10,000 in accounts receivable. B has taken the $10,000 into income, but has deducted $4,000 of the receivables as an uncollectible bad debt.[90] If B forms a corporation in a transaction governed by § 351, must B report gain to the extent of the previous deduction?

In *Nash v. United States*,[91] the Supreme Court held that § 351 was not inconsistent with the tax benefit rule since the transferor received stock equal to the net value of the assets transferred—in the example above, $6,000 of stock. The holding in *Nash* does not preclude application of the tax benefit rule if the transferor in the example above received $10,000 of stock since receipt of property equal to the face value of the receivables would be inconsistent with

---

88. See, e.g., *Brown v. Commissioner*, 115 F.2d 337 (2d Cir.1940).

89. See e.g., *Estate of Kluener v. Commissioner*, 154 F.3d 630 (6th Cir. 1998).

90. See § 166(a).

91. 398 U.S. 1 (1970).

the earlier deduction.[92] Note also that the basis taken by both the transferor and the transferee-corporation will be $6,000 reflecting the bad debt deduction. If and when the transferee-corporation collects the full $10,000 face value of the receivable, it will be taxed on $4,000, and the transferor faces the possibility of a $4,000 tax upon disposition of his stock.

92. See, e.g., *Hillsboro Nat. Bank v. Commissioner,* 460 U.S. 370 (1983), for a discussion of the tax benefit rule.

CHAPTER 3. THE CORPORATION AS A TAXABLE ENTITY

3.01 Corporate Tax Rates and Base. The corporate tax rate schedule[1] is a funny creature, progressive for some corporations, regressive for others, and flat for most. For corporations with taxable income of $100,000 or less, the rates are progressive, with brackets of 15 percent (on taxable income up to $50,000), 25 percent (on taxable income between $50,000 and $75,000), and 34 percent (on taxable income in excess of $75,000). There is a 35 percent bracket for corporate taxable income in excess of $10 million. What little graduation there is disappears for corporations with taxable income in excess of $18,333,333. These corporations are taxed at a flat 35 percent rate because Congress wanted to restrict the benefits of lower rates to smaller businesses.

The elimination of graduation is implemented in a convoluted manner. First, there is an additional tax on taxable income in excess of $100,000. The additional tax is equal to 5 percent of the income in excess of $100,000 with a maximum additional tax of $11,750, which occurs at $335,000 of taxable income. The $11,750 figure represents the difference between taxing the first $75,000 of taxable income at a flat 34 percent ($25,500) and taxing it at the graduated rates ($13,750). As a corporation's taxable income increases from $100,000 to $335,000, the benefits of the reduced tax rates on the first $75,000 vanish. Note that for taxable income in the range of $100,000 to $335,000, the marginal tax rate is not 34 percent but rather 34 percent plus the 5 percent surtax—39 percent. A similar surtax phases out the 34 percent bracket for corporate taxpayers with taxable income exceeding $15 million. These corporations pay 3 percent of taxable income in excess of $15 million or $100,000, whichever is less. Accordingly, for taxpayers with taxable income in excess of $15 million and less than $18,333,333, the marginal tax rate is 38 percent. For taxpayers with taxable income exceeding $18,333,333, there is a flat 35 percent rate.

What little graduation exists in corporate tax rates is denied to "qualified" personal service corporations. § 11(b). Such corporations are "qualified" to be treated more harshly than other corporations by paying taxes at a flat 35 percent tax rate. A corporation is a qualified personal service corporation if it meets a function and

---

1. See § 11.

an ownership test. § 448(d). Under the function test, substantially all of the activities of the corporation must involve the performance of services in the fields of health, law, engineering, architecture, accounting, actuarial science, performing arts or consulting. Under the ownership test, substantially all of the stock (by value) of the corporation must be held directly or indirectly by employees (or by their estates) performing the services or who performed the services in the past two years.

Congress both giveth to and taketh away from qualified personal service corporations. While such corporations are subject to a flat 35 percent rate, they are entitled to use the cash basis method of accounting.[2] There does not appear to be a well founded policy reason that justifies treating personal service corporations differently from manufacturing or sales corporations. Moreover, it is not always apparent whether a corporation constitutes a qualified personal service corporation. For example, a corporation that engages in financial planning is a qualified personal services corporation if the corporation is paid for its advice regardless of outcome. On the other hand, if payment is based on trade orders executed, the corporation is not a qualified personal service corporation.[3]

The current income tax rate structure generally creates an incentive for taxpayers to use the corporate form to shelter income from the top individual rates. This incentive is furthered by the tax-favored capital gains rate. For individuals, the tax rate applicable to most capital gains is 20% and a top rate of 39.1 percent on ordinary income. For corporations, § 1201 provides for an alternative tax on net capital gains in lieu of the § 11 tax if the § 1201 tax is less. The § 1201 tax is the sum of (1) the § 11 tax on the corporation's taxable income minus net capital gains and (2) 35 percent of the net capital gains. Section § 1201 takes effect if the tax rate under § 11 exceeds 35 percent. Therefore, for corporations the maximum rate on net capital gains is 35 percent. Capital losses of corporations are also treated differently than those of individual taxpayers. A corporation can deduct capital losses only to the extent of capital gains.[4] Unlike individuals who can carry forward capital losses indefinitely, corporations generally can only carry losses back three years (perhaps resulting in a tax refund) and forward five years, if necessary. A loss unused in the current year is first carried back three years and then carried forward chronologically until the

---

2. Section 448 prohibits the use of cash method accounting by C corporations other than qualified personal service corporations.

3. Regs. § 1.448–1T.

4. § 1211(a). Other taxpayers can use capital losses to offset up to $3,000 of ordinary income. § 1211(b).

entire loss is used to offset income, or the carryforward period expires.

Because corporate distributions often are taxed to the recipient shareholders as ordinary income while gains from the disposition of stock are taxed as capital gain, the capital gains preference historically has encouraged shareholders to eschew dividends and similar distributions in favor of corporate retention of capital. Alternatively, taxpayers and their advisors have divined innumerable strategies to cause corporate distributions to be taxed as capital gain.

The corporate tax is applied to taxable income. Unlike an individual, a corporation has no adjusted gross income from which deductions are taken to determine taxable income. Corporate taxable income is determined by subtracting deductions directly from gross income. Deductions allowed to corporations differ from deductions available to individuals in a number of ways. For example, corporations have no standard deduction, personal exemption deduction, or personal deductions under §§ 211–220 (including items such as medical expenses and alimony). Section 162 does allow corporations to deduct expenses incurred for the production of income even if the income is not derived in a trade or business. Corporations are also allowed to deduct charitable contributions up to 10 percent of taxable income. § 170(b)(2).

Once a corporation's taxable income is determined, corporate tax liability may be offset by tax credits which offset corporate tax liability dollar-for-dollar. While the foreign tax credit (§§ 27 and 901) often is the most significant for a corporation, credits are also available for research (§ 41), targeted job expenditures (§ 51), and rehabilitation and energy expenditures (§§ 46–48).

Companion to the regular corporate income tax is the corporate alternative minimum tax. Perhaps in response to television and newspaper stories focusing on large corporations paying little or no income tax, Congress has acted to limit the advantages that any one corporation can obtain from the various tax incentive provisions appearing throughout the Code. Under § 55(a), each corporation pays the excess, if any, of its minimum tax liability over its regular tax liability. In effect, a corporation's total federal income tax liability equals the *greater of* its regular tax liability or its minimum tax liability.

The corporate minimum tax equals 20 percent of a corporation's "alternative minimum taxable income" less an exemption amount of $40,000 or less. This "alternative minimum taxable income" (or "AMTI") is intended to be a better measure of a corporation's economic income than is the regular taxable income as defined under § 61. AMTI is defined in § 55 as regular taxable income increased by specified tax preferences and other adjustments. The exemption amount is set at $40,000 less one-quarter of the corporation's AMTI above $150,000, so that the exemption amount is zero for corporations with AMTI equal to $310,000 or more.

Many of the adjustments made to taxable income to arrive at AMTI modify the *timing* of corporate deductions but not the *amount.* §§ 56–58. For example, under § 168 the cost of depreciable residential real estate used in a trade or business is recovered ratably over 27.5 years. For the AMTI, however, the recovery period is lengthened to 40 years. For example, the cost recovery deduction for a piece of residential real estate costing $275,000 is $10,000.[5] That annual deduction for the AMTI is reduced to $275,000 divided by 40, or $6,875.

This adjustment is simple to make in the first 27.5 years: taxable income is increased by $3,125 each year to arrive at AMTI. But what about years 28 through 40? In these years, there is no further cost recovery deduction for computing regular taxable income but there should continue to be a cost recovery deduction of $6,875 for the AMTI. That is, taxable income should be adjusted *downward* in the latter years to arrive at AMTI.

While such a downward adjustment to a corporation's AMTI is permitted,[6] it may produce no tax benefit to the corporation. Recall that a corporation's effective tax liability is the greater of the regular tax or the alternative minimum tax. In the first 27.5 years, the depreciation adjustment may cause a tax increase by increasing the AMTI over taxable income. Unfortunately, the subsequent reduction of AMTI in years 28 through 40 will produce no tax benefit because the corporation will still be required to pay its regular tax liability, a tax liability no longer reflecting any cost recovery deduction.[7]

However, some relief may be offered by the alternative minimum tax credit. This is a credit for payments of the alternative minimum tax and it is credited against the corporation's *regular* income tax liability for subsequent years. In the depreciation example above, the corporation's payment of an alternative minimum

---

5. In these computations, it is assumed that all property is purchased on the first day of the taxable year and the mid-month convention of § 168(d)(2) is ignored.

6. See § 56(a).

7. Of course, because of other possible adjustments to AMTI, the different tax rates applicable to taxable income and to AMTI, and the exemption amount applicable only to the minimum tax, it is impossible to know in advance the over-all effect of such timing problems on a corporation's tax liability.

tax liability in the early years may produce a credit against its regular tax liability in the later years.

Even with tax preferences added back to taxable income to form alternative minimum taxable income, Congress was concerned that some highly profitable corporations might still pay insufficient taxes. This might occur because some transactions might increase a corporation's "earnings and profits" but not taxable income.[8] For example, tax-exempt interest increases earnings and profits but not taxable income. To deal with these situations, a corporation with earnings in excess of alternative minimum taxable income must include a portion of such excess in alternative minimum taxable income. § 56(g).

Corporate AMTI includes three-quarters of a corporation's "adjusted current earnings" over AMTI (determined without this addition).[9] Adjusted current earnings consist of AMTI less the alternative net operating loss deduction and less adjustments intended to better reflect the economic picture of the corporation. For example, accelerated depreciation deductions are replaced by straight-line deductions. In addition, amounts not otherwise taken into account in computing AMTI but affecting a corporation's earnings and profits account contribute to the "adjusted current earnings" stew.

3.02 Associations Taxable as Corporations. Both the regular corporate tax of § 11 and the alternative minimum tax of § 55 are imposed on "corporations." Under § 7701(a)(3), the term "corporation" includes "associations, joint-stock companies, and insurance companies" but it does not include "partnerships." For several decades regulations tried to distinguish entities taxable as partnerships from associations taxable as corporations by reference to certain supposed "corporate characteristics" such as continuity of life, centralization of management, limited liability; and free transferability of interests. Reg. § 301.7701–2(a)(1) (repealed 1996) While these regulations were not by their terms elective, taxpayers usually could structure their unincorporated business organizations to be taxed as partnerships or as corporations as they preferred by manipulating relatively insignificant aspects of the organization.

In the late 1980s and early 1990s, most states enacted limited liability company statutes, thereby permitting businesses to have all the non-tax characteristics of corporations (including limited liability for all investors) while technically not being corporations. Thus, the organizer of a limited liability company files articles of

---

8. For the definition of "earnings and profits," see Section 4.02 *infra.*   **9.** See § 56(g).

organization and an operating agreement instead of articles of incorporation and corporate by-laws, investors contribute cash or property to the limited liability company and receive membership certificates instead of shares, and these investors are called "members" instead of "shareholders." Somewhat surprisingly, courts and the Service were willing to treat such corporate look-alikes as unincorporated entities, and so limited liability companies could then qualify for taxation as partnerships by manipulating their various "corporate characteristics."

As the efficacy of the old association regulations was declining, Congress enacted § 7704 providing that publicly-traded partnerships (including limited liability companies and similar business organizations otherwise taxable as partnerships) would be taxed as corporations if their interests were traded on an established securities market or for which their was a secondary market making the interests readily tradable. These two factors—the increasing failure of the meaningless "corporate characteristics" in the association regulations and the more objective standard imposed by § 7704— ultimately convinced the Treasury to repeal the old association regulations and replace them with an explicitly elective regime for distinguishing entities taxable as partnerships from associations taxable as corporations. However, because the statutory term "partnership" explicitly excludes all corporations, the regulations continue to provide that incorporated entities may not be taxed as partnerships.

Under Reg. § 301.7701–2(b)(1)–(8) (excluding (2)), a variety of business organizations are denied elective classification and must instead be taxed as corporations. These entities include all incorporated entities, heavily regulated entities such as insurance companies and banks, entities wholly owned by a state or municipality, and a variety of foreign business entities traditionally treated as corporations under domestic and foreign laws. All other business organizations are classified as "eligible" entities, see Reg. § 301.7701–3(a), and such organizations can elect to be taxed as a partnerships or as a corporations, with the default rule generally favoring partnership treatment. See Reg. § 301.7701–3(b)(1)(i). However, if an eligible entity has a single owner and elects not to be taxed as a corporation, the electing entity is ignored for tax purposes and so will be treated as a division if its parent is a corporation or a partnership or as a sole proprietorship if its parent is an individual. Reg. § 301.7701–3(b)(1)(ii). Thereafter, the entity need only file a new election if it is changing its status. Reg. § 301.7701–3(c)(1)(i). An eligible entity make change its election at any time, but once such a change is made a subsequent change may not be made for 60 months. Reg. § 301.7701–3(c)(1)(iv).

Some foreign business organizations are not eligible entities. See Reg. § 301.7701–2(b)(8). For example, a Naamloze Vennootschap (NV) formed in the Netherlands is always taxable as a corporation. Reg. § 301.7701–2(b)(8)(i). If in response to our current elective classification regime the Netherlands creates a new form of business organization (say, a NNV) with all the attributes of an NV but with a new name, will such an entity be eligible for elective classification or will the Treasury amend its list of ineligible foreign entities? If we have truly moved to elective classification, then presumably foreign governments will be able to exploit elective classification by creating their own versions of limited liability companies.

In fact, invariably there is a corporate form in every country that can be treated as a corporation for foreign purposes and as a flow-through entity for U.S. tax purposes (*i.e.,* a hybrid entity). The ability of a U.S. business to structure its foreign operations in this manner opens up a Pandora's box of opportunities. For example, suppose that USCO has an entity in High Tax Land and an entity in Low Tax Land. Both entities are transparent for U.S. tax purposes but corporations for foreign tax purposes. An "interest payment" from High Tax Entity to Low Tax Entity will decrease overall foreign taxes and is completely ignored for U.S. purposes (*i.e.,* USCO pays interest to itself).[10] Similar opportunities exist when a foreign entity is treated as transparent for foreign tax purposes but as a corporation for U.S. tax purposes (*i.e.,* a reverse hybrid). Consider USCO which wholly owns an entity in country X that is treated as a corporation for country X purposes but as a transparent entity for U.S. purposes. When the entity earns income, country X may not tax it because the tax authorities think the income is earned in the US while the US may not tax because the IRS thinks the income is earned by a country X corporation.

In § 7704(a), Congress has provided that certain publicly traded partnerships will be taxed as corporations. For this purpose, a "publicly traded partnership" is one whose partnership interests are (1) traded on an established securities market or (2) are readily traded on a secondary market. § 7704(b). This provision was enacted as part of the Revenue Act of 1987 in response to the growth of "master limited partnerships," huge entities having thousands of partners and assets worth tens (or hundreds) of millions of dollars.

---

10. If the entities were corporations for U.S. tax purposes, the interest received by Low Tax Entity might be subject to U.S. taxation even if not distributed. See § 951.

Note, though, that if the income of a partnership consists of 90% or more of investment income as defined in § 7704(d), the partnership will avoid the clutch of § 7704(a). The legislative history of this provision explains that no corporate-level tax need be imposed because a corporate-level tax was imposed on the underlying income-producing investment. The definition of "qualifying income" in § 7704(d), however, imposes no requirement that the passive-type income come from a corporate taxpayer.

3.03 Ignoring the Corporation: Dummy Corporations.

Under some circumstances, taxpayers will use the corporate form but try to avoid the corporate income tax by ignoring their own corporation. In some of these cases, the taxpayers simply ask the courts to pierce the corporate veil and attribute the corporation's income to its shareholders, arguing that the corporation should not be respected for tax purposes. In other cases, the taxpayers argue that income nominally earned by the corporation should be taxed to some other taxpayer because the corporation was acting as an agent.

The first argument—that the corporate form should be ignored—rarely succeeds. In *Moline Properties v. Commissioner*,[11] the Supreme Court held that a corporation engaging in any business activity will be treated as a taxpayer distinct from its shareholders. The taxpayer, having sought the advantages of incorporation, must live with the disadvantages as well. On the other hand, if it is the Commissioner who seeks to challenge the bona fides of the corporation, the challenge may be more successful. In such circumstances, the Commissioner should be free to make the traditional "substance over form" argument because the Commissioner did not choose the taxpayer's form.

Hard-pressed to avoid the corporate income tax by piercing the corporate veil after *Moline,* taxpayers often argue that their corporations are dummies not properly taxable on income nominally received. For example, the taxpayers in *Commissioner v. Bollinger*,[12] formed a corporation to hold title to land on which the taxpayers constructed apartment complexes. The corporate structure was used in order to acquire bank financing. The loan commitment was structured in this fashion because Kentucky's usury law at the time limited the annual interest rate for noncorporate borrowers. Lenders willing to provide money only at higher rates required the nominal debtor and record title holder of mortgaged property to be a corporate nominee of the true owner and borrower.

---

11. 319 U.S. 436 (1943).   **12.** 485 U.S. 340 (1988).

The loan documents referred to the corporate borrower as the "corporate nominee" of Bollinger. Moreover, Bollinger and the corporation entered into an agreement specifying in detail the agency relationship, with Bollinger assuming full responsibility for the property and agreeing to hold the corporation harmless from any liability it might sustain as his agent and nominee. In fact, Bollinger acted as general contractor for the construction and hired a resident manager for the operation of the completed project.

While Bollinger reported all income and losses generated by the corporate activities on his individual tax return, the Commissioner argued that the income and losses should be reported by the corporation. According to the Service, because the corporation held title to the real estate, its transactions could not be directly reported by its shareholders under the *Moline* doctrine.

The taxpayers argued that the corporation was their *agent*. Just as a Sears clerk is not taxable on profits he rings up for Sears, so, too, the taxpayers argued, should the corporation not include the income and losses from their real estate project. In *National Carbide Corp. v. Commissioner*,[13] the Supreme Court indicated that, under some circumstances, a corporation could be the true, nontaxable agent for its shareholders. In its *National Carbide* opinion, the Supreme Court set forth six factors that determine whether a corporation should be treated as such an agent.

(1) Whether the corporation operates in the name and for the account of the principal; (2) whether the corporation binds the principal by its actions; (3) whether the corporation transmits money received to the principal; and (4) whether receipt of income is attributable to the services of employees of the principal and to assets belonging to the principal; . . . (5) If the corporation is a true agent, its relations with its principal must not be dependent upon the fact that it is owned by the principal, if such is the case. (6) Its business purpose must be the carrying on of the normal duties of an agent.

The Service argued that the taxpayer failed to satisfy the fifth factor because the corporation's actions were wholly dependent on its being controlled by the taxpayers, its shareholders. For a controlled corporation to satisfy the fifth *National Carbide* test, according to the Service, the relationship between the corporation and its shareholders must reflect an arm's length agreement between principal and agent. Paying nothing to the corporation for its services as agent is inconsistent with an arm's length agreement.

---

13. 336 U.S. 422 (1949).

The Supreme Court ruled that the fifth *National Carbide* factor serves only as a generalized statement of the concern that the separate-entity doctrine of *Moline* not be subverted. The Court in ruling for the taxpayer reasoned that an agency relationship is established if a writing memorializes the principal-agency relationship, the corporation indeed functions as an agent, and the corporation is held out as an agent and not the principal in all third party dealings.

The issue wrestled with by the courts in *Bollinger* is a difficult one in part because it arises in such counter-intuitive settings. Ignoring the corporation in these cases is natural—what is surprising is that they should be recognized under state usury law. Tax law has matured to the point where form usually will be disregarded in favor of substance. Somehow, state usury laws seem not to have been developed that far. After all, what is the difference between individual liability and corporate liability when the corporation has no assets and the shareholders individually guarantee the debt?

In many areas of the tax law, taxpayers are forced to take the bad as well as the good implications of a form they have adopted. The *Moline* doctrine discussed above is one such example. To the extent that taxpayers win cases like *Bollinger,* their victories may be explained, at least in part, with judges' discomfort with state or local laws, such as the usury statute in *Bollinger,* drawing seemingly arbitrary distinctions, distinctions which can have substantial legal impact far beyond the jurisdiction of the enacting legislatures. On the other hand, perhaps these judges ought to be more concerned with the need for certainty in application of the tax laws, forcing taxpayers to accept the tax consequences of the organizational form selected.

3.04 Ignoring the Corporation: Reallocation of Income and Related Issues. The previous section considered ways in which taxpayers seek to attribute corporate income away from the corporation and to other taxpayers. Sometimes a taxpayer may wish to attribute income *to* a corporation. For example, suppose that a taxpayer earns a salary of $400,000 per year. If the taxpayer can cause his wholly-owned corporation to report $50,000 of that salary, he can reduce the rate of tax on this $50,000 from his 39.1 percent rate to the corporation's 15 percent.[14] In such circumstances it is the Commissioner who wants to reallocate income, and

---

14. This rate of 15 percent assumes that the corporation has no other taxable income.

there are a variety of statutory and common law weapons available to him. Somewhat surprisingly, the common law assignment of income doctrine is, in general, not part of the Commissioner's arsenal.

A leading case is *Rubin v. Commissioner.*[15] In that case, Richard Rubin was the majority shareholder of Park International, Inc. Park was formed exclusively to provide management services to Dorman Mills, Inc., a corporation owned by an unrelated third-party (although Rubin voted the third-party's stock and had an option to acquire it). All the management services were in fact performed by Rubin as Park's employee, and Rubin was paid a salary for these services provided on behalf of Park.

Because of Rubin's management abilities, Dorman Mills turned a substantial profit, one-quarter of which was paid to Park as the price of its management services. At issue in the case was whether the payments from Dorman Mills to Park were taxable to Park or to Rubin. In arguing that they should be taxed to Rubin, the Commissioner argued that the assignment of income doctrine of *Lucas v. Earl*[16] demanded that earned income be taxed to the earner.

The Circuit Court was unwilling to apply the rule of *Earl,* saying that the case

> reveal[s] a tension between competing policies of the tax law. On the one side is the principle of a graduated income tax rate, which is undercut when individuals are permitted to split their income with others or to spread it over several years.... Opposing this is the policy of recognizing the corporation as a taxable entity distinct from its shareholders in all but extreme cases.[17]

While the Court in fact held only that broad, common law doctrines should not be used when more narrow statutory provisions are available,[18] the case has come to stand for the proposition that the assignment of income doctrine cannot be used to reallocate income from a corporation to its shareholder-employee. This reading of *Rubin*—supported by the quotation above—is unfortunate because there is no reason why the assignment of income doctrine cannot be applied with full vigor in the corporate context.

The *Rubin* court saw a conflict between the assignment of income doctrine and the principle that corporations should general-

---

15.　429 F.2d 650 (2d Cir.1970).

16.　281 U.S. 111 (1930).

17.　429 F.2d at 652.

18.　The court remanded the case for reconsideration under § 482, a provision discussed *infra.*

ly be recognized as distinct taxpayers. If such a conflict existed, surely it also would be present in the noncorporate context because individuals, at least as much as corporations, are respected as distinct taxpayers. Was the Supreme Court in *Lucas v. Earl* holding that Mrs. Earl was not a legitimate or recognizable taxpayer? Of course not.

In *Rubin*, the taxpayer worked for a Park Corp. as an employee loaned to Dorman Mills. Dorman Mills paid Park Corp. for the services provided, and the taxpayer received a salary in his capacity as employee of Park Corp. Under the court's holding, Park Corp. was taxable on what it received less what it paid to the taxpayer as salary. Suppose that the taxpayer had accepted a salary of $1.00. Is it not clear that what should have been paid—and taxed—to the employee as salary will now be taxed to the corporation?

Why should such income-shifting be countenanced? Suppose that Park Corp. was not a corporation but rather was the taxpayer's sister. Could the taxpayer have circumvented the doctrine of *Lucas v. Earl* simply by signing an employment contract with his sister? If not, why should such a technique work as between the taxpayer and his corporation?

Would application of the assignment of income doctrine to corporations and their employee/shareholders vitiate the corporate income tax? Mrs. Earl, for example, could earn her own income and be taxable on it. A corporation, of course, cannot physically earn anything.

Consider General Motors Corp. It builds cars and makes a profit on them. Is this corporate profit nothing but income of GM workers improperly assigned to the corporation? Surely not, because the GM workers are paid fair market value for their labor. The profit that GM makes on its cars equals the sale price of the cars over the fair market cost of production. That profit is a return on GM's capital, for when consumers buy a GM car, they receive not only the workers' labor but also part of the value of the GM plant and equipment. The corporation's profit represents a return on this capital as well as on the capital invested in producing a favorable business reputation, in maintaining that reputation (e.g., advertising), and in a host of other benefits sold to the consumers as part of their cars.

The Tax Court in the *Rubin*[19] case had agreed with the Commissioner that the assignment of income doctrine could be used to reallocate income from a corporation to its shareholder-employee. Despite its reversal in *Rubin*, the Tax Court maintained

---

19. 51 T.C. 251 (1968), rev'd, 429 F.2d 650 (2d Cir.1970).

that position in *Foglesong v. Commissioner*.[20] The Tax Court was again reversed,[21] however, and in *Keller v. Commissioner*,[22] the Tax Court followed the circuit courts and rejected its prior position.

In *Keller*, the Tax Court did not reject application of the assignment of income doctrine entirely, but rather limited it to the case of a corporation failing to satisfy the *Moline* test of viability.[23] This limitation of the doctrine by the Tax Court reflects a complete misunderstanding of the assignment of income doctrine.

The assignment of income doctrine determines which of two taxpayers must report certain income. In the case of a corporation failing the *Moline* test, the corporation is ignored entirely for tax purposes so that all corporate income is taxable directly it's shareholder. In such circumstances, there is no room for—or need of—the assignment of income doctrine because there is only one taxpayer (the shareholder) to whom the income can be allocated. The assignment of income doctrine, in other words, cannot be applied in the one case to which the Tax Court purported to limit it. Each reported case makes it even less likely that this area of the law will ever be straightened out.[24]

In *Rubin,* the circuit court remanded the case for reconsideration under § 482. That section empowers the Commissioner to reallocate income, deductions, credits and other tax items among related taxpayers to more clearly reflect income. Suppose that B owns two corporations, X and Y. X has sustained substantial losses in prior years, giving it a net operating loss carryforward. Y, on the other hand, has been profitable. If X and Y jointly manufacture and sell some product, B will prefer that most of the income be taxed to X so as to be sheltered by the NOL carryforward. However, if B fails to allocate the joint profit in a manner properly reflecting Y's contribution to the venture, the Commissioner will reallocate some of the income to Y and away from X under § 482.

Although the Commissioner has broad discretion under § 482, it is discretion only to reallocate tax items. Thus, § 482 cannot be used to deny deductions or credits. In addition, the reallocation under § 482 is limited to commonly owned or controlled "organizations, trades or businesses."

20. T.C. Memo. 1976–294, rev'd, 621 F.2d 865 (7th Cir.1980).

21. *Foglesong v. Commissioner,* 621 F.2d 865 (7th Cir.1980).

22. 77 T.C. 1014 (1981).

23. *Moline Properties v. Commissioner,* 319 U.S. 436 (1943), discussed in Section 3.03 *supra.*

24. See, e.g., *Johnson v. Commissioner,* 78 T.C. 882 (1982) (income from personal services taxed to employee rather than corporation only because payor would not agree to arrangement).

It is this last limitation which makes the application of § 482 to the facts of *Rubin* and similar cases so problematic. Recall that the taxpayer in *Rubin* worked for Park Corp., and the issue was whether payments received for the taxpayer's services were properly taxed to Park Corp. or to the taxpayer. Surely Park Corp. was one organization controlled by the taxpayer, but what was the second? In order for § 482 to apply to *Rubin,* presumably the "business" of being an employee must be considered as the second business controlled by the taxpayer.

Section 482 may be susceptible to such a reading,[25] but even so, problems remain. Since the only activity engaged in by Park Corp. was that of employing the taxpayer to perform services on its behalf, was there any business in the case *other than* that engaged in by the taxpayer in his individual capacity? At least one court has held that § 482 cannot be applied in similar circumstances.[26]

Consider the case of K Corp., a personal service corporation owned entirely by Dr. K. K Corp. becomes a partner in a medical partnership in which each partner is required to perform medical services for the partnership in exchange for a share of partnership profits. Because K Corp. cannot perform such services directly, it hires Dr. K as its sole employee to perform the services.[27]

Assume that K Corp. will receive one-fourth of the partnership's profits, anticipated to be about $100,000. Assume also that Dr. K's salary from K Corp. is set at a fixed amount of $60,000 cash plus pension and other fringe benefits costing the corporation $20,000. If a court is willing to apply the assignment of income doctrine or § 482 to Dr. K and his corporation, how much (if any) of the corporation's income should be reallocated to Dr. K?

Under both the assignment of income doctrine and § 482, income should be reallocated between the corporation and its shareholder/employee only if the salary is less than that which would be paid in an arm's-length agreement. One is tempted to say that all of K Corp.'s income should be allocated to Dr K., but that may not be true for at least two reasons. First, although the cost of the fringe benefits may be $20,000, their worth to Dr. K may be substantially more. For example, if the corporation provides Dr. K with a medical expense reimbursement plan, the cost of the plan to the corporation will be less than its value to Dr. K because of the

---

25. See Regs. § 1.482–1(a)(1).

26. *Foglesong v. Commissioner,* 691 F.2d 848 (7th Cir.1982) (§ 482 cannot apply when individual works exclusively for his corporation; only one business present). *But see* Rev.Rul. 88–38, 1988–1

C.B. 246 (§ 482 can apply to allocate income between a corporation and its shareholder-employee).

27. This example is based on the facts of *Keller,* discussed *supra.*

tax-preferred status given to such plans.[28] Indeed, any fringe benefit given to Dr. K which represents a tax expenditure ought to be worth more than it costs, with the excess being the amount of the tax expenditure captured by Dr. K and his corporation. Thus, it may be the case that Dr. K's total compensation has an after-tax value to Dr. K in excess of the income generated by his services. If so, no reallocation of income is appropriate.

In addition, even if the value of the fringe benefit package does not fully offset the reduction in salary that Dr. K has accepted by working for his corporation, Dr. K enjoys an additional benefit of the arrangement that may have some value. Dr. K's salary is a guaranteed $60,000 (plus fringe benefits) independent of the partnership's profits. Even if the corporation's partnership share is less than $60,000, Dr. K must be paid his full salary. This freedom from uncertainty may be worth something. If so, its value ought to be added to Dr. K's compensation package to determine if he has sold his services for less than they are worth.

However, this freedom from uncertainty is worthless if it is illusory. For example, suppose that the corporation is capitalized with only $100. It is clear that the corporation will be unable to meet its salary obligation to Dr. K unless its partnership share is sufficient, and so Dr. K's compensation is as dependent on the partnership's profits as it would be if he worked directly for the partnership. In this case, Dr. K's arrangement really offers no risk avoidance.

On the other hand, if the corporation has substantial assets, then its promise of $80,000 (or more) in salary and other compensation may be worth more than an uncertain draw from the partnership. In this case, any partnership profits retained by the corporation reflect a return on its capital, since only by having capital available was it able to ensure Dr. K his full compensation arrangement.

Section 482 has implications well beyond that of personal service corporations. The regulations under § 482 list several situations in which § 482 may be applicable including: (1) below-market loans between related enterprises; (2) performances of services by one business enterprise on behalf of a related one for less than market compensation; and (3) intercompany sales at less than fair market value.[29] In each case, § 482 will be used by the Commission-

---

28. Medical reimbursements described in § 105(b) are deductible to the employer/payor although excludible to the employee/recipient.

29. Regs. § 1.482–2(a) through (e).

er if the effect of the transaction is to shift income from a high-bracket taxpayer to a related, low-bracket one.

The most important use of § 482 is in the international arena—often referred to as the transfer pricing issue. In many cases U.S. corporations subject to U.S. taxation have an incentive to shift income to a related foreign corporation which may not be subject to U.S. taxation and is often subject to little foreign taxation. For example, suppose a U.S. corporation with a foreign subsidiary in a low tax jurisdiction manufactures thermostats at a cost of $100 which it sells to the subsidiary which resells the thermostats to unrelated purchasers in the subsidiary's jurisdiction at a price of $500. If the U.S. parent charges the subsidiary $140 for the thermostats, it will have $40 subject to U.S. taxation. The $360 gain the subsidiary realizes on the resale is typically not subject to U.S. taxation. Often the IRS in this type of situation will attempt to reallocate some of the subsidiary's income to the U.S. parent., arguing that the transfer price between parent and subsidiary is not an arm's length price and should be adjusted upwards.

Similarly, suppose a foreign corporation manufactures automobiles at a cost of $4,000 per automobile which are sold to the foreign corporation's U.S. subsidiary which resells the automobiles to unrelated purchasers at a cost of $15,000 per automobile. If the foreign parent corporation charges a transfer price of $12,000 to its U.S. subsidiary, then most of the profit would be allocated to the foreign corporation which typically will not be subject to taxation in the United States. The IRS often will argue that the transfer price between parent and subsidiary is not an arm's length price and should be adjusted downwards.

Section 482 applies to commonly controlled enterprises, even those whose common control is only "indirect." The use of the term "indirect" suggests that some set of attribution rules should be used to attribute ownership—stock or otherwise—from one taxpayer to related taxpayers. Although the Code has several such attribution rules,[30] § 482 fails to incorporate any of them. Despite the lack of explicit incorporating language, the Courts have been willing to look to these attribution rules in making determinations under § 482.[31]

The Commissioner has statutory weapons beyond § 482 in his arsenal. Under § 269, the Commissioner may disallow any deductions, credits or other corporate tax benefits when the principal

---

30. See §§ 267(b), 318(a).

31. E.g., *Hall v. Commissioner,* 294 F.2d 82 (5th Cir.1961) (using the rules of § 318).

purpose for forming or acquiring control of a corporation is tax avoidance. This section has been used, for example, to disallow a corporate net operating loss carryover following a change of corporate control.[32]

Prior to the Tax Equity and Fiscal Responsibility Act of 1984, the tax-preferred pension benefits available to employees of corporations far exceeded those available to self-employed individuals. Highly-compensated professionals such as doctors and lawyers formed professional service corporations for which they would work solely to take advantage of the greater pension opportunities. The Commissioner challenged these arrangements under § 269, arguing that the professional service corporations were formed for tax avoidance.

It was conceded that the corporations were formed to obtain a tax *advantage,* but does that mean that they were formed for tax *avoidance?* Tax-preferred pension plans, like all other tax expenditures, represent an implicit congressional subsidy of an activity determined by Congress to be desirable. The whole point of enacting tax-expenditures is to create incentives for taxpayers to change their behavior. How can it be wrong to follow those incentives? For example, although it is hard to explain why Congress might have wanted to encourage incorporations by professionals to obtain pension plans not available to the self-employed, the Tax Court nevertheless came to that conclusion in *Achiro v. Commissioner.*[33]

What role should § 269 play? Statutes cannot be drafted with absolute precision, and sometimes a taxpayer may fit himself within the terms of a provision without fulfilling its spirit. Presumably § 269 speaks to such incidents. That is, § 269 should apply only when it fairly can be said that a taxpayer formed or acquired control of a corporation to obtain a tax advantage not intended by Congress to be available to one in the taxpayer's position. Read this way, though, is § 269 necessary?

Related to sections 482 and 269 is 269A. Under § 269A, the Commissioner may reallocate income from a professional service corporation to its shareholder/employee. In its remedial feature, then, § 269A is like § 482. However, application of § 269A is triggered by a tax avoidance motive, just like § 269. This peculiar marriage of the two sections is attributable to congressional dissatisfaction with the victories of taxpayers like Mr. Foglesong and Dr.

---

32. Section 382 now addresses this issue. See Section 11.03 *infra.*

33. 77 T.C. 881 (1981). Substantial equalization of employee and non-employee pension plans under recent tax acts has repudiated this holding of *Achiro.*

Keller in the courts. According to the legislative history of § 269A, the reach of § 269A should extend to "corporation[s] serv[ing] no meaningful purpose other than to secure tax benefits which would not otherwise be available."

3.05　The Passive Loss Limitations. Enacted as part of the Tax Reform Act of 1986, § 469 seeks to ensure that deductions from passive investments (typically limited partnership tax shelters) not be used to offset unrelated income such as salary and portfolio income. Although the reach of § 469 extends well beyond the corporate tax and corporate taxpayers, one should not forget that many corporations are subject to its provisions. For those who have not had an introduction to § 469, the following is a brief description of its interplay with corporations.

To curtail investments made solely or primarily for tax advantages, Congress enacted the passive loss rules of § 469. These rules limit a taxpayer's ability to use deductions and credits from passive activities to offset active income such as income from a trade or business or from services and portfolio income such as interest and dividends. Passive losses and credits disallowed in the current year are suspended and treated as deductions or credits in subsequent years available to offset passive income of such years. In addition, suspended passive losses can offset any income in the year in which the taxpayer disposes of his entire interest in the passive activity.[34]

In general, an activity is "passive" if it involves the conduct of a trade or business in which the taxpayer does not materially participate. Material participation in this context means participation on a regular, continuous and substantial basis.[35] By definition, the ownership of a limited partnership interest is passive as is any rental activity. However, the rental of real estate is subject to special rules which, in effect, allow up to $25,000 of excess net real estate deductions to offset non-passive income if the taxpayer "actively" participates in the real estate activity.[36] If a closely held corporation derives more than 50 percent of its income from a real property trades[37] in which the corporation materially participates, then the rental activities are not considered passive. § 469(c)(7).

34.　See § 469(b), (g).

35.　To materially participate, one or more of the shareholders having a 50 percent interest in the corporation must spend more than 500 hours on the activity (§ 469(h)(4)) or meet one of the other tests under the regulations. Regs. § 1.469–1T(g),–5T.

36.　See § 469(i).

37.　A real property trade is any real property development, construction, acquisition, conversion, rental, operation, management, leasing, or brokerage trade or business.

Although the passive loss rules do not, in general, apply to corporate taxpayers, they do apply to personal service corporations, closely-held C corporations, and to shareholders of S corporations.[38] For example, a personal service corporation that also rents computer equipment may not offset any of its personal service income by its excess rental losses stemming from depreciation, interest deductions, etc. The definition of a personal service corporation includes any corporation no matter how large if employees of the corporation own at least 10 percent of the corporation's stock and the principal activity of the corporation is the performance of services by employee/shareholders.[39]

Material participation for a personal service corporation subject to § 469 is achieved if one or more shareholders owning 50 percent or more of the corporation's stock materially participate in the activity. For a closely-held S corporation, a further requirement is added to ensure that the corporation engages in at least one active business.[40]

Closely-held C corporations[41] (other than personal service corporations) are permitted to offset active income with passive loss deductions and credits. § 469(e)(2). This is not a complete elimination of the passive loss restriction to such corporations because passive losses still cannot offset portfolio income. Nevertheless, the ability to shelter active business income offers a substantial benefit to taxpayers who need to operate a closely-held business in corporate form. If the corporation conducts a passive activity that produces excess deductions (*e.g.,* depreciation), those deductions can offset taxable income from the corporation's business.

3.06 A Corporation's Capital Structure. A corporation needs capital to begin business and to expand. To raise needed capital, a corporation must offer prospective investors a return on their money. This promised return might take the form of periodic payments of a sum certain (interest payments), periodic returns of net profits (dividends), or some combination of the two. The return also might be in the form of accumulated earnings that can be realized by the sale of stock.[42] The investor also will expect to recover his principal at some point down the road, either at a

---

38. See § 469(a)(2).

39. See § 469(j)(2).

40. See §§ 469(h)(4)(B), 465(c)(7)(C).

41. A "closely-held C corporation" is a corporation taxed under the rules of subchapter C (and not under the rules of Subchapter S) that has more than 50

percent of its stock held by 5 or fewer shareholders. See §§ 469(j)(1), 465(a)(1)(B), and 542(a)(2).

42. It is the ultimate distribution of these earnings that makes a purchaser of stock willing to pay a price that reflects prior undistributed profits.

specified time in the future (retirement of debt instruments or of callable stock) or on final liquidation of the corporation.

The classic equity interest in a corporate enterprise is a share of common stock. The owner of such a share is entitled to participate in the earnings of the corporation, but payments with respect to such stock are made only after all persons with more preferred interests in the corporation (e.g., holders of debt instruments and preferred stock) have received their due. Such an interest in the corporation is called a *residual* interest because it comes after all other interests. Note, though, that the residual interest in a corporation is also unlimited: whatever profits have not been paid to creditors and preferred shareholders are available for distribution to the common shareholders.

The interest in a corporation at the opposite end of the spectrum is a corporate note. The holder of such a note normally receives a fixed return on his investment for a limited period, followed by a return of capital. Thus, the investment in the corporation is both *limited* and *preferred:* limited in the sense that the return will not increase even if the corporation's profits climb and preferred in the sense that payments made on corporate debt must be paid before dividends may be declared on corporate stock. In particular, if a corporation has insufficient funds with which to pay interest on its debts and to pay a dividend, the interest must be paid and the dividend deferred.

You should not think of equity and debt as qualitatively different but rather as the two extremes of a continuous spectrum. All investments in a corporate enterprise are made in the expectation of profit and with the recognition of risk. Common stock and notes simply offer different *returns* subject to differing amounts of *risks*.

Looking first at relative *returns* on investment, we have seen that returns can be either unlimited or fixed. Some instruments can have elements of both: for example, a class of stock could share ratably in corporate profits subject to a minimum return of 6 percent per year. Convertible bonds are another example of such hybrid instruments because they guarantee the fixed return of a bond but offer the opportunity through conversion of an unlimited return as stock. Also the return on a debt instrument can be tied to the performance of the corporation, sometimes referred to as an "equity kicker."

Similarly, the *risk* associated with an interest in a corporation can be large, small, or somewhere in between. For example, the risk associated with common stock of a corporation is always greater than that associated with the corporation's debt. If a corporation has sufficient assets to meet the claims of its creditors, any excess may be distributed to shareholders. But if there are insufficient assets, the creditors will take everything and the shareholders will receive nothing.

If a corporation has two or more classes of stock, it may provide that the claims of one class come before those of another. Such preferred stock will have a lower risk than the non-preferred common stock but will have a greater risk than corporate debt. So, too, the corporation may have subordinated debt, the holders of which take a greater risk than the holders of unsubordinated debt but less than that of shareholders. And, of course, the holders of one corporation's equity may be subject to less risk than the holders of another corporation's debt.

Although the risks and returns of preferred stock blend into that of unsubordinated debt on our spectrum, the Code treats debt and equity very differently. The most important tax distinction between debt and equity is that periodic payments on debt—called interest—can be deducted by the corporation while the equivalent payments on equity—dividends—cannot be. From the "corporation's perspective"[43] and all other things being equal, the corporation is better off raising needed capital in the form of debt rather than equity.

How about from the holder's perspective? For non-corporate taxpayers, most dividends now are taxed at the same rate as long term capital gain, generally 15%,[44] while interest payments are subject to the usual ordinary rates up to a maximum rate of 35%. On the back end, the retirement of corporate debt qualifies for exchange treatment[45] while the retirement of stock may qualify for exchange treatment or may be taxed be treated as ordinary income, but because dividends are now taxed at the same rate as capital gain, this . Thus, individual taxpayers have two reasons for preferring debt to equity: their individual tax position *may* be improved and the corporation's tax position *will* be improved. Do not forget that any taxpayer having a stake in the corporation profits when the corporation profits[46], and taxpayers having residual (i.e., unlimited) interests profit very much.

---

43. There is of course no "corporate" perspective, only the perspectives of its investors, employees, suppliers and customers. Nevertheless, we sometimes refer to the "corporation's perspective" as short-hand for the perspective of one who wishes to maximize the corporation's net worth.

44. § 1(h)(11).

45. Section 1271(a)(1).

46. It may seem as though those persons having limited interests in the corporation (such as bondholders) are indifferent to the corporation's tax liability. However, the lower a corporation's tax

For corporate taxpayers, the analysis is altered because of the dividends-received deduction of § 243. The ability of a corporate shareholder to deduct all (*e.g.,* dividends from a wholly-owned subsidiary) or a portion of dividends received reduces the effective rate of taxation on dividends. Interest payments, on the other hand, are taxed at the usual rates without reduction. Thus, the corporate taxpayer may be better off owning stock rather than debt.

However, consider the case of X Corp. with two shareholders outstanding, individual B and corporation C. These shareholders agree to invest additional funds in their corporation in proportion to their current ownership interests. Should they contribute the additional funds as debt or equity?

Assume that B owns 40 percent of X and that C owns 60 percent. Whether B and C make debt or equity investments, B will continue to have a claim to 40 percent of X's profits and assets. Similarly, C will continue to have a claim to 60 percent of X's profits and assets. By investing in debt, B and C increase X's after-tax profits, and that profit redounds directly to their benefit.

In this situation, the corporate shareholder as well as the non-corporate shareholder benefits from debt more than from equity. Assume that the infusion of capital will produce additional pre-tax profits to X Corp. of $100, and assume that this $100 represents a reasonable return on the shareholders' new investment. If the shareholders invested in additional equity, the $100 of pre-tax profit is equivalent to $66 of after-tax profit.[47] Of that amount, $26.40 (40 percent of $66) will be distributed to B and $39.60 (60 percent of $66) will distributed to C. C will be entitled to deduct 80 percent of the dividend received, leaving only $7.92 to be taxed. If C is in the 34 percent bracket, C will pay a tax of $2.70, giving C an after-tax return of $39.60 less $2.70, or $36.90.

On the other hand, if B and C loaned money to X Corp., the deductibility of interest would permit the corporation to distribute the entire $100 after taxes. Of that amount, $60 would go to C. Because interest received by a corporation is fully taxable, C would pay a tax of $20.40, leaving $39.60 after-taxes. Thus, C is better off if both B and C invest in debt rather than equity.

Why is the influence of § 243 less significant in this case? The usual "cost" of investing in debt is that one's return is fixed. Thus, investing in debt saves the corporation taxes, but that profit flows

liability, the more likely it is that the corporation will be able to meet its debt and equity obligations in the future. Thus, debt as well as equity holders

profit as a result of a reduction in the corporation's tax liability.

47. Assuming that X Corp. is in the 34 percent tax bracket.

for the most part to the equity owners. However, if the X Corp.'s current equity owners make pro rata debt investments, this cost is avoided because they recapture the corporation's profits in their capacity as shareholders. That is, the debt holders make more profits for the equity owners, so that if the debt owners *are* the equity owners, they create more profits for themselves.

In the example above, investment as equity subjects the profits to full taxation at the corporate (X Corp.) level and partial (20 percent) taxation at the shareholder (C Corp.) level, for a total 120 percent tax inclusion. Investment as debt, though, avoids all corporate level tax, so that the over-all tax inclusion is only 100 percent.

It should not be surprising that taxpayers often seek to characterize as debt that which the Commissioner asserts is equity. Because there really is no hard and fast line to be drawn between the two, courts are hard-pressed to resolve such a dispute. Resolve it they must, though, because as we've seen the tax consequences of debt and equity are very different.

In deciding whether a corporate interest should be classified as debt or equity, the courts consider a large number of factors, the most important of which usually is the ratio of debt to equity. While no ratio is necessarily too high or low enough, if a corporation has a high ratio of debt to equity, the risk associated with the corporation's debt becomes very high, high because the corporation may not have sufficient assets to meet the needs of the debt holders. Consequently, the debt holders, in effect, become holders of residual interests. High risk, of course, is usually associated with the unlimited but subordinated return of equity.

A second important factor is the proportion in which the nominal debt is held by shareholders. As shown above, if the shareholders own the corporation's debt in the same proportion as they own the stock, the debt gives them all the benefits associated with debt without the loss of residual interest. On the other hand, if corporate debt is owned substantially disproportionate to stock (e.g., one 50 percent shareholder invests an additional $1,000 in corporate debt while the other 50 percent shareholder invests in stock), the debt holder will reduce his residual return as well as his risk by investing in debt rather than in equity.

Other factors considered by the courts include whether the formalities associated with debt (such as the execution of a promissory note) were observed, whether interest obligations were met by the corporation, and whether the purported loans were made during the corporation's formative stage and used to acquire "essential" corporate assets.[48] These other factors, especially the last, are hard to justify. For example, why must a corporation purchase its first assets with equity capital rather than with debt capital? Would a court recharacterize an early loan as an equity investment if made by a non-shareholder commercial lender?

A particular area of difficulty in the debt/equity characterization arena is the treatment of a guarantee. Often a commercial lender will require a shareholder guarantee in order to make a loan to a corporation. In some cases, the IRS may regard the loan as being made to the guaranteeing shareholder. If a shareholder/guarantor is treated for tax purposes as the true borrower under a third party loan to a controlled corporation, the following is generally the result: (1) the guarantor is deemed to have received the funds directly under a loan from the lender; (2) the guarantor is treated as having contributed the funds to the underlying corporation as a capital contribution; (3) any interest or principal payments made by the controlled corporation to the third party lender are treated as dividend distributions to the guarantor (subject to the existence of earnings and profits); and (4) the guarantor is treated as having made potentially deductible interest payments to the lender.

The leading case in the area is Plantation Patterns, Inc. v. Commissioner.[49] In that case an individual, Mr. Jemison, and his wife established New Plantations to acquire the assets of an existing business from Old Plantations, a corporation owned by unrelated persons. Mr. Jemison contributed $5,000 of capital to New Plantations, and New Plantations then received an advance of $150,000 from an unrelated third party in exchange for its non-guaranteed, subordinated note. New Plantations then acquired the business of Old Plantations in exchange for cash and a combination of interest bearing and non-interest bearing notes. The interest bearing notes were payable over ten annual installments and were guaranteed by Mr. Jemison and Mr. Jemison's wholly owned investment company. New Plantations claimed deductions for interest payments made on the guaranteed debt. The Commissioner challenged this treatment on the basis that the guarantees were the "real undergirding" for the debt and that Mr. Jemison should be treated as the true borrower under the loans for federal income tax purposes. The Commissioner argued that, as a result of the guarantees, Mr. Jemison should be treated as having made a direct contribution of capital to New Plantation in the principal amount of the debt and that the subsequent payments made by New Plantations on the debt should be treated as dividends paid by New

---

48. See *Bauer v. Commissioner*, 748 F.2d 1365 (9th Cir.1984).

49. 462 F.2d 712 (5th Cir.1972).

Plantations to Mr. Jemison. The Tax Court held for the Commissioner and was affirmed on appeal by the Fifth Circuit on the basis that the corporation was "thinly capitalized."

Unhappy with the judicial uncertainty in this area, Congress enacted § 385 as part of the Tax Reform Act of 1969. This section instructs the Treasury to issue regulations distinguishing corporate debt from equity. While several sets of regulations have been proposed under § 385, none have survived public criticism. The inability of Treasury to promulgate regulations distinguishing debt from equity over more than 30 years strongly suggests that such a distinction cannot be made. Because both debt and equity investments in a corporation reflect ownership interests, albeit with different rates of return and associated risks, drawing a line between the two probably cannot be done in a way that will engender widespread support. How then should debt be distinguished from equity? "No answer is what the wrong question begets...."[50]

In any case, Congress has taken piecemeal steps to prevent perceived misuse of the interest deduction by corporations. In some cases the Service has been "whipsawed" by inconsistent treatment of instruments by the issuer and holders. A corporate issuer may prefer to designate an instrument as debt so that it can deduct the interest. However, a corporate holder of that instrument may prefer to treat it as stock so that a dividends-received deduction is available under § 243. Under § 385(c)(1) the issuer's characterization is binding on the holder.

Section 385 has been amended to allow the Service to bifurcate the treatment of "hybrid securities"—debt instruments with both equity and debt characteristics—so that part of the return on the investment is treated as interest and part as a nondeductible equity distribution.[51] For example, debt instruments that provide for a fixed return (e.g., 6 percent of the face value) as well as an "equity kicker" (e.g., 2 percent of the corporation's profits) may be bifurcated so that the fixed return is treated as deductible interest while the contingent return is treated as an equity distribution.

Congress has applied the bifurcation technique as well with regard to certain high yield discount obligations issued by corporations. § 163(i). The "disqualified portion" of such instruments is

---

50. A. Bickel, The Least Dangerous Branch 103 (1962).

51. Hybrid securities often have the following characteristics: (1) ownership solely by shareholders and in the proportion to the stock held; (2) transferability permitted only if accompanied by stock transfer; (3) lengthy or no fixed maturity dates; (4) interest payments that are discretionary or linked to corporate income; (5) payment of interest and/or principal subordinate to general creditor claims; and (6) issuance to a current shareholder for no new consideration.

not deductible and even the remaining deductible portion of the original issue discount is only deductible upon payment rather than as the interest accrues which is normally the case. The details of this provision are not as important as its general philosophy.

Suppose X Corp. issues a debt instrument which has an issue price of $100 and matures in five years at which time the lender receives $250. No interest payments are required, but the yield to maturity is approximately 20 percent. If at the time the instrument is issued, the applicable federal rate on certain government debt instruments is 9 percent, a portion of the original issue discount which X Corp. would normally deduct each year will be disallowed. The "disqualified yield" is the portion of the yield that exceeds the applicable federal rate plus a cushion of six percentage points. Because the 20 percent yield exceeds the applicable federal rate (9 percent) plus the 6 percentage point cushion, or a 15 percent total, the nondeductible disqualified portion of the $20 of original issue discount in the first year (20 percent _ $100) is $5 ((20 percent yield minus 15 percent) divided by 20 percent yield).

Even when treatment of an investment return as interest is questionable, normally there is a maximum loss of one level of taxation. That is, the corporation's deduction may wipe out a corporate level tax on the earnings generated by the borrowed funds, but the lender will be taxed on the receipt of the interest. A potentially more serious problem is presented by those situations where two levels of taxation are avoided by characterizing certain payments as interest rather than equity distributions. This occurs when the recipient of the purported interest is tax-exempt. For example, a private foundation that owns stock in a corporation or a foreign taxpayer who is not subject to U.S. taxation because of an applicable income tax treaty can strip away the earnings of a corporation that would otherwise be subject to one and maybe two levels of taxation.

To deal with this "earnings stripping" problem, Congress has enacted a provision that denies a deduction for "disqualified interest" paid to (or guaranteed by) a related party exempt from U.S. tax on such interest payments. § 163(j). The related party requirement is designed to distinguish bona fide loans from independent parties from intercorporate loans undertaken to generate interest deductions. A taxpayer cannot avoid the reach of § 163(j) by borrowing from a bank if a tax-exempt related party guarantees the loan. For example, § 163(j) may apply to a U.S. subsidiary that borrows from a bank if a foreign parent corporation guarantees the loan.

There are additional requirements before an interest deduction will be disallowed. Because Congress was concerned with equity masquerading as debt, the deductibility of interest paid to tax-exempt, related parties hinges on whether the ratio of debt to equity of the paying corporation exceeds 1.5 to 1, as measured on certain specified days of the year. In addition, interest deductions will be disallowed only if the interest is deemed to be excess interest, as determined under a formula measuring the relationship of the interest expense to taxable income with certain adjustments.

Given the complexity and ad hoc nature of these provisions designed to distinguish debt from equity perhaps Congress should provide that debt and equity be treated equivalently, using the current treatment of debt or equity as the role model. For example, dividends as well as interest payments could be deductible by the corporation. This change would equalize the taxation of debt and equity, although it would do so by, in effect, abolishing the corporate tax.

An alternate approach is to tax all corporate investments as equity is treated under current law; that is, do not permit corporations to deduct interest paid. This would equalize the treatment of corporate debt and equity without eliminating the corporate double tax. In fact, denying the interest deduction would substantially increase the efficacy of the corporate income tax by increasing its base. If such an implicit raising of the effective corporate tax rate is thought to be inappropriate by Congress, an offsetting downward adjustment to the nominal rates could be made.

CHAPTER 4. CASH AND PROPERTY DISTRIBUTIONS

4.01 Introduction. As noted in Chapter 3, a corporation generally reports income and deductions in much the same ways as individuals. As a corporation earns income, its shareholders may at some point want to get their hands on the corporate earnings. Much of what follows in this and subsequent chapters focuses on the different ways shareholders can obtain corporate earnings. Perhaps the most direct way is for the corporation to distribute those earnings.

Section 61(a)(7) includes "dividends" in gross income. But not every corporate distribution is a dividend. Suppose B forms X Corp. by contributing $1,000 in exchange for all of the X Corp. stock. In year 1 X Corp. has no gain or loss, but makes a $200 distribution to B. Should B be taxed on the distribution? B has not experienced any accession to wealth. Nor has B realized a previously unrealized gain. Before the distribution B owned X Corp. stock with a basis of $1,000 and a fair market value of $1,000. § 358. After the distribution, B owns $200 in cash and stock with a basis of $1,000 and a fair market value of $800. B has simply received a return of the original investment and should not be taxed on the distribution, but B's stock basis in X Corp. should be reduced.

Suppose instead that in year 1 X Corp. earned $200 which it distributed to B. First, X Corp. would be taxed on its earnings.[1] What about B? B would like to claim that the distribution comes from B's original $1,000 contribution. If so, the distribution would reduce B's basis from $1,000 to $800. B would hold $200 in cash and stock with a basis of $800 and fair market value of $1,000, thereby deferring B's taxation on the $200 earned by X Corp. On the other hand, one could argue that the distribution represents the earnings of X Corp. in year 1 and should be taxable to B.

Note that B is no better off after the distribution than immediately before. Just prior to the distribution, B holds X Corp. stock with a basis of $1,000 and a fair market value of $1,200. After the distribution, B holds stock with a basis and fair market value of $1,000 and $200 in cash. The "undeniable accession to wealth"[2] to the shareholder occurred when X Corp. earned the $200. The

---

1. The quantitative effect of corporate taxes on amounts distributed or available for distribution is ignored throughout this chapter.

2. *Commissioner v. Glenshaw Glass Co.*, 348 U.S. 426 (1955).

treatment of corporate nonliquidating distributions is a question of timing—when is it appropriate to tax the shareholders on their previously accrued accession to wealth?

Both ways of treating distributions draw strength from other areas of tax law. For example, under the open transaction doctrine of *Burnet v. Logan*,[3] a taxpayer can recover basis first if the amount realized cannot be determined. Arguably, it is impossible to determine how much will be distributed during the life of the corporation. Following *Burnet v. Logan,* shareholders should be allowed to recover their investment before reporting gain. On the other hand, where a taxpayer holds property, periodic returns are taxed under the general principles of *Commissioner v. Glenshaw Glass Co.*[4] Thus, rent is fully taxable to a holder of real estate and interest is fully taxable to a holder of a debt instrument.

The arguments supporting either treatment give way to a web of statutory provisions. Section 301(a) addresses distributions of "property," as defined by § 317(a). Note that § 317(a) specifies that a corporation's own stock does not constitute property for purposes of § 301.[5] Section 301(a) applies only to a corporation making distributions of property *with respect to its stock:* that is, distributions to shareholders in their capacity as shareholders. Other distributions such as salaries or interest payments on debt obligations are not addressed by § 301(a). If a corporation makes a distribution with respect to its stock, the amount of the distribution is computed in accordance with § 301(b). While the amount of a cash distribution is self-evident, the amount of a property distribution is more problematic. Should the amount distributed be the property's fair market value, its adjusted basis or some other measure? How do liabilities encumbering the distributed property affect the amount distributed?

Once these issues have been resolved, the tax treatment of the distribution is determined under § 301(c)—a three tiered provision. Section 301(c)(1) states that dividends are to be included in gross income. Considering that the statutory journey started with § 61(a)(7), we have not made much progress. However, § 301(c)(1) references § 316 for the definition of a dividend. Section 316(a) provides that distributions out of specified "earnings and profits" are treated as dividends. The earnings and profits concept was enacted to distinguish a distribution of a shareholder's contribution to the capital of the corporation from a distribution of income

---

3. 283 U.S. 404 (1931).

4. *Commissioner v. Glenshaw Glass Co.*, 348 U.S. 426 (1955).

5. Stock distributions are treated separately under § 305. See Chapter 6 *infra.*

earned by the corporation. No definition of "earnings and profits" appears in the Code.

Those distributions which are not dividends under § 301(c)(1) are next treated under § 301(c)(2) as a return of the shareholder's investment in the corporation. Accordingly, the distributions reduce the basis of the shareholder's stock. If a shareholder has fully recovered his investment in the corporation, any further distributions are given sale or exchange treatment, generally producing capital gain for the shareholder. § 301(c)(3).

Note that distributions taxed under both (c)(1) and (c)(3) are includible in the shareholder's income but the (c)(1) component is includible as a "dividend" while the (c)(3) component is includible as gain. Historically, "dividend" income was taxable at ordinary rates, but since 2003 most dividends (called "qualified" dividends) have been taxed to individuals at the same rate as long-term capital gain; that is, at 15%. See § 1(h)(11). Note, however, that qualified dividends are *not* capital gain. In particular, dividend income is includible without any offset for basis and dividend income will not free up capital losses suspended under § 1211. For corporate shareholders, even qualified dividends are includible as ordinary income.

Qualified dividends include dividends paid on stock of domestic corporations and on most foreign corporations so long as the stock has been held for at least 61 of the immediately prior 121 days. A shareholder can elect the lower tax rate applicable to qualified dividends or can treat the dividend as "investment income" for purposes of the investment interest limitation in § 163(d)

Section 301 and the other provisions briefly sketched address the treatment of shareholders. A distribution may also trigger tax consequences for the distributing corporation. Should a distribution of appreciated property cause the distributing corporation to recognize income? If the property has declined in value, is a loss appropriate? Historically, a distributing corporation did not recognize gain or loss on a distribution. Now, however, § 311 requires a corporation to recognize gain on the distribution of appreciated property.

It is important to note at this point that the distributions addressed in this chapter are not the only type of distributions made by corporations. Distributions *of* stock are addressed by § 305. Distributions *in exchange for* a shareholder's stock (called "redemptions") are addressed by § 302. Liquidating distributions are described in §§ 331–338. Finally, distributions in connection with a reorganization are discussed in §§ 354–368. In Chapter 2, we looked at distributions in connection with the formation of a corporation.

4.02 Earnings and Profits. While the term "earnings and profits" is not defined in the code, the concept plays an important role in the characterization of distributions. The backbone of our corporate taxation system is that corporate earnings be taxed twice—once when earned at the corporate-level and once again when distributed to shareholders. The earnings and profits account helps to measure whether a distribution originates from corporate earnings or from other sources.

At the outset it is important to note that the earnings and profits concept is not synonymous with "earned surplus" "retained earnings" or any other financial reporting or accounting concept of corporate earnings. For example, a nontaxable, pro rata distribution of common stock by a corporation decreases earned surplus but has no effect on earnings and profits. Otherwise a corporation could sweep away its entire earnings and profits account by making such distributions. This would enable a corporation to subsequently distribute cash or other property that would not be taxable to its shareholders.

Similarly, the term "dividend" may not mean the same thing for income tax and state law purposes. For example, a distribution may be a dividend under § 316(a) although under state law the distribution impairs capital.[6] Conversely, a dividend under state law may not be a dividend under § 316(a).

Put aside for the moment how the earnings and profits account is calculated in order to consider how the account works.[7] Suppose B forms X Corp. by exchanging $50,000 for all of X Corp.'s stock in a transaction that falls under § 351. B's basis in the stock is $50,000 under § 358. In year 1, X Corp. is profitable, increasing its earnings and profits account from $0 to $20,000. Suppose X Corp. makes a $20,000 distribution at the end of year 1. Under § 301(c)(1), B must include in ordinary income that part of the distribution that is a dividend. Under § 316(a), since X Corp. has current earnings and profits of $20,000, the entire distribution is a dividend.[8]

---

6. See, e.g., *United States v. Lesoine*, 203 F.2d 123 (9th Cir.1953) (claim of right doctrine requires dividends be taxed in year of receipt even if distribution was illegal under state law).

7. For a good presentation of how the earnings and profits account works, see Rev. Rul. 74–164, 1974–1 C.B. 74.

8. Note that corporate-level taxes would actually decrease the earnings and profits account below $20,000. See note 1 *supra*.

Suppose instead that X Corp. has operating losses in year 1 which produce negative earnings and profits of $20,000. In year 2, X Corp. has $20,000 of earnings and profits. If X Corp. makes a $20,000 distribution at the end of year 2, B will have a $20,000 dividend despite the fact that X Corp. has no overall earnings and profits. Section 316(a)(2) employs a "nimble dividend" rule whereby distributions will be taxable to shareholders regardless of any accumulated earnings and profits deficit if there are current earnings and profits.[9] If there is more than one distribution during the year, the current earning and profits are prorated among the distributions for purposes of determining if a distribution is a dividend. Accumulated earnings and profits are allocated to distributions on a first come, first served basis.[10]

Earnings and profits are decreased at the end of the year in which a distribution was made. To the extent that a corporation has both accumulated and current earnings and profits, distributions are deemed to come first from the current earnings and profits. § 316. Once a distribution is made, the earnings and profits account must be adjusted so that future distributions will be treated correctly. Section 312(a)(1) requires that the earnings and profits account be decreased by the amount of any cash distributed. Note that earnings and profits cannot be decreased below zero by a distribution. How then can there be an earnings and profits deficit? A corporation which has an operating deficit may have an earnings and profits deficit.

Suppose X Corp. has $20,000 of earnings and profits in year 1, and on the last day of year 1, B sells her stock to C. C receives a distribution of $20,000 from X Corp. after the purchase and before X Corp. has any additional earnings. At first glance, it may seem somehow unfair that C will have ordinary income when the corporation earned that income while B was a shareholder. From C's perspective, the distribution is merely a return of part of C's investment in the corporation. However, the rules of § 301(c)(1) and § 316 are unremitting. Since X Corp. has earnings and profits, C must report a dividend.

The Supreme Court in *United States v. Phellis*[11] long ago explained why this "miracle of income without gain" is not as

---

9. Interestingly, the rule originated in 1936 as a pro-taxpayer relief measure from the since-repealed undistributed profits tax. Taxpayers were able to reduce their undistributed profits only by making dividend distributions and the predecessor to § 316(a)(2) facilitated the characterization of distributions as dividends.

10. Regs. § 1.316–2(b), (c).

11. 257 U.S. 156, 171–172 (1921).

troublesome as it may seem.[12] Suppose B owns 1 share of X Corp. stock with a fair market value of $100 and an adjusted basis of $60. In one month, X Corp. will distribute $10 per share as a dividend, reducing each share's value to $90. If B wants to sell his share prior to the dividend, what price will the share fetch? Assume that income is taxed at a flat rate of 30 percent.

A prospective purchaser will know that with the share comes a tax liability of $3.00 attributable to the impending dividend. Accordingly, B should receive the current value of the share *less the anticipated tax liability.* B will bear the burden of the tax not by actually paying it but rather by receiving a reduced sales price. The purchaser, on the other hand, will actually pay the tax but will not bear its burden.

Of course, this example depends on two assumptions. First, it was assumed that the seller and purchaser knew when the corporation would make a distribution and the amount thereof. More realistically, the seller and purchaser can only estimate this information, and to the extent they err, the tax burden may be shifted from the seller to the purchaser.

In addition, it was assumed that the seller and purchaser were taxed at the same rate. This often will not be true. If their tax rates differ, the failure to tax corporate profits to those taxpayers who are shareholders when the profits are earned may result in reduced (or increased) income to the Treasury.

To compute a corporation's earnings and profits, it is helpful to start with taxable income. A corporation's taxable income and its current earnings and profits will normally not coincide since the earnings and profits account is intended to measure what the corporation has available for distribution while taxable income reflects a number of preferences and incentives. Three types of adjustments are necessary to convert taxable income into earnings and profits.[13] First, some items that are excluded from taxable income are included in the earnings and profits account because they represent an accretion to the corporation which can be distributed without impairing the corporation's original capital. For example, interest on obligations excluded by a corporation under § 103 is nevertheless available for distribution to shareholders and, therefore, increases a corporation's earnings and profits account.

In computing taxable income a corporation can sometimes defer recognition in a manner that may not reflect the corporation's

---

12. The phrase comes from Powell, *Income from Corporate Dividends,* 35 Harv. L. Rev. 363 (1922).

13. See Regs. § 1.312–6.

ability to make distributions without impairing its capital. For example, a corporation might sell property under the installment method of § 453, thereby including as taxable income for the year of sale only the proceeds received (minus some allocated basis). From an economic standpoint though, the corporation has earned the present value of all expected payments regardless of when they are actually paid. Indeed, the notes themselves are available for distribution. Consequently, for purposes of computing earnings and profits, the entire gain is included in earnings and profits to reflect this dividend paying capacity.

The second category of adjustments are for those items that are deductible in computing taxable income but are not deductible in computing earnings and profits. Some of these are "artificial" deductions in that no immediate cash outlay is required that would deplete what is available for distribution. For example, while a corporation can take a dividends-received deduction under § 243 for purposes of computing taxable income,[14] the full amount of the dividend received is available for distribution. A corporation must therefore add the § 243 deduction to taxable income in computing earnings and profits. Similarly net operating losses under § 172 and capital loss carrybacks under § 1212 do not reduce earnings and profits since these are accounting conventions. The actual losses reduce earnings and profits in the year they occurred. To reduce earnings and profits again would be double counting.

Congress has shown signs of mild schizophrenia in its treatment of depreciation for taxable income and earnings and profits purposes.[15] Under § 168, corporations (and other taxpayers) can depreciate property rapidly and often in an accelerated manner. Yet for purposes of computing earnings and profits, accelerated depreciation is not permitted and even the straight-line depreciation must be computed over longer time periods. § 312(k). Presumably these differences stem from a congressional belief that the deductions permitted under § 168 are more generous than economic depreciation—perhaps to encourage investment—and therefore understate a corporation's true economic income and accordingly a corporation's ability to make distributions.

The third category of adjustments is the converse of the second category. Some items that cannot be deducted in computing taxable income are deductible in determining earnings and profits. While various policy reasons may preclude deduction of these items for

---

14. See discussion at Section 4.03 *infra.*

15. For computation of the corporate minimum tax, depreciation is treated in the same manner as it is for computation of earnings and profits. See Section 3.01 *supra.*

taxable income purposes, these items do represent economic costs that deplete what is available for distribution. For example, expenses that are not deductible on policy grounds (e.g., fines and kickbacks) under § 162(c), (f) or (g) can be subtracted in the computation of earnings and profits. Similarly, unreasonable compensation and nondeductible expenses under § 265 (e.g., interest incurred to produce tax-exempt income) are subtracted in the earnings and profits calculation. Dividends paid in previous years also are subtracted in determining earnings and profits as are federal income taxes.

To see how the three types of adjustments work consider the following problem where X Corp. is an accrual basis taxpayer taxed at a flat 30 percent rate.

	Income
Gross income from business	$30,000
Dividend income (dividends-received deduction under § 243 = $14,000)	20,000
Interest on municipal bonds	8,000
Long-term capital gain	6,000
	$64,000

	Expenses
Wages, rent, supplies, etc.	$17,000
Fines and kickbacks	5,000
Depreciation (§ 312(k) recapture amount = $6,000)	9,000
Capital losses	7,000
	$38,000

In order to compute current earnings and profits, we start with X Corp.'s taxable income. X Corp. has gross income of $30,000 from operations plus $20,000 of dividends plus $6,000 of long-term capital gain, or a total gross income of $56,000. X Corp.'s taxable income is $56,000 minus $17,000 of deductible expenses under § 162 minus $9,000 of depreciation minus $6,000 of capital losses[16] minus the $14,000 dividends-received deduction, or taxable income of $10,000.

The first adjustment made to the $10,000 of taxable income is to increase it by certain items that are not includible in taxable income such as the $8,000 of tax-exempt interest. Next, the $18,000

---

16. Capital losses are permitted to the extent of a corporation's capital   gain. See §§ 165(f) and 1211.

subtotal is increased by items that are deductible in computing taxable income, but not in determining earnings and profits such as the $14,000 dividends-received deduction. Under § 312(k), excess depreciation of $6,000 must be added to the subtotal,[17] bringing the subtotal to $38,000. Finally, nondeductible items must be subtracted from the subtotal since they are economic costs. In this example, these items include the $5,000 in fines and kickbacks, the $1,000 excess capital loss over the capital gain and the $3,000 of accrued tax liability.[18] X Corp.'s earnings and profits for the year would be $29,000.

Considering all of the complexity involved in the earnings and profits concept, might it not be better to eliminate it?[19] This could be done by taxing the shareholder on all distributions rather than distinguishing distributions of earnings from distributions of invested capital.

For example, suppose B forms X Corp. by exchanging $10,000 for all of the X Corp. stock. In year 1 X Corp. has no earnings and profits, but distributes $2,000. Under current law, the $2,000 would not be a dividend under § 301(c)(1) and would reduce B's stock basis from $10,000 to $8,000. § 301(c)(2). Without the earnings and profits concept, B would report the $2,000 as a dividend. B would then hold the X Corp. stock with a basis of $10,000 and a fair market value of $8,000. When B disposes of the stock through sale or liquidation, the $2,000 loss deduction would offset the earlier inclusion.[20] B, who started off with $10,000, ends up with $10,000—$2,000 on the distribution and $8,000 on the sale. From a tax standpoint, B has a $2,000 inclusion and a $2,000 deduction.

Whatever appeal this treatment might have, it is time to reconsider a question raised at the outset of this chapter—why are distributions taxed at all? Suppose in the previous example, X Corp. produces $2,000 of earnings in year 1. On the last day of the year, B holds the X Corp. stock with a basis of $10,000 and a fair market value of $12,000. B will not be taxed on the appreciation in the

---

17. Note that for earnings and profits purposes not only must straight-line depreciation be used, but the time periods are increased. §§ 312(k) and 168(g)(2).

18. Regs. § 1.312–6(a) provides that the method of accounting used to compute taxable income should also be used to compute earnings and profits. X Corp. as an accrual basis taxpayer can accrue the federal income taxes to be paid.

19. See Colby, Blackburn & Trier, *Elimination of Earnings and Profits*

from the Internal Revenue Code, 39 Tax Lawyer 285 (1986).

20. This somewhat simplistic analysis ignores the time value of money problem—the fact that the taxes paid on the inclusion occurred in a year prior to the taxes saved by the deduction. Also unless the limitations on the deductibility of capital gains are revised, the capital loss deduction may not fully offset the ordinary income inclusion, even ignoring differences in timing. §§ 165(f), 1211 and 1212.

stock until it is realized. If X Corp. makes a distribution on the last day of year 1, B will hold $2,000 in cash and the X Corp. stock with a basis and fair market value of $10,000, or total assets of $12,000. There is no accession to a shareholder's overall wealth which is $12,000 whether or not there is a distribution. Yet, under our tax system we tax B on the distribution because we consider it to be the appropriate time to tax the unrealized gain that occurred earlier. This policy is a manifestation of the realization doctrine—that the cash or other property received by the shareholder cannot be offset by the corresponding decrease in the value of the shareholder's stock.

4.03 Relief From Dividends. By now it is clear that Congress has legislated a system whereby corporate earnings are generally taxed twice—once at the corporate-level and once at the shareholder-level. For example suppose B owns all of the stock of X Corp. and is taxed at a 15 percent rate. If X Corp. earns $100 and is taxed at a 35 percent rate, it must pay a tax of $35. When B receives the $65 distribution, B will pay an additional $9.75 in income tax, leaving $55.25 for B out of the original $100.[21]

Suppose instead that X Corp. operates its business through a wholly-owned subsidiary Y Corp. Now Y Corp. earns $100, pays $35 in taxes and distributes $65 to X Corp. If X Corp. is taxed on receipt of the dividend, it will pay $22.75 to the government and distribute the remaining $42.25 to B who must pay an additional $6.34 in federal income tax. The result is that out of the original $100 earned, B ends up with $35.91. If more corporate layers are interposed, B will end up with less.

One must ask whether the tax results should vary depending on the number of corporate entities involved. There was only one productive activity—the earning of $100 by performing services or selling goods. If enough corporate entities are interposed, the $100 would almost completely be taxed away.

Because of this cascading tax problem, the Code makes a special allowance for dividends received by corporate shareholders. Section 243 provides for a deduction equal to a specified percentage of dividends received by a corporation from a domestic corporation depending on the degree of ownership.[22] For those corporations

---

21. This example assumes that X Corp. has sufficient earnings and profits so that the distribution would be a dividend under §§ 301(c)(1) and 316 and that both X Corp. and B are taxed at a flat rate on the additional $100 of income.

22. The provision does not generally extend to dividends from foreign corporations since they are not subject to U.S. taxes. But see § 245 providing a dividends-received deduction for certain for-which own less than 20 percent (by vote or value) of the stock of the distributing corporation, § 243 provides a 70 percent dividends-received deduction. There is an 80 percent deduction for corporations which own 20 percent or more of the stock (by vote and value) of the distributing corporation but which do not qualify for the 100 percent dividends-received deduction of § 243(a)(3) which is available for certain affiliated corporations. At the current 35 percent corporate rate, the maximum tax rate on dividends received by a corporation is 10.5 percent—i.e., the highest corporate rate of 35 percent imposed on 30 percent of the distribution includible in taxable income for a less than 20 percent shareholder.

The dividends-received deduction (*i.e.*, DRD) presents corporations with an arbitrage opportunity. Suppose that stock of Y Corp. regularly pays dividends of $6.00 per year on its common stock selling for $100 per share, a 6 percent return. If X Corp. can borrow funds at 8 percent interest, it would not, absent tax considerations, purchase the stock of Y Corp. In the absence of tax considerations, it does not make sense to borrow at 8 percent in order to earn a 6 percent return. But suppose X Corp., in the 35 percent tax bracket, borrows $100 to buy one share of Y Corp. stock. The after-tax cost of borrowing $100 at 8 percent is $5.20 because of the interest deduction. The after-tax return on the $6.00 dividend is $5.58, assuming an 80 percent dividends-received deduction, thereby resulting in a $.42 tax on the $1.20 that enters taxable income. With tax considerations, the investment becomes profitable, producing a $5.58 return at a cost of $5.28.

You may recall that in § 265 Congress prohibits a deduction for interest incurred to produce tax-exempt income. For a corporate shareholder, dividend income is tantamount to tax-exempt income by virtue of the § 243 deduction. In § 246A, Congress has chosen to limit the tax-exemption rather than the deduction. The amount of the dividends-received deduction otherwise permitted under § 243 is reduced by a percentage related to the amount of debt used to purchase the stock. Thus, if a taxpayer purchases stock with some cash and some debt such that the "average indebtedness percentage" is 50 percent, then the § 243 deduction will be 40 percent rather than 80 percent. § 243A(a) and (d).[23] Section 246A

eign corporations subject to U.S. taxation.

A distribution from a foreign corporation not subject to U.S. taxation to a U.S. corporation shareholder does not qualify for the § 243 dividends-received deduction, but may entitle the receiving corporation to a foreign tax credit for foreign income taxes imposed on the income that made the dividend possible. *See* §§ 901 and 902.

23. Section 246A applies to "portfolio stock" only. Stock will be considered portfolio stock if the corporate shareholder owns less than a 50 percent interest in the subsidiary. Where there is at

requires the Service to try to trace what proceeds were used to make the purchase. Not surprisingly, tracing creates administrative headaches.

Even when a corporation does not use debt to acquire the stock of another corporation there are arbitrage possibilities. Suppose X Corp. purchases all of the stock of Y Corp. for $1,000 and shortly thereafter receives a dividend of $100. Immediately before the distribution, Y Corp. has assets worth $1,000; after the distribution, Y Corp. has assets worth $900. If X Corp. now sells the Y Corp. stock, X Corp. will report a $100 loss.[24] In total X Corp. which started with $1,000 ends up with $1,000—$100 from the distribution and $900 from the sale. However for tax purposes, X Corp. may be able to deduct the full $100 distribution under § 243, thereby reducing income to $0. At the same time, X Corp. might use the $100 loss deduction under § 165 to offset a full $100 of income. In short, for no net investment, X Corp. would produce a net $100 deduction. Assuming a 35 percent tax rate, X Corp. would profit by keeping the $35 that would otherwise have been paid in taxes.

Section 1059 now mandates a reduction of basis for corporate shareholders on the receipt of "extraordinary dividends" if the stock on which the dividends are paid is sold before it has been held for two years.[25] In the example above, X Corp. would reduce its basis in the Y Corp. stock by $100—the amount excluded under § 243—from $1,000 to $900. When X Corp. sells the Y Corp. stock, it would realize and recognize no gain, reflecting the fact that X Corp. which started with $1,000 ends up with $1,000.[26]

But is it clear that § 1059 should cause a basis reduction in this case? Suppose, in the example above, that X Corp. purchased the Y Corp. stock from W Corp. for $1,000. W Corp. had formed Y Corp. by contributing $900 in exchange for all of the Y Corp. stock. After its formation, Y Corp. had earned $100 on which it was taxed. When W Corp. sells the Y Corp. stock to X Corp., W Corp. is taxable

---

least 50 percent ownership, perhaps it suggests that the parent is interested in more than the subsidiary's dividends— the corporations are likely to be part of a multicorporate structure.

24. Short- or long-term depending on the holding period.

25. See § 1059(c) for the definition of "extraordinary dividends." For common stock, dividends in excess of 10 percent of a taxpayer's stock basis (5 percent for preferred stock) generally are considered extraordinary. Dividends

with respect to certain preferred stock are subject to § 1059 even if the stock is not held for two years, § 1059(f), as are certain redemptions taxable as distribution, see § 1059(e)(1)(A).

26. If the amount of the extraordinary dividend excluded under § 243 exceeds the corporate shareholder's adjusted basis in the stock on which the dividend was declared, that excess amount is taxable gain as of the date of the dividend. § 1059(a)(2).

on $100—a second corporate-level tax. If X Corp. is allowed a $100 loss deduction when it sells the Y Corp. stock, after receiving the nontaxable dividend from Y Corp., the deduction will, in the aggregate, offset one of the corporate-level taxes, thereby preserving a single-level corporate tax. Of course there will be a second level of tax when the corporate earnings are ultimately distributed to individual shareholders.

Note that if the Y Corp. stock is originally held by W, an individual, it would be inappropriate to allow X Corp. a deduction on the sale of the Y Corp. stock following the dividend from Y Corp. That is because the Y Corp. earnings were taxed once when earned and once again at the individual-shareholder level when W sold the appreciated stock to X Corp. No deduction is needed by X Corp. on the sale of the Y Corp. stock because there has only been a single level of corporate tax. By mandating a reduction in X Corp.'s basis in the Y Corp. stock in this situation, § 1059 preserves two levels of tax—one at the corporate level and one at the shareholder level.

Perhaps because it is administratively difficult, if not impossible, to determine from whom it purchased the Y Corp. stock (i.e., from an individual or a corporate seller), the automatic rule in § 1059 to reduce X Corp.'s basis in the Y Corp. stock if the dividend is "extraordinary" (but not otherwise) may be a reasonable accommodation.[27] This is not an unreasonable result even if X Corp. purchased the Y Corp. stock from W Corp., a corporate seller. After all, W Corp. had within its own power the ability to prevent two levels of corporate tax by causing Y Corp. to distribute a dividend prior to the sale of the Y Corp. stock to X Corp. If § 243 would have rendered the dividend nontaxable to W Corp., then W Corp. would have sold the Y Corp. stock to X Corp. for $900. In the aggregate, there would have been one level of corporate tax—the tax imposed on Y Corp. when it earned the $100.[28]

Section 1059 can apply to any transaction taxed as a dividend including distributions in redemption of stock, see § 302(d), as well

---

27. To eliminate all possibility of a triple tax on corporate earnings, the corporate and individual taxes would have to be integrated completely with respect to corporate taxpayers. Recall from Chapter 1 how difficult such integration can be.

28. Regardless of whether W is a corporation or an individual, to the extent that the distribution from Y Corp. is not out of its earnings and profits, it is appropriate for X Corp. to reduce its basis. Suppose that W had formed Y Corp. by exchanging $1,000 for all of the Y Corp. stock which was then sold to X Corp. which then caused Y Corp. to make a $100 distribution. The distribution is a nontaxable return of capital to X Corp. which then reduces its basis in the Y Corp. stock to $900. If X Corp. then sells the Y Corp. stock for $900, no gain or loss is recognized on the sale. In the aggregate, there is no corporate gain or loss because there have been no corporate earnings.

as redemptions through related corporations, see § 304(a). If a sale of stock in one corporation (called the issuing corporation) to another corporation (called the acquiring corporation) is taxed as a distribution under § 304(a)(1), the sale is recast as (1) a transfer of the stock sold for stock of the acquiring corporation (2) which is then redeemed by the acquiring corporation in a transaction described in § 302(d). If the shareholder engaging in this § 304 transaction is itself a corporation (call it the "selling" corporation), then the effect of this hypothetical stock acquisition and redemption is to ensure that if the selling corporation excludes more than its basis in the shares sold by reason of the § 243 dividends received deduction, that excess will be taxable immediately as gain under § 1059(a)(2).

For example, assume Parent Corp. owns all the outstanding stock of Brother Corp. with an adjusted basis of $5,000 as well as all the outstanding stock of Sister Corp. with an adjusted basis of $50,000, and assume that the fair market value of each subsidiary corporation equals $50,000. If Parent Corp. sells the stock of Brother Corp. to Sister Corp. for cash of $50,000, this transaction is a redemption by related corporations as described in § 304(a)(1), and because Parent Corp. retains complete control of Brother Corp. after the transaction, it is taxable as a distribution pursuant to § 304(a)(1).

Suppose that the combined earnings and profits of Brother and Sister exceed $50,000, so that the entire distribution is taxed as a dividend. See §§ 304(b)(2), 301(c)(1). If this is treated as an extraordinary distribution, Parent Corp. is deemed to contribute its stock of Brother Corp. to Sister Corp. for Sister Corp. stock which is then redeemed and taxed as a dividend. The Sister Corp. stock hypothetically received by Parent has a substituted basis of only $5,000 under § 358(a)(1), so that the subsequent hypothetical $50,000 redemption produces not only a $50,000 dividend and a $50,000 dividends-received deduction but also a taxable gain of $45,000 under § 1059(a)(2). Note in particular that Parent Corp. was unable to offset that gain with its pre-existing basis in the stock of Sister Corp. that it actually owns.

4.04 Treatment of the Distributing Corporation. Suppose X Corp. holds an asset with a basis of $100 and a fair market value of $500. If X Corp. sells the asset and distributes the proceeds, X Corp. will be taxed on the $400 gain and the shareholders would be taxed on the $500 distribution as a dividend (assuming X Corp. had sufficient earnings and profits). On the other hand, if X Corp. distributed the property to its shareholders who then sold the asset, should the tax consequences be any different?

The shareholders will still be taxable on a $500 dividend distribution under § 301(b). There would be no further shareholder-level tax on the sale since the shareholders take a fair market value basis in the assets received. See § 301(d) discussed in more detail *infra*. Unless there is a corporate-level tax on the distribution, the tax system would seem to reward the form of the transaction. Under both scenarios, the shareholders end up with the cash from the sale and a purchaser ends up with the asset.

To the extent that the form of a transaction is dictated by non-tax considerations (e.g., easier transfer of title), it makes no sense to have economically identical situations treated differently for tax purposes. To the extent that a taxpayer has latitude in choosing the form of a transaction, a tax system is wasteful and inefficient if it causes taxpayers to invest resources (e.g., money or time) in a nonproductive search to determine the best form for tax purposes of economically equivalent transactions.[29]

In 1935 the Supreme Court decided *General Utilities & Operating Co. v. Helvering*,[30] a case that shaped corporate taxation for more than 50 years. In that case, the corporate taxpayer contemplated a sale of stock in another corporation. Realizing that a sale by the corporation followed by a distribution of the proceeds would result in corporate-level and shareholder-level taxes, the corporation distributed the appreciated stock to its shareholders who reported a shareholder-level dividend. Pursuant to the predecessor of § 301(d), the shareholders took a fair market value basis in the distributed stock and reported no further gain when the stock was sold to the purchaser by the shareholders at fair market value.

Before the Board of Tax Appeals (the predecessor to the Tax Court), the Commissioner argued that the taxpayer should be taxed on the distribution since it had declared a dividend of $1 million and satisfied that obligation through a distribution of appreciated property. The trial court rejected that argument because in fact the dividend was declared to be a dividend of stock and not a dividend of cash. On appeal, the Commissioner added a second argument—that the sale should be attributed to the corporation rather than to the shareholders.

While this second argument convinced the circuit court, the Supreme Court held that the argument was raised too late. In its

29. There may be equity problems as well since it is the wealthy that have better access to informed tax advice.

30. 296 U.S. 200 (1935).

Supreme Court brief, the Commissioner raised a third argument—that a distribution of appreciated property constituted a "sale or other disposition" under § 1001, thereby triggering a corporate-level tax. The Supreme Court ignored this argument. Whether the argument was ignored because it was raised belatedly or rejected on the merits is not clear. What is clear is that the latter interpretation gave rise to the *General Utilities* doctrine—a distributing corporation recognized no gain or loss on a distribution of property with respect to a shareholder's stock. The doctrine was codified in § 311(a).

The Tax Reform Act of 1986 substantially repealed the *General Utilities* doctrine. Section 311(a) still provides nonrecognition of gain or loss on a distribution with respect to stock. But § 311(b) now provides that a distributing corporation must recognize gain on a distribution of property (other than the distributing corporation's own obligation) where the fair market value exceeds the adjusted basis of the property. The gain will be recognized as if the property had been sold to the shareholders at fair market value.

The reach of § 311(b) is quite broad. Not only must a distributing corporation recognize post-incorporation appreciation, but pre-incorporation appreciation is also captured by the provision. Suppose C forms X Corp. in a § 351 transaction by exchanging property including one parcel with a basis of $300 and a fair market value of $1,000 for all of the X Corp. stock. Before X Corp. earns any income, the corporation distributes the property to C. Under § 311(b), X Corp. is treated as having sold the asset to C for $1,000. The $700 gain to X Corp. will be capital or ordinary depending upon the nature of the underlying property. The $700 gain recognized by X Corp. will enter taxable income and therefore the earnings and profits account. Consequently, C will have a shareholder-level tax on the distribution as well.

Note that these two levels of taxation stem from appreciation that occurred prior to the incorporation of X Corp. Could Congress have written a provision that distinguished between pre-and post-incorporation gain? Curiously, Congress did make similar distinctions involving liquidating distributions of property whose basis at the time of incorporation exceeded its fair market value. It is not clear why such distinctions are reserved for liquidating distributions and for property with a built-in loss rather than built-in gain.

The repeal of *General Utilities* embodied in § 311(b) does not apply to the distribution of property whose basis exceeds its fair market value—loss property. Suppose X Corp. (with ample earnings and profits) holds property with a basis of $1,000 and a fair market value of $300. Assume further that the decrease in the asset's value occurred while it was held by the corporation. If X Corp. sells the property and distributes the proceeds, the corporation will recognize a $700 loss and the shareholders will be taxed on the distribution as a dividend to the extent of X Corp.'s earnings and profits. If instead X Corp. distributes the property to its shareholders who then sell it, the shareholders will be treated in the same manner, but there will be no corporate-level recognition of the $700 loss. Moreover, because the shareholders take the distributed property with a basis equal to fair market value or $300, the loss is not preserved when the shareholders sell the property for $300.

Why should Congress countenance a difference in form when loss property is involved while eliminating form considerations when gain property is involved? Perhaps Congress was concerned that shareholders could exploit the realization doctrine by causing a corporation to distribute loss property but not gain property, thereby triggering loss recognition while keeping the gain unrealized. If that is the problem, the solution does not seem to fit.

It is always in a taxpayer's power to exploit the realization doctrine by selling loss property rather than gain property. This power gave rise to the enactment of §§ 165(f), 1211 and 1212 which limit the amount of loss immediately available from the sale of capital assets. Generally, capital losses can only be used to offset capital gains plus up to $3,000 of ordinary income. If these provisions are deemed inadequate, perhaps Congress should somehow limit the deduction of losses that do not arise from the sale of capital assets, but it should limit such losses on sales as well as distributions.

Not surprisingly, Congress *has* enacted provisions that further curtail the exploitation of the realization doctrine. Suppose a taxpayer sells loss property under circumstances where the capital loss limitations are ineffective. Perhaps the taxpayer has sufficient capital gains from other transactions so that the loss would not be limited by § 1211. Or perhaps the asset sold would not give rise to a capital loss. If the property is sold in a manner that permits the taxpayer to control the property after sale, Congress has deemed that recognition of the loss is inappropriate. In effect the continued taxpayer control means that the loss has not truly been realized.

Section 267 prohibits the deduction of losses resulting from the sale or exchange between related parties. Conceptually not unlike the "wash sale" provision of § 1091, § 267 disallows a loss where the transferor is deemed to retain control of the asset (or in the case of § 1091, substantially identical assets). A corporation and a more than 50 percent (by value) shareholder either through direct or indirect stock ownership are considered related for purposes of

§ 267. If X Corp. sells property with a basis of $1,000 and a fair market value of $300 to a shareholder, C, who owns more than 50 percent (by value) of X Corp. stock, X Corp. is not allowed a loss on the sale. A similar result follows if C is a 5 percent shareholder as long as more than 45 percent of the remaining stock is held by someone related to C within the meaning of § 267(b) such as C's son. If this last condition is not met, then § 267 would not disallow the deduction on the sale to C.

In light of § 267, why doesn't § 311(b) allow a loss on a distribution of loss property to a shareholder subject only to the rules of § 267? In fact, the language of § 311(b) treats the distributed property as if it had been sold to a shareholder at fair market value. It would have been easy enough to subject the deemed sale to § 267. If the distribution were to a more than 50 percent shareholder, then no loss would be allowed to the distributing corporation. On the other hand, if the distribution were to a 50 percent or less shareholder, a loss would be allowed.

There are some peculiar side effects resulting from the application of § 267 to actual sales and not deemed sales under § 311(b). On a sale governed by § 267, a purchaser takes a cost basis under § 1012. But if the purchaser sells the property at a gain, the loss that was disallowed to the original seller is available to the purchaser to offset any gain recognized on the subsequent sale. § 267(d). If X Corp. sells property with a basis of $1,000 and a fair market value of $300 to C, its only shareholder, X Corp. will recognize no loss pursuant to § 267, and C's basis is $300. If C later sells the asset to D for $1,000, C can offset the gain with the loss disallowed to X Corp.

Even though § 311(b) disallows losses, there is no provision that preserves the loss. If X Corp. distributes property with a basis of $1,000 and a fair market value of $300 to C, X Corp. is unable to deduct the loss. C's basis in the property is its fair market value or $300. § 301(d). If C subsequently sells the asset for $1,000, C will recognize a $700 gain which cannot be offset by the previously disallowed loss.

In light of the discontinuities created by § 311(b), it may be expected that distributing corporations will try to sidestep the application of § 311(b). Suppose X Corp. intends to distribute property with a basis of $1,000 and a fair market value of $300 to its shareholders. X Corp. will not be allowed a $700 loss on a distribution. § 311(a). Suppose instead that X Corp. declares a cash dividend of $300. The corporation then satisfies the cash dividend with a distribution of the loss property. Can X Corp. now deduct the $700 loss (subject to § 267) since it has used property to satisfy a pecuniary obligation?[31] Note that this position is precisely what the Service argued in *General Utilities*—only in that case the distributed property had appreciated prior to the distribution.

Similar techniques may be employed when the property distributed is appreciated. Suppose X Corp. distributes property with a basis of $300 and a fair market value of $1,000 to its shareholders with respect to their stock. Under § 311(b) X Corp. must recognize the $700 gain in the year of distribution as if the property were sold at its fair market value. Suppose instead that X Corp. sells the property to its shareholder in exchange for a note bearing appropriate interest. If the sale is respected, X Corp. would be entitled to defer the $700 gain pursuant to the installment provisions of § 453 while the shareholder would not have to treat the property as a dividend distribution.

If the shareholder ultimately honors the note, it is appropriate that the treatment of X Corp. and the shareholder differ from distribution treatment since there has been an exchange and not merely a distribution. But what if the shareholder ultimately defaults on the note? Under this scenario, the shareholder ends up in much the same way as if the property had been distributed except that by casting the transaction as a sale, X Corp. has avoided recognition of gain and the shareholder has avoided dividend treatment.

It is true that some correction will occur upon the discharge of indebtedness, but the parties have enjoyed the benefits of deferral and the correction is incomplete. Presumably, the shareholder will have discharge of indebtedness income of $1,000 under § 61(a)(12) which is in effect a deferred recognition of what would have been a dividend if the property had been distributed. On the discharge, X Corp. would seem to be entitled to a bad debt deduction under § 166 equal to the basis in the note, or $300. Stated differently, X Corp. not only avoids the recognition of gain but is entitled to a loss deduction when the note is discharged. Of course these and other attempts to circumvent the reach of § 311(b) will be closely scrutinized. The Service will press to recharacterize such transactions as distributions falling within the confines of § 311(b).

Aside from the recognition or nonrecognition of gain or loss on the distribution of property, § 311 raises some other unanswered questions relating to the treatment of liabilities associated with a distribution. Suppose X Corp. distributes property with a basis of $300 and a fair market value of $1,000. The property is subject to a

---

31. See *Kenan v. Commissioner*, 114 F.2d 217 (2d Cir.1940) (satisfaction of a cash legacy with appreciated stock treated as a sale or disposition).

$200 mortgage. Section 311(b) treats the distribution as if X Corp. had sold the property for $1,000, its fair market value. Of course, a purchaser would not pay $1,000 but instead would pay $800 because of the $200 liability encumbering the property. However under *Crane v. Commissioner*,[32] the amount realized would include the encumbering liability and would therefore equal the $1,000 fair market value measure used in § 311(b).

Suppose instead that the property is subject to a $1,300 liability. X Corp. is treated as having sold the property for its fair market value, but under § 311(b)(2), the fair market value is considered to be the amount of the liability or $1,300. This rule codifies the treatment mandated by *Crane* and *Commissioner v. Tufts*,[33] that the amount realized includes indebtedness even if it exceeds the fair market value of the property.

But conceptually there is an alternative way of characterizing the situation where a corporation distributes property subject to a liability in excess of the property's fair market value.[34] Taking the example above, it is as if the shareholder makes a contribution to the corporation's capital of $300 which the corporation uses to pay off the $300 excess liability. Viewed in this manner, the distribution by the corporation would produce a $700 gain to the distributing corporation, rather than a $1,000 gain. Of course the shareholder has not actually contributed $300 to the corporation but in effect has contributed a promise to discharge the $300 excess liability.[35] Conceptually, such a promise might be equated to an actual cash contribution.

As indicated above, the formulation under § 311(b) is an inexact way of providing that a distributing corporation be treated as if it sold the appreciated asset to the shareholder followed by a distribution of the proceeds. The formulation might cause a problem where the liability encumbering the property is a deductible one. Suppose X Corp. distributes an asset with a basis of $300 and a fair market value of $1,000 secured by accounts payable in the amount of $200. Under § 311(b), it appears as if the distributing corporation must recognize a $700 gain since the corporation is treated as if it had sold the property for the $1,000 fair market value. Of course if a purchaser were to pay $1,000 for the property,

---

32.   331 U.S. 1 (1947).

33.   461 U.S. 300 (1983).

34.   Crane, *Toward A Theory of the Corporate Tax Base: The Effect of A Corporate Distribution of Encumbered Property to Shareholders,* 44 Tax L. Rev. 113 (1988).

35.   This characterization may be inappropriate if the liability is nonrecourse because a shareholder would not normally advance funds to pay off a liability in excess of the encumbered property if there was no personal liability.

it would be conditioned on the corporation removing the encumbrance. If the distributing corporation were deemed to pay off the account payable, it would have a $700 gain on the sale, but would have a $200 deduction.[36] If the distributing corporation is not permitted to deduct the $200 on the deemed § 311(b) sale, the deduction would seem to be lost since the acquiring shareholders would not be entitled to take a deduction when the accounts payable were paid.[37]

It is not clear how the regulations or the courts will deal with the distribution of deductible liabilities. But prior to the enactment of § 357(c)(3), courts demonstrated great ingenuity in overcoming § 357(c)(1) on the transfer by a shareholder to a corporation of accounts payable. For a discussion of this issue, see Section 2.06(b) *supra.*

4.05 Effect of Property Distributions on Earnings and Profits. At Section 4.02 *supra,* the effect of earnings and profits on the treatment of a corporate distribution was considered. But it is also important to consider the effect of a distribution on earnings and profits in order to evaluate subsequent distributions. Conceptually, it makes sense that the earnings and profits account is decreased to the extent that there is a distribution. If a corporation distributes all of its earnings, the earnings and profits account should be $0. Section 312(a)(1) provides that earnings and profits are decreased by the amount of money distributed.

But what happens to earnings and profits if a corporation distributes property whose basis does not equal its fair market value? A corporation distributing appreciated property must recognize the appreciation on the distribution. § 311(b). Suppose X Corp. distributes property with a basis of $5,000 and a fair market value of $14,000 to its shareholders. On the distribution, X Corp. must recognize a $9,000 gain. That gain enters X Corp.'s taxable income and therefore the earnings and profits account for purposes of evaluating the tax consequences to the shareholders on the distribution. Following the distribution, the earnings and profits account should be decreased to reflect the distribution. Under §§ 312(b)(2) and 312(a)(3), earnings and profits are decreased by the *fair market value* of the property distributed. Because the appreciation was recognized for tax purposes by X Corp., it is appropriate to decrease earnings and profits by not only the distributed asset's basis

---

36. For a discussion of this issue see *Commercial Security Bank v. Commissioner,* 77 T.C. 145 (1981) (allowing a comparable deduction in a liquidation context).

37. See, e.g., *Hyde v. Commissioner,* 64 T.C. 300, 306 (1975).

($5,000) but also the recognized appreciation ($9,000) which togetherer sum to the fair market value.

Notice that §§ 312(b)(2) and 312(a)(3) work by indirection. Section 312(a)(3) decreases earnings and profits by the "adjusted basis" of the property distributed while § 312(b)(2) defines "adjusted basis" to mean "fair market value" in the case of a distribution of appreciated property. You might ask why Congress did not directly amend § 312(a)(3) to decrease earnings and profits by the fair market value of property distributed. The answer emerges from the treatment of distributed property whose basis exceeds fair market value—loss property.

Suppose X Corp. distributes property with a basis of $14,000 and a fair market value of $5,000. Under § 311(a), X Corp. cannot deduct the unrealized loss on the distribution. But if X Corp. could recognize the $9,000 loss, that loss would decrease taxable income and consequently the earnings and profits account. Accordingly, it would be appropriate to decrease earnings and profits by the fair market value of the property as a result of the distribution itself. This follows from the fact that the total reduction of earnings and profits would be $14,000—$9,000 from the loss deduction and $5,000 from the distribution itself.

But where the loss is not recognized to the distributing corporation, earnings and profits must be decreased by the adjusted basis of distributed property to reflect the fact that $14,000 of corporate earnings were used to acquire the property and have now been distributed to the shareholders.

To illustrate the operation of §§ 311 and 312, suppose X Corp. with no earnings and profits distributes property with a basis of $0 and a fair market value of $2,000 to its shareholders. On the distribution X Corp. recognizes a $2,000 gain under § 311(b). That gain increases X Corp.'s earnings and profits for purposes of evaluating the tax consequences to the shareholders. Under § 301(c)(1), the shareholders will have dividend treatment on the distribution since there are sufficient earnings and profits (ignoring the effect of corporate taxes paid on the distribution) to cover the distribution. Following the distribution, X Corp.'s earnings and profits will be reduced from $2,000 to $0 under §§ 312(b)(2) and 312(a)(3) since X Corp.'s earnings were fully distributed.

Suppose X Corp., with $50,000 of earnings and profits, distributes its own debt obligation with a face value of $50,000. The note bears no interest and matures in 20 years. The distribution of the note does not trigger a tax to X Corp. on the distribution since it is a distribution of X Corp.'s own obligation. §§ 311(b) and 317. As discussed in more detail in the following section, the shareholders will be taxed on the fair market value of the distributed obligations. At a 10 percent discount rate, the obligation has a present value of $7,432.

While individual shareholders include the present value as a dividend (to the extent of earnings and profits), how should X Corp. adjust its earnings and profits account? Prior to the Deficit Reduction Act of 1984, a distributing corporation was permitted to reduce its earnings and profits by the face value of the obligation. The effect of this Congressional largesse was to allow a corporation to wipe out its earnings and profits account at a small tax cost to its shareholders on the issuance of a debt obligation with original issue discount.

This technique paved the way for future nontaxable distributions under § 301(c)(2). In the example above, X Corp. would have reduced its earnings and profits account to $0 by a distribution producing only $7,432 of taxable income at the shareholder-level. Section 312(a)(2) now provides that earnings and profits are decreased by the issue price, or $7,432 in our example. Each year, the corporation can reduce its taxable income and accordingly its earnings and profits by the portion of the original issue discount that the shareholders must report. § 163(e).

4.06 Treatment of Shareholders. The treatment of shareholders receiving a property distribution has been alluded to in much of the foregoing discussion. However, it seems appropriate to defer the discussion to this point because the tax consequences to the distributing corporation may have an effect on the treatment of the shareholders. If earnings and profits are increased as a result of a distribution of appreciated property, dividend treatment is more likely for the shareholders. § 301(c).

If X Corp. distributes property with a basis of $4,000 and a fair market value of $10,000, what is the amount of the distribution for purposes of § 301? Section 301(b) provides that it is the fair market value of property that is the amount distributed, or $10,000 in the example. Suppose the property is subject to a $3,000 mortgage. Under § 301(b)(2), the amount distributed is $7,000.

The basis rule for distributed property is found in § 301(d). Not surprisingly, shareholders will take a fair market value basis in the property. Notice that assuming or taking subject to a mortgage has no effect on the basis of the distributed property. This too should not be surprising. Section 301(d) simply confirms the

Crane[38] doctrine that basis includes assumed or "subject to" indebtedness.

4.07 Constructive Dividends. Often dividend treatment is undesirable to shareholders. After all, a corporation is taxed when it earns income, and a dividend distribution will result in a second tax at the shareholder level while the distributing corporation receives no deduction. There has been no shortage of imaginative ways to disguise a dividend distribution as some non-dividend distribution.

Notwithstanding the variety of techniques, the attempts to disguise seem to fall under one of three prototypes. First, the distribution might be disguised as a deductible expense even though the receipt by the shareholder would be taxable. This prototype eliminates the corporate-level tax by providing a deduction that will offset the corporate inclusion of the earnings which were distributed. The second prototype is a distribution which is excludable from income by shareholders while the distributing corporation receives no deduction. This prototype eliminates the shareholder-level tax rather than the corporate-level tax. To the extent that corporate tax rates exceed individual tax rates, this prototype may be less advantageous than the former. But note that both are preferable to dividend treatment. There is also a third prototype—the best of all worlds from the taxpayer's point of view—which is a distribution that generates a deduction and yet is not includable.[39]

Perhaps the most common illustration of the first prototype is in the compensation area. While dividends are not deductible by a distributing corporation, reasonable compensation is deductible under § 162. From the shareholder perspective, both dividends and compensation produce ordinary income, but shareholders generally will benefit to the extent the corporation has a lighter tax burden. In light of the foregoing, the tax system provides an incentive for corporations to characterize distributions as deductible reasonable compensation. Determining whether a distribution should be treated as a nondeductible dividend or deductible compensation calls for artificial distinctions engendered by the Code's disparate treatment of different distributions. In a world where corporate earnings are taxed only once at shareholder rates, the nature of the distribution would assume less importance.

38. *Crane v. Commissioner,* 331 U.S. 1 (1947).

39. It is difficult to disguise dividends in this manner, but compensation frequently can be disguised. For example, if a corporation rents a car for an employee's use, the corporation may deduct the rental payments under § 162 while the employee may attempt to exclude the value of the rental car from income as a "working condition" fringe benefit under § 132.

But until that world arrives, taxpayers, the Service and courts must wrestle with the dividend/compensation distinction. The mere fact that a shareholder-employee receives a large salary—say $1 million—will not necessarily mean that part or all of the distribution will be treated as a dividend distribution. It must be determined whether the shareholder-employee has performed services commensurate with the payment. This determination is made by looking at payments to other employees, payments to other similarly situated employees in other companies, what services the employee actually performed for the corporation and how those services affected the corporation's performance.[40]

One might think that the free market will assure that a corporation pays reasonable compensation. If a corporation pays unreasonable compensation, it will be disciplined by the market, finding it more difficult to compete because of its higher costs of production. Or perhaps shareholders will object to the unreasonable levels of compensation paid to certain shareholder-employees that might deplete the amount otherwise available for distribution to all shareholders.

There are at least two problems with reliance on the market to ensure reasonable compensation levels. First, there may be high transaction costs that make it difficult or costly for shareholders to prevent some level of over-compensation to shareholder-employees. For example, the costs of bringing a lawsuit against the corporation can be significant. Second, while the market may in fact dictate a level of return for both employees and shareholders, in the case of a shareholder-employee, the market does not care how that return is allocated.[41] Whether the payments are considered to be dividends or compensation will not be determined by the market so long as the shareholder-employee's overall return is commensurate with the level of investment and services rendered. Predictably, it is the closely-held corporation where most or all of the shareholders are employees that is most susceptible to recharacterization.

In addition to gauging the level and value of services rendered, the Service and the courts may also look to the history of dividends paid by the corporation. In general, it is probably true that if the corporation has a history of dividend distributions that reflect a "reasonable" rate of return on investment, amounts denominated as compensation are more likely to pass muster. Conversely, if a

---

40. See, e.g., *Elliotts, Inc. v. Commissioner,* 716 F.2d 1241 (9th Cir.1983).

41. More accurately, the market will value those corporations that minimize

taxes more favorably than those corporations that do not.

corporation has never paid dividends, the level of compensation will be closely scrutinized.

In at least one case, a court recharacterized purported compensation as a dividend even where the compensation was found to be reasonable. The court found that no dividends had ever been declared and that a 15 percent return on shareholders' investment was appropriate.[42] If the court found the payments for services and other factors of production to be reasonable, what justification is there for recharacterizing some of those payments as dividends? It just might be that after meeting its obligations the corporation had no earnings left for the residuary claimants—the shareholders.

A variation on the excessive compensation issue occurs where a controlling shareholder causes a corporation to pay excessive compensation to a relative of the shareholder—a child, for example—who might do some work for the corporation. The excessive compensation will be treated as a distribution to the shareholder, who then will be deemed to make a gift to his child. There will be no deduction for the excess compensation and, assuming sufficient earnings and profits, the shareholder will have dividend income.

The second prototype for disguised dividends covers those transactions where the corporation receives no deduction, but the shareholder has no inclusion. Corporate loans serve as a good illustration. Suppose X Corp. has just earned $50,000 on which it was taxed. Its shareholder, B, would like to get the $50,000 out of the corporation and into her hands. If X Corp. makes a distribution, B will have a dividend under §§ 301(c)(1) and 61(a)(7) since X Corp. has earnings and profits, and X Corp. receives no deduction for the distribution.

Suppose instead that X Corp. "loans" B $50,000. If the transaction is respected, X Corp. still receives no deduction,[43] but now B has no inclusion. While it is true that in the loan situation B has an obligation to repay X Corp., until repayment is made B does have the tax-free use of the funds. Moreover, if repayment is never made, then it is only in the year that the indebtedness is discharged (not the year the loan is made) that B will have ordinary income under *United States v. Kirby Lumber Co.*[44]

---

42. *Charles McCandless Tile Service v. United States,* 422 F.2d 1336 (Ct.Cl. 1970). But see *Laure v. Commissioner,* 70 T.C. 1087 (1978), and Rev. Rul. 79–8, 1979–1 C.B. 92, rejecting the automatic dividend rule.

43. While a distribution will reduce X Corp.'s earnings and profits under § 312(a), a loan will not.

44. 284 U.S. 1 (1931). The corporation may then be entitled to a bad debt deduction under § 166.

The corporate loan situation raises two issues. First, the Service or the courts must determine whether the transfer of funds is in fact a loan. If it is not a loan, there is no need to resolve the second issue. If it is a loan, the second issue is whether the loan bears an appropriate level of interest.

In resolving the first issue, the Service and the courts first look to see if the transaction on its face seems to be a loan—whether there is a written loan agreement, whether an adequate interest rate is provided, whether the note is secured, whether a repayment schedule is provided, whether any repayments have been made, etc. The purported loan is then viewed in a broader context by looking at factors such as whether any previous loans have been repaid. The corporation's dividend history may also be important. If a corporation has been successful and yet has made few or no distributions to shareholders, it is more likely that a purported loan will be closely scrutinized.

Finally, the capitalization of the corporation may influence the loan/dividend determination. To the extent that the corporation has a high ratio of outstanding debt to equity, it is more likely that a purported loan will be recharacterized as an equity investment so that the purported interest payments will be recharacterized as dividend payments. This is particularly the case where the purported loans are made in proportion to the outstanding equity. For example, suppose X Corp., with ample earnings and profits, has ten shareholders, each holding 10 percent of the outstanding stock. If X Corp. purports to make equal loans to each shareholder, it is likely the Service will recharacterize the loans as dividend distributions, with the subsequent interest payments treated as contributions to the corporation's capital.

Suppose that a $50,000 loan X Corp. made to its shareholder B is respected as a loan, but that the loan makes no provision for interest.[45] Beneath the surface of the loan, B is still receiving a distribution: she receives the free use of X Corp.'s money. For example, B may be able to accelerate a purchase she was planning to make and the concomitant enjoyment of the purchased item. The free or below-market use of corporate property by a shareholder will often give rise to recharacterization of the transaction as a dividend.

Section 7872 performs this function in the case of below-market interest loans. Where a loan is payable on demand, § 7872 recharacterizes the transaction as though a market rate of interest

---

45. While the lack of interest may be one factor that suggests a loan is not a loan, it is not determinative. The con-cept of a no-interest loan is not an oxy-moron.

applies.[46] For example, suppose the applicable market rate of interest is 10 percent. B will be treated each year as paying $5,125 in interest to X Corp.[47] In fact, B makes no such payment. To conform the recharacterization to reality, X Corp. is treated as though it not only loaned $50,000 but also made a distribution of $5,125. B is treated as having received the $5,125 distribution which she turns around and pays back to X Corp. in the form of interest. The $5,125 distribution and the $5,125 interest payment are deemed to occur each year the loan is outstanding.[48]

Historically, the fact that the amount of the deemed distribution and the deemed interest payment were the same in the case of a demand loan led to taxpayers offsetting the income with the deduction.[49] However, under § 7872 the offsetting deduction is not automatic. For example, if the taxpayer uses the borrowed proceeds to purchase tax-exempt securities, § 265 will not allow the shareholder to deduct the deemed interest payment. Similarly if the shareholder uses the borrowed funds for personal purposes, § 163(h) will not permit a deduction. If a deduction is not permitted, the shareholder who receives a below market interest loan may have dividend income without an offset.[50]

A related transaction that purports to generate no deduction and no inclusion is a loan between related corporations. Suppose

46. The market rate of interest is determined by looking at certain specified federal rates. See § 7872(f)(2).

47. Section 7872 uses semiannual compounding. Accordingly, a 10 percent rate of interest is equivalent to 10.25 percent when compounded semiannually.

48. If the loan is a term loan (that is, a loan made for a set period of time rather than a loan payable on demand) the timing of the deemed distribution and deemed interest repayment differs. Suppose the loan were for a 5–year period. In the year the loan was made B would be deemed to receive a loan of $30,696, assuming a 10 percent interest rate compounded semiannually. B would also be deemed to receive a distribution of $19,304, the difference between the deemed loan amount and the amount B actually received. At the end of year 1, B would be deemed to pay interest on the $30,696 loan of $3,146 (10.25 percent _ $30,696). In year 2 there would be no deemed distribution but B would have a deemed interest payment of $3,469

(10.25 percent _ ($30,696 + $3,146)). At the end of 5 years, B will have received a deemed distribution of $19,304 and will be deemed to have paid the same amount in interest, but the distribution is all in year 1 while the deemed payments occur in each of the 5 years. The large inclusion in year 1 is appropriate since B could put aside the $30,696 which by the end of 5 years would grow to $50,000—the amount necessary to repay the loan—at a 10.25 percent interest rate. Meanwhile the excess $19,304 can be spent without using it to repay the loan.

49. See *Dean v. Commissioner*, 35 T.C. 1083 (1961) (no taxable income since deemed interest deduction offsets deemed income).

50. Dividend treatment assumes the distributing corporation has adequate earnings and profits. The corporation that makes the below market interest loan will have no deduction for the deemed distribution and will have income for the receipt of the deemed interest payment.

that all of the stock of X Corp. and Y Corp. are owned by B and that X Corp. lends $300,000 to Y Corp. If the Service cannot find a business reason for the loan and if the loan formalities are not observed (e.g., executed loan agreement, repayment schedule), it might recharacterize the transaction as though X Corp. had made a $300,000 distribution to B who in turn will be deemed to make a $300,000 contribution to the capital of Y Corp. Viewed in this manner, the transaction will produce a dividend for B, assuming sufficient X Corp. earnings and profits.[51] However, if X Corp. had a valid business purpose for the loan, then treatment as a constructive dividend may not be appropriate.[52]

It is not only loans that fall into the second prototype. Suppose X Corp. owns an asset (e.g., an apartment, yacht, car) which it leases to B, a shareholder, for $5,000 a year. Just as a below market interest loan can be a disguised dividend, so too can a bargain purchase or lease. If the fair market value for leasing the asset is $7,000 a year, B will be deemed to have received a $2,000 distribution. Conversely, suppose B leases an asset to his corporation for $7,000 a year. If the fair market rental value of the asset is only $5,000 a year, B will be treated as receiving a $2,000 distribution.

The third prototype—a corporate deduction with no shareholder inclusion—might arise where the corporation makes a payment on behalf of a shareholder, claiming it to be for the benefit of the corporation. Suppose X Corp. pays for a trip to Bermuda for several prospective investors or lenders including B, a controlling shareholder. X Corp. might seek to deduct the expense under § 162, arguing that there is benefit to the corporation. At the same time, B might argue that the benefit to the corporation exceeds the incidental personal benefit, thereby justifying an exclusion from income. Not enough facts are presented to resolve the issue. If in fact the trip to Bermuda was filled with conferences, presentations, etc., arguably the transaction could produce a corporate deduction with no inclusion. On the other hand, if the trip were filled with snorkeling and deep sea fishing, dividend recharacterization may be appropriate.

If the transaction is recharacterized as a distribution with respect to B's stock, then B will have a dividend if X Corp. has sufficient earnings and profits. Note that if the transaction is

---

51. See, e.g., *Stinnett's Pontiac Serv., Inc. v. Commissioner,* 730 F.2d 634 (11th Cir.1984). When a transaction is recharacterized in this manner, it is not at all clear what tax treatment occurs if Y Corp. should in fact make interest payments or repay the loan. It is certainly not inconceivable that the Service may recharacterize those payments also as disguised dividends to B—this time from Y Corp.

52. See *Rapid Electric Co. v. Commissioner,* 61 T.C. 232 (1973).

recharacterized not only would B have a dividend but also X Corp. would lose its deduction. It is as though X Corp. made a cash distribution to B equal to the fair market value of the Bermuda trip and then B used the cash to purchase the trip.

Note that in any of these disguised dividend situations, whether the deemed distribution will be treated as a dividend depends on the earnings and profits of the distributing corporation.[53] If the distributing corporation has no earnings and profits, the deemed distribution will first offset the shareholder's stock basis and upon the exhaustion of basis will normally produce a capital gain. §§ 301(c)(2) and (c)(3).

In *Truesdell v. Commissioner*,[54] the sole shareholder of two corporations diverted income earned by the corporations to himself. Neither the taxpayer nor his corporations reported the income on their returns. The Service argued that the full amount of the diverted funds was taxable to Truesdell as ordinary income without regard to the earnings and profits of the corporations. The Tax Court rejected the Service's position, holding that Truesdell was taxable on the constructive dividend only to the extent of the corporations' earnings and profits. Because the corporations did not have sufficient earnings and profits to cover the entire amount of the distribution, only a portion of the diverted funds was taxable. The Service neglected to assess additional income to the corporations. Had it done so, the corporations would have owed additional tax and the increase in the taxable income of the corporations would have increased earnings and profits, thereby making the constructive distributions to Truesdell fully taxable as a dividend.

4.08 Constructive Dividends and Corporate Shareholders. The last few pages were devoted to transactions in which the taxpayers were attempting to disguise dividend payments as other transactions. The disguise can be played out in reverse when a corporate shareholder is involved. Suppose X Corp. owns all of the Y Corp. stock which has a basis of $500,000 and a fair market value of $2 million. If X Corp. sells the stock, there is a potential gain of $1.5 million. Suppose instead that X Corp. causes Y Corp. to distribute $1.5 million to X Corp. Even assuming that Y Corp. has sufficient earnings and profits to give X Corp. dividend treatment, under § 243 X Corp. can deduct 80 percent[55] of the $1.5 million dividend or $1.2 million. Of course X Corp. will be taxed on $300,000 but will have no gain when it sells the Y Corp. stock (now

53. *DiZenzo v. Commissioner,* 348 F.2d 122 (2d Cir.1965).

54. 89 T.C. 1280 (1987).

55. Or perhaps 100 percent in the case of certain affiliated corporations under § 243(b).

worth $500,000 after the distribution) since X Corp. can offset the amount realized with its $500,000 basis.

Whether corporate shareholders will be successful in trying to turn sales proceeds into dividends may depend on events surrounding the distribution. For example, if the purchaser were to infuse Y Corp. with $1.5 million in cash shortly after completing the purchase of the stock from X Corp., the Service might ignore the distribution from Y Corp. and treat X Corp. as though it realized $2 million on the sale.

Timing will often dictate the outcome in these constructive dividend cases. In *Waterman Steamship Corp. v. Commissioner*,[56] the Fifth Circuit reversed the Tax Court and held that the distribution of a note would not be treated as dividend even though the declaration of the dividend occurred after the negotiations began with the purchaser, and even though the purchaser of stock provided the cash to the purchased corporation to pay off the note. However, in *Litton Industries, Inc. v. Commissioner*,[57] the Tax Court reaffirmed its majority opinion in *Waterman Steamship*. In *Litton Industries*, prior to selling the stock of its Stouffer subsidiary to Nestle, Litton arranged for Stouffer to declare a $30 million dividend in the form of a debt instrument. Litton, an accrual basis taxpayer, reported the dividend income for tax purposes and took a fair market value basis in the note.[58] Litton also took an 85 percent (now 80 percent) dividends-received deduction. When Nestle purchased the Stouffer stock, it presumably paid $30 million less for the stock than it would have paid if Stouffer did not have a $30 million liability. Nestle also paid $30 million to satisfy the debt instrument. Litton reported no gain on the payment of the debt instrument with a $30 million basis and $30 million less gain on the sale of the stock than it would have reported if no dividend had been declared.

In ruling for Litton, the Tax Court distinguished *Waterman Steamship's* outcome where the purported dividend was treated as part of the purchase price of the stock because the dividend was declared after negotiations for the stock sale commenced. The Tax Court noted that the dividend in *Litton Industries* was declared two weeks prior to the time that Litton announced that Stouffer was for sale. Consequently, the declaration of the dividend and the sale of the Stouffer stock were not interdependent.

Conceptually, it is difficult to reconcile the outcomes in *Waterman Steamship* and *Litton Industries* solely on the basis of whether

56. 430 F.2d 1185 (5th Cir.1970).   **58.** Regs. § 1.301–1(h)(2)(i).
57. 89 T.C. 1086 (1987).

the dividend precedes or follows negotiations for a stock sale. In any case, *Litton Industries* provides a blueprint for using a constructive dividend to reduce overall gain on the sale by a parent corporation of the stock of its subsidiary.

Because a distribution cannot be a dividend unless the distributing corporation has sufficient earnings and profits, corporate shareholders, desiring dividend treatment, have incentives to increase the amount of earnings and profits. One method of immediately increasing the earnings and profits without an immediate recognition of gain is an installment sale.[59] Earnings and profits are increased immediately by the full amount of gain from an installment sale even though recognition of that gain is deferred under the installment method. Potentially, such an installment sale paves the way for dividend treatment (and a dividends-received deduction) on a subsequent distribution. Section 301(e), however, prevents this result by providing that adjustments to earnings and profits mandated by § 312(k) and (n) are not made for purposes of determining the taxable income (and adjusted basis) of any "20 percent corporate shareholder."[60] Under § 301(e), the distribution reduces the shareholder's basis in its stock. The reduction in stock basis will result in increased capital gain (or decreased capital loss) on a sale of the shareholder's stock. For example, if the distribution to Litton was not a dividend but was treated as a return of basis, Litton would recognize the same gain as if the distribution had not taken place. That is, Nestle would pay less because of the distribution but Litton's basis would be decreased by precisely the amount of the distribution.

4.09 "Fast pay" or "Stepped-down preferred" stock.

Tax advisers can be a clever lot. Many devote much of their professional lives to parsing complex code provisions in an effort to create tax savings that may never have been intended. Recharacterizing transactions to create constructive distributions is one method of dealing with this phenomenon. In the transaction described below, the taxpayer was attempting to shift taxable income to a taxpayer who is not subject to tax while not affecting the economic positions of the participants.

59. Under § 312(n), certain items deferred from currently taxable income are included for purposes of computing earnings and profits. Installments sale gains are such an item.

60. A "20 percent corporate shareholder" is a corporation, entitled to a dividends-received deduction, that owns, directly or indirectly, 20 percent of the total voting power or value (excluding nonvoting preferred stock) of the distributing corporation.

In the basic fast-pay transaction, a U.S. corporate sponsor (the "sponsor") forms a closely-held real estate investment trust (called a REIT)[61] with accommodating tax-exempt investors (the "exempt participants" might be foreign investors not subject to US taxation). The REIT, generally treated as a corporation but with the ability to deduct dividends, issues common stock to the sponsor and fast-pay stock to the exempt participants. The fast-pay stock is structured to have an above-market dividend rate for a fixed period of time, after which the dividend rate "steps down" to a de minimis rate. In addition, after the step down, the arrangement generally gives the sponsor (or the REIT) the right to redeem the fast-pay stock for its then-fair market value, a small fraction of its issue price. As an economic matter, the fast-pay stock performs much like self-amortizing debt: to the exempt participants, the high periodic dividend payments represent in part distributions of income and in part returns of capital.

For federal income tax purposes, by contrast, the periodic dividend payments on the fast-pay stock prior to the enactment of remedial legislation were entirely deductible distributions of income by the REIT. This mischaracterization of the dividends (entirely as income when economically a portion represented a return of capital) effectively allowed the REIT to overallocate its taxable income to the exempt participants. This overallocation resulted in a corresponding underallocation to the taxable sponsor. If the sponsor eventually sold its interest in the REIT, the underallocation would allow the sponsor to defer its economic income from the transaction to the time of the sale and convert its character from ordinary to capital gain. If the sponsor liquidated the REIT in a tax-free parent-subsidiary liquidation, the sponsor's economic income from the transaction would permanently escape tax.[62]

The following hypothetical example illustrates the intended tax benefits of the transaction: A U.S. corporation forms a REIT by contributing $1,000 in exchange for substantially all of its common stock. At the same time, a tax-indifferent party contributes $1,000 in exchange for fast-pay stock that has a stated dividend rate of 14 percent. The REIT invests its $2,000 in a 10–year, 7 percent, balloon payment mortgage. The mortgage provides for 10 annual payments of $140 (7 percent x $2,000) and a single payment of its $2,000 principal at the end of the ten year term. The fast-pay stock provides for annual dividend distributions of $140 (14 percent x $1,000) for ten years. After the initial 10–year period, the dividend

---

61. A REIT is a statutory entity that generally invests in real property or mortgages. See § 857.

62. See Section 8.03 *infra*.

rate on the fast-pay stock steps down to 1 percent per year. At that time, the REIT has the ability to redeem the fast-pay stock for its then-fair market value of, say, $100. If the fast-pay stock is redeemed, the U.S. corporation that owns the corporation can then liquidate the REIT in a tax-free manner.

The U.S. corporation expects that it will realize a predictable economic benefit over the anticipated 10–year term of the transaction without ever incurring any tax liability for that benefit. In particular, the U.S. corporation anticipates that the dividends-paid deduction on the fast-pay stock will eliminate the REIT's income for the initial 10–year period. Immediately after this period, the U.S. corporation anticipates that the fast-pay stock will be redeemed for $100 and that the REIT will then be liquidated in a tax-free manner. Upon the liquidation, the U.S. corporation will succeed to the $1,900 cash on hand ($2,000 cash on hand less the $100 payment to redeem the fast-pay stock) without incurring a tax. Thus, the U.S. taxpayer will have realized a $900 economic benefit ($1,900 amount received less $1,000 initial investment) over the 10–year term of the transaction without ever incurring a tax on it.

In response to fast-pay transactions, the IRS has issued regulations that treat the fast-pay stock as if the stock were a security issued by the sponsor, instead of the REIT.[63] Consistent with this recharacterization, the regulations treat the fast-pay distributions as if they were made by the REIT to the sponsor and then by the sponsor to the exempt participants. The payments from the sponsor to the exempt participants would only be deductible to the extent they constituted interest. Repayments of principal would not be deductible. This recharacterization ensures that the sponsor is taxed on its economic income from the transaction.[64] In effect, the fast pay stock rules treat the sponsor as receiving a constructive distribution.

63. *See* Regs. § 1.7701(*l*)–0 *et seq.* The "security" may be treated as debt or stock depending on its characteristics.

64. In the example, the sponsor would be taxable on $140 each year, but each $140 payment to the exempt participants would in most cases be partly interest and partly a return of the loan principal. Only the interest portion would be potentially deductible.

CHAPTER 5. REDEMPTIONS

5.01 Introduction. A "redemption" (more correctly, a "distribution in redemption of stock") is the purchase by a corporation of some of its own stock. § 317(b). How should a redemption be taxed to the corporation and to the selling shareholder? On the one hand, a redemption might be treated as any other distribution made with respect to a shareholder's stock, producing ordinary income, recovery of basis, and capital gain to the distributee shareholder depending on the corporation's earnings and profits account and on the shareholder's stock basis. See § 301. Consistent with this approach, the distributing corporation would recognize gain but not loss on the distribution. See § 311(b). On the other hand, a redemption could be treated like any other purchase and sale of a capital asset, giving the selling shareholder exclusively recovery of basis and capital gain, independent of the corporation's earnings and profits account. Were this characterization followed at the corporate level, gain or loss could be recognized on the exchange.

The shareholder-level taxation of redemptions is governed by § 302, and this section incorporates both approaches.[1] Under § 302, those redemptions resembling the sale of stock to a third party will qualify for exchange treatment, while those redemptions more closely resembling dividend distributions are subjected to the general distribution rules of § 301. The rules of § 302 distinguish one type of redemption from the other by reference, in general, to the effect of the redemption on the distributee shareholder's interest in the corporation. Exchange treatment offers to the shareholder whose stock is redeemed the recovery of basis implicit in the definition of "gain": only the excess amount realized over the shareholder's basis is taxable to the shareholder (generally as capital gain).

For example, consider the case of individual B who owns 100 outstanding shares of X Corp. with adjusted basis of $70 per share and fair market value of $100 per share. If X redeems 10 of B's shares for fair market value, taxation under the distribution rules of § 301 produces dividend income to B of $1,000 (assuming sufficient earnings and profits) while exchange treatment produces capital gain of $300. With most dividends now taxable at the same rate as long-term capital gain, a shareholder owning stock with a

---

1. The corporate level taxation of redemptions is discussed at Section 5.04 *infra*.

very low basis may be practically indifferent to the distinction between exchange and distribution treatment. Conversely, a shareholder with high share basis generally will prefer exchange treatment. In fact, with a sufficiently high stock basis exchange treatment can generate a taxable loss while distribution treatment can at best be tax-free.

The possibility of exchange treatment becomes even more significant in the case of inherited stock because of the fair market value basis given to property at death by § 1014. Thus, if B in the example above dies and devises his shares to children C and D, each child will take a $100 basis in each share. If the corporation then redeems all of C's stock, distribution treatment produces income of $100 per share while exchange treatment results in no gain or loss. As this example demonstrates, qualifying for exchange treatment can mean, for the devisee of stock, the difference between taxation on the entire amount distributed and no taxation at all.

The structure of § 302 is as follows. Exchange treatment is given to the recipient shareholder under § 302(a) if and only if[2] the redemption qualifies under one of the provisions of § 302(b). Thus, one *obtains* the benefit of § 302(a) by *qualifying* under § 302(b). A redemption that fails to qualify under § 302(b) is subjected to the distribution rules of § 301 pursuant to § 302(d). Thus, subsections (a) and (d) are the taxing provisions while subsection (b) contains the qualifying rules.

Subsection (b)(1) gives (shareholder-level) exchange treatment to redemptions "not essentially equivalent to a dividend." Until enactment of the 1954 Code, only this ambiguous language distinguished qualifying from non-qualifying redemptions. As you might expect, substantial litigation and transactional uncertainty was the result.[3] Congress responded by creating the safe harbor provisions now found in § 302(b)(2)–(4),[4] provisions giving exchange treatment to redemptions based upon objective criteria. These rules are explored in detail in Section 5.02 below. Section 302(b)(1) now is a residuary provision, a last resort for taxpayers who fail to navigate into the safe harbors of § 302(b)(2)–(4).

In focusing on the effect of a redemption on the recipient shareholder's stock interest in the distributing corporation, Con-

---

2. See also § 303 (exchange treatment for certain redemptions used to pay death taxes).

3. See, e.g., B. Bittker & J. Eustice, Federal Income Taxation of Corporations and Shareholders ¶ 9.01 (7th ed. 2000).

4. The safe harbor provision for partial liquidations in § 302(b)(4) was, until 1982, in § 346, now repealed in its entirety.

gress recognized that stock owned by a relative of the recipient shareholder might appropriately be imputed to the recipient shareholder. For example, if B and C are equal co-owners of X Corp., the redemption by X of all the stock of B has a substantial effect on B's control of the corporation if B and C are strangers and perhaps only a nominal effect if B and C are husband and wife. Accordingly, Congress provided in § 302(c) that a set of *attribution rules* are to be applied to determinations under § 302(b), rules that are exceedingly complex and which apply with varying degrees of rigor. These attribution rules also impute stock ownership from (and to) entities (corporations, partnerships, estate and trusts) and to (and from) their equitable owners.

For example, with two exceptions[5] the redemption of stock from a sole shareholder is taxed as a distribution rather than as an exchange.[6] On the other hand, the redemption of all the stock held by one taxpayer will, in general, qualify for exchange treatment.[7] Suppose that X Corp. has two shareholders, individual B and Y Corp. If B has no relationship to Y, then the redemption of all of B's stock by X will qualify as an exchange. On the other hand, if B owns all the stock of Y as well as half the stock of X, the redemption by X of B's stock will be treated as a distribution: Y's ownership of stock of X will be imputed to B and B will be deemed to be the sole shareholder of X both before and after the distribution.[8]

Section 304 takes these attribution rules one step further, treating the purchase of one corporation's stock by a second corporation as a redemption if the two corporations have sufficient commonality of ownership. The attribution rules are discussed in Section 5.02 below, while discussion of § 304 is deferred until Section 5.07.

Redemptions often occur in the context of larger transactions. For example, a sale of a corporation often is structured as the part sale, part redemption of a controlling shareholder's stock. As a second example, employment agreements of key corporate employees sometimes provide that the employee's stock must be redeemed if the employment relationship is terminated. These and similar transactions are discussed in Section 5.05 below.

---

5. The two exceptions are redemptions constituting partial liquidations, see § 302(b)(4), and redemptions to pay death taxes, see § 303.

6. *United States v. Davis,* 397 U.S. 301 (1970).

7. See § 302(b)(3) discussed at Section 5.02(a) *infra.*

8. See § 318(a)(2)(C).

5.02   Redemptions Taxed as Exchanges

(a) Complete Terminations. Consider the case of a shareholder whose entire stock interest in the corporation is redeemed. The effect of the redemption on this shareholder is identical to that of a sale of his shares to a third party, and Congress has recognized that such a redemption presents a compelling case for exchange treatment to the shareholder. Under § 302(b)(3), a redemption is taxed as an exchange if the redemption "is in complete redemption of all the stock of the corporation owned by the shareholder."

As indicated above, a set of attribution rules are applicable to determinations made under § 302(b) by virtue of § 302(c)(1). That section expressly incorporates the attribution rules of § 318, rules that attribute stock between family members, between business entities and their beneficial owners, and between corporations and owners of options to purchase shares of the corporation's stock. While a general discussion of the § 318 attribution rules can be deferred, there is a special relationship between the family attribution rules of § 318(a)(1) and the complete termination safe harbor of § 302(b)(3).

In general, a shareholder wishing to qualify under the complete termination safe harbor of § 302(b)(3) must have neither actual nor constructive ownership of stock of the redeeming corporation after the redemption. In the case of closely held corporations, this burden might be very difficult to meet because, under § 318(a)(1), any stock owned by the shareholder's spouse, children, grandchildren and parents will be imputed to the shareholder. In particular, this safe harbor would be essentially unavailable for parents wishing to pass control of the family corporation to the younger generation by means of a redemption.

For example, suppose X Corp. is owned by Father and Daughter. If X redeemed all of Father's stock, in the absence of a remedial provision Father would not have completely terminated his interest in the corporation within the meaning of § 302(b)(3). Rather, he would be deemed to continue to hold a stock interest because Daughter's stock would be imputed to him.[9] Thus, although his actual stock ownership of X would be reduced to zero, his constructive stock ownership would be 100 percent.

However, Congress has provided that a shareholder seeking qualification under § 302(b)(3) can elect to have the family attribution rules waived under certain circumstances. The terms of this waiver are set forth in § 302(c)(2), but before examining that

---

9. See § 318(a)(1)(A)(ii).

section in detail, it is worthwhile to recognize precisely what the waiver does and does not cover. First, it only applies to the *family* attribution rules of § 318(a)(1): the entity and stock option attribution rules of § 318(a)(2)–(4) continue to apply. Second, this waiver only applies to determinations under § 302(b)(3), the complete termination safe harbor: it does *not* apply to the general rule of § 302(b)(1) nor to the other safe harbors in §§ 302(b)(2) and 302(b)(4).

One further limitation is imposed on the waiver by virtue of § 302(c)(2)(B). If a shareholder acquired any of his stock within 10 years of the redemption from a family member (as defined by § 318(a)(1)) or transferred any of his stock to a family member within the same period, no waiver can be obtained unless the transfer in question was not made to avoid Federal income tax. This limitation prevents, for example, the following obvious abuse of the complete termination safe harbor. Individual A owns all the stock of X Corp. A gives 25 percent of his stock to his spouse, and that stock is redeemed one week later. But for § 302(c)(2)(B), this redemption would fall within the complete termination safe harbor as long as A's spouse filed the § 302(c)(2) waiver form. Similarly, the limitation of § 302(c)(2)(B) would apply to the redemption of A's 75 percent stock interest if it occured within 10 years of the transfer to his spouse. In each case, the tax avoidance potential is clear—cloaking a dividend distribution as an exchange—and Congress reasonably has excluded such transactions from the reach of § 302(b)(3) unless the taxpayer can establish an absence of a tax avoidance motive for the initial transfer.[10]

On the other hand, if a § 302(c)(2) waiver is effective, it will allow a shareholder to obtain exchange treatment under § 302(b)(3) even if the shareholder's spouse, child or grandchild (for example) continues to own stock of the corporation after the redemption. Thus, this waiver makes the complete termination safe harbor a viable possibility for shareholders of closely held corporations.

A shareholder who seeks to obtain the benefit of the § 302(c)(2) waiver must file a form with the Service in which the shareholder agrees (1) that he will have no interest in the corporation immediately after the redemption other than as a creditor, and (2) that he will not acquire any interest in the corporation within 10 years of the redemption. The effect of such a filing is to keep open the statute of limitations for the 10 year period so that if an

---

10. See Rev. Rul. 85–19, 1985–1 C.B. 94, for an example of transfer of stock not triggering application of § 302(c)(2)(B) for lack of a tax avoidance motive.

impermissible interest in the corporation is acquired, the Commissioner can reopen the redemption year and assert a deficiency based upon a recharacterization of the redemption as failing to qualify for exchange treatment under § 302(b)(3).

Not surprisingly, substantial litigation has centered on the definition of an interest in a corporation "as a creditor." The regulations offer little guidance in this area, saying only that "a person will be considered to be a creditor only if the rights of such person with respect to the corporation are not necessarily greater or broader in scope than necessary for the enforcement of his claim. Such claim must not in any sense be proprietary and must not be subordinate to the claims of general creditors."[11] This regulation is seeking to distinguish the claim of a *creditor* from that of an *equity owner*. Accordingly, all the problems plaguing the debt/equity issues in other contexts[12] can reappear here.

In *Lynch v. Commissioner*,[13] the Tax Court held that a taxpayer did not run afoul of this regulation even though he permitted the corporation to subordinate his debt to that of a note acquired after the redemption. In addition, the Service has ruled that a taxpayer can obtain the benefit of the § 302(c)(2) waiver despite retaining his interest as lessor of the corporation's office building.[14] Presumably the "creditor" exception in § 302(c)(2)(A) was intended to permit exchange treatment to retiring shareholders even if they were the continuing beneficiaries of a company pension plan. The Tax Court's opinion in *Lynch* and the IRS ruling indicate how far "creditor" can be stretched.[15]

The Code specifically provides that a § 302(c)(2) waiver is invalid if the shareholder retains or acquires an interest in the corporation as "officer, director, or employee." See § 302(c)(2)(A)(i)–(ii). Further, it is clear that a waiver will be invalid if such an interest is retained by the shareholder solely as a result of ignorance of the law.[16] However, it has been held that § 302(c)(2)(A) does not prohibit retention of an interest as an officer or director if the shareholder performs no duties, receives no compensation, and exercises no influence over the affairs of the corporation,[17] and in a surprising opinion, the Tax Court held that continuing to work for the corporation as an independent contrac-

---

11. Regs. § 1.302–4(d).

12. See Section 3.06 *supra*.

13. 83 T.C. 597 (1984), rev'd, 801 F.2d 1176 (9th Cir.1986).

14. Rev. Rul. 77–467, 1977–2 C.B. 92.

15. *Lynch* was reversed on other grounds and the proper treatment of a subordinated note expressly was left undecided. 801 F.2d 1176 (9th Cir.1986).

16. *Seda v. Commissioner*, 82 T.C. 484 (1984).

17. *Lewis v. Commissioner*, 47 T.C. 129 (1966).

tor is not a tainted interest akin to the explicitly forbidden interest of being an employee.[18] This dubious distinction was reversed, however, on the theory that Congress intended to impose a bright-line test in § 302(c)(2)(A). Whether the Tax Court's precarious reliance on the distinction between "employee" and "independent contractor" can withstand the test of time remains to be seen.[19]

While the § 302(c) waiver limits application only of the *family* portion of the attribution rules, the waiver itself can be made by entities as well as by individuals.[20] Because entities have no spouses, children or other family members, the ability to waive the family attribution rules is important to entities only because, under § 318(a)(5), the attribution rules can be used to form *chains* of attribution between individuals and entities.

For example, suppose that Father's estate owns shares in X Corp., and assume that the only beneficiary of Father's estate is Mother. If X Corp. redeems all of the estate's shares, the estate will fail to qualify for exchange treatment under § 302(b)(3) if Mother owns any stock of X. To be sure, the estate can file for a waiver of the family attribution rules, but because Mother's stock is imputed to the estate under one of the *entity* attribution rules, the waiver will not prevent attribution from Mother to the estate. Thus, the redemption will not work a complete termination of the estate's interest in the corporation, so § 302(b)(3) will not apply.

Suppose, however, that Mother owns no stock of X Corp. but that Son does. In the absence of a § 302(c) waiver by the trust, the redemption of all of its stock once again will fail to qualify under the complete termination provision of § 302(b)(3) because Son's stock will be imputed to Mother under the family attribution rules[21] and that constructive ownership will be imputed to the estate under the entity attribution rules.[22] If a § 302(c) waiver *is* filed by the trust, though, the chain of attribution will be broken at the link from Son to Mother, so that the estate will have no actual or constructive ownership of X Corp. after the redemption and § 302(b)(3) will apply.

While individual shareholders ordinarily will prefer redemptions to qualify for exchange treatment, corporate shareholders often prefer distribution treatment because of the dividends-re-

---

18. *Lynch v. Commissioner,* 83 T.C. 597 (1984), rev'd, 801 F.2d 1176 (9th Cir.1986).

19. See also *Cerone v. Commissioner,* 87 T.C. 1 (1986), in which the Tax Court reasoned that a former shareholder performing services for the corporation will fail § 302(c)(2)(A) only if the individual has a significant financial stake in the corporation or continues to control the corporation.

20. See § 302(c)(2)(C).

21. See § 318(a)(1)(A)(ii).

22. See §§ 318(a)(3)(A), 318(a)(5).

ceived deduction of § 243. The safe harbor provisions of § 302(b) are not elective, thus encouraging corporate shareholders to structure redemptions so as to fall *outside* the terms of § 302(b). Can a corporate shareholder structure a complete termination as a series of partial redemptions to avoid exchange treatment on all of the redemptions other than the last? In *Bleily & Collishaw v. Commissioner*,[23] such a series of redemptions was telescoped into a single redemption taxable as an exchange under § 302(b)(3).

If a redemption fails to qualify for exchange treatment, it is treated as a corporate distribution subject to the general distribution rules of § 301. Ordinarily, § 301 can be applied to failed redemptions without difficulty: the basis of the shares redeemed flows into the shareholder's remaining stock,[24] and the amount distributed is taxed as a dividend to the extent of the corporation's earnings and profits. However, consider the case of a shareholder whose stock is completely redeemed but whose constructive ownership does not decrease to zero (because, for example, a relative continues to own stock of the corporation and a valid § 302(c) waiver is not, or cannot be, filed).

For example, suppose that individual B and corporation C each owns half the stock (50 shares) of X Corp. with adjusted basis of $10 per share and fair market value of $100 per share. Suppose further than B is the sole shareholder of C. If X redeems all the stock owned by B for fair market value of $5,000, that amount will be taxed under the distribution rules of § 301 because C's shares will be attributed to B. Assuming that all of the distribution is taxed as a dividend, what happens to the shareholder's basis in the redeemed shares? Does that basis simply disappear? In *Levin v. Commissioner*,[25] the court ruled that the shareholder's basis is transferred to the shares held by the related shareholder whose stock was imputed to the distributee-shareholder.

(b) Substantially Disproportionate Redemptions. If a redemption reduces a shareholder's interest significantly but not completely, exchange treatment on the redemption may be obtained pursuant to § 302(b)(2). That section taxes as an exchange those redemptions satisfying a three-part test: (1) the redeemed shareholder owns less than 50 percent of the voting power of the corporation immediately after the redemption; (2) the shareholder's voting power after the redemption is less than 80 percent of his pre-redemption voting power; and (3) the shareholder's percentage ownership of common stock of the corporation after the

---

23. 72 T.C. 751 (1979), aff'd without opinion, 647 F.2d 169 (9th Cir.1981).

24. Regs. § 1.302–2(c).

25. 385 F.2d 521 (2d Cir.1967).

redemption also is less than 80 percent of his pre-redemption ownership.

As an example of the more computational aspects of § 302(b)(2), consider individual A owning 90 of the 300 outstanding shares of X Corp. X redeems 20 of A's shares, leaving 280 shares outstanding. Does A qualify for exchange treatment under § 302(b)(2)?

After the redemption, A owns 70 of 280 outstanding shares, or 25 percent. Thus, A's ownership is less than 50 percent and part (1) of the three-part test is satisfied. Prior to the redemption, A owned 90 of 300 shares, or 30 percent. Since 80 percent of 30 percent is 24 percent, A's post-redemption voting percentage of X is *not* less than 80 percent of his pre-redemption voting percentage, so A fails the second test. (A also fails the third test because his ownership of common stock also decreases from 30 percent to 25 percent while a decrease below 24 percent is required.) Note that tests two and three require a computation of A's pre-and post-redemption ownership of X Corp.: it is *not* sufficient to determine whether 20 percent of A's stock has been redeemed.

Compare the tax treatment to A if the corporation had redeemed 50 of his 90 shares. In that case, A's post-redemption ownership of the corporation would be 40 of 250 shares, or 16%. A would thus have dropped below 80 percent of his former ownership percentage (because 80 percent of 30 percent is 24 percent) and would qualify for exchange treatment.

Determinations made under § 302(b)(2) must take into account the attribution rules of § 318, and there is no waiver available under § 302(b)(2) corresponding to that available under § 302(b)(3). Accordingly, a shareholder's actual and constructive ownership always must be considered under § 302(b)(2). It is thus time for a thorough examination of the attribution rules.

The attribution rules of § 318 consist of *family attribution rules,* § 318(a)(1), *attribution-from-entity rules,* § 318(a)(2), and *attribution-to-entity rules,* § 318(a)(3). In addition, there is the *stock option rule* of § 318(a)(4) and a series of *operating rules* in § 318(a)(5). It is the operating rules that permit the other rules to be chained together to attribute stock between shareholders whose relationship can be quite distant.[26]

---

26. For example, if F and S are father and son, S is a 75% shareholder in X Corp., and X is a 25% partner in the P partnership, stock of any unrelated corporation owned by F will be imputed to P via the chain: (1) F to S under § 318(a)(1)(A)(ii); (2) S to X under § 318(a)(3)(C); and (3) X to P under § 318(a)(3)(A).

We already have been exposed to the family attribution rules in the discussion of complete terminations under § 302(b)(3). While those rules are perhaps the most natural set, they hold their own surprises. For example, while there is attribution from grandchild to grandparent, there is no attribution in the other direction. Thus, the redemption of stock held by grandchildren is unaffected by the stock holdings of grandparents and more distant relatives.

In addition, there is no attribution between siblings. However, there *is* attribution between parents and children, raising the possibility of constructing a chain of attribution from brother to mother to sister, thereby attributing stock between siblings at least when one of their parents is alive. However, by virtue of the anti-sidewise operating rule of § 318(a)(5)(B), such chains are not allowed. The familial relations warranting attribution are set forth in § 318(a)(1), and the anti-sidewise rule prohibits enlarging that class: it provides that stock imputed to a taxpayer under the family attribution rules may not then be reattributed under the family attribution rules. For example, the congressional failure to impute stock from grandparents to grandchildren cannot be circumvented by attributing the grandchildren's stock to the parent and then reattributing it to the grandparents. Of course, any stock *actually* owned by the parents will be imputed to the grandparents without recourse to the operating rules.

Attribution from trusts, estates, partnerships and corporations to the beneficial owners of such entities is pro rata according to percentage ownership of the entity. Thus, a one-quarter partner will be deemed to own one-quarter of any stock owned by the partnership. Of course, describing a partner's interest in a partnership by reference to a single percentage is impossible in many of today's complex partnerships, but the attribution rules assume that it can be done. In the case of trusts, ownership is determined by reference to actuarial interests, except that grantor trusts are deemed to be owned by their grantors.

Attribution from corporations to their shareholders is based on the fair market value of each shareholder's stock interest as compared with the total value of all of the corporation's outstanding shares. Such a rule recognizes the existence of corporations having multiple classes of stock outstanding. However, Congress specifically provided that there is no attribution from a corporation to any shareholder owning less than 50 percent of the value of the corporation's outstanding stock. Thus, attribution from corporations to their shareholders is limited to closely-held corporations and their majority shareholders.

There also is attribution *to* entities from their beneficial owners, but it is a much simpler rule: all stock owned by partners, trust and estate beneficiaries and shareholders is attributed to their entities without regard to percentage ownership. The only limitations on this rule are (1) there is no attribution to an estate from any beneficiary having a contingent interest having a maximum actuarial value of five percent or less of the trust corpus, and (2) there is no attribution to a corporation from any shareholder owning less than 50 percent of the value of the corporation's outstanding stock. Once again, attribution between corporations and their shareholders effectively is limited to closely-held corporations and their majority shareholders.

Just as chains between family members is limited by the anti-sidewise operating rule, there is a limitation imposed on chains of attribution linked by the entity attribution rules. Congress did not provide for attribution from, for example, one partner to another, and the operating rule of § 318(a)(5)(C) prohibits circumvention of that rule: it provides that stock ownership imputed to an entity from a beneficial owner may not then be attributed out of the entity to another beneficial owner.

Do these operating rules eliminate all possibilities of constructing chains of attribution? Certainly not. For example, if X Corp. stock is owned by the ABC partnership, that ownership will be imputed to partner A based upon his ownership interest in ABC. That constructive ownership can then be imputed to W, A's wife. If W is a beneficiary of the T Trust, the constructive ownership will be reattributed to T. And on it goes.

The last operating rule is the stock option rule. That rule provides that any person having an option to acquire stock of a corporation is to be treated as owning the option stock. This rule often can be used by taxpayers to their advantage because it increases the total number of shares outstanding, thereby implicitly reducing the ownership interests of all shareholders other than the optionee. For example, granting an option to one shareholder while redeeming some of the shares held by a second shareholder will make it easier for the second shareholder to qualify under the disproportionate redemption rule of § 302(b)(2).[27]

(c) Redemptions Not Essentially Equivalent to a Dividend. A redemption that fails to satisfy both the complete termination requirements of § 302(b)(3) and the disproportionate redemption requirements of § 302(b)(2) still can be taxed as an exchange at the

---

27. See, e.g., *Henry T. Patterson Trust v. United States,* 729 F.2d 1089 (6th Cir.1984), in the context of a § 302(b)(1) redemption.

shareholder level if, considering all the facts and circumstances, the redemption "is not essentially equivalent to a dividend." § 302(b)(1). However, the Supreme Court in *United States v. Davis*[28] adopted a very narrow interpretation of this language in § 302(b)(1), limiting its application to redemptions resulting in a "meaningful reduction" in the distributee shareholder's stock ownership of the distributing corporation.

In *Davis,* the corporation had been required to increase its working capital by $25,000 to qualify for a Reconstruction Finance Corporation loan. The taxpayer, then a major shareholder of the corporation, purchased 1,000 shares of $25 par value preferred stock, it being understood that the preferred stock would be redeemed once the loan was repaid. By the time of the debt's repayment, the taxpayer and his family were the corporation's only shareholders. As agreed, the corporation redeemed the preferred stock for $25 per share, and the taxpayer reported the transaction as a tax-free return of basis.

The Supreme Court held that the redemption was taxable to the taxpayer as a distribution and, because the corporation had adequate earnings and profits, was includible as a dividend in full. The Court held that in making determinations under § 302(b)(1), the attribution rules of § 318(a) are fully applicable. Accordingly, the taxpayer's actual and constructive ownership both before and after the redemption was 100 percent. Therefore, "this case viewed most simply involves a sole stockholder who causes part of his shares to be redeemed by the corporation. We conclude that such a redemption is always 'essentially equivalent to a dividend' within the meaning of that phrase in § 302(b)(1)....'" In particular, the Supreme Court held that any corporate-level motivation for the redemption transaction is irrelevant to the determination under § 302(b)(1).

The *Davis* case once again illustrates the extreme difference in treatment of corporate debt and equity. Had the shareholder contributed the additional funds in exchange for a debt instrument of the corporation, the *Davis* case could not have arisen because the retirement of corporate debt, unless it is recharacterized as equity, always qualifies for exchange treatment. Corporate equity, on the other hand, must on occasion be tested by the rules of § 302.

Since the *Davis* case, the role of § 302(b)(1) has been small. The legislative history of § 302(b)(1) indicates that it was intended to cover redemptions of minority holdings of preferred, nonvoting stock. However, § 302(b)(1) is not expressly so limited so that any

---

28.   397 U.S. 301 (1970).

time a redemption works a reduction in a shareholder's percentage interest in the corporation, the claim can be raised that the reduction was "meaningful." For example, in *Henry T. Patterson Trust v. United States*,[29] it was held that a reduction from 80 percent to 60 percent was "meaningful," and the court in that case indicated that a reduction from 97 percent to 93 percent also could be "meaningful." Has the court in this case confused "meaningful" and "nonzero"?

Courts and the Service have looked to factors other than the change in percentage ownership to determine whether a reduction is meaningful. For example, in *Wright v. United States*,[30] it was held that a reduction from 85 percent to 61.7 percent was meaningful because state law imposed a two-thirds voting requirement on certain corporate actions. On the other hand, in Rev. Rul. 78–401[31] the Service ruled that a reduction from 90 percent to 60 percent was not meaningful because no corporate action requiring a two-thirds vote was anticipated.

One issue that has plagued the courts is whether family hostility can mitigate application of the attribution rules. For example, suppose Father and Daughter each own 40 of 100 of the outstanding shares of X Corp. If 20 of Father's shares are redeemed, can the redemption qualify under § 302(b)(1)?

Father's actual ownership of the corporation prior to the redemption was 40 of 100 shares, or 40 percent. After the redemption, Father's actual ownership drops to 20 of 80 shares, or 25 percent. However, although Father's actual ownership drops substantially as a result of the redemption, his constructive ownership barely changes.[32]

Prior to the redemption, Father's actual plus constructive ownership was 80 of 100 shares, or 80 percent. After the redemption, Father's actual plus constructive ownership is 60 of 80 shares, or 75 percent. Ordinarily, such a minor reduction in percentage ownership would fail to qualify under § 302(b)(1). However, if Father can prove that great antagonism has come between himself and his daughter, should the § 302(b) determination be based on the effect of the redemption on Father's actual ownership of the corporation?

Both the Tax Court[33] and the Fifth Circuit Court of Appeals[34] have said in dicta that such family hostility should be irrelevant to

---

29.   729 F.2d 1089 (6th Cir.1984).

30.   482 F.2d 600 (8th Cir.1973).

31.   1978–2 C.B. 127.

32. The drop in *actual* ownership would qualify under § 302(b)(2) were there no attribution.

33. *David Metzger Trust v. Commissioner,* 76 T.C. 42 (1981), aff'd, 693 F.2d

application of § 302(b)(1), but Judge Tannenwald of the Tax Court has argued strongly that issue merits further consideration.[35] At least one court has affirmatively entertained the suggestion that family hostility *can* mitigate application of the attribution rules to § 302(b)(1) determinations.[36] Should the courts ignore family hostility under § 302(b)(1) to avoid costly factual determinations in favor of applying an easy, bright-line test? Probably not. After all, the "not essentially equivalent to a dividend" rule of § 302(b)(1) is not a bright-line under the best of circumstances.

(d) Partial Liquidations. A redemption qualifying as a "partial liquidation" within the meaning of § 302(b)(4) is taxed to the distributee shareholders as an exchange under § 302(a). The definition of a partial liquidation is in § 302(e). That section makes clear (see § 302(e)(1)(A)), in contradistinction to determinations made under § 302(b)(1)–(3), that the determination whether a redemption is a partial liquidation is made by examining the *corporate-level* effects of the redemption. Note also that to qualify under § 302(e)(1)(B), the distribution must occur no later than the year following the year in which the plan of partial liquidation was adopted.

The taxation of partial liquidations dates back at least to 1935 and passed through old § 346 on its way to its present form in § 302(b)(4).[37] The essence of a partial liquidation is that of a *corporate contraction* in which a distinct part of the corporation's business is discontinued and the assets (or the proceeds from a sale of those assets) are distributed to the corporation's shareholders. Because qualification under § 302(b)(4) is made at the corporate level, shareholder-level aspects of the distribution (including, for example, that the distribution is made pro rata) are irrelevant.[38]

Shareholder-level exchange treatment of partial redemptions can be justified by reference to shareholder-level taxation of complete liquidations. In general, a shareholder receiving corporate assets as part of a complete liquidation of the corporation will receive exchange treatment on the distribution. Thus, if multiple businesses are each conducted in distinct corporations, one of the businesses can be discontinued and liquidated in a non-dividend transaction. Exchange treatment for partial liquidations gives the

---

459 (5th Cir.1982).

34. *David Metzger Trust v. Commissioner,* 693 F.2d 459 (5th Cir.1982).

35. *David Metzger Trust v. Commissioner,* 76 T.C. 42, 80–84 (1981) (Tannenwald, J., concurring), aff'd, 693 F.2d 459 (5th Cir.1982).

36. *Haft Trust v. Commissioner,* 510 F.2d 43 (1st Cir.1975).

37. Because the wording of old § 346 is continued in current § 302(b)(4), the regulations promulgated under § 346 should continue their validity.

38. See § 302(e)(4).

same tax advantage to those taxpayers conducting multiple businesses in the form of distinct divisions within a single corporation.

Any distribution "not essentially equivalent to a dividend" (determined at the corporate level) will meet the statutory definition of a partial liquidation in § 302(e)(1)(A). In the well-known case of *Imler v. Commissioner*,[39] a fire destroyed the top two floors of the corporation's seven-story factory. Rather than rebuilding, the corporation scaled down its business operations and distributed the insurance proceeds and some of its working capital in what was held to be a partial liquidation. In an attempt to inject more certainty into this area of the law, Congress has added an alternative set of objective criteria also defining a partial liquidation. Under § 302(e)(2), any redemption meeting the cessation of business test and the continuing business test of § 302(e)(2)(A) and (B) automatically will be treated as being not essentially equivalent to a dividend at the corporate-level. Consistent with the underlying policy of § 302(b)(4) giving exchange treatment to redemptions analogous to complete liquidations, these tests ensure that the redemption is attributable to a genuine corporate cessation of a business and not to the mere reduction in scope of a continuing business.

The cessation of business test requires only that the redemption be attributable to the distributing corporation ceasing to conduct a "qualified" trade or business, and the continuing business test requires the distributing corporation to be in a "qualified" trade or business immediately after the redemption. In each case a "qualified" trade or business is one which has been actively conducted (by the distributing corporation or otherwise) for at least five years and, if the distributing corporation acquired the business during the five year period, that the acquisition was entirely tax-free.

These requirements ensure that a corporation cannot invest accumulated earnings in property that the shareholders are willing to hold as individuals and then distribute the newly-acquired property in a transaction qualifying for exchange treatment to the shareholders. In addition, the "active" trade or business requirement prevents the partial liquidation provision from being used to bail out passive corporate investments.

It has been held that a distribution of less than the entire proceeds from the sale of an active trade or business cannot qualify as a partial liquidation.[40] Will a distribution of more than the

---

39. 11 T.C. 836 (1948).

40. *Gordon v. Commissioner*, 424 F.2d 378 (2d Cir.1970); see also Rev.Rul.

proceeds from the sale of one active business qualify for partial liquidation treatment? For example, suppose X Corp., which actively conducts two businesses, sells one. X Corp. then distributes not only the sale proceeds but also the accumulated earnings attributable to the business sold. Such a distribution should qualify as a partial liquidation because, going back to the theory underlying § 302(b)(4), the distribution is akin to the complete termination of a single corporate entity. On the other hand, if X Corp. also distributes some of the accumulated earnings of the second business, giving full exchange treatment to the liquidation will work an end run around the dividend distribution rules of § 301. Presumably the Service will bifurcate the distribution into a partial liquidation component and a dividend component. The same problem can arise if the earnings from one business are invested in a second business prior to a partial liquidation of the second business, and the Service has indicated that it will see through such a charade.[41]

The partial liquidation provisions have much in common with divisive reorganizations. Under § 355, a corporation actively conducting two trades or businesses can place one into a subsidiary and then distribute all of the subsidiary's stock, thereby splitting up the corporation's business activity into two corporate entities. Because such a transaction is entirely tax-free under § 355, such a reorganization will be preferred to a partial liquidation by most taxpayers. However, if the corporation's shareholders wish to terminate one of the two businesses or conduct it outside of the corporate form, the reorganization route becomes unavailable and favorable taxation will be found only in the partial liquidation format.[42]

Since 1982, partial liquidation characterization of a redemption has been unavailable to shareholders of the distributing corporation who are themselves corporations.[43] However, because of § 1059(e), partial liquidations in redemption of stock held by corporate share-

67–299, 1967–2 C.B. 138, in which the Service ruled that a transaction failed to qualify for partial liquidation treatment when the proceeds from the sale of one active business were temporarily invested in a second trade or business prior to distribution.

41. See Rev. Rul. 59–400, 1959–2 C.B. 114, in the context of a § 355 distribution.

42. Divisive reorganizations under § 355 are discussed at Section 10.04 *infra*.

43. This limitation can be traced to a congressional concern that selective use of partial liquidations, coupled with the consolidated return provisions and the *General Utilities* doctrine, allowed acquiring corporations to step-up the basis in the assets held by acquired corporations without the imposition of any corporate level tax. The demise of *General Utilities* eliminates this problem, but the limitation to non-corporate shareholders in § 302(b)(4)(A) remains.

holder's effectively will be taxed as if § 1001(a) applied by reason of § 1059(a).

Because the shareholder-level effect of a redemption is irrelevant in the case of a partial liquidation, it could be the case that a partial liquidation occurs without the tendering of any shares by any shareholder. Indeed, in the case of a pro rata partial liquidation, pro rata stock exchange would be a needless formality. The legislative history of § 302(b)(4) indicates that such stockless partial liquidations should qualify for exchange treatment at the shareholder-level.[44] In such case, the basis to be used for computing each shareholder's gain or loss on the exchange must be a percentage of his stock basis equal to the percentage of corporate assets distributed in the partial liquidation.[45]

(e) Redemptions to Pay Death Taxes. In general, § 303 gives exchange treatment to redemptions from estates in which more than 35 percent of the estate's net value consists of the stock of a single corporation. In addition, stock of two or more corporations can be combined if the value of the stock of each corporation is at least 20 percent of the value of the corporation. When § 303 applies, its benefits are limited in amount to the taxes and expenses incurred by the estate.

The motivation behind § 303 is a congressional concern that the burden of death taxes could force some taxpayers to liquidate their holdings of stock in family corporations. In light of the attribution rules applicable to determinations under § 302(b), redemptions of such stock might fail to qualify for exchange treatment under § 302(a). Accordingly, the shareholders may sell the stock to a third party to obtain exchange treatment, even though, in the absence of tax considerations, they would prefer to continue to run the family business themselves. Note, though, that the benefit of § 303 is available only to stock actually owned by the estate and does not include, for example, stock includible in the estate under § 2035. See Rev. Rul. 87–76, 1984–1 C.B. 91. However, in that Ruling the Service allowed such stock to contribute to the 35% threshold required by § 303, thereby allowing stock actually owned by the estate to qualify under § 303. Note also that the attribution rules of § 318 cannot be used to satisfy the 35% test of § 303 because § 303 does not explicitly reference § 318.[46]

Should a provision like § 303 be in the Code? No special provision is made for other needy redemptions, such as redemptions

---

44. H.Rept. No. 760, 97th Cong., 2d Sess. 530 (1982); see *Fowler Hosiery Co. v. Commissioner,* 301 F.2d 394 (7th Cir. 1962).

45. See Rev. Rul. 90–13, 1990–1 C.B. 65.

46. *Estate of Byrd v. Commissioner,* 388 F.2d 223 (5th Cir.1967).

to pay for medical expenses. Further, no showing must be made under § 303 that the estate lacked sufficient liquid assets to meet its liabilities. Recall that when combined with § 1014, exchange treatment under § 303 means that an estate will pay no taxes on the redemption of its stock. At least in some cases, § 303 will be nothing more than an opportunity to bail-out earnings and profits of a corporation without shareholder-level taxation and without justification.

5.03 Redemptions Taxed as Distributions. If a redemption fails to qualify for exchange treatment under §§ 302(a) or 303, the amount distributed is subject to the distribution rules of § 301. As you will recall, those rules treat the amount distributed as dividend income to the extent of the distributing corporation's earnings and profits, then as a return of basis and finally as gain from an exchange.

If the entire amount distributed in redemption is taxed as a dividend, the shareholder will not obtain a recovery of basis on the redemption. Accordingly, his basis in the shares turned in flows into his remaining stock of the corporation, and it will be recovered when those shares are sold or exchanged.

For example, suppose that Father and Daughter each owns 40 of the 100 outstanding shares of X Corp. with adjusted basis of $10 per share and fair market value of $100 per share. If X redeems 20 of Father's shares for fair market value, Father's actual plus constructive interest drops from 80 percent to 75 percent. Assuming that this reduction is not "meaningful," Father will be taxed on the distribution of $2,000 under § 301. If X has sufficient earnings and profits, Father will recognize the full amount as ordinary income. Father's basis in the shares redeemed will flow into his remaining shares, leaving Father with actual ownership of 20 shares with an adjusted basis of $20 per share.

This rule works in most cases, but what if the shareholder has no more shares in the corporation? Usually, this problem will not arise because the shareholder will qualify for exchange treatment under the complete termination safe harbor of § 302(b)(3). However, if a related party owns stock in the corporation, the shareholder may not qualify for the complete termination safe harbor, and so distribution treatment is a possibility.

Reconsider the example above, but assume that all 40 of Father's shares are redeemed in one transaction. Father's actual and constructive ownership will fall as a result of the redemption from 80 of 100 shares (80 percent) to 40 of 60 shares (67 percent).

If Father fails to file a valid waiver under § 302(c)(2),[47] the redemption will be taxed under the distribution rules of § 301 unless the reduction from 80 percent to 67 percent is considered "meaningful." Assuming that Father is taxed on a dividend equal to the full $4,000, what happens to Father's basis in the shares redeemed?

One case has held that the shareholder's basis flows into the basis of the stock held by the related party.[48] That is, Father's basis is transferred to Daughter. While no alternative readily presents itself, one cannot help but wonder if this rule might not, in some extreme cases, be counter to the shareholder's desires. For example, might not the shareholder be given the right to elect whether the basis is lost rather than transferred to the related party? After all, but for the related party (and the attribution rules), the taxpayer would have obtained exchange treatment on the redemption.

If this was the rule, the shareholder might have some ability to force the related party to pay for the windfall basis. Do not assume that all parties "related" under § 318(a) necessarily share love and affection or that they regard themselves as having common interests and goals. Indeed, family hostility sometimes might cause a shareholder to prefer a lost basis over a transfer of basis simply out of spite. Should the Code preclude such a choice? Recall that the basis in the shareholder's stock presumably reflects an investment by the shareholder, an investment the shareholder in most circumstances can transfer or not transfer, in his absolute discretion.

An additional question arises when a redemption fails to qualify as an exchange and related parties own stock of the corporation. If the distributing corporation lacks sufficient earnings and profits to cover the distribution, the amount distributed is applied first to offset basis. Since an amount not offsetting basis is treated as taxable gain, it is to the shareholder's advantage to maximize the basis offset. Is the stock basis of the related party available to the shareholder for a recovery of basis?

Reconsider the Father/Daughter example above, but assume that the corporation has only $3,000 of accumulated and current earnings and profits. Father will have ordinary income of $3,000, and the remaining $1,000 can be treated as a recovery of basis. Unfortunately, Father's basis in his shares was only $400, leaving $600 to be taxed as capital gain. Can Father argue that this additional $600 be offset against Daughter's $400 stock basis before

---

47. Father might fail to file a valid § 302(c)(2) waiver out of ignorance of the law or because he remains as an officer, director or employee of the corporation and for that reason is statutorily incapable of filing the waiver.

48. *Levin v. Commissioner*, 385 F.2d 521 (2d Cir.1967).

producing recognized gain, gain in this case of only $200? Presumably the rule is no, although allowing the shareholder to steal basis from the related party in this way seems to be the opposite of the basis transfer rule discussed above. Particularly if it was the related party's stock ownership that caused the redemption to be taxed as a distribution, would it be so unfair to allow the shareholder to steal a little basis in this way to avoid the recognition of gain?

5.04 Corporate–Level Taxation of Redemptions. A distribution in redemption of stock can have two distinct tax consequences for the distributing corporation. First, because a redemption is simply one kind of corporate distribution, if appreciated property is used in a redemption, the distributing corporation will recognize gain according to the rule of § 311(b) applicable to nonliquidating corporate distributions generally. Any gain recognized under § 311(b) on the distribution will increase the corporation's earnings and profits account.

The second consequence of the redemption is the reduction, if any, of the corporation's earnings and profits by reason of the distribution. We know that distributions in general reduce the distributing corporation's earnings and profits under § 312(a), usually by the fair market value of the property distributed. However, if a redemption is taxed to the distributee as an exchange, some part of the amount distributed might properly be treated as a distribution of the corporation's paid-in capital. If so, then this amount of the distribution ought not be charged against the corporation's earnings and profits account. In fact, § 312(n)(7) expressly limits the reduction of earnings and profits in just this way.

Under § 312(n)(7), the reduction in the earnings and profits account of the distributing corporation, if the distribution in redemption of stock is taxed to the distributee as an exchange, is limited to "an amount which is not in excess of the ratable share of the earnings and profits of [the] corporation ... attributable to the stock so redeemed." In some cases, this limitation is easy to apply and understand. For example, suppose that X Corp. owns cash of $1,000,000, and assume that X has only 1,000 shares of stock outstanding, all being part of a single class of common stock. Each share is worth $1,000, and if the corporation redeems 100 shares in a transaction taxed as an exchange under § 302(a), the distributee should receive 10 percent of the corporation, or $100,000.

If X Corp.'s earnings and profits account stands at $400,000, then it should be reduced by 10 percent to $360,000. That is, of the $100,000 amount distributed, $40,000 is treated as a distribution of earnings and profits and $60,000 as a return of paid-in capital.

Note that X Corp.'s paid-in capital should total $600,000 prior to the redemption because the corporation has $1,000,000 in cash, only $400,000 of which is attributable to earnings and profits.

The problem becomes more difficult if X Corp. owns appreciated property. Suppose X Corp., while still worth $1,000,000, has cash of $200,000 and Blackacre with adjusted basis of $500,000 and fair market value of $800,000. Because the appreciation in Blackacre is as yet unrealized, the corporation's earnings and profits plus its paid-in capital should total only $700,000: the appreciation in Blackacre will contribute to the corporation's earnings and profits only upon disposition of Blackacre. If the corporation has earnings and profits of $400,000, then its paid-in capital should equal $300,000. How should a distribution of $100,000 in redemption of 100 shares affect the corporation's earnings and profits, assuming that the redemption is taxed as an exchange to the distributee?

Ten percent of $400,000, or $40,000, is properly allocable to the redeemed shares from the earnings and profits account. Similarly, 10 percent of $300,000, or $30,000, is properly allocable to the corporation's paid-in capital. But what of the remaining $30,000? Conceptually, this amount is properly allocable to the unrealized appreciation in Blackacre. State law will not permit the corporation to reduce its paid-in capital account by this amount, leading the Tax Court to conclude that reduction of the earnings and profits account was appropriate. See *Anderson v. Commissioner*.[49] However, Congress enacted what is now § 312(n)(7), overruling *Anderson* by limiting the earnings and profits reduction in this example to $40,000.

The rule of § 312(n)(7) ensures that a distribution in redemption of stock will not reduce the earnings and profits account for gain not yet in the earnings and profits account. However, because the rule of § 312(n)(7) *eliminates* rather than *delays* the proper earnings and profits reduction, a discontinuity will be created once Blackacre is sold and its gain recognized.

After Blackacre is sold by the corporation for $800,000, the corporation's earnings and profits will increase to $660,000.[50] At that time, the paid-in capital will equal $270,000.[51] Note that the sum of the earnings and profits account and the paid-in capital account equals $930,000 although the company is worth but

49. 67 T.C. 522 (1976), aff'd per curiam, 583 F.2d 953 (7th Cir.1978).

50. The pre-redemption amount of $400,000 less the redemption charge of $40,000 plus the $300,000 gain recognized on the sale of Blackacre produces earnings and profits of $660,000.

51. Paid-in capital of $300,000 minus $30,000 distributed in the prior redemption.

$900,000. This extra $30,000 is the gain in Blackacre properly allocable to the shares redeemed prior to the recognition of gain on Blackacre, the same $30,000 that was not charged to any corporate account at the time of the redemption. Although there are only $630,000 of earnings in the corporation, its earnings and profits show $660,000.

Under § 312(n)(7), the proper charge to the corporate earnings and profits account turns on the earnings and profits properly allocable to the shares redeemed. If common stock is redeemed, this allocation can be determined by reference to the share's proportionate interest in a hypothetical liquidating distribution. On the other hand, if preferred stock is redeemed, presumably no charge to the earnings and profits account is appropriate because, in general, preferred stock entitles the holder only to a return of capital on liquidation. Of course, if dividends on the preferred stock are in arrears at the time of the distribution, the redemption amount should include the dividend arrearages and the corporate earnings and profits account should be reduced in the same amount.

One further corporate-level question arises in connection with redemptions, and that is the proper tax treatment of redemption expenses. Consider, for example, the case of a large, publicly held corporation that avoids a hostile take-over by redeeming all the stock of a "corporate raider." The corporation may incur substantial legal and accounting fees in connection with the redemption, expenses that seem to fall within the reach of § 162(a). However, § 162(k) denies a deduction for all expenses incurred in connection with the redemption of its stock. The legislative history of § 162(k) indicates that the phrase "in connection with the redemption" should be construed broadly. Further, the committee reports list legal fees, accounting fees, appraisal fees, and premiums paid for the stock itself (i.e., greenmail) as items specifically disallowed under § 162(k).

Section 162(k) does not limit the deduction of an interest expense incurred on funds used by a corporation to reacquire its own stock? § 162(k)(2)(A)(i). Suppose, though, that X Corp. pays an investment banker $100,000 to guarantee that a loan of $1,000,000 will be available if that amount is needed to redeem some shareholder's stock. Assuming the loan eventually is made and the redemption occurs, what is the proper tax treatment of the loan guarantee fee of $100,000 paid to the investment banker? The fee does not seem to fall within the definition of "interest" as that term is used in §§ 163 and 162(k)(2)(A)(i). However, because such a guarantee fee presumably is "properly allocable to indebtedness" and because the fee should be recoverable over the term of the loan, the fee will be deductible despite the general rule of § 162(k)(1) because of § 162(k)(2)(A)(ii).

Note that § 162(k) does not say how amounts paid by a corporation in connection with a redemption should be treated other than no deduction should be allowed. Can such amounts be capitalized by the corporation and recovered when it liquidates or sells its business? It long has been the case that an amount paid to a shareholder by a corporation in exchange for the corporation's stock (that is, the actual amount used by the corporation to effect the redemption) can be neither deducted nor capitalized.[52] But what of other corporate expenditures falling within § 312(k) such as legal and accounting fees? Can these be capitalized by the corporation. The legislative history of § 162(k) describes such corporate expenditures as nonamortizable capital expenses. Recall that § 197 now generally permits the amortization of intangibles over 15 years. Can a redemption premium be characterized as payment for an intangible? Does *INDOPCO* have any relevance to resolution of the matter?[53]

5.05 Redemptions Related to Other Transactions. In certain corporate acquisitions, called "bootstrap" acquisitions, part of the consideration used to acquire the target corporation consists of assets of the target corporation. If such a transaction seems like a minnow swallowing itself, consider the case of T Corp. owning the assets of an active business worth $600,000 as well as cash and other liquid assets worth $400,000. All the stock of T is owned by individual B, with an aggregate basis of $100,000 in his T Corp. stock. X Corp. would like to acquire the business run by T, but X has no special interest in T's liquid assets, and X will pay only $600,000 for the productive assets of T. To ensure that no corporate tax is incurred on the transaction, X insists on buying the stock of T rather than the productive assets.

If X is able to raise the full $1,000,000 value of T's stock, a direct stock purchase is possible and may be the best way to structure the transaction. But it might be the case that X has only $600,000 available to fund the acquisition. Because that is enough

---

52. But see *Five Star Mfg. Co. v. Commissioner*, 355 F.2d 724 (5th Cir. 1966), an opinion which has engendered substantial criticism and which was expressly overruled by enactment of § 162(k).

53. Congress deliberately excluded the expenses at issue in *INDOPCO* from amortization under § 197, see § 197(e)(8), but that exclusion should

not apply to redemption premiums because a redemption is a taxable transaction. However, to the extent that a redemption premium or related expense is treated as part of the price paid for by the corporation for its own stock, arguably § 197 will not apply by reason of § 197(e)(1)(A), although that provision does not seem to have been written with treasury stock in mind.

to purchase T's operating assets, if the liquid assets are removed prior to the sale, the sale can proceed without X needing to acquire additional funds. Thus, $400,000 could be distributed by T to B prior to the acquisition by X.

Historically, this was a tax-disadvantaged way to structure the transaction. A direct sale of the shares without a prior distribution would give B basis recovery followed by capital gain. But the pre-sale distribution would be taxable to B under § 301 as dividend income if X had earnings and profits sufficient to cover the distribution. When dividend income could not qualify for a preferential rate of taxation (that is, prior to 2004), this technique adversely converted some of B's capital gain into ordinary income. A distribution to B in redemption of some of his stock would prove no better, because the redemption of stock held by a sole shareholder always is essentially equivalent to a dividend within the meaning of § 302(a) under *Davis*.[54] Such a redemption also could not qualify for exchange treatment as a partial liquidation because a partial liquidation requires a distribution attributable to an active trade or business rather than liquid assets representing accumulated earnings and profits.

B could, of course, get exchange treatment by selling all of the stock of T for $1,000,000, but that would require X to raise $400,000 more than the value of the assets it seeks to acquire and possibly more than X can obtain. To satisfy X without compromising B's tax result, the acquisition could be structured as a part sale/part redemption, with B selling 60 percent of his stock to X while simultaneously causing T to redeem the remaining 40 percent with its liquid assets. X Corp. would acquire only the productive assets of T, and the full $1,000,000 received by T will qualify for exchange treatment.[55]

Of course, B will only obtain exchange treatment on the redemption if he falls within § 302(b)(1)-(4), most likely § 302(b)(3) (complete termination of interest). The various intricacies of § 302(b)(3), including application of the constructive attribution rules, waiver of the family attribution rules, and the like, must be reconsidered in this context. If B does not completely terminate his interest in T, he still may qualify for exchange treatment under the other provisions of § 302(b). In particular, the Service has ruled that the sale and redemption can be linked so as to satisfy the

---

54. See Section 5.02(c) *supra*.

55. See *Zenz v. Quinlivan*, 213 F.2d 914 (6th Cir.1954). In tax jargon one refers to B as having been "zenzed" out. The Service has ruled that the redemp-

tion may precede the sale in a *Zenz* transaction as long as the redemption and sale are part of a single transaction. See Rev. Rul. 75–447, 1975–2 C.B. 113.

requirements of § 302(b)(2),[56] the substantially disproportionate redemption safe harbor.

If T Corp. is owned by a corporation rather than by an individual, the analysis always has been and continues to be different. In such circumstances, the seller will seek to convert taxable gain on the sale into effectively tax-exempt dividend income by causing T to distribute its liquid assets as a dividend prior to the sale. Because of the dividends-received deduction of § 243, this will reduce the taxable gain by $400,000.[57] Not surprisingly, the Service typically argues in such cases that the dividend should be taxed as if made to the buyer (X Corp.) who then uses it as part of the consideration for the acquisition.[58]

In this case of the corporate seller, the issue should be resolved by statute in favor of nontaxation. The rules of subchapter C are premised on the double taxation of corporate profits, once when earned at the corporate level and a second time when distributed to shareholders. When tiers of corporations are formed, intercorporate distributions should be tax-free to avoid a triple (or greater) tax: corporate profits should be taxed only when earned and then when removed from corporate solution, not at every rung of the corporate ladder. Indeed, this is precisely the role that § 243 plays today.[59]

While intercorporate dividends effectively are excluded from the tax base of the recipient corporation, the same is not true for gain from the sale of corporate shares by a corporate shareholder. Such gain, though, reflects either corporate profit earned by the subsidiary corporation but not yet distributed or appreciation in the subsidiary's assets. Such profit either was or will be subjected to the corporate tax when earned. Accordingly, it should pass through all corporate tiers unscathed by further taxation for the same reason that intercorporate distributions do: the second level of taxation should be imposed only when the profit is removed from corporate solution.[60]

---

56. Rev. Rul. 75–447, 1975–2 C.B. 113.

57. The corporate parent of a wholly-owned subsidiary may be entitled to a 100% deduction for dividends received from the subsidiary. § 243(a)(3).

58. See *Waterman Steamship Corp. v. Commissioner*, 430 F.2d 1185 (5th Cir.1970); *Basic, Inc. v. United States*, 549 F.2d 740 (Ct.Cl.1977); *Dynamics Corp. of America v. United States*, 449 F.2d 402 (Ct.Cl.1971).

59. That less than 100% of intercorporate dividends are excluded in many situations under § 243 is better explained by revenue needs of the government than by tax policy.

60. Note that this proposal not only reduces the over-all tax burden but also defers the corporate-level tax from when the appreciated stock is sold by a top-or middle-tier corporation to when the bottom-tier corporation earns the income.

The failure of the drafters of subchapter C to take a compre-hensive view of corporate profits attributable to the business activi-ty of another corporation creates not only the potential of a triple tax of corporate profits but also the possibility for creation of phantom loss. Suppose P Corp. purchases all the stock of Sub Corp. for $1,000,000. The assets of Sub consist exclusively of cash, and assume that Sub has earnings and profits of the full $1,000,000. If P causes Sub to distribute all but one dollar of its cash, P will receive $999,999 without tax due to the dividends-received deduc-tion of § 243. P can then sell the stock of Sub for its fair market value of $1 and realize a taxable loss of $999,999. No economic loss has been sustained by P or by Sub, yet P's loss deduction on its disposition of the Sub stock may be allowable. Congress has in piecemeal fashion tried to attack these phantom losses.[61]

Why has Congress limited relief from the corporate triple tax to intercorporate dividends, and even then complete relief is limited to dividends paid by controlled corporations to their parent corpora-tion?[62] Why has Congress not generally provided that no gain or loss is recognized by a corporation on the receipt of an intercorpo-rate distribution or on the disposition of stock? In part, the expla-nation may be a case of cognitive dissonance: it is easy to see the potential for a triple tax in the case of intercorporate dividends, less easy in the case of gain or loss from the casual sale of shares in unrelated corporations, especially given the paradigm upon which subchapter C is based that each corporation is a separate taxpayer distinct from its (corporate or noncorporate) shareholders. But whatever the reason, the effect is clear: corporate shareholders should eschew recognizing gain on the disposition of stock in favor of receipt of intercorporate distributions.

Redemptions can play a substantial role not only in the sale of a corporation but also in the retention of corporate control. Suppose that X Corp. is owned equally by individuals A and B. If A and B come to a parting of the ways, one can buy the stock of the other. However, if instead they have the corporation redeem all the stock of one of the two shareholders, they have accomplished their goal while removing substantial assets from corporate solution without triggering the recognition of any ordinary income. However, case law has developed a trap for the unwary using a redemption in such circumstances.

---

61. See Section 4.03 *supra* discussing §§ 246A and 1059.

62. The American Law Institute adopted a set of proposals aimed at sim-plifying the corporate income tax. In those proposals, the ALI, although adopting a slightly broader perspective in this context, also has limited its pro-posal to the case of controlled corpora-tions.

Suppose X Corp. is owned 95 percent by Owner and 5 percent by Employee. Owner and Employee have agreed that Employee must sell his stock back to Owner if he ever terminates his employment with X Corp. One day Employee quits, tendering his shares to Owner for purchase at fair market value.

At this point, it may occur to Owner that he should have X Corp. redeem Employee's shares. By restructuring the transaction in this way, Owner effectively obtains the funds to purchase Employee's shares from the corporation without having to recognize any dividend income. However, the Service will argue that by redeeming the shares, X Corp. has made a constructive distribution to Owner, taxable (if X Corp. has adequate earnings and profits) as a dividend. If Owner in fact had an unconditional obligation to purchase Employee's shares, the Service will win on this issue.[63]

Note that the stakes at issue are high: if the transaction is characterized as a dividend to Owner followed by a purchase from Employee, Owner will recognize dividend income equal to the fair market value of Employee's shares. If the transaction is simply treated as a redemption, Owner will recognize no income whatsoever. In either event, Employee should qualify for exchange treatment on the disposition (if the transaction is characterized as a redemption, exchange treatment should be available under the complete termination provision of § 302(b)(3)). What should Owner have done?

Owner should have provided initially that when Employee terminated his employment with X Corp., Owner would purchase Employee's stock *or would have the shares acquired by some other person or entity.* That is, Owner should have preserved the redemption possibility *ab initio.* If Owner had, the redemption would not be recharacterized and he would not have to recognize any dividend income.[64] If this seems like an overly formalistic distinction, it is. Yet, so long as redemptions have no adverse tax consequences on shareholders not participating in the redemption, such lines must be drawn.

If Owner has an unconditional obligation to purchase the shares owned by Employee, and if those shares are instead redeemed by the corporation, we have seen that the transaction will be taxed as if the redemption proceeds were distributed by the corporation to Owner and then used by Owner to purchase the

---

63. *Sullivan v. United States,* 363 F.2d 724 (8th Cir.1966); *Wall v. United States,* 164 F.2d 462 (4th Cir.1947).

64. *Holsey v. Commissioner,* 258 F.2d 865 (3d Cir.1958); *Fox v. Harrison,*

145 F.2d 521 (7th Cir.1944); *Niederkrome v. Commissioner,* 266 F.2d 238 (9th Cir.1958).

shares owned by Employee. But since those shares in fact end up in the corporate treasury, to close the circle we must treat Owner as if he contributed the shares to the corporation after purchasing them from Employee. This should suggest an alternate characterization of the transaction: we could treat Owner as purchasing the shares from Employee and then treat the corporation as redeeming those shares from Owner. While this alternate characterization is unlikely to change the tax consequences to Owner—the redemption of shares from a sole shareholder generally will be taxed as a distribution under § 301 pursuant to the Supreme Court's decision in the *Davis* case[65]—it will offer Owner the opportunity to argue for exchange treatment under § 302(b)(4) if the transaction includes a corporate contraction.

The same issue can arise in the context of divorce. For example, H and W might each own stock in X Corp. Incident to divorce and pursuant to the decree, H might be obligated to purchase any stock of X Corp. owned by W. If instead X Corp. redeems that stock, should the transaction be taxed as if (1) W transferred the stock to H under § 1041 and then (2) the stock was redeemed by X Corp from H? Courts have applied differing standards in this context, with the result that in one case the redemption was not taxed to *either* spouse.[66] To prevent future whipsaws, the regulations now generally provide that the same analysis applicable outside of the divorce context be applied within it.[67] As a result, the transaction should be treated as a stock transfer from W to H only if H had an unconditional obligation to acquire the stock directly. However, such an unconditional obligation will be ignored if so provided in a divorce decree, separation instrument, or written agreement between the spouses (or ex-spouses).[68] Similarly, a redemption of stock held by one spouse (or ex-spouse) will be imputed to the other spouse if such a decree, instrument, or written agreement so provides.[69] Thus, the parties largely can control whether the form of the transaction will be respected or ignored, but in all events the parties must treat the transaction consistently.[70]

5.06 Redemptions for More or Less Than Fair Market Value.

(a) Redemption Premiums. There are a variety of reasons why a corporation might pay more than fair market value for stock it redeems from a shareholder. One possibility easy to forget is that,

---

65. See Section 5.02 *supra.*

66. *Arnes v. United States,* 981 F.2d 456 (9th Cir.1992) (transferor spouse); *Arnes v. Commissioner,* 102 T.C. 522 (1994) (transferee spouse).

67. Regs. § 1.1041–2.

68. Regs. § 1.1041–2(c)(1).

69. Regs. § 1.1041–2(c)(2).

70. Regs. § 1.1041–2(c)(3).

because the fair market value of nonreadily traded stock often is difficult to determine, a price that after the fact appears to be a redemption premium might before the fact have seemed to be a fair price. To the extent a corporation pays no more than fair market value for stock it redeems, certainly it would be improper to allow the corporation to deduct or capitalize the expenditure: in measuring a corporation's profit or loss, amounts paid in redemption of stock should be irrelevant, a result now codified in § 162(k).

A redemption premium might also represent a disguised dividend or similar payment. For example, suppose a minority shareholder complains that dividends are declared too infrequently. A troublesome shareholder might be removed and a lawsuit avoided by purchasing the shares of this minority shareholder at some premium over fair market value. Yet, treating the redemption premium as part of the amount realized to the shareholder would convert what seemingly should be ordinary income into capital gain. Presumably courts will have little difficulty in recharacterizing the transaction as a redemption for fair market value coupled with a dividend or other payment.

Similarly, suppose a corporation redeems the shares held by an employee/shareholder, and as part of the transaction the employee/shareholder gives the corporation a covenant not to compete. Amounts received for a covenant not to compete are ordinary income, and an individual should not be able to transmute such ordinary income into capital gain simply by combining the covenant with a stock transfer. Once again courts should have no difficulty in recharacterizing the transaction as a redemption coupled with the purchase of a covenant not to compete.

Now consider these transactions from the perspective of the redeeming corporation. If removal of a troublesome minority shareholder allows the corporation to conduct its affairs more easily or more cheaply, should the corporation be permitted to deduct the redemption premium? While the answer might seem to be yes, that possibility is foreclosed by application of § 162(k).

And what is the proper corporate-level treatment of the redemption premium paid in exchange for a covenant not to compete? Note that § 162(k) provides that no deduction is allowable for such expenditures, but it does not speak to the possible capitalization of such amounts. Indeed, the legislative history repeatedly speaks of expenditures captured by § 162(k) as being nonamortizable capital expenditures. If, though, corporate expenditures falling within the ambit of § 162(k) can be capitalized, the reach of § 162(k) is small. After all, few expenditures described in § 162(k) would otherwise be deductible, especially in light of *INDOPCO*. Further, § 197 now permits the cost of most intangibles to be recovered over 15 years. To the extent that a redemption premium can be characterized as made to improve business rather than as a cost of acquiring stock, § 197 may be applicable.

The legislative history of § 162(k) further makes clear that payments otherwise deductible will not be rendered nondeductible merely because they are paid simultaneously with a redemption. For example, payment by a corporation to a retiring employee for accrued vacation time will be deductible as compensation under § 162(a) even if accompanied by a redemption of the retiring employee's stock in the corporation.

Consider in this vein the proper tax treatment of greenmail: that is, a redemption premium paid to a substantial minority shareholder threatening a potential hostile takeover. Such a payment might represent an attempt by entrenched management to retain its position, or it might be a cost incurred to find a more profitable corporate suitor. How should the redeeming corporation treat such a payment? The possible deduction of greenmail payments was the major impetus for enactment of what is now § 162(k). In this context consider also a corporate payment made in exchange for a standstill agreement (i.e., an agreement by a shareholder not to acquire additional shares of the corporation). The legislative history of § 162(k) specifically identifies payments made for standstill agreements as falling within the reach of § 162(k). Note that the no-deduction rule of § 162(k) also applies to appraisal fees, accountants' fees, lawyers' fees, and similar costs incurred in connection with a redemption.

(b) Stock Surrenders. Shareholders sometimes accept less than fair market value for stock turned in to the corporation. For example, in *Schleppy v. Commissioner,*[71] a dispute arose between the holder of $1,000,000 of corporate convertible securities and the issuing corporation. In settlement, it was agreed to lower the conversion ratio from $7 to $5 per share, in effect allowing the securities holder to acquire 57,142 additional shares on conversion. Two major shareholders of the corporation, owning in aggregate just over 70 percent (810,500 of 1,155,833 shares) of the corporation's outstanding stock, turned in 57,142 shares to the corporation. The shareholders claimed losses on the transaction equal to their bases in the shares turned in.

Is such a loss appropriate? The only effect of the stock surrender is to rearrange shareholder interests in the corporation: the surrendering shareholders' interests decline in favor of the nonsur-

---

71. 601 F.2d 196 (5th Cir.1979).

rendering shareholders (including the holder of convertible securities). Precisely the same effect could have been obtained by paying a stock dividend to the nontendering shareholders, a transaction never thought to produce a loss to nonrecipient shareholders. In *Schleppy*, the court disallowed the deduction on the ground that the stock surrender was made to protect the tendering shareholders' remaining stock, and so no gain or loss from the transaction is appropriate until the remaining stock is sold or exchanged.[72]

In *Commissioner v. Fink*,[73] a struggling closely-held corporation was told by its lender to acquire $900,000 of new capital, $700,000 of equity and $200,000 of subordinated debt. The corporation decided to raise the new equity by issuing 700,000 shares of $1 par preferred stock convertible into 1,400,000 shares of common stock. Two major shareholders of the corporation surrendered just under 13 percent of the corporation's outstanding common shares so that, prior to the issuance of the new preferred stock, there would be less than 1,400,000 shares of common stock outstanding. Thus, a purchaser of all of the new convertible preferred stock could be assured of obtaining control of the corporation.

The circuit court allowed the taxpayers in *Fink* to deduct their bases in the surrendered stock, except to the extent that the surrender increased the value of the taxpayers' remaining shares. The court was not bothered that the surrendering shareholders then purchased the newly issued convertible preferred stock, thus obviating the need to offer control of the corporation to an outside purchaser. In addition, the court did not seek from the taxpayers an explanation why the stock surrender was necessary at all: majority control of the corporation could have been given to any purchaser of the convertible preferred stock without a stock surrender simply by increasing the conversion ratio. The court wrote that "[t]he purpose of the stock surrender was to improve [the corporation's] financial position, to preserve its business, and to increase the attractiveness of the corporation to outside investors." Yet, a non-pro rata surrender of stock does not change the financial structure of the corporation at all—it merely rearranges the relative interests of the current shareholders.

The Supreme Court reversed the decision in *Fink* and disallowed the deduction. Following the reasoning of the Circuit Court in *Schleppy*, the Supreme Court held that the taxpayers' non-pro rata stock surrender was made to enhance the value of their remaining shares and thus was nondeductible under § 263. In

72. Accord, *Frantz v. Commissioner*, 83 T.C. 162 (1984), aff'd, 784 F.2d 119 (2d Cir.1986).

73. 483 U.S. 89 (1987), rev'g 789 F.2d 427 (6th Cir.1986).

addition, the Court said that the stock surrender was akin to a shareholder's forgiveness of a corporate debt and so should be nondeductible as a contribution to capital.

Taking these explanations in order, is it true that a non-pro rata stock surrender is made to enhance the value of the surrendering shareholder's remaining shares? If the stock surrender does not increase the overall worth of the corporation in the eyes of outside investors, the only effect of the surrender is to rearrange relative shareholder interests in the corporation. And while it is true that the value of the surrendering shareholder's remaining shares will increase, that increase will never offset the value lost to the surrendering shareholder by reason of the surrender. For example, suppose that X Corp. has 120 shares of stock outstanding, with 100 shares owned by individual P and the remaining 20 shares owned by individual Q. Further, assume that the corporation is worth $120,000, so that each share is worth $1,000.

If P surrenders 20 shares to the corporation, the number of outstanding shares will drop from 120 to 100. Because the value of the corporation remains at $120,000, the per share value increases to $1,200. Accordingly, P's interest in the corporation drops from $100,000 (100 shares at $1,000 each) to $96,000 (80 shares at $1,200) each. The net loss to P occurs because the value in the surrendered shares inures, after the surrender, in part to Q, the remaining shareholder. That is, P loses the full value of the surrendered shares by reason of the transaction but regains only a part of it through his non-surrendered shares of the corporation. The remaining value of the surrendered shares is transferred to the other shareholder. Here, that remaining value is $4,000.

Why then would a shareholder make a non-pro rata stock surrender? In *Fink*, the taxpayers argued that the surrender was intended to increase the net value of the corporation. The Supreme Court accepted this explanation as the basis for its holding that the stock surrender was non-deductible under § 263, an outlay made to increase the value of the shareholder's total investment in the corporation. A similar argument was made and accepted in *Schleppy*.

Yet, a stock surrender should have no appreciable effect on the value of the corporation. The surrender does not change the assets available to the corporation for investment or other productive use nor change its obligations to creditors and other investors.[74] Simply

---

74. The surrender of preferred stock may increase the value of the corporation vis-a-vis holders of the corporation's common stock because such a surrender reduces the corporation's obligation to

changing the number of common shares outstanding, whether increasing the number by a stock surrender or decreasing it by a stock split, should not affect the market value of the on-going corporate enterprise.

The second reason offered by the Supreme Court for its holding in *Fink* was that the stock surrender should be treated as a contribution to the capital of the corporation. This reasoning, also found in the Circuit Court's opinion in *Schleppy,* is even more troubling. The Supreme Court likened a stock surrender to a shareholder forgiveness of corporate debt, but the flaw in this reasoning is that the surrender of common stock adds nothing to the capital of the corporation while the debt forgiveness does. When a true capital contribution is made to a corporation, whether of cash, property, or forgiven indebtedness, the net value of the corporation increases. No such increase results from a stock surrender because no assets are added to the corporate treasury and no obligations upon it are removed. This point was not lost on Justice Scalia, who observed in concurrence: "I do not believe that the Finks' surrender of their shares was, or even closely resembles, a shareholder contribution to corporate capital."[75]

So how should a non-pro rata stock surrender be treated under the Internal Revenue Code? One approach would be to treat the transaction as a redemption in which the redemption price is $0 per share. Under this reasoning the surrendering shareholder would recognize a loss only if the effect on the shareholder's interest in the corporation was significant as judged by the tests of § 302(b). A second approach would be to treat the transaction as a stock dividend to all non-surrendering shareholders. From this perspective there would be no income or loss recognized to any shareholder unless the surrendering shareholder received some form of compensation, in which case the non-surrendering shareholders would be taxable under § 305(b)(2) and the surrendering shareholder would be taxable on the additional compensation. Indeed, now that the Supreme Court has held in *Fink* that the surrendering shareholder will not recognize a loss on the transaction, presumably shareholders will refuse to make non-pro rata surrenders unless some form of compensation is offered. While both the redemption and stock dividend recharacterizations of the stock surrender have advantages, no true solution to the problem will be found until Congress provides a unified treatment of all rearrangements of shareholder interests. Until that time, the form of a rearrangement—whether

make distributions ahead of distributions on the common.

75. See also the discussion in *Tilford v. Commissioner*, 705 F.2d 828 (6th Cir. 1983), discussed at Section 5.06(b) *infra.*

as redemption, stock dividend, or stock surrender—will be important in determining its tax consequences.

Non-pro rata stock surrenders can arise in other settings. Consider the case of a sole shareholder who transfers stock of his corporation to a corporate employee as an inducement for the employee to remain with the corporation. Should the transferor be entitled to a deduction on account of the transfer? To bring the issue into clearer focus, assume that A owns all 100 outstanding shares of X Corp. with adjusted basis and fair market value of $9.50 per share. E agrees to perform $50 worth of services for the corporation in exchange for some of A's shares. How many shares should A transfer to E?

Prior to the transaction, the corporation is worth $950. After the transaction, the corporation should be worth $1,000, its prior value plus the value of the services performed by E. Since there are 100 shares outstanding, each share is now worth $10.00. Accordingly, E should be entitled to receive 5 shares for his services.

Should A be entitled to deduct his basis in the shares transferred to E?[76] Regulations disallow such a deduction,[77] treating the transaction as if A contributed the shares back to the corporation as a contribution to its capital, followed by a distribution of the shares by the corporation to E. Under this analysis, A is not entitled to a deduction for the shares transferred but rather adds his basis in those shares to the shares that he retained.

This analysis and the regulation in question were upheld in *Tilford v. Commissioner*.[78] While the result seems correct, the analysis is open to question: in what sense is the transfer to a corporation of its own stock a "contribution to its capital"? No assets were put into corporate solution by A nor were any assets received by X Corp. Accordingly, it is hard to find any capital contribution.

The transaction is better viewed in two steps: (1) the contribution of shares by A, and (2) the distribution of those shares by X to E. Since A was the sole shareholder at the time of the contribution, the contribution had no effect other than a formal reduction in the number of shares held by A: both before the contribution and immediately after, A was the sole shareholder of X Corp. This first step, which the regulations consider to be a contribution to capital,

---

76. A more aggressive taxpayer in A's position might argue for a deduction equal to the fair market value of the shares transferred, but that result cannot be correct: since any appreciation in the shares is as yet unrealized, it cannot be deducted. Perhaps, though, the shareholder should argue for an ordinary deduction and an equal capital gain.

77. Regs. § 1.83–6(d).

78. 705 F.2d 828 (6th Cir.1983).

cannot be so treated because a contribution to a corporation's capital made by a shareholder increases the shareholder's stock basis. Here, no such increase is appropriate.

Step 2, the distribution of stock to E, should not produce a loss deduction to A for several reasons. First, no economic loss has been sustained by A or X Corp. As to X Corp., it exchanged stock worth $50 for services worth $50. As to A, he began as the 100 percent shareholder of a corporation worth $950 and ended up as a 95 percent shareholder of a corporation worth $1000—A's position has not changed in any substantial way.

Note that the transaction could have been structured without the transfer by A. X Corp. could have issued 5 shares[79] (newly issued or treasury) directly to E. Had this been done, A would have made no transfer and would have no argument for a loss deduction.

5.07 Redemptions Through Related Corporations. The rules of § 302 ensure that a redemption will not produce exchange treatment to the shareholder unless the transaction produces a meaningful reduction in the shareholder's interest in the corporation. Similar rules do not, in general, apply to a sale of shares to another shareholder, even though the sale may have an insignificant effect on the selling shareholder's relation to the corporation. Indeed, if the purchaser is related to the selling shareholder, application of the attribution rules might suggest that the sale has no effect at all. Nonetheless, the selling shareholder will be entitled to exchange treatment on the disposition, limited only if the sale produces a loss.[80]

For the most part, exchange treatment on a sale of shares presents no abuse because the transaction removes no funds from corporate solution. Even if the purchaser is a related party, no bailout of earnings and profits has occurred because no assets have been distributed.[81] However, if the purchaser is itself a corporation, the sale *does* result in a corporate distribution (by the purchaser) and the potential for a bailout occurs.[82]

---

79. Actually X Corp. would have to issue 5.263 shares to E because E should end up with 5% of the company, and if 5 new shares are issued to E, there will be 105 shares outstanding. If 5.263 shares are issued, E will own 5.263 of the 105.263 shares outstanding, or 5% of the total outstanding shares.

80. See § 267.

81. Under some circumstances, the sale could set the stage for a subsequent redemption and bailout. See the discussion at Chapter 7 *infra*.

82. A "bailout" of corporate earnings refers to a transaction in which such earnings are removed from corporate solution as capital gain rather than as dividend income under circumstances in which exchange treatment is inappropriate. For more on bailouts, see Chapter 7.

For example, suppose individual T owns all the stock of X Corp. and all the stock of Y Corp. A redemption by X or Y of any stock will produce distribution treatment to T under the *Davis* rule absent a partial liquidation or qualification under § 303. However, if T simply sells some of his X stock to Y, T seemingly can avoid § 302 without relinquishing any effective control of X. Indeed, if after the purchase a dividend is paid to Y on its X shares, T will have obtained exchange treatment without regard for § 302 even though the purchase price ultimately will have been paid by X itself.[83]

Section 304 speaks to this and similar transactions in which a sale of stock of one corporation is made to a second corporation. Consistent with the abuse to which it speaks, § 304 recharacterizes the transaction as a redemption to which the rules of § 302 apply. See § 304(a). Thus, a sale covered by § 304 will not necessarily produce distribution treatment to the taxpayer. Rather, distribution or exchange treatment will turn on the effect (if any) of the transaction on the taxpayer's relation to the corporation whose stock nominally is being sold.[84]

Section 304 applies in both the brother/sister and parent/subsidiary contexts. The example above illustrates the brother/sister context, because X and Y, both controlled by the taxpayer T, form a pair of sibling corporations. In the parent/subsidiary context, the taxpayer controls P Corp. which in turn controls S Corp. A sale of P stock by T to S will be captured by § 304 and subjected to the redemption rules of § 302.

The touchstone of a § 304 transaction is the sale of stock of one corporation to another, where the seller controls both corporations. Note that "control" for § 304 is defined in § 304(c) to mean ownership of 50 percent of the voting stock or 50 percent of the total value of all stock. In computing control under § 304(c), the attribution rules of § 318 are used, § 304(c)(3), and the entity rules of § 318(a)(2)-(3) are modified to increase the expanse of the attribution rules. See § 304(c)(3)(B). Note that stock acquired in the transaction is counted in determining whether the shareholder

---

83. Note that § 243 will allow Y to deduct most or all of the distribution from income.

84. If a transaction described in § 304 is taxed as a distribution, the transferor is treated as receiving stock from the acquiring corporation which is then immediately redeemed, and this redemption is then taxed under § 301. This peculiar hypothetical redemption (which only arises if the transaction has *already* been determined to be taxable as a distribution, and so the redemption rules of § 302(b) are not implicated) is important if the transferor is itself a corporation; in such circumstances, this hypothetical redemption affects the transferor's tax treatment because the transaction will be taxed as a extraordinary dividend under § 1059, see § 1059(e)(1)(A).

is in control of the transferee (i.e., "acquiring") corporation. § 304(c)(2)(A).

The corporation whose stock is being sold in the § 304 transaction is called the "issuing corporation," while the corporation purchasing the stock is called the "acquiring corporation." For example, suppose that individual B owns 50 of 100 shares of X Corp. and all 100 shares of Y Corp. If B sells 10 shares of X to Y, X is the "issuing corporation" and Y is the "acquiring corporation."

Under § 304(a), the rules of § 302(b) are applied to the taxpayer's ownership interest in the *issuing* corporation. See § 304(b)(1). Note that, because of the attribution rules, some or all of the taxpayer's stock sold to the acquiring corporation will be attributed back to the taxpayer under § 318(a)(2)(C). In the X/Y example above, the rules of § 302 will be applied to B's ownership in X Corp. In this example, B has constructive ownership of 50 percent of X Corp. both before and after the transaction. The following rule can be generalized from this example: if the taxpayer owns 100 percent of the stock of the *acquiring* corporation, the sale will work no change in the taxpayer's constructive ownership of the issuing corporation.

To determine whether the § 304 sale qualifies for exchange treatment, one must compare the taxpayer's pre-sale ownership of the issuing corporation with his post-sale ownership interest. In making this comparison, the rules of § 302(b) apply. A taxpayer might qualify for exchange treatment under the substantially disproportionate safe harbor of § 302(b)(2) or under the general rule of § 302(b)(1). Indeed, if the transaction is coupled with a contraction of the *acquiring* corporation's business, the taxpayer may qualify under the partial liquidation provision of § 302(b)(4).[85]

In the X/Y example, the sale by B of 10 shares of X to Y has no effect on B's constructive ownership of X because of the attribution rules. Thus, under the *Davis* case,[86] B cannot qualify for exchange treatment unless the transaction qualifies as a partial liquidation. Suppose, though, that B sells 10 shares of Y stock to X.

Prior to the transaction, B has complete ownership of Y. After the transaction, B's actual ownership drops to 90 percent. However, because B is a 50 percent shareholder of X Corp., half of X's stock in Y must be attributed to B.[87] Thus, B's total constructive owner-

85. *Blaschka v. United States,* 393 F.2d 983 (Ct.Cl.1968).

86. See Section 5.02(c) *supra*

87. See § 318(a)(2)(C). In applying these attribution rules in the context of § 304, attribution from a corporation to a shareholder is required whenever the shareholder owns 5% or more of the corporation's stock. See § 304(c)(3)(B)(i). The same is true for

ship is 95 of 100 shares, or 95 percent. Such a reduction is unlikely to qualify as "meaningful" under § 302(b)(1), thus denying exchange treatment to B on the exchange. If, however, B had transferred all of his stock of Y to X, his total constructive ownership would have dropped from 100 percent to 50 percent, a reduction that probably would be held to be "meaningful."

One question that often arises is whether the complete termination provision of § 302(b)(3) can be useful in a § 304 transaction? Suppose that Father owns all the stock of P Corp. and that Son owns all the stock of Q Corp. If Father sells all of his P stock to Q, how should he be taxed?

This transaction falls within the reach of § 304(a)(1) because Father has constructive ownership of both corporations. Can Father file a § 302(c)(2) waiver and thereby avoid application of the family attribution rules in making the § 302(b)(3) determination? Since such a waiver is permitted in the context of a true redemption, surely Father should not be worse off by reason of selling his stock to a related corporation. Yet, it is unclear if such a waiver is permitted in the context of § 304. See the introductory clause in § 302(c)(2)(A).

If a taxpayer qualifies for exchange treatment on the § 304 sale, gain or loss will be recognized under § 1001(a) subject to the loss limitation of § 267. However, if distribution treatment is mandated because the taxpayer fails to qualify under the tests of § 302(b), dividend treatment will be accorded up to the earnings and profits of *both* corporations. See § 304(b)(2).

For example, if B is the sole shareholder of X Corp. and Y Corp., the sale by B of X stock to Y will be covered by § 304. Further, because of the attribution rules, the sale will work no change in B's ownership of X, the issuing corporation. Accordingly, B will be taxed on the amount received from Y under the distribution rules of § 301. B's basis in the X shares sold will flow into his stock of Y. See the last sentence in § 304(a)(1).[88]

Section 304 applies only to sales of stock to related corporations, where a "sale" means the exchange of stock for "property." The definition of "property" in § 317(a) is applicable to § 304, and thus "property" under § 304 does not include stock of the acquiring corporation. Accordingly, the transfer of Brother Corp. stock to Sister Corp. will not fall within § 304 if all that is received in

---

attribution from a shareholder to the corporation. See § 302(c)(3)(B)(ii).

88. In the parent/subsidiary context, the basis consequences are less clear.

Presumably the basis will flow into the shareholder's remaining stock of the issuing corporation (i.e., into his remaining stock of the parent).

exchange is stock of Sister. In particular, a bootless incorporation under § 351 cannot fall within § 304.[89]

But what of a § 351 incorporation in which boot is received by the transferor/taxpayer? Suppose for example that stock of Brother Corp. is transferred to Sister Corp. in exchange for stock of Sister and $10,000 of cash. If the transferor meets the 80 percent control tests of § 368(c) with respect to Sister, this transaction meets the definition of an incorporation taxable under § 351(b). Under that provision, the gain (up to $10,000) on the exchange would be taxable, possibly as capital gain.

However, if the transferor also meets the 50 percent control test of § 304(c) with respect to Brother Corp., § 304(a)(1) also seems to apply. (The 50 percent control test also must be met with respect to Sister, but if the 80 percent test of § 368(c) has been met, so has the 50 percent test of § 304(c) *a fortiori*.) In this case, must the transferor run the hurdles of § 302(b) via § 304 to obtain exchange treatment, or does § 351(b) provide it automatically?

This question, once a thorny one for the courts, has been resolved by statute. Under § 304(b)(3), the rules of § 351(b) must give way to those of § 304. Thus, taxation of the boot will turn on the application of § 304 and § 302(b). Of course, § 351 applies to the receipt of the Sister stock because § 304 can only apply to "property."

Consider the following example. B owns all 100 shares of X Corp. with adjusted basis of $10 per share and fair market value of $30 per share. B also owns 50 of the 70 outstanding shares of Y Corp. with adjusted basis of $1 per share and the other 20 shares are owned by an unrelated taxpayer. B transfers all his shares of X to Y in exchange for 30 treasury shares of Y as well as $1,200 of cash. Assume that the treasury shares are worth a total of $1,800.

In effect, B has received Y stock for 60 percent of his X shares and cash for 40 percent. As to the 60 percent, the transaction is described in § 351 because B is in "control" of Y immediately after the transaction (because 80 of 100 shares constitutes "control"). Section 304 cannot apply to this part of the exchange because B receives only stock of Y. Thus, no gain or loss is recognized and B's basis in the shares received in the transaction is $600.[90]

---

89. See also the discussion of *Bhada v. Commissioner*, 89 T.C. 959 (1987), aff'd sub nom. *Caamano v. Commissioner*, 879 F.2d 156 (5th Cir.1989), discussed at Section 10.04(d) *infra*, for the acquisition by a subsidiary corporation of stock of its parent in exchange for its own stock.

90. Sixty shares with a basis of $10 per share, carried over to the Y stock received under § 358(a).

As to the other 40 percent of the transaction, B has exchanged stock of X for property. This transaction meets all the tests of § 304, so that B will be taxed on the $1,200 received as dividend income unless § 302, applied to B's interest in X, gives exchange treatment. B's interest in X drops from 100 percent (all actual ownership) to 80 percent (all constructive). If this reduction is not "meaningful" enough to qualify under § 302(b)(1), the $1,200 will be taxed under the distribution rules of § 301.

The examples so far have all involved brother/sister transactions implicating § 304(a)(1). Recall that § 304 also can apply to distributions by a subsidiary corporation in exchange for stock of its parent. § 304(a)(2). Unfortunately, the application of § 304 to parent/subsidiary transactions is problematic.

Before looking at the difficult aspects of the parent/subsidiary application of § 304, note that at least one aspect of § 304 is appreciably simpler here than in the brother/sister context. Recall that for § 304(a)(1) to apply to a brother/sister pair, the taxpayer must "control" both corporations. In the parent/subsidiary case, though, § 304(a)(2) requires only that the parent corporation control the subsidiary, where control continues to mean direct or indirect ownership of at least 50 percent (by vote or by value) of the stock of the controlled corporation. Accordingly, § 304(a)(2) can apply even if the shareholder's ownership interest in the parent corporation is small.

That aspect of the statute aside, the problem becomes much more difficult. For example, assume that individual J owns all 100 outstanding shares of P Corp. and that P owns all 100 shares of S Corp. If J sells 60 of his P shares to S in exchange for property, is the sale taxed under § 304(a)(2) as an exchange or as a distribution? Exchange treatment will permit J to recover his basis in the shares transferred before reporting any gain. Distribution treatment, on the other hand, will cause J to report the entire consideration received as ordinary income, subject only to the limitation that there must be sufficient earnings and profits in the two companies to cover that amount. See § 304(b)(2).

Under § 304(a)(2), exchange or distribution treatment to J will turn on application of the redemption rules of § 302 to the transaction. From § 304(b)(1) we know that it is J's change in ownership interest of the issuing corporation (i.e., P Corp.) that must be examined. Prior to the transaction, J owns 100% of P Corp. After the transaction, J has actual ownership of 40 of the 100 outstanding shares. Can the remaining shares be imputed to J under the attribution rules of § 318(a)? A technical reading of that section permits the attribution from S to P under § 318(a)(2)(C) and then from P to J under a second application of § 318(a)(2)(C). However, two challenges can be mounted to this application of § 318(a)(2). First, the second link in the chain (from P to J) will impute to J only a proportion of the 60 shares depending on J's (direct or indirect) percentage ownership of P. But what is J's percentage ownership of P? That is the precise question we are trying to answer, thus showing that the application of the attribution rules in this context is circular. Note that this problem in the application of the § 318 attribution rules occurs only because P owns stock of S and S owns stock of P at the same time.

In addition, the attribution of shares owned by S Corp. to J through P requires the attribution from P Corp. of its own stock. We do not attribute P stock actually owned by P (i.e., treasury shares) to its shareholder. Is it appropriate to attribute P stock owned only constructively by P to its shareholders?

One approach is to treat the P Corp. shares acquired by S on the transaction as no longer outstanding. Indeed, state law presumably would prohibit S from voting the shares. Should we then treat J as having 100% actual ownership of P Corp. because his 40 shares are the only P Corp. shares properly considered outstanding? While this approach is a reasonable one, Congress should clarify the application of the § 318(a) attribution in the context of a parent/subsidiary transaction described in § 302(a)(2).[91] Of course, if J is deemed to own 100 percent of P Corp. after the transaction, the proceeds of the sale received from S Corp. will be taxed as a distribution.

---

91. See generally Land, Strange Loops and Tangled Hierarchies, 49 Tax L. Rev. 53 (1993).

CHAPTER 6.   STOCK DIVIDENDS

6.01 Overview and History. Before considering the taxation of stock dividends, it is worthwhile to reconsider the taxation of cash and property dividends.[1] Recall that a "dividend" is a distribution by a corporation made to a shareholder with respect to the shareholder's stock, taxable as ordinary income.[2] Why is it that cash dividends, for example, are includible by the recipient as income?

At first blush, cash dividends seem to be "undeniable accessions to wealth, clearly realized, . . . over which the taxpayers have complete dominion."[3] Yet, upon closer inspection we see that such dividends are *not* accessions to wealth, because cash dividends, or at least pro rata cash dividends, reduce *pro tanto* the value of the corporate stock held by the shareholders. More generally, no pro rata distribution of corporate assets increases the wealth of the shareholders but only transmutes part of the value of their shares into the form of distributed property.

Why then are dividends includible in gross income? The answer to that question touches on both the realization doctrine and the double taxation of corporate profits. For better or worse, Congress has decided that corporations should be treated as taxable entities distinct from their shareholders. As a consequence, corporate profits are subjected to a double tax, once to the earning corporation and a second time to the corporation's shareholders. In theory, both layers of taxation could be imposed as corporate profits are earned at the corporate-level, with the shareholders taxed in some manner akin to that of partners and S corporation shareholders. Congress has always provided as to C corporations, however, that the shareholder-level taxation is imposed only when the corporate profits are distributed as dividends.

Imposition of the shareholder-level tax on only *distributed* corporate profits follows from the principle that corporations and their shareholders are distinct taxpayers. Undistributed corporate profits increase shareholder wealth by increasing the value of the corporation's shares. Under the realization doctrine, the mere increase in value of an asset is not taxable until that increase is

---

1. See Chapter 4 *supra*.

2. Throughout this discussion it is assumed that the distributing corporation has sufficient earnings and profits to cover any distribution.

3. *Commissioner v. Glenshaw Glass Co.*, 348 U.S. 426, 431 (1955).

converted into some new form, usually by sale or exchange. Accordingly, while corporate profits can be taxed to the corporation as earned, the realization doctrine protects the shareholders from taxation until such profits are converted into some form other than an increase in stock value.[4]

With this in mind, how should stock dividends be taxed? Consider first the case of a corporation having only a single class of common stock outstanding, and assume that the stock dividend consists of additional shares of the same class of stock distributed to the shareholders in proportion to their predividend stock ownership. Should such a distribution be taxable to the shareholders?

The distribution does not increase the wealth of the distributees, but of course no pro rata distribution does. The form of each shareholder's wealth undergoes a change: the number of shares held increases although the aggregate value of those shares does not. This change in form is particularly minimal: each shareholder's wealth remains in the form of corporate stock.

Note that this common on common stock dividend does not remove any assets from corporate solution. Whatever corporate profits have been earned, therefore, still can be taxed when distributed even if the stock dividend goes untaxed. Since imposition of a tax liability other than when funds are generated to pay the tax is difficult to administer, taxation of a pro rata common on common stock dividend seems inappropriate.

Perhaps for these reasons, Congress does not now seek to tax common on common stock dividends. But once it did, as part of the Revenue Act of 1916. In *Eisner v. Macomber*,[5] the Supreme Court held that common on common stock dividends were constitutionally immune from federal income taxation. Justices Holmes and Brandeis dissented in *Macomber*, Holmes on the ground that the purpose of the Sixteenth Amendment was to "get rid of nice questions" as to what could be taxed. Justice Brandeis wrote a lengthy dissent, arguing that stock dividends were sufficiently akin to cash dividends to preclude a *constitutional* line between the two. History seems to have borne out Justice Brandeis: it is practicality rather

---

4. Note that the value of the property distributed to any particular shareholder will, in general, bear no relationship to the corporate profits earned since that shareholder acquired his stock. However, the price paid for shares of a corporation should reflect not only the value of the corporation but also the potential tax liability to be incurred by the purchaser. In fact, though, because corporate earnings often have been bailed out of corporate solution at less than ordinary rates, the value of corporate shares traded on the market probably reflects little discounting for potential taxes owed.

5. 252 U.S. 189 (1920).

than constitutional mandate that precludes the taxation of common on common stock dividends.[6]

The taxation of stock dividends is covered by § 305. Subsection (a) states the general rule that "gross income does not include the amount of any distribution of the stock of a corporation made by such corporation to its shareholders with respect to its stock." Exceptions to this general rule in subsection (b), though, limit its application to little more than pro rata stock dividends made with respect to common stock.

6.02 The General Rule of § 305(a). The general rule of nontaxability under § 305(a) only applies to distributions made with respect to a shareholder's stock. It does not apply, for example, to a distribution of stock to an employee as compensation or to a lender in discharge of a debt. Such stock distributions are taxable under other provisions of the Code.[7] In addition, § 305 does not apply to the distribution by one corporation of stock in a second corporation.[8] On the other hand, § 305 *does* apply to distributions of stock rights as well as to stock itself.[9]

Stock received tax-free under § 305(a) is treated as a continuation of the recipient's old stock. Accordingly, the recipient's old basis in the old shares is divided among the old and new shares in proportion to relative fair market values. § 307(a); Regs. § 1.307–1(a).[10] The identification of the old and new shares is continued in § 1223(5), which provides that a taxpayer's holding period of the old shares is tacked onto the holding period of the new shares. Of course, because stock distributions described in § 305(a) result in no taxation to the recipients, such distributions do not reduce the earnings and profits account of the distributing corporation. § 312(d)(1)(B).

---

6. See, e.g., Surrey, *The Supreme Court and the Federal Income Tax: Some Implications of Recent Decisions,* 35 Ill. L.Rev. 779 (1941). See also § 951 et seq. taxing shareholders of controlled foreign corporations on unrealized "subpart F" income.

7. See, e.g., § 83 (distribution of stock in exchange for services).

8. Distributions of "property" (as defined in § 317(a) to include stock of any corporation other than the distributing corporation) are covered by § 301.

9. Section 305(d).

10. In the case of a distribution of stock rights qualifying for nonrecognition under § 305(a), there is a de minimis rule in § 307(b) applicable only if the distributed stock rights have a fair market value less than 15% of the value of the shareholder's stock. In such a case, a taxpayer may elect to avoid the basis allocation and take the stock rights with a zero basis. To prevent manipulation, if stock rights not covered by the de minimis rule lapse, no loss to the shareholder is allowed. Rather, the basis of the lapsed rights flows back to the taxpayer's stock. Regs. § 1.307–1(a).

For example, suppose that individual B owns all outstanding 100 shares of X Corp. with adjusted basis of $20 per share. If X pays a one-for-one stock dividend (that is, distributes one share of stock for every share outstanding), B will own 200 shares after the transaction. Because such a stock dividend is tax-free to B under § 305(a), B allocates his pre-dividend stock basis among his old and new shares, leaving him with a stock basis of $10 per share after the distribution.

6.03 Exceptions to the General Rule Under § 305(b). Despite the broad language used in the nonrecognition provision § 305(a), its application is quite narrow. Under § 305(b), many distributions of stock (and of stock rights) are treated as distributions of property subject to the usual distribution rules in § 301. Since nonrecognition under § 305(a) is appropriate only when the stock distribution does not substantially alter the form of the recipient's investment in the distributing corporation, the rules in § 305(b) tax most stock distributions rearranging the relative interests of the shareholders in the distributing corporation. In addition, stock distributions appropriately considered to be property distributions followed by a reinvestment of the distributed property also are removed from the protection of § 305(a) by the rules of § 305(b). Note, though, that a stock distribution falling within § 305(b) is not automatically taxable to the recipient as dividend income. Rather, such stock distributions are simply subject to the usual rules covering corporate distributions in § 301, rules which can produce dividend income, tax-free recovery of basis, and capital gain. See § 301(c).[11]

Section 305(b)(1) covers stock distributions in which any shareholder could have elected to receive money or property in lieu of stock. Of course, shareholders electing to receive cash or property will not be taxed under § 305: such shareholders will be subject to the rules of § 301 by the express terms of that section. The reach of § 305(b)(1) is thus limited to shareholders electing to receive their distribution in stock and to shareholders having no choice but forced to receive stock *if* any other shareholder had the opportunity to receive cash or property. As to each group, the distribution will

---

11. In the case of a stock dividend taxable under §§ 305(b) and 301, the distributing corporation does not have income on the distribution because the corporation could have sold the stock tax-free under § 1032 and then distributed the cash. For the same reason, the corporation's earnings and profits account will be reduced (but not below zero) by the fair market value of the distributed stock. See § 312(a), which applies to distributions of property, and § 305(b), which treats the distribution of stock as a distribution of property under specified circumstances.

be taxed as if the distribution had been in cash, followed by a purchase of additional stock with the cash received.

As the simplest example, suppose that X Corp. declares a dividend payable in cash of $10 or 1 share of $10 par value preferred stock. Those X Corp. shareholders electing to receive cash will be taxed directly under § 301. Those shareholders electing to receive the stock also will be taxed under § 301 by virtue of § 305(b)(1). This example shows that the rule of § 305(b)(1) can be justified at least in part by reference to the *constructive receipt* doctrine: because the shareholders had the freedom to elect between cash and stock, shareholders electing to receive stock are taxed as if they received the cash and used it to purchase additional stock.

As a second example, suppose that X Corp., having only one class of common stock outstanding, declares a one-for-one stock dividend. However, the terms of the dividend provide that any shareholder holding 4 or more shares may elect to receive a $50 bond in lieu of the dividend stock. Once again all shareholders will be taxed under § 301, those receiving the bond without implicating § 305 and those receiving stock by virtue of § 305(b)(1). Note that even shareholders holding fewer than 4 shares of the corporation will be taxed under § 301 via § 305(b)(1) even though they had no choice as to the form of the dividend.[12]

An election to receive stock in lieu of cash or property will trigger application of § 305(b)(1) whether made before or after the stock distribution. In addition, an indirect election to receive stock rather than cash or property will suffice. For example, suppose X Corp. has two classes of common stock outstanding, identical in all respects except that dividends on one class must be paid in cash while dividends on the other class must be paid in stock. A taxpayer who purchases shares receiving stock dividends rather than cash dividends has elected to receive stock dividends in lieu of cash within the meaning of § 305(b)(1)[13], and so subsequent stock distributions will be taxed under the rules of § 301.

Compare the case of two related corporations jointly engaged in a single productive activity. One of the two corporations pays its dividends in cash while the other pays in stock. Although the decision to buy the stock of one of these two corporations rather than the other is in effect a decision to receive dividends in cash or stock, § 305(b)(1) does not capture such an implicit election: the

---

12. See Regs. § 1.305–2(a).   **13.** See Regs. § 1.305–2(a)(4).

language of § 305(b)(1) will not support its application *among* corporations.

Corporations sometimes offer dividend reinvestment plans to their shareholders. Such a plan might provide that shareholders can elect to receive 105 percent of the value of declared cash dividends in the form additional stock. Shareholders electing to participate in such a plan will be taxed on the fair market value of the stock received by virtue of § 305(b)(1).[14] The only exception to this rule is for certain dividend reinvestment plans of public utilities, and even then the exception is limited to distributions of common stock.[15]

Suppose a corporation declares a stock dividend and then offers to redeem the dividend shares of any shareholder wishing to tender them. Of course, the tendering shareholders will be taxed under one theory or another, but should this sequence of events constitute the equivalent of a dividend optionally paid in stock or in property within the meaning of § 305(b)(1) so that those shareholders who keep the dividend stock should be taxed? In *Frontier Savings Association v. Commissioner*,[16] the Tax Court refused to apply § 305(b)(1) in such circumstances even though the distributing corporation habitually offered to redeem its shares.

The rule in § 305(b)(2) for disproportionate distributions is the cornerstone of § 305(b). This rule captures stock distributions increasing the recipients' interest in the distributing corporation, but only if some other shareholder receives a distribution of cash or property. Thus, the rule of § 305(b)(2) embodies two distinct tests: the increased interest test and the companion distribution test.

The increased interest test will be satisfied by an increased claim to the assets or the earnings and profits of the distributing corporation. Consider the case of X Corp. having two classes of stock outstanding, class A common and $100 par class B 10 percent cumulative preferred. A distribution of class B shares to the holders of the common or holders of the preferred will satisfy the increased interest test. Since the holders of class B shares are entitled to 10 percent dividends each year, receipt of class B shares increases any recipient's interest in the earnings and profits of the corporation. In addition, because the holders of class B shares are entitled to $100 in liquidation per share, receipt of class B shares increases a recipient's interests in the assets of the corporation.

---

14. See, e.g., Rev.Rul. 78–375, 1978–2 C.B. 130.

15. See § 305(e).

16. 87 T.C. 665 (1986), aff'd, 854 F.2d 1001 (7th Cir.1988).

A distribution of class A shares, on the other hand, will not necessarily satisfy the increased interest test. Consider a distribution of class A shares only to holders of class A shares. Since common stock has only a residual interest in dividends and on liquidation, the additional shares of the class A stock do not give a recipient an increased interest in the earnings and profits or in the assets of the corporation. Accordingly, the increased interest test is not satisfied by this distribution. But if the common stock is distributed to holders of preferred stock, the increased interest test will be satisfied because a recipient will hold not only a preferred interest but a residuary interest in the corporation as well.

The companion distribution requirement of § 305(b)(2) usually will be met with respect to any stock distribution satisfying the increased interest test because those shareholders not receiving stock of the corporation ought to receive something else of value in exchange for a reduction in their ownership of the corporation. A dividend of cash or property will of course satisfy the companion distribution requirement, and so will less obvious corporate distributions such as excess salary payments constituting disguised dividends. Indeed, any payment to a shareholder not participating in the stock distribution will qualify as the companion distribution so long as the payment is made to the shareholder in his capacity as shareholder.[17] While cash or property distributed as part of a plan to give some shareholders an increased interest in the corporation obviously will qualify as the companion distribution, so too will a distribution of cash or property *not* made pursuant to such a plan if made within 36 months of the stock dividend.[18]

Suppose a distribution of stock satisfying the increased interest test of § 305(b)(2) is closely followed or preceded by a corporate distribution in redemption of some of the corporation's shares held by taxpayers *not* receiving any of the dividend stock. Since a redemption of stock technically is a distribution of property with respect to stock, will this redemption distribution satisfy the companion distribution test of § 305(b)(2)? One might expect that it would, at least if the redemption is essentially equivalent to a dividend within the meaning of § 302(d) and therefore taxed as a distribution under the rules of § 301. Nonetheless, the regulations under § 305 provide that a distribution of property in redemption of stock will not satisfy the companion distribution requirement of § 305(b)(2) unless the redemption is part of a periodic plan to increase the proportionate interests of some of the shareholders.[19]

---

17. Regs. § 1.305–3(b)(3).
18. See Regs. § 1.305–3(b)(4).

19. See Regs. § 1.305–3(b)(3); Rev. Rul. 78–60, 1978–1 C.B. 81.

The regulations excuse from § 305(b)(2) one common situation that technically falls within the statute's terms. A stock dividend will not be covered by § 305(b)(2) simply because cash in lieu of fractional shares is distributed by the corporation. To be sure, the effect of such a distribution is to increase ever so slightly the interests of those shareholders entitled to receive integer numbers of shares at the expense of those receiving cash in lieu of fractional shares. Furthermore, the cash paid in lieu of the fractional shares seems to satisfy the companion distribution requirement. Nevertheless, such distributions will escape § 305(b)(2) "[p]rovided the purpose of the distribution of cash is to save the corporation the trouble, expense, and inconvenience of issuing and transferring fractional shares."[20]

Note that the companion distribution requirement of § 305(b)(2) causes one taxpayer (who receives a stock dividend having a disproportionate impact) to have his taxation turn on events happening to another taxpayer (any shareholder receiving a companion distribution). Why *should* the tax consequences of a stock dividend to one shareholder be influenced by the distributions to another? Congress apparently has been satisfied that there is an answer to this question, because several of the other provisions of § 305(b) echo § 305(b)(2).

For example, the disproportionate distribution rule of § 305(b)(2) is extended in § 305(b)(3) to include distributions of common stock to some common shareholders and preferred stock to other common shareholders. Such stock distributions satisfy the increased interest test of § 305(b)(2) as to both the common and preferred shareholders but they fail the companion distribution test imposed by that subsection since the definition of "property" applicable to § 305 excludes stock of the distributing corporation.[21] The rule of § 305(b)(3) overcomes this deficiency in the definition of "property," at least in the specific context of disproportionate distributions of stock to common shareholders.

Any stock distribution on preferred stock will alter the preferred shareholders' investment in the corporation, either by increasing the shareholders' preferred claim to earnings and profits as well as liquidation proceeds (if preferred stock is distributed) or by adding residual rights to the shareholders' preferred claims (if common stock is distributed). For this reason, § 305(b)(4) makes taxable any stock distribution made with respect to (that is, any stock distribution *on*) preferred stock.

---

20. Regs. § 1.305–3(c)(1).   **21.** Section 317(a).

Consider the distribution of preferred on common as well as preferred on preferred. Depending on the values of the common and preferred shares as well as on the terms of the distribution, it may be the case that no shareholder's interest in the corporation is changed *as measured by fair market value of the stock held.* Why then are the shareholders taxed?[22] Because the focus of § 305(b), like that of most nonrecognition provisions, is not on a change in *value* but on a change in *form.* After all, if an equal-value exchange were always the proper occasion for nonrecognition, no arms'-length exchange would be taxable!

The last provision of § 305(b), that contained in § 305(b)(5) applicable to distributions of convertible preferred stock, is very peculiar. It provides that distributions of convertible preferred stock are taxable unless the distribution does not have the result described in § 305(b)(2), the disproportionate distribution provision. The situations intended to be covered by this provision, as identified in the regulations,[23] involve the distribution of convertible preferred stock in which the right to convert is limited to a short time and the price of the common stock into which the preferred is convertible is greater than that of preferred stock lacking the convertibility feature. Because the convertibility premium must be exploited quickly if at all, those shareholders wishing to hold additional convertible stock will exercise their conversion rights and those not wishing to convert will sell their preferred shares immediately. In effect, some shareholders will end up with additional common stock and others with cash, the situation covered by § 305(b)(2).

Section 305(b)(5) does not cover all distributions of convertible preferred stock but only those having a disproportionate effect on the recipients' interests in corporate earnings and profits or assets. Such an effect will obtain only if some but not all of the distributed stock is converted. Consistent with the legislative history of § 305(b)(5), the regulations provide that such an effect will not be presumed if the conversion right can be exercised over many years and the dividend rate is consistent with market factors.[24]

The peculiar aspect of § 305(b)(5) is that it seemingly fails to address another situation to which it quite easily might speak. If

---

22. The shareholders receiving preferred on preferred are taxed under § 305(b)(4). The shareholders receiving preferred on common are taxed under § 302(b)(2) because the stock dividend gives them an increased interest in the corporation and the preferred stock distributed to the preferred shareholders, because it is taxed under § 305(b), qualifies as a companion distribution of "property." See the flush language in § 305(b) preceding subsection (1).

23. See Regs. § 1.305–6(b) (example 2).

24. Regs. § 1.305–6(a)(2).

any convertible preferred stock is distributed by a corporation (whether or not there is a convertibility premium), some shareholders may retain the stock while others may convert it into common stock. The effect of the distribution, in other words, may approximate that of a distribution composed in part of preferred stock and in part of common stock. That effect would be described in § 302(b)(2) and thus the distribution would be captured by § 305(b)(5) except that neither common stock nor convertible preferred stock is "property" within the meaning of § 305. Thus, the companion distribution requirement of § 305(b)(2) is not met. To close this loophole, § 305(b)(5) should cover distributions of convertible preferred stock having the effect described in § 305(b)(2) *or in § 305(b)(3)*.[25]

6.04 Deemed Distributions Under § 305(c). Many transactions not involving an actual distribution of stock nevertheless can have the effect of a stock dividend. Consider X Corp. having 300 shares outstanding, 150 owned by B and 150 owned by C. Assume that each share is worth $100 because X Corp. has assets worth $30,000.

If X distributes cash of $5,000 to B and 75 shares to C, the distribution will be taxable to both shareholders: B will be taxed under § 301 directly while C will be taxed under the same section pursuant to § 305(b)(2). After the transaction, B will own 150 of the 375 (40 percent) outstanding shares of X Corp., each share having a value of $66.67, or $10,000 in the aggregate.[26] C, on the other hand, will own the remaining 225 shares (60 percent), having an aggregate value of $15,000. Accordingly, the value of the distributed shares is $5,000 (75 shares at $66.67 per share), and C will be taxed on that amount under the rules of § 301.[27]

The same effect can be obtained by replacing the two distributions with a single redemption by X of 50 of B's shares. If that is done, B will receive the same $5,000 (50 shares at $100 per share), and B's ownership in X will drop to 100 of 250 shares outstanding, or 40 percent. C's percentage ownership of X will increase to 60 percent (150 of 250 shares outstanding). Each share will continue to be worth $100, making the aggregate value of C's stock $15,000,

---

25. Note that distributions of convertible preferred stock to holders of preferred stock need not be covered by § 305(b)(5) because such distributions already are covered by the general rule of § 305(b)(4) applicable to all stock distributions on preferred stock.

26. After the distribution, X Corp. has assets worth $25,000.

27. Note that C is taxed on the fair market value of the shares distributed to him without any offset for the decrease in value of his remaining shares. That decrease under § 305(b) remains unrealized until disposition by C of his shares.

just as in the case of the two distributions considered above. Should C, who is totally passive in this case, be taxed under § 305(b)(2)?

To ensure that this transaction and others having the same effect as a stock dividend do not offer a potential for abuse, § 305(c) provides that, under regulations promulgated by the Secretary of the Treasury, certain transactions having the effect of a stock distribution are to be subjected to the rules of § 305. These transactions include the change in conversion ratio of stock, a change in stock redemption price, a difference between stock issue and redemption price, and a redemption taxed to the recipient shareholder under § 301. While the thrust of § 305(c)—that transactions having the effect of a stock dividend should be taxed like a stock dividend—makes sense, its arbitrary lines and mechanical application undercut its coherence.

For example, the statute recharacterizes as stock distributions only those redemptions failing to qualify for the exchange treatment of § 302(a). Yet, it is precisely those redemptions qualifying for exchange treatment that work the greatest rearrangement of shareholder interests. No explanation leaps to mind that would explain why highly disproportionate stock distributions should trigger § 305 although redemptions having the same effect do not. The best that can be offered in defense of this rule is that the companion distribution requirement of § 305(b)(2) is not met when the redemption is taxed as a sale or exchange.[28]

A change in conversion ratio also can trigger application of § 305(c). However, not all changes in the conversion ratio of preferred stock are proper candidates for § 305(c). Consider X Corp. having 2 classes of stock outstanding, 100 shares of class A common and 100 shares of class B preferred convertible one-for-one into class A stock. If the class A stock splits (or if a stock dividend payable in shares of class A stock is declared on the class A shares), then the conversion rights of the class B shares must be adjusted to avoid dilution of the class B shares. For example, if the class A shares split one-for-one, then the conversion ratio of the class B shares must be increased from one-to-one to two-to-one. Such antidilution conversion increases are explicitly permitted by statute without taxation.[29]

Reconsider the example above, but assume that the class B shareholders do not benefit from an antidilution provision increas-

---

28. That is, a redemption taxed as an exchange should not be treated as a distribution with respect to stock, just as the sale of property to a corporation for cash is not a "distribution with respect to stock" if the corporation pays no more than fair market value.

29. Section 305(b)(4).

ing their conversion ratio in the case of stock splits or dividends. Suppose X Corp. declares a stock dividend on the class A shares payable with one share of additional class A stock for each share of class A stock held. In addition, to prevent dilution of the class B shareholders' interests, they too receive a stock dividend, payable in one share of class A stock for each share of class B stock held. Is such an antidilution distribution protected from taxation? No—the only antidilution provision sanctioned by the Code is an increase in conversion ratio. The stock dividend declared on the class B shares, even though having the effect of avoiding a disproportionate impact by the stock dividend declared on the class A, is simply a stock distribution made with respect to preferred stock and thus taxable according to the rule of § 305(b)(4).[30] Of course, if the conversion ratio of the class B shares had been adjusted and then half of the shares converted, the same result would have been obtained without taxation to the class B shareholders (except they would have had less preferred stock).

6.05 Poison Pills. When corporate takeovers became common in the 1980s, anti-takeover practices blossomed. And these practices continue today. One such practice is the "poison pill," by which the corporation ensures that the cost of a hostile takeover will be too expensive to pursue. For example, the corporation might provide that each shareholder can purchase additional shares of the corporation at a 50% discount if an outsider acquires 20% or more of the company's stock or announces its intention to mount a tender offer without the approval of the corporation's board of directors. Until such a triggering event, such rights to buy discounted stock cannot be separated from the actual shares and can be redeemed by the corporation for a nominal amount. Once triggered, though, the discounted stock rights can be sold and are not subject to redemption.

Should the adoption of such a poison pill be treated as a distribution of stock rights to current shareholders of the corporation? In Rev.Rul. 90–11,[31] the Service ruled that the adoption of a similar poison pill is not subject to taxation under § 305. Unfortunately, the ruling provides no analysis whatsoever in support of its conclusion that the adoption of the pill "does not constitute a distribution of stock or property by [the corporation] to its shareholders, an exchange of property or stock (either taxable or nontaxable), or any other event giving rise to the realization of gross income by any taxpayer." The only hint of any justification for this very broad Ruling was the assumed fact that "[a]t the time [the

---

30. Rev. Rul. 83–42, 1983–1 C.B. 76.   **31.** 1990–1 C.B. 10.

corporation] adopted the [poison pill], the likelihood that the [shareholders' rights] would, at any time, be exercised was both remote and speculative."

Despite the lack of a conceptual underpinning, it is hard to fault Rev.Rul. 90–11. If the adoption of the poison pill were treated as a distribution subject to § 305, the rights would have to be valued as if there were a companion distribution of cash or property to some shareholders. How would these rights be valued given their highly contingent nature? Indeed, given that adoption of a poison pill is intended to stave off hostile takeovers—and if there are no hostile takeovers, exercise of the poison pill stock rights will never be triggered—do the rights have any significant current value? The Revenue Ruling explicitly did not consider the tax consequences of the exercise or transfer of the poison pill stock rights following a triggering event, but because such rights are created to inhibit all triggering events, the tax implications of this remote possibility are of little concern to most corporate lawyers.

CHAPTER 7. TAINTED STOCK

7.01 The Preferred Stock Bailout. It may seem as if the exceptions in § 305(b) swallow the general rule of nonrecognition in § 305(a). To be sure, many stock dividends will be taxable under § 305(b). On the other hand, many stock dividends will be tax-free, at least those made with respect to common stock. Indeed, a pro rata distribution of common stock on common stock will always be tax-free under § 305(a), while a pro rata distribution of preferred stock on common stock will be tax-free in the absence of a companion distribution of cash or property to other shareholders.

The rule allowing a tax-free, pro-rata distribution of preferred stock to common shareholders created what has come to be known as the "preferred stock bailout." Consider the case of X Corp. having 100 shares of appreciated common stock outstanding. X Corp. has earnings and profits of $10,000 that the shareholders would like to remove from corporate solution as capital gain. Declaration of a cash dividend will not work, nor will a pro rata stock redemption. If the shareholders are unwilling to dissolve the corporation, it seems that the shareholders must recognize dividend income (without any basis recovery) according to the rules of § 301.

Suppose, though, that the corporation declares a stock dividend payable in one share of a newly-created class of $100 par preferred stock for each share of common stock outstanding. Such a distribution will be tax-free under § 305(a). If the shareholders then sell the preferred stock, they will recognize capital gain on the sale, thereby accomplishing their goal. Of course, the $10,000 has not been removed from corporate solution, but that is done easily enough. The purchaser, having a cost (fair market value) basis in the preferred stock under § 1012, simply has it redeemed, a transaction taxed as an exchange under § 302(a) and (b)(3) and producing no gain.[1]

In one sense, a taxpayer always can bail out corporate earnings and profits as capital gain by the simple expedient of selling some or all of his stock. However, if common stock is sold, the taxpayer may lose some or all of his interest in the future profits of the corporation. The virtue of the *preferred* stock bailout is that earnings and profits can be bailed out by a taxpayer without reduction

---

1. An alternate form of the preferred stock bailout is for preferred stock to be distributed tax-free under § 305(a), followed by a redemption of the preferred stock under circumstances qualifying for exchange treatment pursuant to § 302(a) via § 302(b)(1).

of the taxpayer's interest in the corporation. Further, if the preferred stock is nonvoting, the bailout will not even involve a reduction in corporate control.

The linchpins of the preferred stock bailout are (1) the tax-free distribution of stock and (2) capital gain on the disposition of the stock so obtained. Congress could have substantially eliminated these bailouts by restricting the nonrecognition rule of § 305(a); that is, impose an immediate tax liability on any distribution of preferred stock. Such an approach, though, works an unnecessary hardship on those distributions of preferred stock not constituting the first step of a bailout. Accordingly, Congress has attempted to eliminate preferred stock bailouts by hitting its other link, the capital gain on disposition of the dividend stock. In § 306, Congress has provided that much (but not all) of the preferred stock distributed by a corporation, if received tax-free by the shareholders under § 305(a), will produce dividend income if subsequently disposed of in a manner constituting a bailout.[2]

7.02 Definition of § 306 Stock. Stock subject to the disabilities of § 306—tainted stock, as it usually is called—is defined in § 306(c). Any stock other than common stock distributed by a corporation is § 306 stock if received by the taxpayer tax-free under § 305(a). The definition of § 306 stock also includes stock (other than common stock) received in a tax-free reorganization if receipt of the stock had the effect of a stock dividend. Stock exchanged for § 306 stock also will be § 306 stock if received in a carry-over basis transaction (such as in a § 351 transaction).

Because a § 306 taint will not, in general, attach to common stock, the definition of "common" stock plays an important role in § 306. Despite this, neither that section nor the regulations promulgated under it define common stock. Recall, though, that the distinction between common and preferred stock was important in the related context of § 305. For purposes of § 305, preferred stock is

> stock which, in relation to other classes of stock outstanding, enjoys certain limited rights and privileges ... but does not participate in corporate growth to any significant extent. The distinguishing feature of "preferred stock" ... is not its privi-

---

2. If the § 306 stock is redeemed, the rules of § 301 will apply directly by reason of § 306(a)(2). If the § 306 stock is disposed of other than by redemption, the amount realized generally will be taxed as dividend income by reason of §§ 306(a)(1)(A) and 306(a)(1)(D).

leged position as such, but that such privileged position is limited....[3]

This definition of preferred stock responds to the abuse presented by preferred stock bailouts. Shareholders of a corporation always can obtain the earnings and profits of their corporation at capital gains rate by selling their stock—that is the essence of the rule that treats a corporation as an entity distinct from its shareholders and which considers stock to be a capital asset regardless of corporate-level activity. The abuse of the preferred stock bailout is that shareholders will bail out the corporation's earnings and profits without recognizing ordinary income *and* without reducing their interests in the corporation.[4] In a number of revenue rulings, the Service has adopted this view of the preferred stock bailout abuse, holding that common stock for purposes of § 306 is any stock, whether voting or not, that participates without substantial restriction in corporate growth.[5]

Consistent with limiting application of § 306 to preferred stock bailouts, Congress provided an exception to the § 306 taint for distributions of stock made by a corporation without earnings and profits.[6] Since such a corporation can distribute cash or property without producing dividend income to its shareholders, the distribution of stock works no end run around the dividend rules of § 301. However, this rule permitted sophisticated taxpayers to avoid the reach of § 306 by using a pair of related corporations.

Consider individual A who owns all the stock of X Corp., a corporation with substantial earnings and profits. A creates Y Corp., exchanging the stock of X Corp. for common and preferred stock of Y. Is the Y preferred tainted under § 306? If not, sale of the Y preferred will work a preferred stock bailout of the earnings and profits of X Corp.

Observe that newly-formed Y Corp. has no earnings and profits. Thus, it would seem as if the Y preferred would not be § 306 stock. However, Congress recognized the abuse in this situation and provided that preferred stock received in a § 351 exchange is tainted under § 306 if, had money been distributed in lieu of the preferred stock, the taxpayer would have had dividend income to

---

3.   Regs. § 1.305–5(a).

4.   A question of timing arises in the preferred-stock bailout: exactly when does the bail-out occur? From the shareholders' perspective, it occurs once the dividend stock is sold because at that moment they possess the cash equal to the corporation's accumulated earnings

and profits. However, nothing yet has been distributed out of corporate solution: the bail-out is not completed until the dividend stock is redeemed.

5.   Rev. Rul. 81–91, 1981–1 C.B. 123; Rev. Rul. 76–387, 1976–2 C.B. 96.

6.   Section 306(c)(2).

any extent.[7] To appreciate the implications of this rule, one must recall the operation of § 304.

Section 304 recharacterizes as a redemption the sale of one corporation's stock to a second, related corporation. If the transferor receives stock of the second corporation in addition to cash or property, then § 304 applies only to the cash and property.[8] This hypothetical redemption is then taxed under the rules of § 302.

The interplay of §§ 306 and 304 is as follows. If our taxpayer—A—exchanges his X stock for common and preferred Y stock, *then for computing the § 306 taint on the Y preferred,* we ask how the exchange would have been taxed under § 304 had cash been used instead of the preferred stock. If any of the cash would have been taxed to A as a dividend, then the Y preferred is tainted under § 306.

In order for there to be dividend income under § 304, the redemption must fail to qualify for exchange treatment under § 302(b)(1)-(4) *and* there must be earnings and profits available to cover some or all of the distribution. Because A owns all of the stock of Y, A will fail to qualify for exchange treatment under § 302(b). Further, under the rule of § 304(b)(2), the earnings and profits of both X and Y are available to cover the distribution. In the case of A's exchange of X stock for Y stock, the Y preferred stock appropriately will be tainted under § 306.

The following problem, although technical, is worth studying closely both because it illustrates the relationship of § 306 to § 304 and because it reviews the mechanics of §§ 304 and 302. X Corp. has 100 shares of stock outstanding, 80 owned by individual A and 20 by individual B. A and C, an unrelated individual, form Y Corp. A contributes his stock of X Corp. to Y in exchange for 60 shares of Y common stock and 600 shares of Y $10 par-value preferred stock. C contributes cash of $4,000 to Y in exchange for 40 shares of Y common stock as well as 400 shares of Y $10 par-value Y preferred stock. Assume that the Y Corp. preferred stock is worth par, that the fair market value of the X stock is $100 per share, and that X Corp. has earnings and profits of $5,000. Is the Y preferred stock tainted under § 306 in the hands of A?

The transfer by A is wholly within the confines of § 351. However, if A had received cash in lieu of the Y preferred stock, the taxation of that cash would have been determined under § 304. If in these circumstances the application of § 304 would produce

---

7. Section 306(c)(3).

8. As this example illustrates, there can be an over-lap of § 304 and § 351, resolved in favor of § 304. See § 304(b)(3).

dividend income to A, then the Y preferred stock *is* tainted under § 306.

Under § 304, A's stock interest in X Corp. must be tested under the rules of § 302. Prior to the formation of Y, A owned 80 percent of X. After the formation of Y, A had no direct ownership of X Corp. but A has an indirect ownership (under the constructive ownership rules of § 318) of 60 percent of 80 percent, or 48 percent. A will fail to qualify for exchange treatment under § 302 (in this case, that is, the preferred stock of Y will be tainted under § 306) unless A meets one of the tests in § 302(b)(1)–(4).

Under § 302(b)(2), a redemption will qualify for exchange treatment if the redemption (or hypothetical redemption under § 304) reduces the taxpayer's ownership interest below 50 percent *and* leaves the taxpayer with less than 80 percent of his preredemption percentage ownership. In this case, the hypothetical redemption reduced A's interest to 48 percent, and that is both less than 50 percent and less than 80 percent of his former interest (since 80 percent of his prior 80 percent interest is 64 percent). Accordingly, A falls within the safe harbor of § 302(b)(2) and his preferred stock is not tainted under § 306.

7.03 Disposition of § 306 Stock. A taxable disposition of § 306 stock will, in general, produce dividend income to the transferor. If § 306 stock is redeemed, the amount realized on the redemption is treated as a distribution subject to the rules of § 301. Thus, if the corporation has adequate earnings and profits at the time of the redemption, the entire amount distributed can be taxed to the shareholder as a dividend.

If § 306 stock is sold, a more complex rule must be followed. The selling shareholder has ordinary income on the sale equal to the lesser of (1) the amount realized on the sale and (2) the stock's ratable share of the amount that would have been a dividend had the corporation distributed cash instead of the § 306 stock in the first place. Thus, the earnings and profits of the corporation at the time of disposition are relevant only if § 306 stock is redeemed; if § 306 stock is sold or exchanged, the earnings and profits of the corporation are relevant only as of the time of distribution of the § 306 stock.[9] In the case of a sale or exchange of § 306 stock, any amount realized in excess of the stock's share of the corporation's earnings and profits and in excess of the stock's adjusted basis is taxed as gain from the sale of such stock. § 306(a)(1). Any ordinary

---

9. Of course, if the distributing corporation has no earnings and profits at the time of distribution of the stock, it is not § 306 stock and the rules of § 306 will not apply to it. § 306(c)(2).

income arising from these rules is treated as dividend income for purposes of § 1(h)(11) providing for the taxation of qualified dividends at the rate applicable to long-term capital gain. § 306(a)(1)(D).

For example, suppose that B is the sole shareholder of X Corp. On January 1, 2007, X distributes 100 shares of preferred stock to B in a distribution that is tax-free under § 305(a). The fair market value of the preferred shares is $10 per share, and assume that B's basis in the preferred shares becomes $3 per share under § 307(a). Assume further that X has accumulated earnings and profits of $600 at the time of the distribution and that X has no current earnings and profits for the entire taxable year.

The preferred stock is tainted by virtue of § 306(c)(1)(A). Suppose that B sells her preferred stock one year later on January 1, 2108, for its then fair market value of $11 per share. B is taxed under § 306(a)(1), producing ordinary income of $600 and capital gain of $200.

These amounts are computed as follows. B's amount realized on the sale is $1,100. Under § 306(a)(1)(A), that entire amount constitutes ordinary income to B except to the extent that the "ratable share" limitation in § 306(a)(1)(A) applies.

The limitation ensures that the dividend income on disposition does not exceed the amount of ordinary income that B would have recognized had she received cash instead of the preferred shares back in 2007. Since the corporation had earnings and profits of $600 for 2007, a cash distribution of $1,100 in 2007 would have produced dividend income to B of $600. Since 100 shares of preferred stock were distributed, each preferred share has a "ratable share" of that dividend in the amount of $6. Thus, under the "ratable share" limitation of § 306(a)(1)(A), B's ordinary income is limited to $6 per share, or $600 total.

The remainder of the amount realized—$500—is first treated as a recovery of basis and then as taxable gain.[10] Since B's basis in the preferred stock was $3 per share (or $300 total), B has $200 of taxable gain. Note that the corporation's earnings and profits at the time of sale are irrelevant in this example.

However, suppose that B's preferred stock is redeemed rather than sold. Now, taxation is determined under § 306(a)(2), and the tax consequences are very different because that section provides the blanket rule that the entire amount realized is taxed as a distribution under § 301.

---

10. See § 306(a)(1)(B).

Does this mean that the entire $1,100 amount distributed is taxed as dividend income without any recovery of basis? Not necessarily, because § 301 limits the amount of ordinary income to the earnings and profits of the corporation. Note, however, that this limitation is determined by reference to the earnings and profits as of the end of the year in which the distribution takes place and *not* as of the end of the prior year. Thus, if X's earnings and profits account has decreased, the amount of ordinary income to B will be less than $600. On the other hand, if the earnings and profits account has risen, the amount of ordinary income will be greater. Indeed, if the corporation's earnings and profits equals or exceeds $1,100, X will be required to recognized the entire amount distributed as ordinary income.[11]

Section 306 contains a number of exceptions to its draconian rules. First, disposition of § 306 stock as part of the complete liquidation of a corporation is not covered by § 306. Since the earnings and profits of a corporation are bailed out at capital gains rates in a complete liquidation, there is no reason to treat the disposition of the § 306 stock in this manner as an abusive bailout. Second, the sale or exchange of § 306 stock will not be subject to the § 306 rules if the disposition terminates the shareholder's entire interest in the corporation. Once again, because earnings and profits can be bailed out at capital gains rates by selling one's stock in the corporation, completely terminating one's interest in a corporation is not an abusive bailout. Similarly, disposition of § 306 stock in a redemption will not be taxed as ordinary income if the redemption qualifies for exchange treatment as a complete termination of the shareholder's interest in the corporation or if it is part of a partial liquidation.

Suppose taxpayer T owns 100 shares of common stock in X Corp. as well as 100 shares of § 306 stock. We know that disposition of the 100 common shares will permit T to avoid the § 306 taint on disposition of the § 306 stock.[12] Can T avoid half of the § 306 taint by selling half of his common shares? This issue was raised but not settled in *Fireoved v. United States.*[13]

In *Fireoved,* the taxpayer began as one of three equal owners of a corporation. Prior to redemption of some of his § 306 stock, the taxpayer and one of the other owners sold some of their common

---

11. Section 306(a) produces the following rules of thumb: (1) if the corporation's earnings and profits are low in the year of disposition, redeem; (2) if the corporation's earnings and profits are low in the year of distribution, sell; (3) if the corporation's earnings and profits are low in both years, you can't go wrong; and (4) if the corporation's earnings and profits are high in both years, hold on to the stock until you die.

12. See § 306(b)(1)(A).

13. 462 F.2d 1281 (3d Cir.1972).

stock to the third owner, leaving the taxpayer and the other selling shareholder each with a 25⅓ percent ownership of the corporation's common stock. However, because the corporate by-laws required at least a 76 percent vote to make substantial changes, this reduction in the taxpayer's voting interest was irrelevant; in fact, the affirmative vote of all three shareholders was necessary both before and after the stock sale.

The court indicated that partial disposition by the taxpayer of his common stock should not remove a proportionate part of the § 306 taint on his preferred stock. However, the court felt that it could avoid that issue in general because, on the facts of the case before it, the partial disposition of the common stock had no effect on the taxpayer's voting control of the corporation and so should have no effect on the § 306 taint. The court's analysis of this issue was unfortunately thin.

Recall that common stock for purposes of § 306 is any stock participating without substantial restrictions in corporate growth. Only non-common stock is tainted under § 306[14] because only such stock presents the bailout abuse. As made clear in Rev.Rul. 76–387, the preferred stock bailout abuse arises whenever a shareholder is able to obtain corporate earnings and profits as capital gain without a concomitant reduction in the shareholder's interest in the future growth of the corporation. Reduction of the shareholder's voting interest in the corporation, if any, should not be relevant. Accordingly, the court's focus in *Fireoved* on the lack of reduction in voting control seems misplaced.

While the language of § 306 does not easily support the conclusion that a partial disposition of common stock should reduce a proportionate part of the § 306 taint,[15] such a rule is consistent with the rationale of § 306 (as that can be determined from examination of the statute itself). That is, a taxpayer can "bail-out" all corporate earnings by giving up all interest in future growth of the corporation. Similarly, a taxpayer should be able to bail-out *part* of the corporate earnings by giving up *an equivalent part* of his interest in the future growth of the corporation.

There are exceptions to the application of § 306 for certain transactions "not in avoidance" of Federal income taxes,[16] and

---

14. Common stock can be tainted under § 306 if it is received in exchange for § 306 stock in a carry-over basis transaction (such as a § 351 exchange). See § 306(c)(1)(C).

15. Under § 306(b)(1), the sale or exchange of § 306 stock will not be sub-

ject to the § 306 rules if the transferee is unrelated to the transferor and the transfer "terminates the *entire* interest of the [transferor] in the corporation." (emphasis added.)

16. Section 306(b)(4).

these exceptions may protect (in part) taxpayers disposing of their § 306 stock subsequent to a partial disposition of their common stock. The first exceptions applies if a taxpayer establishes that the distribution and disposition of the § 306 stock were not in pursuance of a plan having one of its principal purposes the avoidance of Federal income tax. The second exception applies regardless of the motivation behind the distribution of the § 306 stock if, "in the case of a prior or simultaneous disposition (or redemption) of the stock with respect to which the section 306 stock disposed of (or redeemed) was issued," the taxpayer establishes that the disposition of the § 306 stock was not for tax avoidance. It is this second exception that was at the heart of the taxpayer's argument in *Fireoved*.[17]

Under what circumstances should it be held that a distribution or disposition of § 306 stock did not have tax avoidance as one of its principal purposes? In *Fireoved*, the court held that a distribution of preferred stock has a tax avoidance motive even if made for a business purpose of the distributing corporation if a taxable dividend could have achieved the equivalent result. Apparently, not adopting the most expensive route possible is tax avoidance. In Revenue Ruling 80–33,[18] the Service ruled that the distribution of preferred stock had as one of its principal purposes the avoidance of Federal income tax because a taxable dividend of corporate debt could have accomplished the same business objective.

---

17. These exceptions by their terms apply only if a taxpayer "establishe[s] to the satisfaction of the Secretary [of the Treasury]" that the transactions lack a tax avoidance motive. Can a taxpayer seek to obtain the benefit of either of these exceptions in court if a prior administrative determination was not sought? This issue was raised but not decided in *Fireoved*. If the failure to seek an administrative ruling on this issue forecloses judicial review, then presumably a taxpayer cannot report a transaction as falling within one of these two exceptions absent an administrative review, even if the taxpayer believes in good faith that one of the exceptions should apply.

18. 1980–1 C.B. 69.

CHAPTER 8. LIQUIDATIONS

8.01 Introduction. Upon the formation of a corporation, a shareholder normally recognizes no gain or loss.[1] Consistent with nonrecognition is the preservation of the unrecognized gain or loss through a carryover of the shareholder's basis in the transferred assets. § 362(a). For example, if B forms X Corp. by transferring an asset with a basis of $8,000 and a fair market value of $15,000 to the corporation in exchange for all of its stock, B will not be taxed on the exchange. § 351. B will take an $8,000 basis in the stock, and X Corp. will take an $8,000 basis in the property. §§ 358, 362.

If B were to liquidate X Corp. at a time when X Corp.'s basis in the asset was $5,000, the asset had a $15,000 fair market value, and B's stock basis was $8,000, one might expect similar nonrecognition treatment. That is, neither X Corp. nor B would recognize gain and B would succeed to X Corp.'s basis in the assets of $5,000. But nonrecognition normally is not the order of the day for liquidations. Instead, a complete liquidation usually is a recognition event to both the distributing corporation and the shareholders. The distributing corporation recognizes gain (or loss) as if the distributed property were sold to the shareholders at fair market value. In the example, X Corp. would recognize a $10,000 gain. The shareholders must recognize gain or loss on the difference between the fair market value of the property received on the distribution and the shareholder's stock basis. In the example, B would recognize a $7,000 gain.

Notice that in general there is nonrecognition treatment for incorporations under § 351 and recognition treatment for liquidations. One reason for the difference may be that there is a continuity of investment when an unincorporated business incorporates often lacking in a liquidation. An incorporation usually signifies the continuation of a business in corporate form. A corporate liquidation, on the other hand, often signifies the discontinuation of the business with the assets sold or converted to personal use.

But of course that is not always the case. It may be that incorporated assets were used for some other purpose prior to incorporation or that following a liquidation the shareholders will continue the business. Congress has chosen to draw a bright line, giving nonrecognition to corporate formations while generally denying nonrecognition treatment to "disincorporations."

---

1. This assumes the absence of boot.

A liquidation presents the last opportunity to tax shareholders on any earnings and profits that the corporation has accumulated. But that reason does not explain why a shareholder will be taxed on a corporation's unrealized appreciation—particularly, as in the example, where the appreciation occurred prior to incorporation. Additionally the taxation of the shareholders in a liquidation is independent of the corporation's earnings and profits account.

In any event, a liquidation is normally treated as if the shareholders had sold their stock to the corporation in exchange for the corporation's assets. Typically, the liquidating corporation recognizes gain (or loss) as if it had sold the distributed assets to the shareholders at fair market value. § 336. Each shareholder recognizes gain (or loss) on the difference between the adjusted basis of the shareholder's stock and the amount realized. §§ 331, 1001. Finally, each shareholder takes a fair market value basis in the assets received on liquidation. § 334(a).

There is an alternative liquidation pattern that applies to the liquidation of a subsidiary into its parent corporation. See § 332. Because the subsidiary's assets remain in corporate form, the likelihood of business continuity is greater here than where individuals liquidate a corporation. A parent which liquidates a subsidiary has merely simplified the corporate structure. Accordingly, § 332 postpones the parent-corporation's recognition, requiring the parent to step into the liquidating subsidiary's tax shoes. The parent receives the liquidated assets with the subsidiary's basis. In the example, assume that B is a corporation and that the corporate asset has a basis of $5,000. Upon a liquidation qualifying under § 332, B Corp. would recognize no gain, but it would take a $5,000 basis in the asset received from X Corp. Note that B's $8,000 basis in the X Corp. stock does not play a role in this liquidation. In this liquidation pattern, the liquidating corporation normally recognizes no gain or loss. § 337.

The term "liquidation" is not defined in the Code although the regulations offer some help.[2] Essentially a liquidation is a distribution of a corporation's assets in complete cancellation of all outstanding stock. A corporation need not dissolve under state law nor adopt a formal plan of liquidation. Note that there is no requirement that assets be converted to cash—an in-kind distribution will qualify. Furthermore, there is no specific time frame during which a liquidation must be completed: A corporation might distribute its assets over a period of time and meanwhile continue some corporate activity. The longer the liquidating process and the more active

2. See Regs. § 1.332–2(c).

the liquidating corporation, the more likely it is that the Service will treat a distribution not as part of the liquidation but rather as a distribution taxable under § 301.[3]

In some cases, a liquidation may occur even when no assets are transferred. Suppose that USCO wholly owns an entity which it has treated as a corporation for U.S. tax purposes.[4] If USCO "checks-the-box" to now treat the entity as a disregarded entity for U.S. tax purposes, the check-the-box election is treated as if USCO liquidated the entity even though nothing has changed, other than filing a form with the IRS. Typically, the check-the-box election with respect to a foreign entity will be ignored for foreign tax purposes which continues to regard the entity as a corporation. An entity that is treated one way in a foreign jurisdiction (here, as a corporation) and a different way for US tax purposes (here, as a disregarded entity) is referred to as a "hybrid" entity.

8.02 Section 331 Liquidations.

(a) Treatment of the Shareholders. Section 331(a) treats a shareholder as having exchanged stock for the amount received in liquidation. This exchange treatment normally provides capital gains treatment on the difference between the amount realized and the shareholder's adjusted basis in the stock. § 1001. If a shareholder acquires stock in the liquidating corporation on different dates or at different prices, gain or loss is determined separately for each block.[5] The distributing corporation's earnings and profits account, which is vital in determining the tax consequences of nonliquidating distributions, does not affect the taxation of shareholders in a liquidating distribution.

Suppose X Corp., with an earnings and profits account of $6,000, has $5,000 of cash and an asset with a basis of $3,000 and a fair market value of $8,000.[6] B holds all of the X Corp. stock with a basis of $2,000 and a fair market value of $13,000. If X Corp. liquidates, B will recognize an $11,000 gain, the difference between the $13,000 amount realized and the $2,000 stock basis. § 1001. Assuming B is not a dealer in stock, the gain will be a capital gain despite the earnings and profits account. § 331.

---

3. Many tax lawyers use the three-year time period described in § 332 as a guide.

4. Regs. § 301.7701–3.

5. Regs. § 1.331–1(e).

6. Recall that the earnings and profits account is just that—an account. It is not synonymous with cash on hand (e.g., corporate earnings might be reinvested in the corporation which would deplete cash available for distribution but not the earnings and profits account).

Since B is treated as having exchanged X Corp. stock in exchange for X Corp.'s assets, B will take a fair market value basis in the assets received—in the example above, the basis will be $8,000 in the assets. § 334(a). Often this is referred to as a step-up in basis, but if an asset has declined in value its basis in the hands of the shareholder will be stepped-down.

Suppose in the example above that the assets were subject to a $4,000 liability. The amount received by B must be reduced to reflect the liability to which the property is subject or which the shareholder assumes. Consequently, B has a $7,000 gain on the liquidation. B's basis in the assets is still $8,000, their fair market value. Sometimes shareholders may inherit liabilities that are disputed (*e.g.,* if the $4,000 liability represented a claim for patent infringement). If a liability cannot be valued, it will not be taken into account in valuing the distributed assets.

Often the assets themselves may be difficult to value even where there are no disputed liabilities. Suppose X Corp.'s assets consisted of a contractual claim on a percentage of some other corporation's future profits. If the claim cannot be valued on liquidation, the shareholder's gain will remain open until valuation is possible.[7] However, the Service requires valuation except in rare and extraordinary circumstances.[8]

Suppose that a corporation sells its assets on the installment method prior to making a liquidating distribution of the installment notes. Although the corporation must recognize the difference between the adjusted basis and fair market value of the installment notes, a shareholder receiving installment notes in a § 331 liquidation may not have to treat the notes as part of the amount realized on the liquidation. § 453(h). Instead, the shareholders can treat payments on the notes as payments for the corporate stock, usually resulting in capital gain or loss treatment.[9] If § 453(h) is not applicable, then the shareholder must treat the fair market value of the installment note as the amount realized on the exchange of stock in the liquidating corporation.

Where liquidating distributions take place over more than one year, shareholders are permitted to recover basis before reporting

7. See *Burnet v. Logan,* 283 U.S. 404 (1931).

8. See Regs. § 1.1001–1(a); see also § 453(j)(2).

9. For § 453(h) to apply: (1) the sale resulting in the installment note must occur within 12 months of adoption of a plan of liquidation; and (2) the liquidation must take place within the same 12–month period. Installment reporting is available to a shareholder on the receipt of notes from the sale of inventory only if the inventory is sold in a bulk sale to one purchaser in one transaction.

gain (or loss).[10] For example, if X Corp. distributed $2,000 in year 1 and the remaining $11,000 of assets and cash in year 2, B recognizes no gain in year 1 and $11,000 of gain in year 2. Compare this treatment with installment reporting under § 453 which, if applicable, would have required B to pro rate the $2,000 basis between years 1 and 2. Note that if B's basis were $22,000, B's $9,000 loss could not be reported until year 2. While § 267(a)(1) usually disallows recognition of losses on the exchange of property between a shareholder and a corporation in which the shareholder owns directly or indirectly more than 50 percent of the stock, losses incurred by shareholders in complete liquidation of a corporation are exempted.

(b) Treatment of the Liquidating Distribution. Prior to the enactment of the Tax Reform Act of 1986, former § 336 codified the *General Utilities* doctrine—that a distributing corporation was not taxable on a distribution of appreciated property.[11] As discussed earlier,[12] the Tax Reform Act of 1986 largely repealed the *General Utilities* doctrine. Under current § 336(a) a liquidating corporation generally will be taxed on a distribution of property as if the property had been sold to shareholders[13] at fair market value.[14]

Note first the sweep of § 336(a). A liquidating corporation must recognize not only the post-incorporation appreciation but pre-incorporation appreciation. Suppose B forms X Corp. by exchanging property with a basis of $5,000 and a fair market value of $20,000 for all of the X Corp. stock. On the exchange X Corp. carries over B's $5,000 basis in the property under § 362(a). B will take a $5,000 basis in the X Corp. stock pursuant to § 358. If X Corp. liquidates later that same day before incurring any gain or loss, it will recognize a $15,000 gain under § 336(a) while B will also recognize a $15,000 gain under §§ 331 and 1001. B will take a $20,000 basis in the property. § 334(a).

Not only has B traded in a low basis asset for gain recognition and a high basis, but X Corp.'s gain recognition reinforces the double tax mechanism of our corporate tax system. It is one thing

---

10. Rev. Rul. 68–348, 1968–2 C.B. 141.

11. Nor could the liquidating corporation recognize a loss on the distribution of property whose basis exceeds fair market value.

12. See Section 4.04 *supra.*

13. Because § 336(a) specifies that a distribution in liquidation is taxed as if the distributed property were sold "to the distributee," a distribution of depreciable property will force the distributing corporation to treat any gain as ordinary income if the corporation and the distributee are "related" within the meaning of § 1239(b).

14. Section 336(b) provides that if property distributed in a liquidation is encumbered by a liability, the amount realized is not less than the amount of the liability.

to tax post-incorporation appreciation at the corporate-level, but is there a justification for taxing a corporation's pre-incorporation appreciation? Congress might have drafted § 336 in a manner that would exclude pre-incorporation gain from the tax base. While a provision drafted in this manner would be more complex than current § 336, Congress knows how to draft such a provision. Indeed, as discussed in more detail below, Congress drafted § 336 in a way to prevent liquidating corporations from recognizing some pre-incorporation *losses*.

Even though some pre-incorporation built-in losses are not recognized on a liquidation, a liquidating corporation generally can recognize post-incorporation and other pre-incorporation losses. Section 336(a) is different in this respect from the operation of § 311(b) dealing with nonliquidating distributions. While § 311(b) prohibits a nonliquidating corporation from recognizing any loss on a distribution, § 336(a) generally permits recognition to a liquidating corporation.

Why the difference? Perhaps the answer lies in the finality of a liquidating distribution. A full repeal of *General Utilities* would permit any distributing corporation a loss on the distribution of property with a basis exceeding fair market value. That principle should be the starting point. On a nonliquidating distribution there is a greater chance for manipulation. An on-going corporation could manipulate the realization doctrine by distributing only loss property. In a liquidation context, the opportunity for manipulation is reduced because all assets are distributed. A liquidation offers the last opportunity to recognize the built-in losses.

Regardless of the reason, § 336(a) applies to losses as well as to gains. Suppose that B owns all the stock of X Corp. whose assets have a basis of $90,000 and a fair market value of $120,000. Assume B's stock basis is also $90,000. B also holds a piece of property with a basis of $130,000 and a fair market value of $80,000. If X Corp. liquidates, it will recognize a $30,000 gain under §§ 336(a) and 1001. B will recognize a $30,000 gain under §§ 331 and 1001. Suppose instead that B exchanges the loss property for additional X Corp. stock in a transaction that qualifies under § 351. (A contribution to capital will achieve the same result). After the exchange, B's basis in the X Corp. stock under § 358 increases from $90,000 to $220,000, and X Corp.'s basis in the aggregate of assets increases to $220,000 pursuant to § 362.

When X Corp. liquidates, it is treated as if it sold the property to its shareholder for $200,000, the property's fair market value. X Corp. would recognize a $20,000 loss under § 336, and B would recognize a $20,000 loss under §§ 331 and 1001.[15] Compare these losses at both the corporate-level and shareholder-level with the $30,000 gain at each level if B did not incorporate the loss property. These losses allow both X Corp. and B to offset other income on which they would have been taxable. B now holds the loss property with a basis of $80,000, its fair market value under § 334(a). B has gladly surrendered the higher pre-incorporation basis in exchange for a double loss deduction.

This multiplication of pre-incorporation losses is addressed by two rules governing the treatment of losses. Under § 336(d)(1), a liquidating corporation cannot recognize a loss on a distribution to a "related person" if the distributed property is "disqualified property" or is not pro rata. A "related person" is defined by § 267. Accordingly, a distribution of property with a basis of $10,000 and a fair market value of $4,000 to a shareholder who directly or indirectly owns more than 50 percent of the liquidating corporation's stock would fall under the loss prevention rule.

It is odd that Congress opted to enact a special provision dealing with transfers of loss property to related persons when § 267 addresses that very problem. Instead, Congress might have opted to treat a liquidating distribution as if the property had been sold to the shareholders and allow § 267 to operate where it will.[16] In the example above, if § 267 applied to the liquidating distribution, it would deny the loss to the liquidating corporation on the deemed sale under § 336(a) since B is a related party under § 267(b)(2).

If there is a liquidating distribution of loss property to a related person, no loss is allowed to the liquidating corporation if the property distributed is "disqualified property." That term is defined in § 336(d)(1)(B) as property which is acquired by the liquidating corporation during the 5–year period preceding liquidation if the property was acquired through a § 351 transaction or a contribution to capital. In the example above, when X Corp. liquidates and distributes the loss property B transferred to the corporation shortly before liquidation, the property constitutes disqualified property. As a result, X Corp. would not be entitled to recognize the $50,000 loss on the distribution of the recently acquired property.

---

15. X Corp. and B each has an aggregate basis of $220,000 and an amount realized of $200,000.

16. Section 267(a)(1) would have to be amended to remove the second sentence which specifically denies the application of § 267(a) in a liquidation context.

However, B would seem to be entitled to deduct the $50,000 loss on the liquidation under §§ 331 and 1001.[17]

If distributed property is "disqualified property," a liquidating corporation will be denied a loss deduction even if the property declines in value while held by the liquidating corporation. Suppose all of the stock of X Corp. is owned by B. Five years after the formation of X Corp., B contributes additional property to X Corp. with a basis of $20,000 and a fair market value of $60,000. Three years later, B decides to liquidate X Corp. At the time of liquidation, this property has a fair market value of $5,000 while its basis still is $20,000. Under § 336(d)(1)(B), X Corp. appears to be precluded from recognizing the $15,000 loss. This result is curious in that the loss is post-incorporation loss rather than pre-incorporation loss.

Indeed, this loss disqualification rule is even more peculiar given the loss limitation provision in § 362(e)(2)(A) generally limiting the corporation's basis in contributed property to adjusted basis.[18] As a result, practically the only losses that § 336(d)(1)(A) will disallow are post-incorporation diminutions in value.[19]

To back up the disqualified property rule, § 336(d)(1)(B) provides that any property with a basis that is determined by reference to disqualified property will constitute disqualified property. Accordingly, if a shareholder contributes loss property to a corporation within 5 years of liquidation and prior to liquidation the corporation exchanges that property for other property in a like-kind exchange under § 1031, the liquidating corporation cannot recognize a loss on the distribution of the newly received property even though it was not contributed to the corporation in a § 351 transaction. In the absence of a rule of this type, taxpayers could circumvent the disqualified property rules by cleansing the property prior to distribution.

Suppose that a controlling shareholder of X Corp. transfers property to Y Corp., a newly formed corporation, in a transaction that qualifies under § 351. Two years after the transfer, Y Corp. is

---

17. Presumably under the right circumstances, the Service would ignore the purported transfer of the loss property to X Corp. prior to the liquidation, thereby denying B a deduction but preserving the $130,000 basis in the asset.

18. Note, however, that when multiple assets are transferred in a single transaction the limitation in § 362(e)(2)(A) applies only to limit an aggregate built-in loss.

19. If an election is filed under § 362(e)(2)(C), the incorporation of loss property can give rise to a built-in loss at the corporate level but only at a cost of losing the loss at the shareholder level. If such a corporate loss is then disallowed by operation of § 336(d)(1)(A)(ii), the pre-incorporation economic loss will never be allowed to any taxpayer.

merged tax-free into X Corp. in a transaction described in § 368(a)(1)(A).[20] One year later, X Corp. liquidates. Does § 336(d)(1)(B) apply? Note that X Corp. did not acquire property under § 351 nor did it acquire property whose basis is determined by reference to property acquired by the *liquidating* corporation in a § 351 transaction.

Suppose X Corp., a liquidating corporation, distributes property to B, a related party (e.g., a 75 percent shareholder) with a basis of $40,000 and a fair market value of $12,000. Even if the property is not "disqualified property," the liquidating corporation may be unable to recognize a loss on the distribution.

Under § 336(d)(1)(A)(i) a liquidating corporation cannot recognize a loss on a non-pro rata distribution of property to a related party. Suppose that X Corp.'s only other asset is $4,000 of cash which it distributes to C, its only other shareholder. X Corp. will not be allowed to recognize a loss on the liquidating distribution of the property since B receives all of the property and none of the cash. If X Corp. had distributed a ¾ interest in both the property and the cash to B and a ¼ interest to C, X Corp. would be able to deduct the loss on the liquidation.

A distribution of a ¾ interest in the property would give B $9,000 of property and $3,000 of cash. C would receive $3,000 of property and $1,000 of cash. This pro rata distribution of property (not disqualified property) would allow X Corp. to recognize a $28,000 loss on the liquidating distribution. Note that whether the distribution is non pro rata or pro rata will have no effect on the shareholders. Either way, B will have an amount realized of $12,000 while C's amount realized is $4,000.

Now suppose that following the pro rata distribution B agrees to purchase C's interest in the property for $3,000. If C sells his ¼ interest for $3,000, there will be no gain since C took a fair market value basis in the asset upon liquidation under § 334(a). B would use the cash received on the liquidation to make the purchase. After the liquidation and purchase, B would hold property with a fair market value and basis of $12,000, and C would hold $4,000 of cash. The only difference between this pattern of a pro rata liquidation followed by a sale and non pro rata liquidation is that if the liquidation and sale are respected for tax purposes, X Corp. will be allowed a loss on the distribution. Otherwise that loss is precluded.

20.   See Chapter 10 *infra.*

Whether the transactions will be respected would turn on the particular circumstances surrounding the transactions. If there was a preconceived and binding plan for B to purchase C's ¼ interest after the transaction, then the Service will successfully recharacterize the liquidation as a non pro rata distribution. On the other hand, if C was under no obligation to sell his ¼ interest to B following the liquidation, the transactions should probably stand for tax purposes.[21]

A corporation faced with the potential loss limitation rule of § 336(d)(1) can sell its loss property prior to liquidation and thereby ensure recognition of the loss. As might be expected, this route is sometimes discovered only after a liquidation has been set in motion. For example, a shareholder, in anticipation of the liquidation, may agree to sell the distributed property once the liquidation is completed. However, upon realizing that the distributed property has a loss in the hands of the distributing corporation that will be eliminate by operation of § 336(d)(1), the sale my be recast as a sale by the corporation with the sale proceeds distributed to the shareholder. Will a last minute conversion of a liquidation followed by sale into a sale followed by a liquidation be respected?

This issue is and its resolution is called the Court Holding doctrine after *Commissioner v. Court Holding* Co.[22] In *Court Holding Co.*, the taxpayer's only asset was an apartment building. All the stock of the corporation was owned by Minnie Miller and her husband. The corporation negotiated to sell the apartment to the lessees of the property. An oral agreement was reached as to the terms and conditions of sale. When the parties met to reduce the terms to writing, the corporation's attorney informed the purchaser that the sale could not be consummated because of the large tax that would be imposed on the seller. The next day, the corporation liquidated with the Millers surrendering their stock for the deed to the building. Three days later, the sale was completed with the Millers selling the property. Under the law then in effect (that is, prior to the repeal of the *General Utilities* doctrine), this reordering eliminated the corporate-level tax.

The Tax Court ruled that the sale had to be attributed to the corporation with the result that the corporation had a gain on the sale and the Millers were taxed on the liquidation in accordance with the rules of §§ 331 and 1001. While the Court of Appeals reversed, the Supreme Court supported the Tax Court, holding that

21. See, e.g., *American Bantam Car Co. v. Commissioner*, 11 T.C. 397 (1948), aff'd per curiam, 177 F.2d 513 (3d Cir. 1949).

22. 324 U.S. 331 (1945).

the steps of the transaction must be viewed as a whole and that the Millers could not serve as a conduit for a sale by the corporation.

On the other hand, in *United States v. Cumberland Public Service*,[23] the Supreme Court refused to recharacterize a transaction. There, shareholders first attempted to sell their stock, but the buyer refused to purchase it.[24] However, the buyer and the shareholders agreed that following the liquidation of the corporation, the shareholders would sell the assets to the purchaser. The Supreme Court upheld the lower court's factual finding that the sale of assets was made by the shareholders. Compared with *Court Holding Co.*, in Cumberland Public Service the plan for liquidation was adopted earlier in the negotiating process.

The results in *Court Holding Co.* and *Cumberland Public Service* put a premium on good tax advice since choosing the wrong form of the transaction could be costly. And while the *Court Holding* doctrine no longer arises in the specific context at issue in these two cases, the more general reordering issue and its resolution remains a mainstay of corporate taxation. Thus, if a liquidating corporation distributes loss property described in § 336(d)(1), the loss is gone forever. But if that same property is sold by the corporation prior to the liquidation, the loss will be recognized. How far along can a liquidation be before it is too late to negotiate a sale of the corporation's loss assets? For such a fact-specific inquiry, no clear line can be drawn.

There is a second rule limiting losses in connection with a liquidation. See § 336(d)(2). This rule does not focus on the relationship between the liquidating corporation and shareholders. Instead the rule can apply to liquidating distributions to any shareholders (related or not) and to sales in connection with a liquidation if the distributed or sold property was acquired by the corporation for the purpose of recognizing loss.

The rule applies to a liquidating corporation which makes a distribution, sale or exchange of property acquired in a § 351 transaction (or as a contribution to capital) if the acquisition "was part of a plan the principal purpose of which was to recognize loss on the liquidating corporation with respect to such property in connection with the liquidation." § 336(d)(2)(B). Note that the disallowance rule applies to sales and exchanges as well as to liquidating distributions.

If a corporation acquires property and then adopts a plan of liquidation within two years, the acquisition is considered to be

---

23. 338 U.S. 451 (1950).

24. Perhaps the buyer did not want to assume any undisclosed liabilities.

part of a plan to recognize a loss even if the actual liquidation takes place more than two years after acquiring the property. For example, if property is acquired by X Corp. on January 1 of Year 1, X Corp. adopts a plan of liquidation on December 31 of Year 2, and X Corp. liquidates on July 15 of Year 3, § 336(d)(2) will apply even though more than two years elapsed between the acquisition of the property and the actual distribution. Notice that the 2–year period in § 336(d)(2) is determined by reference to the date a plan of liquidation is adopted while the 5–year period of § 336(d)(1) is determined by reference to the date of the liquidating distribution.

Suppose the § 351 transaction occurs six months before a plan of liquidation is adopted, but the acquisition was not motivated by a loss recognition purpose. For example, a shareholder might contribute loss property that the liquidating corporation will use in its trade or business. Under these circumstances, the Secretary is given authority to enact regulations that will exempt this and other non-abuse transfers occurring within the 2–year period. Instead, suppose that a § 351 transfer occurs more than 2 years before a plan of liquidation is adopted. If, the purpose of the transfer *is* to allow the liquidating corporation to recognize a loss. Section 336(d)(2) might still apply since the 2–year period is merely illustrative. However the conference report states that for transfers occurring outside the 2 year period, loss disallowance will apply "only in the most rare and unusual cases under such circumstances."[25]

Where this second loss disallowance rule (i.e., § 336(d)(2)) applies, a liquidating corporation is not denied the entire loss deduction relating to the offending property. Instead, the amount of loss that can be recognized is decreased by the built-in loss at the time of the property's acquisition by the corporation. § 336(d)(2)(A). As a result, this loss disallowance rule should now play a minor role since § 362(e)(2) now generally precludes using a § 351 transaction to create a corporate built-in loss.[26] Suppose X Corp. acquires property in a § 351 transaction one year prior to liquidation. The property has a basis of $40,000 and a fair market value of $25,000 at the time of acquisition. The property continues to decrease in value, and on the date of the liquidating distribution the property has a basis of $40,000 and a fair market value of $15,000. On the liquidating distribution, X Corp. will be able to recognize a $10,000 loss—the decline in value that occurred while X

---

25. H.R. Rep. No. 841, 99th Cong., 2d Sess. (1986).

26. Corporate-level built-in losses can be created when multiple assets are contributed in a single transaction (some of which have built-in gain and some of which have built-in loss) and

Corp. held the asset. Similarly, if X Corp. sold the property for $15,000 and distributed the proceeds, X Corp. would be allowed to recognize a $10,000 loss on the sale.

It is interesting to note that in § 336(d)(2)(A) Congress evidences the ability to draft a provision that precludes a liquidating corporation from deducting pre-incorporation losses. One must ask why Congress didn't draft § 336(d) and § 311, the later dealing with nonliquidating distributions, to preclude recognition of pre-incorporation gains that are unrealized when the corporation acquires the property.

Ever vigilant that taxpayers may seek to avoid recognizing a corporate level gain thus circumventing the repeal of the *General Utilities* doctrine, Congress authorized Treasury to issue regulations where necessary.[27] For example, suppose that a corporation qualified to become a real estate investment trust (a REIT)[28] in what would normally be a nontaxable event. After becoming a REIT, the corporation could sell appreciated assets and distribute the proceeds with only a tax at the shareholder level.[29] Pursuant to § 337(d), regulations have been issued to prevent the elimination of a corporate-level gain on the appreciated property.[30] In this case, the corporation would be deemed to sell the asset, resulting in gain to the corporation and a stepped-up basis in the hands of the REIT.[31]

(c) The Corporate Triple Tax. While our corporate tax system generally seeks to tax corporate earnings twice—once when earned and once when distributed. Congress has taken steps to minimize the imposition of triple, quadruple or more taxes on corporate earnings: Section 243 was enacted to provide a dividends-received deduction for dividends received by a corporation.[32]

The repeal of the *General Utilities* doctrine created the potential for a corporate triple tax in the context of a liquidation. Suppose B owns all of the stock of X Corp., a holding company, whose only asset is all of the stock of Y Corp. P, an unrelated purchaser, wants to acquire all of Y Corp.'s assets. Assume that all of the stock and assets are appreciated in value. There are a variety

---

when an election under § 362(e)(2)(C) is made.

27. Section 337(d).

28. A REIT is a special kind of corporation that has a variety of requirements, including the type of property held (generally real estate).

29. While generally treated as a corporation, a REIT can generally deduct

dividends it pays, thereby functioning as a flow-through entity.

30. Regs. §§ 1.337(d)–6 and–7.

31. No recognition and no basis adjustment occurs for loss property—property the basis of which exceeds the fair market value.

32. See discussion at Section 4.03 *supra.*

of ways that the parties can complete the transaction. Suppose P buys the Y Corp. stock from X Corp. and then both B and P liquidate their wholly-owned corporations. P, who will take a cost basis in the purchased stock under § 1012, will have no gain or loss on the liquidation of Y Corp., but Y Corp. will recognize gain under § 336. X Corp. already recognized gain on the sale of the Y Corp. stock to P. When B liquidates X Corp., B will recognize gain in accordance with §§ 331 and 1001.

The result is a triple tax on the unrealized gain inherent in Y Corp.'s assets. Y Corp. recognizes the gain on the liquidation, X Corp., whose stock was appreciated because of the unrealized gain in the underlying assets, recognizes the gain on the sale to P, and B, whose stock has appreciated to reflect the appreciated Y Corp. stock held by X Corp., recognizes gain on the liquidation.

Suppose the transaction is structured in a different manner. Y Corp. sells its assets directly to P. Y Corp. and then X Corp. liquidate. On the sale, Y Corp. would recognize gain. When Y Corp. liquidates into its parent, X Corp., X Corp. would not recognize gain.[33] Finally, on the liquidation of X Corp., B would recognize gain. If the parties proceed in this manner, there will only be a double tax on the unrealized appreciation in Y Corp.'s assets—a tax to Y Corp. and a tax to B.

Regardless of which method is used, P ends up with the assets of Y Corp. with a fair market value basis[34] and B ends up with the sale proceeds. To allow the tax consequences to differ depending on the form raises the cost of consummating the transaction since the parties must spend more on tax advice in order to insure that they have not used the wrong form. Moreover, a triple tax would place a high cost on operation of a business in corporate form.

Congress addressed the problem by enacting § 336(e) which authorizes the Treasury to promulgate regulations that will treat a sale of stock as if the underlying assets were sold. In the example above, X Corp.'s gain on the sale of stock would be the difference between amount realized for the Y Corp. stock and the adjusted basis of the Y Corp. assets. The Y Corp. assets would then take a fair market value whether or not P liquidated Y Corp. No other gain or loss would be recognized on the sale of the Y Corp. stock by X Corp. B would recognize gain on the liquidation of X Corp. under §§ 331 and 1001. This treatment which reduces the triple tax to a double tax is available if a corporation meets substantial ownership

---

33. See the discussion of subsidiary liquidations, *infra.*

34. Under § 334(a) if the first method is used and under § 1012 if the assets are purchased directly.

tests under § 1504(a)(2).[35] Where the ownership tests are not met, it is likely that the *Court Holding Co.* doctrine may play a role in determining who sold what to whom and when. Where § 336(e) does not apply, the triple tax problem endures.

8.03 Subsidiary Liquidations.

(a) Treatment of the Parent–Corporation. Section 332 provides that no gain or loss shall be recognized by a parent corporation which liquidates a subsidiary. Congress decided in 1935 that taxation upon that event was inappropriate because the result of the liquidation would be a simplified corporate structure. Since the shareholder-parent corporation does not recognize gain or loss on the liquidation, it is inappropriate to step-up (or step-down) the basis of the distributed assets. Instead, § 334(b)(1) requires the parent corporation to take over the basis that the assets had when held by the subsidiary. The parent also inherits the holding periods of the subsidiary's assets. § 1223(2). In effect, the parent is treated as though it had stepped into the shoes of the subsidiary.

Viewed together, §§ 332 and 334(b)(1) remove any unrealized gain or loss in the parent's stock from consideration for tax purposes. Consider the following two situations:

	1	2
Parent's stock basis	$15,000	$15,000
Subsidiary's asset basis	6,000	24,000
Fair market value of subsidiary's assets	9,000	17,000

In situation 1, the parent has a potential $6,000 loss in the stock of the subsidiary. However, if the subsidiary liquidates under § 332, no loss will be recognized by the parent which will take a $6,000 basis in the asset. A sale by the parent of the asset will produce a $3,000 gain. In situation 2, the parent has an unrealized $2,000 gain on the subsidiary's stock, but will recognize no gain on the liquidation. Instead, the parent will take a $24,000 basis in the asset and will have a potential $7,000 loss if the asset is sold.

The American Law Institute has suggested one method of eliminating these types of discontinuities.[36] When a parent-corporation forms a subsidiary under § 351, normally the basis of the subsidiary's stock in the hands of the parent is the same as the

---

35. Section 1504(a)(2) imposes two 80 percent tests—one for voting control and one for total value of outstanding stock.

36. American Law Institute, Federal Income Project—Subchapter C 60–61 (1982).

basis of the assets in the hand of the subsidiary. See §§ 358 and 362. Under the ALI proposal the parent's stock basis would be set continuously equal to the subsidiary's net asset basis. Accordingly the gain or loss on the sale or exchange of the stock in the subsidiary would always equal the gain or loss on the sale of the assets. On the liquidation of a subsidiary, no gain or loss would be recognized by the parent which would then step into the subsidiary's shoes with respect to the basis in the subsidiary's assets. Unfortunately, nothing like this proposal has ever been enacted by Congress.

Section 332 does not govern every liquidation involving a corporate shareholder. Moreover, even where § 332 does apply, it governs the treatment of only certain shareholders while § 331 might dictate the treatment of other shareholders. For example, suppose X Corp., owned by B and C Corp., has assets with a basis of $60,000 and a fair market value of $100,000. B, an individual, owns stock with a basis of $6,000 and a fair market value of $20,000. C Corp. holds stock with a basis of $30,000 and a fair market value of $80,000. Upon the liquidation of X Corp. (assuming a pro rata distribution), B would recognize a capital gain of $14,000 under §§ 331 and 1001 and would have a $20,000 fair market value basis in the assets received. If § 332 applied to C Corp., it would recognize no gain on the liquidation and would take a $48,000 carryover basis in the $80,000 of assets received under § 334(b).[37]

In order for § 332 to apply, § 332(b)(1) requires that the parent own stock that (a) possesses at least 80 percent of the total voting power of the outstanding stock of the subsidiary and (b) has a value equal to at least 80 percent of the stock of the subsidiary. § 1504(a)(2).[38] The 80 percent tests must be met on the date a plan of liquidation is adopted and continuously thereafter until the final liquidating distribution. These tests are designed to distinguish a true parent-subsidiary relationship from a corporate shareholder holding stock as an investment.

While § 332 is formally a mandatory provision, the 80 percent control tests offer a de facto means of avoiding the provision's coverage if desired. A corporate shareholder whose stock basis in a subsidiary exceeds the fair market value of the assets received in liquidation may prefer the loss recognition available under §§ 331

---

37. C Corp. receives 80 percent of X Corp.'s assets and 80 percent of X Corp.'s $60,000 basis in those assets.

38. Nonvoting stock that is limited and preferred as to dividends is excluded from the calculation. Corporations often issue preferred stock to investors in or-der to raise capital. Congress did not want this use of preferred stock to spoil the benefits of § 332. But note that for purposes of control in § 351, the 80 percent tests apply to *all* classes of stock. § 368(c).

and 1001 to nonrecognition under § 332. In some circumstances it may be possible for a parent corporation to sell enough stock to fall under the 80 percent thresholds. Since § 332 does not invoke the attribution rules, the purchaser can be even a related party so long as the price paid reflects fair market value. Since there is no intent test, a motive to avoid the coverage of § 332 should not defeat this effort.[39] Conversely, a parent corporation that lacks the necessary 80 percent control can avail itself of § 332 by acquiring stock immediately before the liquidation.

If the 80 percent control tests are met, the liquidation must comply with one of two prescribed time periods. If there is a shareholders' resolution authorizing a liquidation that does not specify a time period, the liquidating distribution must be completed within the taxable year. § 332(b)(2). On the other hand, if the plan of liquidation provides for a distribution of all assets within a three year period from the close of the year during which the first distribution takes place, § 332 again will apply. § 332(b)(3).

(b) Treatment of the Subsidiary–Corporation. The same rationale that produces § 332 at the parent-corporation level creates the need for a nonrecognition provision at the subsidiary-corporation level. The tax-free contraction of a multiple corporation structure would be thwarted if the liquidating corporation's gain (or loss) were subject to recognition under § 336. Section 337 provides that no gain or loss shall be recognized to the liquidating corporation on a distribution to a corporate shareholder meeting the 80 percent ownership requirements of § 332(b).

The combination of §§ 337, 332 and 334(b)(1) means that the unrealized gain (or loss) in the assets of the subsidiary will be preserved when the assets are received by the parent-corporation. Suppose Y Corp. is wholly-owned by X Corp. Y Corp. holds assets with a basis of $10,000 and a fair market value of $16,000. X Corp. has a basis in its Y Corp. stock of $7,000. If Y Corp. is liquidated, neither X Corp. nor Y Corp. recognizes gain, and X Corp. holds the Y Corp. assets with a basis of $10,000. If and when X Corp. sells, or distributes the property the $6,000 unrealized gain may be recognized.

Where the parent-corporation is tax-exempt, nonrecognition under § 337 would be the equivalent of a permanent exclusion. For that reason, § 337(b)(2)(A) contains an exception to the general

---

39. See, e.g., *Commissioner v. Day & Zimmermann, Inc.,* 151 F.2d 517 (3d Cir.1945). But see *Associated Wholesale Grocers, Inc. v. United States,* 927 F.2d 1517 (10th Cir.1991) (transaction structured to avoid § 332 recharacterized as § 332 liquidation).

nonrecognition of § 337(a).[40] Similarly, if the parent-corporation is a foreign corporation beyond the jurisdiction of the federal tax system, the liquidating subsidiary will be taxed on the distribution of its appreciated assets that are being removed from US taxing jurisdiction.[41] Conversely, if a US parent corporation liquidates a foreign subsidiary, the US parent is subject to tax on the foreign subsidiary's earnings and profits.[42] Otherwise, the earnings and profits might never be subject to US taxation at the corporate level. Note that this treatment applies if the foreign subsidiary makes a check-the-box election to be treated as a disregarded entity.

If a subsidiary-corporation is owned by both a parent-corporation and minority shareholders, the tax consequences to the liquidating corporation will be determined under both §§ 337 and 336. Suppose the stock of Y Corp. is 80 percent owned by X Corp. and 20 percent owned by B, an individual. Suppose that Y Corp. owns assets, some with unrealized gain and some with unrealized losses. If Y Corp. liquidates, it will not recognize gain or loss on the distribution to X Corp. What about the distribution to B? Curiously, while § 336 applies to the portion of the liquidating distribution made to B, it does not apply entirely. Under § 336(d)(3), Y Corp. cannot recognize any loss on the distribution of loss property to B.

Perhaps Congress worried (if Congress worries) that a liquidating corporation would take advantage of §§ 336 and 337 by distributing a disproportionate amount of the loss property to shareholders other than the parent-corporation while distributing a disproportionate amount of gain property to the parent-corporation. Such manipulation would allow the liquidating-corporation to recognize loss while avoiding the recognition of gain. It is not clear that this result is inappropriate manipulation if in fact only the loss property is removed from corporate solution. Moreover, § 336(d)(3) denies a loss to the liquidating corporation even in the event of a pro rata distribution where there is no manipulation.

More likely, Congress elected to treat the distribution to the non-corporate shareholder as a non-liquidating distribution viewed at the corporate level. Recall that § 311 denies a loss deduction to the distributing corporation for a distribution of loss property.

---

40. If the property distributed will be used in an unrelated trade or business of the tax-exempt organization, there is an exception to the exception. Unrealized appreciation will not be recognized by the liquidating corporation since the parent-corporation will be taxed on a sale of the property. §§ 511 and 512.

41. § 367(e)(2).

42. § 367(b). Note that the liquidation of a foreign subsidiary by a US parent cannot be used to import loss property into the US because the parent will take a fair market value basis in such loss property under § 334(b)(1)(B).

Because nonrecognition in the context of a parent-subsidiary liquidation is justified by the continuation of the subsidiary's business in a simplified corporate structure, it may make sense to treat the distribution to non-corporate shareholders as non-liquidating distributions incidental to, and a part of, the larger non-liquidating distribution—in effect, the distribution to the non-corporate shareholder is treated as a distribution in redemption under § 311.

One final aspect of § 337 deserves comment. Normally when a taxpayer transfers appreciated property in satisfaction of a debt, gain is recognized.[43] However where such a transfer occurs in the context of a subsidiary liquidation, it is often difficult to trace whether appreciated property is transferred to a parent-creditor to extinguish the debt or in liquidation of the stock. As a result, § 337(b)(1) provides nonrecognition of gain or loss on the distribution of property to extinguish a debt in connection with a liquidating distribution. Section 334(b)(2) gives the parent-corporation the subsidiary's asset basis.

What if the indebtedness of the subsidiary exceeds the value of the subsidiary's assets; that is, what if the subsidiary is insolvent at the time of the liquidation? Regulations have long provided that in such circumstances § 332 does not apply to the transaction (and so § 337 does not apply as well) because there is no "property distributed incomplete liquidation" within the meaning of § 332(a).[44] As a result, the transaction is fully taxable to both parties (with the parent corporation generally entitled to a worthless security deduction under § 165(g)).[45] If the parent wishes to make the transaction tax-free, can it contribute assets immediately prior to the liquidation of the subsidiary so that the subsidiary is then solvent? Under familiar step-transactions principles, such a pre-liquidation infusion of value will be ignored.[46]

(c) Carryover of Tax Attributes. When a parent-corporation liquidates a subsidiary, nonrecognition is deemed appropriate because the corporate structure is being simplified. Generally, the tax system is indifferent as to whether a corporation conducts a business directly or through a subsidiary. The price paid for nonrecognition on a liquidation is the carryover of the subsidiary's basis in its assets under § 334(b). Consistent with this treatment, § 381(a) provides that the subsidiary's tax attributes also are absorbed by the parent. These tax attributes include net operating losses, the earnings and profits account and capital loss carryovers. § 381(b).

---

43. See, e.g., *United States v. Davis,* 370 U.S. 65 (1962).

44. Regs. § 1.332–2(b).

45. Rev. Rul. 2003–125, 2003–2 C.B. 1243.

46. Rev. Rul. 68–602, 1968–2 C.B. 135.

However, any time that one taxpayer acquires tax attributes of another taxpayer, the transaction will be closely scrutinized. In general, the Code frowns on trafficking in tax attributes where the transaction is not motivated by non-tax, business reasons. Sections 269 and 382 serve as a check on the carryover of tax attributes under § 381.[47]

47. See Chapter 11 *infra*.

CHAPTER 9. TAXABLE ACQUISITIONS

Suppose that X Corp. holds assets with a basis of $150,000 and a fair market value of $450,000, along with $102,000 in cash. X Corp. is wholly owned by B, an individual, who has a 200,000 basis in the X Corp. stock. P, an unrelated individual, wants to buy X Corp. for its fair market value. Among the acquisition choices available are:

(1) an asset purchase where either

(a) X Corp. sells its assets to P and then liquidates, or

(b) X Corp. liquidates and B sells the former X Corp. assets to P;

(2) a stock purchase where P purchases the stock of X Corp. from B and either

(a) liquidates X Corp., or

(b) continues to operate X Corp. as a corporation;

P and B also have other options. The nontaxable reorganization provisions discussed in Chapter 10 may allow B to exchange X Corp. stock for P stock (if P is a corporation) or for stock in a corporation P sets up for purposes to facilitate the acquisition. X Corp. could also merge into P or a subsidiary of P. Since a reorganization can be nontaxable, why would taxpayers ever structure a taxable acquisition? In order to qualify for a nontaxable reorganization, a taxpayer must meet stringent requirements. Often taxpayers cannot meet those requirements.

9.01 Asset Purchases. In the example above, if P buys the assets from X Corp. for $450,000, X Corp. recognizes a $300,000 gain on the sale. If X Corp. is taxable at the 34 percent rate, the tax is $102,000, which X Corp. pays with its available cash. When X Corp. liquidates, B is taxed on $250,000 of gain under §§ 331 and 1001. If B if taxed at the 36 percent rate, B pays a tax of $90,000 and ends up with $360,000. P takes a cost basis in the assets of $450,000. § 1012.[1] The same treatment occurs if X Corp. merges

---

1. If X Corp. had sold its assets to P on the installment method, upon liquidation X Corp. would have to recognize all deferred gain. § 453B. B would have to immediately recognize the fair market value of the note and would have a basis equal to the fair market value. However, if B had received the installment obligation after the adoption of a plan of liquidation that was completed within 12 months, then B would be able to recognize any gain on the stock exchanged in the liquidation as the note was paid. § 453(h).

into P Corp. with X Corp. shareholders receiving cash—a taxable merger.

Instead of selling its assets, if X Corp. liquidates and B sells the assets to P, then the tax consequences would be the same as in the previous example. On liquidation, X Corp. would recognize a gain of $300,000 under § 336, using the cash to discharge the tax liability. B would be taxed on $250,000 of gain—the difference between the 450,000 fair market value of the X Corp. assets and B's $200,000 basis in the X Corp. stock. Under § 334(a), B would take a fair market value basis in X Corp.'s assets, and upon sale to P, B would recognize no gain.

In both patterns there are two levels of taxation—a corporate-level tax on X Corp. and a shareholder-level tax on B. When there are two levels of taxation, the purchaser, P, takes a fair market value basis in the acquired assets. As explained below, it is possible to avoid a corporate-level tax on a stock sale. However, without a corporate-level tax, P would take a carryover basis, rather than a fair market value basis, in the acquired assets.

Both the seller and buyer have an interest in the allocation of purchase price to the various assets sold. For the seller, gain or loss and its character as ordinary income (loss) or capital gain (loss) is determined asset-by-asset. For the buyer, allocation of purchase price determines how much basis is allocated to inventory, depreciable assets, and to nondepreciable assets.

Historically, the parties to a sale often had adverse interests in allocating the purchase price among assets. Sellers wanted to allocate as much of the purchase price as possible to assets yielding tax-favored capital gain, such as land and goodwill. In contrast, buyers benefited from allocating as much as possible to inventory, depreciable property (e.g., buildings, equipment) and amortizable intangibles (e.g., a covenant not to compete) in order to decrease the amount of ordinary income that the buyer would have to recognize in the future. Because of these adverse interests, the Service typically respected negotiated purchase agreements that specifically allocated the purchase price to each asset sold. Both buyer and seller were bound by the agreement unless mistake, undue influence, fraud or distress were shown.[2]

However, agreements often contain no specific allocation of purchase price. In these situations the seller and buyer historically have often taken inconsistent positions whipsawing the government. For example, a buyer often allocated a portion of the purchase price to a covenant not to compete which was amortizable

---

2. See, e.g., *Commissioner v. Danielson*, 378 F.2d 771 (3d Cir.1967).

over the life of the covenant (but produced ordinary income to the seller) while the seller wanted to allocate a portion of the purchase price to goodwill which resulted in capital gain to the seller (but was not amortizable by the buyer). Also, if there was no, or little, differential between the rate of tax on capital gain and ordinary income, a seller often did not care about the allocation of purchase price and along with the buyer "ganged up" on the Service.

Section 1060 now requires a specific method of allocation that must be followed by both seller and buyer in the case of "any applicable asset acquisition." An "applicable asset acquisition" is any transfer (direct or indirect) of assets which constitute a trade or business and with respect to which the transferee's basis in the purchased assets is determined wholly by the consideration paid for the assets (i.e., cost basis). § 1060(c).

The Regulations under § 1060 divide all assets into seven classes. Class I assets include cash and cash equivalents. Class II includes certificates of deposit and foreign currency. Class III includes accounts receivable, mortgages and credit card receivables. Class IV includes stock in trade or other inventory property. Class V is comprised of all assets not in the other classes. Class VI contains most intangibles, other than goodwill or going concern value. Finally, Class VII includes goodwill and going concern value. The purchase price paid is allocated first to Class I assets based on aggregate fair market value, then to Class II assets, and so on. Within each class, the price is allocated to each asset according to fair market value. Notice that any premium paid by the purchaser above the fair market value of the "hard" assets (e.g., tangible assets and specific intangibles such as patents, and trademarks) is allocated to goodwill (and going concern value) rather than allocated proportionately to the "hard" assets.

Some of the allocation disputes under § 1060 may be lessened by the enactment of § 197. Generally, § 197 requires 15–year, straight-line amortization for all purchased intangibles. Among the assets covered by § 197 are: goodwill and going concern value; workforce in place; customer lists and other customer-based intangibles; favorable contracts with suppliers and other supplier-based intangibles; business books and records and any other information base; patents, copyrights, formulas, processes, know-how, designs and similar items; computer software; franchises, trademarks and trade names; licenses, permits and other governmental rights; and covenants not to compete.

Some assets are specifically excluded from § 197 including: off-the-shelf intangibles (e.g., computer software sold in stores); interests in tangible property leases (e.g., a lease premium); interests in debt obligations; certain intangibles requiring contingent payments (e.g., payments for a franchise based on productivity); financial interests; interests in land; and some fees for professional services (e.g., *INDOPCO*-type expenses).[3] Some intangibles, including patents, copyrights and covenants not to compete are covered by § 197 only when there is a related acquisition of the assets (or in some cases the stock) of a business.

9.02 Stock Purchases. Instead of P purchasing the assets of X Corp. either from X Corp. or from B after X Corp. liquidates, suppose that P purchases the X Corp. stock from B for $450,000.[4] On the sale, B recognizes gain of $250,000, pays tax of $90,000 and ends up with $360,000 of cash. Notice that P has acquired X Corp. and, compared with the asset purchases described above, there has been only a shareholder-level tax rather than a shareholder-level and corporate-level tax. But also notice that P has acquired (indirectly through X Corp.) assets (other than the cash) which still have a $150,000 basis. In an asset purchase, P acquires the X Corp. assets with a basis of $450,000.

Note that if P is a corporation, the same result and the same tax treatment can be achieved if P Corp. forms a transitory subsidiary, MergerCo, that merges into X Corp. with shareholders of X Corp. receiving cash in exchange for their X Corp. stock. This is known as a taxable reverse subsidiary merger.[5] In the end, P wholly owns X Corp. and the former X Corp. shareholders receive cash. Gain or loss is recognized by the former X Corp. shareholders on the transaction, but there is no corporate-level gain and the assets carry over their historic bases. A taxable reverse subsidiary merger can have advantages over a stock purchase if there are many X Corp. shareholders or some are recalcitrant when approached about a sale.

Now suppose that the purchaser, P, is an individual. If P wants to step up the basis of the X Corp. assets to $450,000, P can do so, but only if a corporate-level tax is paid. If, after buying B's X Corp. stock, P liquidates X Corp., under § 336, X Corp. recognizes a $300,000 gain on the liquidation and a tax liability of $102,000 which is paid with X Corp.'s cash. P has no gain on the liquidation

---

3. *INDOPCO, Inc. v. Commissioner*, 503 U.S. 79 (1992).

4. Although X Corp. has assets worth $552,000, if P anticipates that X Corp. will soon either sell its assets or liquidate (thereby recognizing a gain), P would be unwilling to pay more for the X Corp. stock than P would pay for the purchase of the assets directly. If P does not anticipate selling the X Corp. assets, P may be willing to pay up to $552,000 for X Corp. The actual purchase price is a function of the demand for B's stock.

5. Nontaxable reverse subsidiary mergers are addressed *infra* in Section 10.02(e).

under §§ 331 and 1001 because P's stock basis in the X Corp. stock is $450,000 which is equal to the fair market value of the distributed assets. P's basis in those assets is $450,000. § 334(a).

Obtaining a higher basis in X Corp.'s assets may be beneficial to P. If the assets are depreciable, the depreciation deductions will be larger. Even if the assets are not depreciable, P will have less gain or a larger loss deduction if the assets are sold. But what price will P pay to acquire a stepped-up basis? P can only acquire a stepped-up basis in the X Corp. assets if X Corp. recognizes a corporate-level gain on the liquidation. Normally, a taxpayer is not willing to trade immediate taxation for future tax benefits (e.g., larger depreciation deductions). However, if X Corp. has a net operating loss carryover that is about to expire, a liquidation might provide a higher asset basis at no immediate tax cost. Also if X Corp.'s assets have bases that exceed fair market value, liquidation may allow X Corp. an immediate loss which P may gladly trade for a lower fair market value basis in the assets upon liquidation.

9.03 Section 338 Elections. If P is a corporation (P Corp.) and P Corp. does not intend to liquidate X Corp. after purchasing the X Corp. stock from B, the tax consequences are the same as if P were an individual. However where P is an individual, P has a choice of recognizing a corporate-level gain and obtaining a stepped-up basis in the X Corp. assets through liquidation or holding the X Corp. assets in corporate solution with a basis of $150,000. Where P is a corporation, if P Corp. liquidates X Corp. X Corp. does not recognize a corporate-level gain and P Corp. does not obtain the X Corp. assets with a stepped-up basis. §§ 337, 332, 334(b).[6] P Corp. can obtain a stepped-up basis in the X Corp. assets if instead of purchasing B's X Corp. stock, P Corp. purchases the assets directly, but can P Corp. obtain a stepped-up basis if it purchases B's X Corp. stock?

Congress has provided P Corp. with a means of obtaining a stepped-up basis in the X Corp. assets if P Corp. purchases B's X Corp. stock, so that from a tax standpoint, P Corp. is more likely to be indifferent whether it acquires X Corp. through an asset or stock purchase. However, in order for P Corp. to obtain a stepped-up basis, X Corp. must recognize the $300,000 gain inherent in its assets.

Before looking at some of the specifics of § 338, it may be helpful to outline the provision. It applies where a corporation purchases within a twelve-month period at least 80 percent of the

6.   See Section 8.03 *supra*.

voting stock and at least 80 percent of all other stock (not including nonvoting, preferred stock, limited as to dividends) of a target corporation and makes a timely election. If applicable, § 338 deems the target corporation, X Corp. in the example above, to have sold all of its assets. And who is the deemed purchaser? The purchaser in this deemed sale is the very corporation that sold the assets—X Corp., the target corporation. In other words, X Corp. sells the assets to itself. The effect of this circular fiction is recognition of gain to the target corporation combined with a cost basis in the target's assets. In the example above, X Corp. would recognize a $300,000 gain and would take a $450,000 basis in the assets.

Note that the application of § 338 does not require P Corp. to liquidate X Corp. in order to secure a cost basis in X Corp.'s assets. If, however, P Corp. does decide to liquidate following a § 338 election, §§ 332 and 334 will apply, and P Corp. takes X Corp.'s $450,000 asset basis. To summarize, § 338 represents Congress's effort to render the form of an acquisition (stock or asset) irrelevant to an acquiring corporation.

Note that § 338 is unavailable (because it is unnecessary) if P is an individual. An individual who purchases B's stock for $450,000 could then liquidate X Corp. under §§ 331 and 336 with X Corp. recognizing a $300,000 gain (i.e., a $102,000 tax liability) and P receiving a $450,000 basis in the X Corp. assets under § 334(a). The election under § 338 is only necessary where §§ 332, 334(b) and 337 would otherwise prevent P Corp. from taking a fair market value basis in a subsidiary's basis. However, there does not appear to be a good reason why § 338 is not available to an individual purchasing stock of a corporation. The availability of § 338 would mean that an individual purchaser would not have to liquidate a corporation in order to step up (or step down) the basis of corporate assets as long as the corporation was willing to recognize gain or loss on the deemed § 338 sale.

Section 338 had greater importance prior to the repeal of the *General Utilities* doctrine when it was possible under § 338 to obtain a fair market value basis without any corporate-level recognition of gain. Under current law, P Corp. gets a stepped-up basis in the assets of X Corp. only if X Corp. recognizes a $300,000 gain. Generally, P Corp. will not make a § 338 election to recognize gain now in order to obtain a stepped-up basis that may increase tax benefits in the future.

However as noted above, there may still be situations where a § 338 election will be made. For example, suppose in the example above that X Corp. has a net operating loss (i.e., NOL) from previous years of $300,000 or more. Then if P Corp. elects under

§ 338, X Corp.'s $300,000 gain will be offset by the net operating loss and X Corp. will take a $450,000 basis in the assets on the deemed purchase. The $450,000 basis rather than a $150,000 basis may allow larger depreciation deductions thereby decreasing X Corp.'s taxable income (or may decrease gain or increase deductible loss on a sale of the assets). Even if X Corp. has an NOL from previous years, a § 338 election may not be advisable because often P Corp. may be able to use X Corp.'s NOL after P Corp. liquidates its subsidiary or perhaps X Corp. can use its own NOL against future earnings. However, if X Corp.'s NOL is about to expire, a § 338 election may provide a tax benefit.

In the international context, a § 338 election can be quite useful. Suppose that USCO purchases all of the stock of Forco. If USCO makes a § 338 election, the deemed sale by Forco is generally not subject to US or foreign tax.[7] The sale purges all of Forco's prior tax history (*e.g.*, earnings and profits account) and provides a higher asset basis for US purposes that can result in increased depreciation deductions for purposes of computing Forco's earnings and profits in the future. The reduced earnings and profits may minimize dividend treatment on any future distributions from Forco.[8] Section 338 also plays an important role in the context of S Corporations.[9]

(a) Qualified Stock Purchases. The 80 percent requirements of § 338 discussed above must be satisfied by a "qualified stock purchase." "Purchase," as defined in § 338(h)(3), in general includes all acquisitions other than those in which the purchasing corporation carries over the transferor's basis. For example, acquisitions by gift or in a § 351 transaction do not qualify. In addition, a "purchase" does not include an acquisition from a related party. § 338(h)(3)(A)(iii). The 80 percent ownership must be acquired within a twelve-month acquisition period that begins with the date of the first acquisition by purchase. See § 338(h)(1).

(b) Election. Under § 338(g)(1), an acquiring corporation can elect to treat the purchase of stock as a purchase of assets any time before the fifteenth day of the ninth month following the month in which the requisite 80 percent control is acquired. The election is irrevocable. See § 338(g)(3).

(c) Operation of § 338. The deemed sale by the target corporation to itself, set forth in § 338(a)(1), will trigger recognition. The

---

7. Forco's deemed sale is generally outside the US taxing authority. For foreign purposes, nothing has happened as § 338 is a US provision that has no foreign significance.

8. Decreased earnings and profits may also increase foreign tax credits available for USCO.

9. See Section 13.09(d) *infra*.

sale is deemed to take place at the close of the acquisition date. The deemed purchase occurs as of the beginning of the day after the acquisition date. The seller's consent is not necessary for the election because the target corporation is deemed to make the sale after the acquiring corporation makes the purchase. Gain recognized by the target on the § 338(g) sale cannot be included on the consolidated return of the purchasing corporation nor can it be included in the consolidated return of the selling corporation. Instead, typically the target must file a one-day return to reflect the § 338 deemed sale.[10] This result can be avoided if the target corporation is a member of a group of corporations filing a consolidated return. See § 338(h)(10), discussed *infra*.

In determining gain, the sale is deemed to take place at fair market value. Fair market value (termed aggregate deemed sales price, or ADSP, in the regulations) is essentially the purchasing corporation's cost of the purchased stock plus liabilities of the acquired corporation. If the purchasing corporation does not purchase all of the stock of the target (but nevertheless acquires the requisite 80 percent), § 338 will still apply with certain adjustments.

Return to our example fact pattern where X Corp. holds assets with a basis of $150,000 and a fair market value of $450,000. If P Corp. acquires all of the stock of X Corp. for $450,000 and makes the § 338 election, X Corp. recognizes a $300,000 gain, and X Corp.'s basis in its assets becomes $450,000. Suppose P Corp. purchases 80 percent of the X Corp. stock for $360,000. If the election is made, X Corp. will still get a $450,000 basis because it will still recognize a $300,000 gain.

Turning from the deemed sale to the deemed purchase, we find even more complexity. The rules contained in § 338(a)(2) and (b) determine the basis that the target has in its assets on the deemed purchase. The rules are set up to deal with two phenomena: First, a purchasing corporation may not purchase all of the target's stock, yet a full step up in basis is allowed; second, the purchasing corporation may have "nonrecently purchased stock" as defined in § 338(b)(6), which is stock not acquired by purchase within the acquisition period and is treated separately from "recently purchased stock" as defined in § 338(b)(6).

Section 338(b) uses an adjusted gross-up basis rule (AGUB) to determine the cost basis of the target's assets on the deemed

---

10. If the target is the parent of a consolidated group, the target's § 338 gain or loss can be consolidated with the income of the subsidiaries.

purchase.[11] The assets of the target are treated as purchased for an amount equal to the grossed-up basis of recently purchased stock, plus the basis of nonrecently purchased stock. In our example, we can ignore the nonrecently purchased stock component because all of the stock held by P Corp. was acquired by purchase within the acquisition period. Where P Corp. acquires all of the X Corp. stock for $450,000, § 338(b)(1)(A) and (b)(4) provide that the basis of the X Corp. assets is $450,000 (P Corp.'s basis in the X Corp. stock) _ 100 percent/100 percent, or $450,000, the same basis as if P Corp. had purchased the assets directly. Where P Corp. acquires 80 percent of the X Corp. stock for $360,000, the new basis of the X Corp. assets is equal to $360,000 (P Corp.'s basis in the X Corp. stock) _ 100 percent/80 percent, or $450,000. Note that the new basis of the X Corp. assets is the same whether P Corp. purchases 80 or 100 percent because in either case X Corp. will recognize a $300,000 gain.

The complexity worsens when nonrecently purchased stock is introduced, since nonrecently purchased stock must be excluded from the gross-up calculation. Suppose in our example that P Corp. acquires 80 percent of X Corp. stock for $360,000 during the acquisition period, and that P Corp. held an additional 8 percent of the X Corp. stock (acquired before the qualified purchase date) with a basis of $10,000 and a fair market value of $36,000 on the acquisition date. The remaining 12 percent of the stock continues to be held by B. If P Corp. elects § 338 after purchasing 80 percent of the X Corp. stock, X Corp.'s basis in its assets will equal $360,000 (purchase price of the stock) _ 92 percent/80 percent, or $414,000, plus the $10,000 basis of the nonrecently purchased stock, or a total basis of $424,000. Notice that the basis in the target's assets reflects the fact that $26,000 of appreciation has not been recognized on the nonrecently purchased X Corp. stock.

However, P Corp. can elect in the previous example to fully step up the basis of the target's assets to $450,000 by recognizing gain on the nonrecently purchased stock (i.e., the 8 percent holding). In the example, the gain would be the difference between the $10,000 basis and the $36,000 deemed sales price under § 338(b)(3) ($414,000 _ 8 percent/92 percent). The effect of this election is to increase the § 338(b)(1)(B) amount to $36,000, which, when added to the $414,000 grossed-up basis, provides a full $450,000 basis. The cost of this additional corporate-level step-up in asset basis is

---

11. The aggregate deemed sales price (ADSP) and the adjusted grossed-up basis (AGUB) may not initially be equal. For example, there may be some contingent liabilities that are taken into account in determining gain that cannot be immediately reflected in the purchaser's basis but will be reflected in basis later. Regs. § 1.338–5.

recognition of what otherwise could eventually be shareholder-level gain.

(d) Adjustments for Liabilities. Suppose in our example that X Corp.'s assets have a fair market value of $450,000 but are subject to a liability of $100,000. Further assume that P Corp. purchases all of the X Corp. stock for $350,000 (i.e., the net value of X Corp.). Section 338(b)(2) and the regulations promulgated thereunder clarify that if P Corp. makes a § 338 election, X Corp. still recognizes a gain of $300,000 and then takes a $450,000 basis in the assets it is deemed to sell to itself.[12] Any tax liability resulting from the deemed sale by X Corp. is treated as a liability that increases X Corp.'s basis on its deemed purchase.[13] In effect, the tax liability inherent in X Corp.'s appreciated asset probably reduced the cash P Corp. was willing to pay for the X Corp. stock in the same manner as a mortgage on the factory would have.

(e) Allocation of Basis. In the example above, if X Corp. holds only one asset the allocation of basis on a deemed § 338 sale by X Corp. to itself is not a problem. However, if X Corp. holds more than one asset (including intangible assets such as goodwill), allocation of basis is necessary. In general, the regulations promulgated under § 338(b)(5) require a residual method of allocation where the basis determined under § 338 is allocated to specified assets to the extent of their fair market values with any balance allocated to goodwill and going concern value. This is the same method of allocation mandated by § 1060 on asset sales.

Suppose that P Corp. purchases the stock of X Corp. from its shareholder B. The stock has a basis of $200,000 and a fair market value of $600,000. P Corp. pays $900,000 in exchange for the stock and B's covenant not to compete for five years. Under § 197, P Corp. must amortize the amount paid for the covenant not to compete over the statutory 15–year period rather than the 5–year period of the covenant itself. Note that because the X Corp. assets carry over their bases when P Corp. purchases the X Corp. stock from B, § 197 does not permit X Corp. to amortize any amount allocated to goodwill even though X Corp.'s assets may be stepped-up for accounting purposes. If P Corp. makes a § 338 election, § 197 will apply to X Corp.'s deemed sale to itself. Any amount of the purchase price allocated to goodwill or other intangibles will be amortizable over a 15–year period.

(f) Consistency Requirements and Deemed Elections. Sections 338(e) and (f) present purchasing corporations with an all-or-

---

12. Regs. § 1.338(b)–1(c).   **13.** Regs. § 1.338(b)–1(f).

nothing choice regarding § 338. If a § 338 election is made, it applies not only to the target corporation but also to any "target affiliates" (as defined in § 338(h)(6)) whose stock is purchased during the "consistency" period. § 338(f). The consistency period basically is a three-year period that includes a year before the acquisition period, the twelve-month acquisition period itself, and a one-year period following the acquisition period. § 338(h)(4). Moreover, if a purchasing corporation does not make a § 338 election, it will be deemed to have made an election if during the consistency period it acquires any asset of the target or an affiliate. § 338(e). This deemed election prevents a purchasing corporation from stepping up the basis of desired assets by purchasing them directly while preserving the basis of other assets (and perhaps avoiding gain) by not electing § 338.

Notwithstanding the statutory requirement of a deemed § 388 election, the regulations take a completely different approach, providing instead that no election under § 388 is deemed made. Suppose as example 1 that Seller Corp. sells all of the stock of Target Corp. to Acquiring Corp. Suppose that Seller's basis is $100 and the fair market value is $130. The sale will produce a $30 gain to the selling group, and no step-up in basis unless Acquiring Corp. makes a § 338 election. Suppose instead as example 2 that prior to the sale, Acquiring purchases a single asset from Target that has a basis of $10 and a fair market value of $40. Acquiring then purchases the stock from Seller Corp. If Seller and Target file a consolidated return the $30 gain on the sale of the asset will automatically increase Seller's stock basis so that no gain would be recognized on the sale. In total, the selling group recognizes $30 of gain (as in example 1) but now Acquiring has a $40 rather than a $10 basis in the purchased asset.

The § 338 regulations no longer permit the Service to impose a deemed § 388 election in example 2.[14] Instead Acquiring is required to take a carryover $10 basis on the asset purchase—thus achieving parity with the straight-forward purchase of Target's stock in example 1. Note that if Seller does not file a consolidated return with Target so that the basis in Target's stock is not stepped up, then the consistency rule will not apply.

Arguably, the regulations are completely inconsistent with the statutory language in § 338 and might therefore be invalid,[15] but who will raise the issue? Note that the rule adopted by the regulations is favorable to Purchase Corp. because it is not saddled with an unwanted § 338 election.

14. Regs. § 1.338–8(a), (d).   **15.** But see § 338(e)(2)(D).

(g) Acquisition of a Subsidiary From a Consolidated Group. There is an election available under § 338(h)(10) that overlaps somewhat with § 336(e). Suppose Target Corp. holds assets with an aggregate basis of $400,000 and a fair market value of $1.5 million. Target Corp. is owned by Parent Corp. which has a stock basis of $200,000 in the Target Corp. stock. Parent Corp.'s stock is held by individual shareholders. Purchase Corp. wants to acquire Target Corp. and to step up the basis of the of the assets acquired. The shareholders of Parent Corp. want to end up with $1.5 million of cash.

If Purchase Corp. bought the assets from Target Corp. directly, Target Corp. would recognize a $1,100,000 gain. There would be no further gain under §§ 332 and 337 if Parent Corp. then liquidated Target Corp. On the liquidation of Parent Corp., the individual shareholders would recognize a shareholder-level gain. In total, Purchase Corp. ends up with a stepped-up basis and the individual shareholders end up with cash at the cost of a corporate-level and shareholder-level tax. The same consequences occur if Target liquidates into Parent which then liquidates, distributing the assets to the individual shareholders. The liquidation of Target would be tax-free, but the liquidation of Parent would generate corporate-level gain under § 336 and shareholder-level gain under §§ 331 and 1001. The basis of the assets in the hands of the shareholder would be fair market value under § 334 so that no further gain would be recognized on the sale of the assets to Purchase Corp. Again the result is one corporate-level tax and one shareholder-level tax.

Now suppose that Parent Corp. sells the stock of Target Corp. to Purchase Corp. for $1,500,000, so that there is a $1,300,000 gain which must be recognized by Parent Corp. If Parent now liquidates, there will be a shareholder-level gain on the distribution of the $1.5 million. Again in the aggregate, there is a corporate-level and shareholder-level gain. But note that because Purchase Corp. acquired stock of Target, Purchase Corp. does not obtain a stepped-up basis in Target's assets. If Purchase Corp. elects to have § 338 apply, the basis of Target's assets will be stepped-up, but Target Corp. would recognize a $1,100,000 gain on the deemed sale of both assets to itself. That is, there would be two levels of corporate tax (as well as a shareholder-level tax) in order for Purchase to get a stepped-up basis.

However, if § 338(h)(10) is elected, Parent Corp. does not recognize gain on the sale of stock. Instead, only Target Corp. will recognize gain ($1,100,000) on the deemed asset sale. In order for § 338(h)(10) to apply, Parent Corp. and Target Corp. must be members of an affiliated group,[16] the purchaser of stock must be a corporation, and both Purchase Corp. and the consolidated group must make the election. Pursuant to the election, Target is treated as selling its assets to Purchase Corp. and then liquidating into Parent Corp in a tax-free § 332 liquidation. Parent Corp. recognizes no gain or loss on the sale of its stock. Purchase Corp. is treated as purchasing Target's assets as of the beginning of the day after the acquisition date. Gain or loss on the § 338(h)(10) sale is reported on Parent's consolidated tax return.[17]

9.04 Expenses in Connection with an Acquisition. In *INDOPCO, Inc. v. Commissioner*[18] the Court ruled that expenses for investment banking, legal fees, etc. incurred during a friendly merger were not ordinary and necessary business expenses and, therefore, not deductible under § 162(a). Instead, the expenses had to be capitalized.[19] *INDOPCO* recognized two categories of acquisition expenses which must be capitalized because they produce long term benefits: (1) benefits generated by the resources of the acquiring company; and (2) benefits obtained by a target on becoming a wholly-owned subsidiary instead of a publicly-held corporation (e.g., avoiding extensive disclosure requirements).

INDOPCO addressed the deductibility of expenses incurred in a friendly takeover. Do the same rules apply to a hostile takeover? Presumably, the *INDOPCO* test should apply: capitalization is required if long term benefits are created. If expenses are incurred primarily to protect rather than to acquire property, a deduction may be appropriate. For example, expenses incurred by a corporation to defend itself in a proxy contest are deductible.[20] Costs associated with specific defensive strategies, such as negotiating with a "white knight," counter-tender offers, poison pill plans, and corporate charter amendments, however, are generally nondeductible capital expenditures if the plans are implemented. If the plans are abandoned, a loss deduction should be permitted under § 165(a).[21] The full scope of *INDOPCO* is being worked out in IRS rulings and court decisions. For example, in *Wells Fargo & Co. v.*

16. Reg. § 1.338(h)(10)–1(d)(1).

17. Even if § 338 is not elected or the § 338(h)(10) election is not made because some of the requirements of that subsection are not met, Parent Corp. can in some cases rely on § 336(e) to report a single gain of $1,100,000. For example, if P, an individual, rather than Purchase Corp. buys the Target Corp. stock, § 336(e) may cause the seller to recognize a $1,100,000 gain rather than a $1,300,000 gain.

18. 503 U.S. 79 (1992).

19. Under § 197(e)(8), these expenses are not subject to amortization.

20. See e.g., Rev. Rul. 67–1, 1967–1 C.B. 28. But see, e.g., Regs. § 1.212–1(k) (expenses to defend title to property must be capitalized).

21. See *Lychuk v. Commissioner*, 116 T.C. 374 (2001).

Commissioner,[22] the court allowed a deduction for officers' salaries and a portion of legal and investigatory expenses incurred in connection with an acquisition.

9.05 Corporate Acquisitions and the Use of Debt. An acquiring corporation may choose to finance the acquisition of a target corporation in several ways including: (1) debt; (2) its own retained earnings; (3) or with new equity contributed by investors.

(a) Stock Acquisitions out of Retained Earnings. If a purchaser uses retained earnings to acquire a target corporation, there are no tax consequences to the shareholders of the purchaser. Shareholders of the target recognize gain or loss on the sale of their shares. Earnings of the target corporation which are distributed as dividends to a purchasing corporation often do not result in tax liability because of either the dividends-received deduction or consolidated return rules.

(b) Debt Financed Stock Acquisitions and Leveraged Buyouts. A purchasing corporation which finances a buyout with debt may use either its own assets or the assets of the target corporation as collateral. When the target's assets are used as collateral, the transaction is often called a "leveraged buyout." In a leveraged buyout, the target corporation may pay the debt obligation out of its cash flow, or the purchasing corporation may sell assets of the target and use to the proceeds to retire the debt. Depending on the degree of leverage and security involved, the debt can range from investment grade to "junk" bonds.

A leveraged buyout is a taxable transaction for the shareholders of the target corporation. Target shareholders recognize gain or loss on the sale or exchange of their shares. At the corporate level, there are no immediate tax consequences. An important consequence of the leveraged buyout is that some of the equity of the target corporation is replaced with debt. As a result, corporate income formerly paid to shareholders as nondeductible dividends is transmuted into deductible interest paid to creditors. Consequently, after a leveraged buyout a corporation may have little taxable income or may claim losses which after an NOL carryback may result in a refund of taxes paid in prior years.[23] Creditors are taxable on any interest received. The effect of a leveraged buyout is a reduction of corporate-level tax, and a redistribution of income from equity holders to debt holders.

---

22. 224 F.3d 874 (8th Cir.2000).

23. But see the discussion of CERTs below.

Consider the following example. X Corp. with 99,000 shares of stock outstanding and no debt, has $750,000 annual income. Assume that X Corp.'s federal income tax is $255,000 ($750,000 _ .34), leaving $495,000 of after-tax income or earnings of $5 per share. Assume that X Corp.'s stock trades at $40 per share (or 8 _ earnings per share). X Corp. is acquired in a leveraged buyout in which the acquirors pay $60 per share of stock, or 50 percent more than the price at which the stock has been trading on the market, for a total price of $5.94 million. Taxable selling shareholders recognize gain or loss on the sale of their shares.

The acquirors put up $440,000 of their own funds and raise the remaining $5.5 million of the purchase price by issuing notes paying 12 percent interest to be secured by the assets of X Corp. The annual income of X Corp. after the leveraged buyout is unchanged.

The distribution of the operating income of X Corp. before and after the leveraged buyout is as follows:

	Before	**After**
X Corp. shareholders	$495,000	$0
Bondholders	0	660,000
Acquirors	0	59,400
Corporate income taxes	255,000	30,600
Total operating income	750,000	750,000

The leveraged buyout has redistributed the income stream of X Corp. The acquirors of X Corp., rather than all of the shareholders (in the case of a distribution with respect to stock) or the continuing shareholders of X Corp. (in the case of a stock redemption) receive the profit of $59,400. X Corp. shareholders who before the transaction received $495,000 a year in dividends now receive no distributions. New bondholders receive interest of 12 percent on $5.5 million, or $660,000. This is one third more than the entire amount of X Corp.'s after-tax income before the leveraged buyout, even though the operating income of X Corp. is the same before and after the leveraged buyout.

The taxable income of X Corp. has, however, been reduced from $750,000 to $90,000 ($750,000 minus $660,000) because most of the income of the company is paid out to investors as interest rather than dividends. Federal income taxes are thereby reduced from $255,000 to $30,600. Acquirors make an after-tax profit of $59,400 (pre-tax profit of $90,000 reduced by Federal income tax of $30,600), a 13.5 percent return on their $440,000 equity investment. The income tax reduction of $224,400 exactly pays for the increased returns to investors (bondholders and shareholders) as a result of the leveraged buyout. Depending on whether the increased investor returns are paid to taxable shareholders or holders of debt, there may be an increase in investor-level Federal income taxes paid.

The engine that drives this example is the assumption that the X Corp. stock initially sells for $40 per share and can be redeemed for $60 per share. Is this a realistic assumption? The example assumes that X Corp.'s pre-tax borrowing cost is 12 percent; presumably its rate of return on investment would be higher than 12 percent. Even assuming that the rate of return on investment is 12 percent, X Corp.'s assets should be worth $6,250,000 ($750,000/ .12) to produce the assumed annual pre-tax profit of $750,000. Yet, the market seems to value the corporation at only $3,960,000 (99,000 shares x $40 per share).

Why might the market value of X Corp. be so much below its asset value? There may be a host of reasons. Perhaps the expected cost of a corporate level tax is one reason. Also, stock may be undervalued because of information failure in the market place or perhaps the assets are not efficiently deployed and transactions costs prevent a more efficient deployment.

In any case, the example not surprisingly shows that if you can borrow at 12 percent to make an investment (i.e. X Corp. stock) which provides a return of almost 19 percent ($750,000 income â (99,000 shares x $40 per share)), it's a good deal.

Notice that in this example the government receives less in taxes when debt is used. The example assumes that the benefits of this tax reduction are shared by the shareholders and the debt holders. However, as noted in Section 1.03 *supra,* the reduction in taxes might also inure to employees, suppliers, customers, etc. Regardless of who benefits from the tax reduction, tax liability is lowered through the use of debt.

(c) Risks of Excessive Corporate Debt. Corporations with high debt ratios must devote large portions of their income to meet interest payments. If the corporation's income decreases or its costs increase, then the corporation may be forced to sell assets, reduce its workforce, and delay or cut back capital expenditures and expansion. If such actions cannot provide sufficient income to meet interest obligations, then the corporation may be forced into bankruptcy, resulting in significant transaction costs.

In the late 1960s, Congress became concerned about the use of debt in corporate acquisitions, and enacted § 279 to discourage leveraged buyouts. Section 279 disallows an interest deduction to an acquiring corporation on specified "corporate acquisition indebtedness." Corporate acquisition indebtedness is a debt obligation issued by an acquiring corporation to purchase a specified amount of stock or assets (i.e. two thirds of the value of the trade or business assets) of another corporation if (1) the obligation is subordinated to trade creditors or unsecured creditors; (2) the obligation is convertible into stock of the issuing corporation; and (3) the ratio of debt to equity exceeds 2:1 or the projected earnings of the acquiring corporation do not exceed three times the interest paid or incurred with respect to the obligation.

Section 279 does not apply if any one of the requirements is absent. If all requirements are met, then § 279 denies an interest deduction in excess of $5 million paid on such corporate acquisition indebtedness. For example, at a 7 percent interest rate, a corporation could have more than $70 million of debt outstanding without triggering § 279.

After the stock market slump of 1987, Congress again acted to curb the use of debt in corporate acquisitions. An interest deduction may be denied to issuers of any "applicable high yield discount obligation." Such obligations usually have an issue price that is significantly lower than their redemption price. The spread between the issue and redemption prices is the original issue discount (OID). Normally, an OID bond issuer accrues and deducts the spread over the life of the bond even though payment is not made until maturity. §§ 1272–1273. A "payment in kind" (PIK) bond is a related instrument in which payments are made in the form of debt or stock of the issuer instead of cash. High yield and PIK bonds are attractive to issuers because they provide deductions before any cash outlay is made.

Section 163(e)(5) divides the OID amount on these bonds between interest that is deductible only when paid and a disqualified portion of interest for which no deduction is allowed, but which may qualify for a dividends received deduction for corporate lenders. The result is a compromise between treating the instrument as debt and treating it as equity. An "applicable high yield discount obligation" is an instrument with: (1) a maturity date of more than five years, (2) a yield at maturity that is at least 5 percentage points higher than a designated federal rate, and (3) a "significant original issue discount." § 163(i).

Congress was also concerned with the perceived abuse of tax refunds to finance leveraged buyouts. Often tax refunds were generated by the acquiring corporation's net operating losses (NOLs) being carried back for 3 taxable years. § 172. With debt financed acquisitions, interest deductions often generated the NOLs that provided the refund. Section 172(h) limits the carryback of NOLs if the losses are created by interest deductions attributable to a "corporate equity reduction transaction" (CERT). A CERT is a "major stock acquisition" or an "excess distribution." A "major stock acquisition" is a planned acquisition by a corporation of at least 50 percent of the voting power or value of stock in another corporation. § 172(h)(3)(B). An "excess distribution" is an unusually large distribution relative to the distributing corporation's distribution history or net worth. § 172(h)(3)(C). When the CERT limitation applies, interest attributable to the CERT (which can occur up to two years after the CERT) cannot be carried back to a year before the CERT.[24]

Congress has enacted a variety of other provisions—not necessarily related to debt-financed acquisitions—that were enacted to curtail perceived corporate acquisition abuses. For example, § 162(*k*) denies a deduction for any amount paid or incurred by a corporation to redeem its own stock.[25] This provision is aimed at "greenmail" payments made by a corporation to a potential corporate "raider" to repurchase the "raider's" stock. Furthermore § 5881 imposes an excise tax of 50 percent on any gain or other income realized by the greenmail recipient.[26]

Section 280G disallows deductions for certain "golden parachute" payments designed to soften the landing of management replaced by new owners in the event of a takeover or other specified event. Some have argued that "golden parachutes" are helpful to shareholders by allowing management to evaluate takeover offers free of financial concerns. Section 280G disallows a deduction for payments to a "disqualified individual" (i.e., officer shareholder or other highly compensated individual), if the payment is contingent on a change of ownership or control and the payment exceeds three times the taxpayer's annual average compensation for the five-year period preceding the change of control. A companion provision, § 4999, imposes an excise tax on 20 percent of the payment a golden parachute recipient.

Section 382, discussed in more detail in Chapter 11, does not attempt to increase the direct cost of corporate acquisitions. Instead, this provision limits the ability of acquiring corporations to use net operating losses of the acquired corporation to offset future income, thereby decreasing the attraction of some corporate takeovers.

---

24. A de minimis rule provides that the limitation applies only if the interest expense in question exceeds $1 million. § 172(h)(2)(D).

25. See Chapter 5 *supra* for a discussion of redemptions. Even before the enactment of § 162(k), it was highly doubtful that such payments were deductible.

26. "Greenmail" is defined as consideration paid by a corporation in redemption of its stock held for less than two years if the holder threatened a public tender offer.

CHAPTER 10. REORGANIZATIONS

10.01 Introduction. The subject of corporate reorganizations is hard to define. In its narrowest sense, corporate reorganizations include only those transactions described in § 368(a)(1); i.e., the so-called A (described in § 368(a)(1)(A)) through G (described in § 368(a)(1)(G)) statutory tax-free reorganizations. More broadly, however, the term encompasses all corporate rearrangements by which the assets of a corporation are transferred to a new corporate entity or are retained by the corporation but controlled by new shareholders.

We adopt the broader interpretation of the term "reorganization" here not only because most tax lawyers use it that way (allowing them to speak of tax-free reorganizations without redundancy as well as of taxable reorganizations without contradiction), but because it is pedagogically better: the statutory reorganizations constitute some but not nearly all the ways of rearranging corporate structures. Sometimes meeting the requirements of § 368(a)(1) will be easily accomplished and will provide the most favorable results. In such cases, the corporate rearrangement will be accomplished by means of a "corporate reorganization" in its narrowest sense. Often, though, meeting the dictates of § 368(a)(1) will be difficult, expensive, or impossible, and in such cases other methods will have to be adopted. In addition, it may well be the case that the tax treatment provided by the reorganization provisions (once again in the narrow sense) may not be what the taxpayer desires, and then a plan must be adopted which deliberately runs afoul of the § 368(a)(1) definitions.

You are already familiar with a number of corporate rearrangements. The bulk sale of a corporation's assets followed by a liquidating distribution of the proceeds is a taxable corporate rearrangement, taxable at both the shareholder and corporate levels.[1] The sale of all the stock of a corporation accomplishes much the same result but is only partially taxable: a shareholder-level tax is imposed on the sale but corporate-level tax may be avoided. Indeed, you are also familiar with a fully tax-free corporate rearrangement: the liquidation by a parent of its wholly-owned subsidiary.[2]

The reorganizations defined in § 368(a)(1) are, in tax effect, most similar to the liquidation of a wholly-owned subsidiary be-

---

1. See Chapter 9 *supra.*   **2.** See Section 8.03 *supra.*

cause the § 368(a)(1) reorganizations can be tax-free at both the corporate and shareholder levels. The shareholder-level taxing provision is § 354(a)(1), providing (with some limitations) for the tax-free exchange of stock or securities of one corporation for stock or securities of another corporation if both corporations are "parties" to a reorganization. The corporate-level taxing provision is in § 361, providing in a complicated way (and with some exceptions) for tax-free treatment to the transferor-corporation in a statutory reorganization. The transactions covered by these sections, the statutory reorganizations, are set-out in § 368(a)(1) (though modified by other parts of § 368). Note that § 368 is a definitional section only: nowhere in § 368 are the tax implications of a reorganization mentioned. The importance of § 368 is that many other sections (e.g., §§ 354 and 361) are triggered by transactions meeting the definitions contained in § 368.

Most broadly, reorganizations can be divided into four groups: (1) amalgamating reorganizations in which two or more corporations are combined into a single corporate structure; (2) divisive reorganizations in which a single corporation is divided into two or more companies; (3) single-party reorganizations in which one corporation undergoes a substantial change in financial structure or modifies its place of incorporation or other similar corporate characteristic; and (4) bankruptcy reorganizations in which a distressed corporation seeks to improve its financial position. In terms of § 368, the amalgamating reorganizations consist of the types A through C as well as some D's; the divisive reorganizations include the remainder of the D's as well as transactions described in § 355 though not falling within the definitions of § 368(a)(1); the single party reorganizations are the types E and F; and the bankruptcy reorganization is the G.[3]

The one unifying aspect of the statutory reorganizations is that of *continuity of interest*. The various definitions in § 368 seek to provide tax-free treatment to corporate rearrangements in which the shareholders continue their investment in modified form. The rationale for tax-free treatment of such reorganizations is the same as that for § 351 incorporations: not enough is changed by the transaction to warrant immediate imposition of tax. You will have to decide for yourself whether you think the lines drawn in § 368 properly distinguish mere changes in form not warranting taxation from sales and other rearrangements that are fully taxable.

---

3. We consider only the tax (and not bankruptcy) aspects of bankruptcy reorganizations.

With few exceptions, the Code provisions specially applicable to the statutory reorganizations do not distinguish among the various types described in § 368(a)(1). Accordingly, it is customary to investigate the various definitions as a group and then consider the tax implications common to all. Before beginning that investigation, recall what we have already learned about the statutory reorganizations: if the detailed provisions of § 368(a)(1) are met, taxation may be avoided at both corporate and shareholder levels.

10.02 Amalgamating Reorganizations: Definitions

(a) "A" Reorganizations. The terms of the A reorganization are beguilingly simple, seemingly applicable to all mergers and consolidations effected pursuant to federal, state or other local law. However, the courts and the regulations have long recognized that a merger or consolidation should be limited to combinations of two or more corporations into a single, combined entity in which the prior owners of the separate corporations maintain a significant ownership interest. For example, a statute will be considered to be a "merger" statute in this context only if it provides that all of the assets of the merging corporations will be combined into a single, surviving entity and all of the other combining entities cease to exist. Regs. § 1.368–2(b)(1)(ii). Thus, a transaction dividing one corporation into two does not become a tax-free "merger" simply because an accommodating legislature puts the word "merger" in the title of the statute. Regs. § 1.368–2(b)(1)(iv) (example 1).

The judicial gloss on the A reorganization is exceedingly thick. Some statutory mergers and consolidations may be little more than outright sales of corporate assets evidencing no continuity of investment, and the courts have struggled to separate those corporate rearrangements deserving of tax deferral from sales and similar transactions habitually taxed in full. In such circumstances what is at stake often is whether the transaction will be tax-free at the corporate-level.

For example, suppose that X Corp. will merge into Y Corp., with the shareholders of X Corp. exchanging their X Corp. stock for cash and preferred stock of Y. Suppose further that for each share of X stock turned in, a shareholder will receive cash of $90 and one share Y Corp. preferred stock worth $10. While the transaction is structured as a merger, the effect of the transaction is to cash out all but 10 percent of the X shareholders' investments.

Long ago, the Supreme Court held that such a transaction could not qualify as a statutory "reorganization" despite meeting the literal language of § 368(a)(1) (or of its ancestors). The Court held that transactions qualifying as tax-free reorganizations must meet both the language and the spirit of the reorganization provisions. This willingness to look beyond the confines of the Code for the definition of a reorganization remains with us today, in both the case law and in the regulations. No clearer statement can be made than that found in Regs. § 1.368–1(b):

> In order to exclude transactions not intended to be included, the specifications of the reorganization provisions of the law are precise. Both the terms of the specifications and their underlying assumptions and purposes must be satisfied in order to entitle the taxpayer to the benefit of the exception from the general rule. Accordingly, ... an ordinary dividend is to be treated as an ordinary dividend, and a sale is nevertheless to be treated as a sale even though the mechanics of a reorganization have been set up.

For example, in *Pinellas Ice & Cold Storage Co. v. Commissioner*,[4] the Supreme Court held that a transfer of corporate assets in exchange for cash plus well-secured promissory notes payable in less than four months could not qualify as a "reorganization." Similarly, in *Le Tulle v. Scofield*,[5] it was held that a transfer of corporate assets in exchange for cash plus bonds payable over 11 years failed to be a tax-free reorganization. The Supreme Court indicated that the hallmark of a reorganization was a continuing proprietary interest by the shareholders of the transferor-corporation[6] in the continuing venture. According to the Court, neither cash nor bonds could supply this essential ingredient.

On the other hand, the Supreme Court upheld the tax-free status of a transfer of corporate assets in exchange for what amounted to $540,000 in stock and $425,000 in cash. Although the stock interest received by the shareholders of the transferor-corporation left them with a minority interest in the ongoing venture (their equity interest represented about 7.5 percent of the transferee's outstanding stock), the Court concluded that the need for a continuing proprietary interest was satisfied because a "material part" of the *consideration* was an equity interest in the transferee.[7]

---

4. 287 U.S. 462 (1933).

5. 308 U.S. 415 (1940).

6. The acquired corporation in a reorganization is variously called the "transferor-corporation" (when it transfers all or substantially all of its assets to the acquiring corporation) and the "target" corporation. Similarly, an additional name for the acquiring corporation is the "transferee-corporation."

7. *Helvering v. Minnesota Tea Co.*, 296 U.S. 378 (1935). If at least 50% of the consideration received is stock of the transferee, continuity should exist. See Rev. Rul. 66–224, 1966–2 C.B. 114, Rev. Proc. 77–37, 1977–2 C.B. 568.

This continuity of proprietary interest doctrine, despite springing from well-founded concerns, has taken some peculiar turns. For example, in *John A. Nelson & Co. v. Helvering*,[8] it was held that receipt of cash of $2 million plus preferred stock worth $1.25 million satisfied the continuity of proprietary interest doctrine even though the preferred stock was redeemable and nonvoting. While the shareholders of the transferor-corporation formally retained an equity interest in the ongoing venture, surely their relationship to the transferred assets became extremely remote.

Compare *Roebling v. Commissioner*,[9] involving a corporation which had leased its assets to a second corporation pursuant to a 900 year lease with rent set at $480,000 per year. The lessor corporation was merged into the lessee, and the shareholders of the lessor received 100 year bonds of the surviving corporation paying interest of $480,000 per year. It was held that this transaction did not qualify as a tax-free reorganization because the shareholders of the lessor failed to acquire a "proprietary" interest in the continuing venture. Rather than asking whether the relationship of these shareholders to the transferred assets became too tenuous or remote (and surely it did not, as no real change was effected by the transaction), the court in *Roebling* applied an arbitrary rule (no stock consideration means no proprietary interest) to tax the transaction.

The Supreme Court in *Paulsen v. Commissioner*[10] addressed the merger of two savings and loan associations, one a state-chartered association authorized to issue "guaranty stock" to its owners and the other a federally-chartered mutual association having no stock of any kind. The federally-chartered association was the survivor corporation of the merger, and the shareholders of the state-chartered association exchanged their guaranty stock for passbook accounts and certificates of deposit as part of the transaction.

The Commissioner argued that the transaction was not a tax-free reorganization because the consideration received by the shareholders of the transferor-corporation consisted exclusively of debt interests in the continuing venture. The Supreme Court upheld the Commissioner's position, saying that the transaction failed to satisfy the continuity of proprietary interest doctrine. Note that the shareholders received as much of a proprietary interest in the transferee as was possible: the federally-chartered institution had no stock.

---

8.   296 U.S. 374 (1935).   **10.**   469 U.S. 131 (1985).

9.   143 F.2d 810 (3d Cir.1944).

By itself, the *Paulsen* decision is unremarkable. While passbook accounts and certificates of deposits in mutual savings and loan associations do have some equity characteristics—they are the only ownership interests available in a non-stock association, they include the right to vote on association matters, and they participate in liquidating distributions—these equity characteristics are relatively insubstantial and do not contribute substantially to the fair market value of the debt interests. Accordingly, it would not be unreasonable to hold that receipt of the passbook accounts and certificates of deposit cannot satisfy the continuity of proprietary interest requirement.

But that is not what the Commissioner argued in *Paulsen,* because the Treasury Department had already ruled that a merger of two non-stock associations could constitute a tax-free reorganization.[11] If, as *Roebling* says, satisfaction of the continuity of proprietary interest test turns on what is received and not on a comparison of what is received with what was given up, the decision in *Paulsen* cannot be explained. The Supreme Court addressed this point in its *Paulsen* opinion, but unfortunately the Court was sufficiently unclear as to leave in doubt the continued vitality of cases like *Roebling.*

The continuity of proprietary interest doctrine applies to a corporate reorganization as a whole and not to the shareholders individually. For example, if 75 percent of the consideration in a merger is stock of the surviving corporation, continuity of proprietary interest exists even if one particular shareholder receives only cash or debt.[12] This does not mean that the recipient of cash will avoid all taxation on the exchange—as we shall see, cash or other boot received as part of a reorganization can give rise to recognition of gain. What it does mean is that all the parties to the transaction will be taxed under those provisions triggered by § 368's definition of a "reorganization."

That reorganization status is determined by reference to the transaction as a whole and not shareholder by shareholder can cut the other way as well. Suppose that the stock of X Corp. is owned equally by 10 individuals. If X merges into Y Corp. under applicable state law, and assuming that 90 percent of the consideration consists of cash, then no shareholder will obtain the benefit of the reorganization provisions even if one shareholder receives only stock of Y in the transaction.[13] Thus, a shareholder's taxation in

---

11. Rev. Rul. 69–3, 1969–1 C.B. 103.

12. See Rev. Rul. 66–224, 1966–2 C.B. 114.

13. *Kass v. Commissioner,* 60 T.C. 218 (1973), aff'd without opinion, 491 F.2d 749 (3d Cir.1974).

these circumstances may turn in part on what is received by other participants in the transaction.

Before leaving the continuity of proprietary interest doctrine, one final issue is worth considering. Suppose that most of the shareholders of the transferor-corporation intend to sell their stock of the surviving corporation as soon as it is received. In practical effect, such shareholders will be cashed out of the transaction just as if they had not received stock as part of the transaction. Should such post-merger sales cause the transaction to lose its reorganization status? If so, such sales will affect the other shareholders who choose to continue to hold their investment in the surviving corporation as well the acquiring corporation whose basis varies depending on whether the transaction qualifies as a reorganization. If not, then the empty formalism of issuing registered shares in a merger involving a publicly-held corporation will eviscerate the continuity of proprietary interest doctrine.

If post-merger sales have an adverse effect on the non-selling shareholders, then the tax implications of a corporate rearrangement cannot be determined with certainty until well after the transaction. In addition, it may be impossible to determine which shareholders sell their shares and when. In *McDonald's of Zion, 432, Ill., Inc. v. Commissioner*,[14] the Tax Court held that anticipated post-merger sales were irrelevant to merger reorganization status as long as the shareholders had no binding obligation to sell, although the circuit court reversed. This difficult issue would not arise if a shareholder's tax treatment was dependent only on what that particular shareholder received; i.e., if the continuity of proprietary interest doctrine were abolished.[15] Note, though, that in many of the statutory reorganization patterns, the common law continuity of proprietary interest doctrine has been superseded by a statutory limitation on the form of consideration that may be used.

One problem with the result in *McDonald's of Zion* (i.e., post-transaction disposition of stock by shareholders defeats the reorganization) is that the IRS can get whipsawed. That is, the acquiring corporation may treat the transaction as a failed merger so it can claim a stepped-up basis in the acquired (perhaps depreciable) assets while the shareholders (especially the shareholders who do not sell their stock) treat the transaction as a tax-free reorganiza-

---

14. 76 T.C. 972 (1981), rev'd, 688 F.2d 520 (7th Cir.1982).

15. There would still be an issue as to timing for the selling shareholders, namely, should they be taxed on receipt of the stock or when it is sold. This issue becomes especially important when they sell their stock shortly after receipt on the installment method.

tion so that they do not report gain on the receipt of the acquiring corporation's stock.[16]

Treasury addressed the problem of the IRS being whipsawed through regulations which now focus primarily on what the acquiring corporation furnishes as consideration and not on how long the target shareholders retain it.[17] For example, suppose A is a shareholder of T Corp. T Corp. merges into P Corp. with A receiving P Corp. stock in exchange for A's T Corp. stock. Immediately after the merger, A sells the P Corp. stock to B, a purchaser unrelated to P Corp.[18] This transaction will qualify as a tax-free merger so that P Corp. takes a carryover basis under § 362 in the assets acquired from T Corp.[19] Note that there is sufficient continuity of interest even where A's sale of the P Corp. stock is prearranged prior to the merger.[20] Indeed, continuity of interest exists even if the stock held by A is redeemed by T Corp. prior to and as part of the merger, so long as none of the property used in the redemption is furnished by P Corp. Regs. § 1.368–1(e)(6) (example 9).

However, a sale immediately following a purported tax-free reorganization will break the continuity of interest requirement if the purchaser is the acquiring corporation or a related corporation. For example, suppose that pursuant to a preconceived plan, P Corp. redeems for cash all the P Corp. stock received by A in the merger. In effect, P Corp. used cash to acquire the T Corp. stock originally held by A. Consequently, the merger would be taxable to all parties, failing the continuity of interest requirement.[21] The result would be the same if A sold the P Corp. stock to B, a corporation, and B Corp. owned 80 percent[22] of the stock of P Corp.[23] The rationale for the related party exception is that because of the dividends-received

---

16. Even those shareholders who immediately sell their stock received in the reorganization may benefit if installment reporting is available on the sale.

17. Regs. § 1.368–1(e).

18. There is also continuity of interest if A sells the T Corp. stock to B immediately prior to the merger pursuant to a prearranged sale and B exchanges the T Corp. stock for the P Corp. stock as part of the merger.

19. Regs. § 1.368–1(e)(6) (examples 1 and 3).

20. The continuity of interest regulations on their face only apply to reorganizations, but should the reasoning also apply to corporate formations as well? Suppose that A forms X Corp. in a purported § 351 transaction and immediately after the formation, A sells half of

the X Corp. stock to B. In *Intermountain*, see Section 2.07(b) *supra*, the court ruled that § 351 did not apply because of the prearranged sale to B who was not a "transferor." Has the result in *Intermountain* (*i.e.*, § 351 not applicable) been effectively eviscerated by the continuity of interest regulations? To date, the continuity of interest regulations have not been expanded beyond the realm of reorganizations.

21. Regs. § 1.368–1(e)(6) (example 4).

22. Corporations are related if they are members of the same affiliated group under § 1504. Regs. § 1.368–1(e)(3).

23. Regs. § 1.368–1(e)(6) (example 2).

deduction and other intercorporate benefits, it is not difficult for P Corp. cash to find its way to B Corp. and then ultimately to A. Rather than actually tracing funds, the regulations conclusively assume that any purchase by a related corporation is funded by P Corp. Note that if B is not a corporation but owns 80 percent of P Corp., A's sale to B would satisfy the continuity of interest requirement. This follows from the fact that the dividends-received deduction under § 243 is not available to individual shareholders.

The continuity of proprietary interest doctrine is not the only non-statutory gloss on the definition of a reorganization. The Service long argued that the surviving corporation must continue the business of the transferor-corporation if a reorganization is to be tax-free. The rationale for this argument is that tax-free treatment of a reorganization is provided when a corporate rearrangement is best viewed as a mere change in form of a corporate enterprise. However, the courts were unwilling to adopt the Service's view,[24] and the regulations now include only a reduced form of this *continuity of business enterprise* requirement. Under Regs. § 1.368–1(d), the acquiring corporation in a reorganization must either continue the historic business of the transferor-corporation *or* use a "significant portion" of the transferor's assets in a different business. However, the acquiring corporation is deemed to use the transferor's assets if the assets are used by any corporation affiliated with the acquiring corporation (*e.g.*, the assets are used by five subsidiaries) even if no one affiliated corporation uses "a significant portion."

What can we conclude from all this? At the very least, an A reorganization is much more than a simple statutory merger or consolidation. In addition, we have seen that the courts have felt free to engraft their conception of what a reorganization should be onto the statute, a statute already full of complexity and detail. Judicial activism in tax is hardly limited to the reorganization arena, but it does seem to be the case that reorganizations have brought forth more than their share of judicial creativity.

There are a variety of business entities that exist for non-tax purposes but which are ignored for all tax purposes. Such entities, called "disregarded entities" include unincorporated entities (such as limited liability companies) that elect not to be taxed as corporation and have a single owner as well as certain wholly-owned subsidiaries of S corporations (called "Q–Subs").[25] Such entities are called disregarded entities because for tax purposes the assets they

---

24. E.g., *Bentsen v. Phinney,* 199 F.Supp. 363 (S.D.Tex.1961).

25. For more on Q–Subs, see Section 13.10 *infra.*

hold are treated as if held directly by their owner. See, e.g., Regs. § 301.7701–2(c)(2)(i).

Suppose X Corp. owns all of the membership interests of X–LLC, a disregarded entity. And suppose Y Corp. owns the membership interests of Y–LLX, also a disregarded entity. There are a variety of ways in which X Corp., Y Corp., and their two disregarded entities might try to combine in an A reorganization.

If X Corp. merges into Y Corp., the existence for state law purposes of the two disregarded entities will have no relevance on the application of § 368(a)(1)(A): under state law, X will disappear and Y will end up owning both X–LLC and Y–LLX while for federal tax purposes Y will survive and be deemed to own directly the assets of X–LLC and Y–LLC.

What if X Corp. merges into Y–LLC? For tax purposes there is no Y–LLC, and so this should be treated as a merger of X Corp. into Y Corp., and the regulations so provide. Regs. § 1.368–2(b)(1)(iv) (example 2). Contrast this transaction with the merger of X–LLC into Y Corp. Such a merger will not qualify as an A reorganization because it in effect divides X Corp. into two parts: one part is X Corp. which survives the merger and the other part consists of the assets of X–LLC (treated for tax purposes as owned prior to the merger directly by X Corp.) transferred to Y Corp. Regs. § 1.368–2(b)(1)(iv) (example 5). Note that the merger of X–LLC into Y–LLC would also not qualify as an A reorganization.

(b) "B" Reorganizations. The B reorganization results in the target corporation becoming a subsidiary of the acquiring corporation. For example, suppose that X Corp. is owned by B and C. If Y Corp. exchanges its voting stock for the stock of X held by B and C, the transaction will qualify as a B reorganization. Note that after the transaction B and C are shareholders of Y Corp. which in turn owns all the stock of X Corp.

Under the terms of § 368(a)(1)(B), the acquiring corporation must end up with "control" of the target corporation, where control is defined in § 368(c) to mean 80 percent of the voting power and 80 percent of all nonvoting classes of stock. The continuity of proprietary interest requirement always will be satisfied in a B reorganization because, per § 368(a)(1)(B), the shareholders of the target corporation must receive only voting stock of the acquiring corporation (or voting stock of its parent).

A variety of different transactions can be fit into the B reorganization pattern. One corporation can acquire control of an unrelated corporation, and if only voting stock of the acquiring corporation is used as consideration, the transaction will be a tax-free B reorganization. On the other hand, a parent corporation already having control of a subsidiary corporation can use the B reorganization to acquire additional stock of the subsidiary in an exchange that will be tax-free to the minority shareholders of the subsidiary. Lastly, a corporation owning less than control of another corporation can use the B reorganization to acquire additional shares of the corporation, so long as its total ownership after the transaction meets the control test of § 368(c).

This last form of the B reorganization is called a "creeping" B because control of the target corporation is obtained in a series of transactions. In *Chapman v. Commissioner*,[26] the acquiring corporation purchased approximately 8 percent of the target corporation's stock for cash.[27] The acquiring corporation then exchanged its voting stock for the remaining stock of the target corporation, and at issue was whether this latter exchange constituted a tax-free B reorganization.

The circuit court conceded that the statute permitted creeping B reorganizations but held that the transaction failed the "solely in exchange for voting stock" requirement of the B reorganization. The taxpayer in *Chapman* argued that the statute required voting stock be used only to acquire control of the target corporation. Since no more than 80 percent of the target's stock need be held by the acquiring corporation after the transaction, the taxpayer argued that any method of obtaining additional stock was consistent with the requirements of the B reorganization. The court rejected this interpretation of the statute, however, holding instead that however much stock of the target is acquired in the transaction, the *total* consideration furnished by the acquiring corporation must be its voting stock or voting stock of its parent.[28]

The "solely for voting stock" requirement of the B reorganization can have impact in other settings. For example, suppose that the shareholders of the target company would like the acquiring corporation to pay their reorganization expenses (such as fees for lawyers and accountants). If the transaction is to qualify as a B reorganization, these expenses of the shareholders cannot be paid

---

26. 618 F.2d 856 (1st Cir.1980).

27. Prior to the reorganization, the acquiring corporation sold this stock to a third party. The terms of this sale were such that the Service could persuasively argue that it was a sham, and for the summary judgment motion at issue in *Chapman,* the court assumed that the acquiring corporation did not sell this stock.

28. The court also held that stock of the target acquired in a prior, unrelated transaction (not the 8 percent purchased and sold prior to the transaction) was irrelevant to the reorganization issue. That is, "old and cold" stock need not have been acquired solely for voting stock. But in *Chapman* the 8 percent stock interest was assumed not to be "old and cold," and the cash paid for it spoiled the B reorganization.

by the acquiring corporation. Similarly, if the target's shareholder has pledged his stock as security for a debt, the acquiring corporation may not pay off that debt. On the other hand, the Service has ruled that cash can be paid in lieu of issuing fractional shares in a B reorganization without running afoul of the "solely for voting stock" requirement.[29]

Additionally, the acquiring corporation can use cash or other property in connection with a B reorganization as consideration for anything *other than* stock of the target. Thus, the acquiring corporation may purchase bonds of the target for cash, or it may issue its own bonds for them. This use of non-voting stock consideration will not disqualify the reorganization for the simple reason that exchanges not involving the target's stock are not part of the definition of the reorganization regardless of the consideration used.

Suppose the acquiring corporation has adopted an anti-takeover poison pill, so that its shares contain the right to purchase additional shares at a discount upon the occurrence of some triggering event such as the acquisition of 20% of the company by an outside investor. Is the B reorganization invalidated automatically because the poison pill stock rights constitute non-stock consideration? In the context of § 305, the Service has ruled that the adoption of a poison pill does not constitute the distribution of stock or of property. Should the poison pill rights also be ignored for tax purposes in this context? In two private letter rulings, the Service ignored poison pill contingent stock rights, thereby implicitly ruling that they do not constitute impermissible other property.[30]

The terms of § 368(a)(1)(B) permit use of voting stock of the acquiring corporation *or* of a corporation "in control of" the acquiring corporation. When stock of the acquiring corporation's parent is used, the transaction often is called a "parenthetical" B reorganization. In a parenthetical B reorganization, shareholders of the target become doubly removed from the target's assets. While the Supreme Court initially held that such transactions violated the continuity of proprietary interest doctrine,[31] Congress has repudiated that position in the parenthetical language of § 368(a)(1)(B) as well as in a variety of other provisions.[32]

In a B reorganization, stock of the acquiring corporation *or* of the acquiring corporation's parent may be used, but not both.[33]

---

29. Rev. Rul. 66–365, 1966–2 C.B. 116.

30. Ltr. Rul. 8808081, Ltr. Rul. 8925087.

31. See *Groman v. Commissioner,* 302 U.S. 82 (1937); *Helvering v. Bashford,* 302 U.S. 454 (1938).

32. See §§ 368(a)(1)(C), 368(a)(2)(C)–(E).

33. Regs. § 1.368–2(c).

This limitation is intended to ensure that a shareholder of the target corporation cannot cash out part of his investment without losing a proportionate part of his interest in the transferred assets. For example, suppose that A Corp. acquired all the stock of T Corp. in exchange for its own stock as well as stock of its parent. If a (former) shareholder of T Corp. sold the stock of A's parent, the shareholder would obtain cash from the transaction without substantially diluting his interest in A (and through A, in T). Were such transactions permitted, the efficacy of the "solely for voting stock" requirement of the B reorganization would be reduced. You may want to reconsider this point when you cover divisive reorganizations, because the effect of using stock of the acquiring corporation as well as stock of the acquiring corporation's parent could be to turn a B into a divisive reorganization.

(c) "C" Reorganizations. The C reorganization is much closer to the A than to the B because it contemplates a transfer of assets (as in a merger) rather than a transfer of stock (as in a B reorganization). In fact, the C reorganization is so similar to the A reorganizations that it often is called the "de facto" (or practical) merger provision.

As an example of a C reorganization, suppose that X Corp. wishes to acquire the assets of Y Corp. in a tax-free transaction. If Y transfers all of its assets to X in exchange for voting stock of X, the transaction will qualify as a C reorganization so long as Y Corp. liquidates immediately after the exchange.

The definition of a C reorganization requires that "substantially all" of the target's assets be transferred to the acquiring corporation. Neither the statute nor the regulations demarcate the line between "substantially all" and less than substantially all, although the Service has ruled that the transfer constituting 90 percent of the target's net assets and 70 percent of the target's gross assets will constitute "substantially all."[34] The D reorganization also includes a "substantially all" requirement, and in that context the courts have held that a transfer of all the operating assets will satisfy the requirement even if the operating assets constitute less than 20 percent of the target's net assets. Presumably the courts should fashion some continuity of business enterprise doctrine to define "substantially all" in this context to ensure that the C reorganization be used to continue a corporate enter-

---

34. Rev. Proc. 77–37, 1977–2 C.B. 568. For example, suppose the target corporation has assets worth $100,000 subject to $20,000 of debt. Seventy percent of the gross value is $70,000, and 90 percent of the net value is $72,000, so the standards of this revenue procedure will be met by any transfer of $72,000 or more of the corporation's assets.

prise in modified form rather than to divide and partially liquidate the company.[35]

As in a B reorganization, the statute ensures continuity of proprietary interest in a C reorganization by limiting the consideration that can be used by the acquiring corporation to voting stock. However, the "solely for voting stock" requirement of the C reorganization lacks much of the bite of the B reorganization because of two provisions: § 368(a)(1)(C) (final clause) and § 368(a)(2)(B).

The final clause in § 368(a)(1)(C) provides that assumption by the acquiring corporation of debts of the target corporation is not to be treated as impermissible consideration in determining qualification as a C reorganization. But for this provision, the assumption by the acquiring corporation of a liability of the target corporation would cause the transaction to fail to qualify as a C reorganization. This provision in § 368(a)(1)(C) overturns the Supreme Court's decision in *United States v. Hendler*,[36] the case in which it was held that assumption of a liability, even in the context of a bulk transfer of corporate assets, should be treated as the equivalent of cash consideration. Because most companies are forced to mortgage their fixed or working assets to obtain commercial credit, continuation of the *Hendler* doctrine would have had the practical effect of making the C reorganization commercially unavailable.

Congress further loosened the C reorganization's "solely for voting stock" requirement by enacting the boot relaxation rule of § 368(a)(2)(B). This provision permits the acquiring corporation to use cash or other boot as consideration in a C reorganization as long as 80 percent of the target's assets are acquired solely for voting stock. Thus, if the acquiring corporation receives 100 percent of the target's assets, up to 20 percent of the consideration may be boot. On the other hand, if the target transfers only 80 percent of its assets to the acquiring corporation, then no boot at all is allowed. In between fall those transactions in which the target corporation transfers more than 80 percent but less than all of its assets. For example, if the target transfers 90 percent of its assets worth $900,000 to the acquiring corporation, the consideration must include at least $800,000 of voting stock of the acquiring corporation (or of its parent). Thus, up to $100,000 of the consideration could be boot.

One peculiar wrinkle of § 368(a)(2)(B) is that taxpayers obtaining its benefits must relinquish the benefit of the anti-*Hendler*

---

35. Compare the partial liquidation provision of § 302(b)(4) discussed at Section 5.02(d) *supra*.

36. 303 U.S. 564 (1938).

language in § 368(a)(1)(C). That is, if boot is used in a C reorganization, then any liabilities assumed by the acquiring corporation are treated as boot for purposes of the boot relaxation rule of § 368(a)(2)(B).

For example, suppose T Corp. has assets worth $100,000 subject to liabilities of $13,000. If A Corp. wants to acquire all of T's assets in a C reorganization, then A must transfer at least $80,000 worth of voting stock to T. Because the net value of T's assets is $87,000, A presumably will provide an additional $7,000 of value. That additional value can be more voting stock, cash, or anything else pursuant to § 368(a)(2)(B). However, if A receives only 90 percent of T's assets, fully subject to the liability of $13,000, then no boot may be provided by A. In fact, the maximum amount of boot that can be used under § 368(a)(2)(B) equals 20 percent of the value of the target corporation's assets *less* the value (if any) of the target's assets not transferred in the reorganization *and less* the target's liabilities (if any) assumed by the acquiring corporation.

Bausch & Lomb Optical Co. v. Commissioner[37] illustrates a court's reading of the reorganization definitions too narrowly. In that case, the acquiring corporation owned 79 percent of the target corporation's stock. In order to obtain the assets of the target corporation, the acquiring corporation exchanged its voting stock for the target's assets. The target then liquidated, distributing 79 percent of the acquiring corporation's stock back to the acquiring corporation and 21 percent of the stock to the target's minority shareholders.

The court held that this transaction failed to qualify as a tax-free C reorganization because the acquiring corporation obtained 79 percent of the target's assets in exchange for its stock of the target and only 21 percent of the target's assets in exchange for its own voting stock. As a result, the transaction was treated as a taxable liquidation rather than as a tax-free reorganization. While the court's holding arguably is consistent with the terms of the statute, the "solely for voting stock" requirement seems intended to ensure that the target shareholders continue a proprietary interest in the continuing enterprise. The holding in *Bausch & Lomb* served to invalidate a transaction when the acquiring corporation is itself a substantial shareholder of the target corporation, a situation in which the continuity of proprietary interest is most evident.

In fact, the taxpayer in *Bausch & Lomb* would have been better off if it had owned either more *or less* of the liquidating corporation's stock. If the taxpayer had owned slightly more stock,

---

37. 267 F.2d 75 (2d Cir.1959).

it would have been over the 80 percent threshold and the transaction would have been tax-free under § 332 as the liquidation of a controlled subsidiary.[38] On the other hand, if the taxpayer has owned less than 20 percent of the liquidating corporation's stock, the transaction would have been a tax-free C reorganization using the boot relaxation rule of § 368(a)(2)(B). Had the court in *Bausch & Lomb* appreciated this, it might have been less willing to impose taxation in the actual, intermediate case. Fortunately, the result in *Bausch & Lomb* has been overruled by regulations which ignore previously acquired stock of the target in a C reorganization for determining whether the "solely for voting stock" requirement has been met. Regs. § 1.368–2(d)(4). Of course, if the target stock is acquired in contemplation of the reorganization, the consideration furnished by the acquiring corporation (unless it consists exclusively of voting stock of the acquiring corporation) will have to fall within the boot relaxation rule of § 368(a)(2)(B). See Regs. § 1.368–2(d)(4) (example 2).

As in the B reorganization, the C reorganization permits the acquiring corporation to use its voting stock or the voting stock of its parent. Once again, voting stock of the acquiring corporation cannot be combined with voting stock of the parent,[39] although if 80 percent of the target's assets are exchanged for voting stock of the acquiring corporation or of its parent, use of the other's stock may be permissible under the boot relaxation rule of § 368(a)(2)(B).[40] Once the target corporation transfers substantially all of its assets to the acquiring corporation, the target must liquidate, transferring whatever consideration it received as well as its remaining assets to its shareholders.[41] This liquidation requirement can be avoided only with permission of the Secretary of the Treasury.[42]

(d) Nondivisive "D" Reorganizations. The definition of a D reorganization includes within it two very different kinds of transactions, distinguished by the way in which each meets the D reorganization distribution requirement. The D reorganization always involves a transfer of assets from one corporation to another followed by a distribution from the transferor-corporation. If that distribution satisfies the requirements of § 354, the effect of the transaction will be to substitute the transferee-corporation for the transferor-corporation, and such transactions often are called "sub-

---

38. See § 8.03 *supra.*

39. Regs. § 1.368–2(d)(1).

40. Note that the definition of "property" in 317(a) applies by its terms only to part I of subchapter C; that is, to 301–318. Accordingly, that definition of

property is not applicable to the reorganization provisions in 368(a).

41. See § 368(a)(2)(G)(i).

42. Section 368(a)(2)(G)(ii).

stitutive" or "nondivisive" D reorganizations. On the other hand, if the distribution meets the requirements of § 355, the transaction will result in the division of the transferor-corporation into two or more corporations, and such transactions are one form of the divisive reorganizations discussed *infra*.[43]

By the terms of § 368(a)(1)(D), a nondivisive D reorganization must satisfy the requirements of § 354, in particular § 354(b). Accordingly, the transferor-corporation must transfer "substantially all" of its assets to the transferee and then liquidate, distributing its remaining assets as well as anything received from the transferee to its shareholders. In addition, the terms of § 368(a)(1)(D) require that the transferor or its shareholders control the transferee immediately after the asset transfer. Thus, once the transferor-corporation liquidates, some or all of its shareholders necessarily will be in control of the transferee. As to these shareholders, the effect of the transaction was to combine the assets of the transferor and the transferee into a single corporation. If the transferee had no significant assets prior to the transaction, then the effect of the transaction is to substitute the transferee for the transferor.

A nondivisive D reorganization is much like a C reorganization. Both involve a transfer of "substantially all" of a corporation's assets, followed (usually, in the case of a C) by a complete liquidation of the transferor. The difference between the two is the statutory implementation of the continuity of proprietary interest doctrine. In the C reorganization, continuity is ensured by the requirement that the transferee-corporation obtain the assets in exchange for voting stock of itself or of its parent. In the nondivisive D reorganization, continuity is ensured by the requirement that the transferor or its shareholders have *control* of the transferee immediately after the exchange.[44]

The definition of "control" is relaxed in the case of nondivisive D reorganizations from the usual 80 percent test down to the 50 percent test of § 304(c).[45] Since § 304 is an anti-abuse provision, you might suspect that the nondivisive D reorganization will on occasion be a tool of the Commissioner rather than of the taxpayer. In fact, the nondivisive D reorganization is the principle statutory provision by which the Commissioner attacks the *liquidation/rein-*

---

43. A D reorganization also can include a distribution meeting the requirements of § 356. Such a D reorganization will be one of the two basic forms but with boot distributed in addition to stock and securities. Thus, a D reorganization qualifying with a distribution taxed under § 356 is either a nondivisive D reorganization with boot or a divisive reorganization with boot.

44. Where a transaction qualifies as both a C and a D reorganization, it is treated as a D. § 368(a)(2)(A).

45. See § 368(a)(2)(H).

corporation problem; that is, the problem of taxpayers liquidating their corporations and then reincorporating some of the assets in an effort to obtain exchange treatment (including the possibility of loss) on what is tantamount to a dividend distribution.

For example, consider the case of X Corp. owning a building with adjusted basis of $1,000,000 and with fair market value of $650,000. Assume that the corporation also has cash of $100,000, and that the shareholders of X would like to have the cash distributed pro rata to them. If X simply declares a dividend, the shareholders will have ordinary income equal to the full amount realized, assuming that X has earnings and profits of at least $100,000. A redemption will do no better, because none of the harbors of § 302(b) will protect the pro rata redemption from § 301 distribution treatment. However, if X liquidates and the building is reincorporated, a far different tax result obtains.

First, the corporation realizes and recognizes a loss of $350,000 under § 336(a) (assuming the inapplicability of the exceptions in § 336(d)). Second, the shareholders apply the amount distributed against their stock bases, reporting any excess as capital gain or any deficit as capital loss. If the shareholders' aggregate basis exceeds $750,000, there will be no net tax at the shareholder-level despite the receipt of cash of $100,000. Regardless of the shareholders' taxation, the corporation will have a loss of $350,000 to apply against its income. A further tax benefit to the corporation is the elimination of its earnings and profits account as a result of the liquidation. The shareholders may then use § 351 to reincorporate the building without recognition of gain.

The Commissioner attacks such transactions under § 368(a)(1)(D), arguing that the liquidation and reincorporation should be treated as a direct transfer to the continuing corporate entity. Because the shareholders of X are in control of the new corporation after the transaction, the terms of the nondivisive D reorganization will have been met. Accordingly, no loss will be recognized at the corporate-level,[46] X Corp.'s earnings and profits account will not be eliminated,[47] and the shareholders will be prohibited from recognizing any loss on the transaction.[48] Moreover, the $100,000 removed from corporate solution will be taxable to the shareholders.[49]

Taxpayers have tried to avoid the D reorganization by reincorporating only a small portion of their assets. For example, the

---

46. See § 361(a)–(b).

47. See § 381(a)(2), (c)(2).

48. See §§ 354(a)(1), 356(a).

49. See § 356 discussed at Section 10.03(b) *infra*.

taxpayers in *Smothers v. United States*,[50] owned two corporations, TIL and IUS. Both corporations were engaged in the business of renting uniforms and cleaning equipment, and because IUS rented most of its heavy equipment, it owned few operating assets. IUS sold its operating assets and some rental property to TIL for $22,637.56 and then liquidated, distributing cash and property worth $149,162.35 to its shareholders. The taxpayers reported the transaction as a complete liquidation of IUS (producing capital gain to the shareholders under § 331) while the Commissioner argued that the transaction was a nondivisive D reorganization producing ordinary income pursuant to § 356(a)(2).[51]

At issue was whether IUS transferred "substantially all" of its assets to TIL.[52] The court in *Smothers* refused to define "substantially all" by reference to a fixed percentage of the corporation's assets. Instead, the court interpreted "substantially all" to mean most of the corporation's operating assets. Such an interpretation by the court ensured that reorganization status would be given to any corporate rearrangement resulting in "a continuance of the proprietary interests in the continuing enterprise under modified corporate form." Because TIL acquired the operating assets of IUS and succeeded to its goodwill, reorganization status was appropriate.

The dissenting opinion in *Smothers* questioned the majority opinion's conclusion that IUS *transferred* substantially all of its assets to TIL. The major operating asset of IUS was its goodwill and knowledgeable employees. Since the employees of IUS could have chosen not to join TIL, in what sense were they "transferred" by IUS? To be sure, the employees did join TIL and TIL did benefit from their experience. But that alone does not mean that they were "transferred" by IUS without straining the meaning of "transfer."

The majority opinion recognized that the business enterprise of IUS was continued in TIL and that TIL was controlled by the IUS shareholders. Accordingly, the transaction met the spirit of the reorganization provisions. But did the court pay sufficient deference to the words chosen by Congress in defining the various forms of reorganization? Congress could have defined a D reorganization to include any transaction which continues the business of one corporation in a new corporate form. Instead, Congress spoke of a

---

50. 642 F.2d 894 (5th Cir.1981).

51. Section 356 is discussed in more detail at Section 10.03(b) *infra*.

52. The transaction formally did not meet the requirement imposed by § 354(b)(1)(A) that the transferee corporation (TIL) exchange its stock or secu-
rities for the assets received. Because the shareholders of IUS also owned TIL prior to the transaction, the receipt of stock by IUS would have added nothing to the exchange. See Temp. Regs. § 1.368–2T.

transfer of "substantially all" of the corporation's assets. For a capital-intensive business, presumably the business cannot be continued without substantially all of its operating assets. But for a service-intensive business such as was involved in *Smothers,* the assets used in the business may have little to do with the business itself. Was it proper for the court in *Smothers* to further the general policy behind reorganizations at the cost of ignoring the words of the statute?

(e) Parent/Subsidiary Combinations. In many circumstances it may be convenient for the acquiring corporation to use a subsidiary corporation in the transaction. For example, if Big Corp. is about to acquire Little Corp. in a tax-free transaction, it may be desirable to continue the business of Little Corp. in a distinct corporation. One way to accomplish this is to employ a B reorganization. However, it may be that some of the shareholders desire consideration other than voting stock of Big Corp. If so, the transaction cannot be fit within the B framework.

The parenthetical C reorganization might be the answer, although recall that § 368(a)(2)(B) limits the actual consideration to the 20 percent less the liabilities assumed. If this restriction is not overly burdensome, the transaction can be structured as a parenthetical C reorganization, with voting stock of the parent constituting the bulk of the consideration.

It may be, though, that even the C form is too restrictive, and in that case the parties would like to look to the A reorganization. Recall that consideration in an A reorganization is limited only by the common law continuity of proprietary interest doctrine; that is, stock (not necessarily voting stock) of the transferee-corporation must constitute a substantial and meaningful portion of the total consideration used in the transaction.

Merging Little Corp. into a subsidiary of Big Corp. may be an ideal form for this transaction. In addition, merging the target corporation into a subsidiary of the acquiring corporation rather than into the acquiring corporation itself may offer non-tax advantages. For example, state law may well provide that a merger of two corporations requires the affirmative vote of both corporate parties. If so, merging Little Corp. into Big Corp. would require approval of the Big Corp. shareholders as well as those of Little Corp. If Big Corp. is publicly held, obtaining the approval of its shareholders may be prohibitively expensive.

On the other hand, if Little Corp. merges into a subsidiary of Big Corp., then approval of the subsidiary's shareholders is easy to obtain, because that approval is nothing but approval by the directors of Big Corp. However, the shareholders of Little Corp. will not want to obtain shares of the subsidiary as part of the transaction. Rather, they will want stock in publicly traded Big Corp. The ideal transaction would be a merger in which the consideration received by the shareholder's of the target company consist in substantial part of stock of the parent of the corporation surviving the merger.

Thus, Big Corp. will form a new corporation, Sub Corp., by contributing its own stock and other property to Sub in exchange for all of Sub's stock. The total value contributed to Sub should equal the value of Little Corp. Then, when Little Corp. is merged into Sub Corp., the shareholders of Little Corp. will give up their Little Corp. stock in exchange for the stock of Big Corp. held by Sub. When the dust settles, the Little Corp. shareholders have become shareholders of Big Corp. and Big Corp. has become the parent of Little Corp.

This type of transaction, the merger of the target corporation into a subsidiary of the acquiring corporation, is explicitly permitted by § 368(a)(2)(D), the so-called "forward subsidiary" merger provision.[53] Under this provision, the only limitation imposed on the consideration transferred to the shareholders of the acquired corporation is that applicable to A reorganizations.[54] This transaction is the A reorganization analog to the parenthetical B and C reorganizations.

It may be the case that Little Corp. rather than Sub Corp. must survive the merger. For example, Little Corp. may own a favorable long-term lease that cannot be transferred. In such circumstances, the parties may want to structure the transaction as follows. As before, Big Corp. creates a subsidiary, Sub Corp. The only asset transferred to Sub is voting stock of Big Corp. Next, Sub Corp. merges into Little Corp. As part of the merger, the Little Corp. shareholders exchange their shares of Little Corp. for the stock of Big Corp. held by Sub. Also as part of the merger, Big Corp. exchanges its shares of Sub for control of Little Corp. In this way, Big Corp. controls Little Corp. after the transaction, and the former Little Corp. shareholders become shareholders of Big Corp. Although slightly more complicated than the forward subsidiary merger, this transaction has the same effect but allows the target corporation to be the survivor of the merger.

---

53. Because these transactions involve three corporate parties, they also are called forward "triangular" reorganizations.

54. See § 368(a)(2)(D)(ii).

This type of transaction, called a "reverse subsidiary merger," is permitted by § 368(a)(2)(E). In contradistinction to the forward subsidiary merger, Congress has added a statutory proprietary interest requirement to the requirements of a reverse subsidiary merger. Under § 368(a)(2)(E), only voting stock of the acquiring corporation (Big Corp. in the example above) may be used to acquire "control" of the target corporation. Thus, the consideration allowed in a reverse subsidiary merger is substantially less broad than that permitted in a forward subsidiary merger.

This voting stock requirement of the reverse subsidiary merger is also very different from that of the B reorganization. On the one hand, if the acquiring corporation in a reverse subsidiary merger exchanges voting stock for control of the target, it can use any consideration to acquire the remaining stock of the target. Thus, the *Chapman* issue is resolved differently in the case of reverse subsidiary mergers, in favor of expanding the reach of the reorganization provision. On the other hand, because the acquiring corporation must *acquire* control of the target in the transaction, the possibility for a creeping reverse subsidiary merger is substantially restricted. For reasons known only to Congress (if to anyone), the reverse subsidiary merger is a strange creature, one part A, one part B, and one part like nothing else.

Technically, the statute requires that the target corporation in a reverse subsidiary merger hold substantially all of its own assets (and the assets of the acquiring subsidiary that is merged out of existence, excluding stock of this corporation's parent) immediately after the transaction. Does this preclude the sale of a significant portion of the target's assets to third parties as part of the plan of reorganization? So long as such a sale does not cause the transaction to fail the continuity of business enterprise doctrine, it will not affect the tax-free status of the transaction.[55]

The reorganization provisions also contemplate the use of a *remote* subsidiary in some circumstances. For example, suppose that H Corp., a multinational holding corporation, plans to acquire M & P Corp., a mom/pop grocery store. In accordance with its corporate structure, H would like the assets of M & P to be held by a wholly-owned subsidiary of G Corp., where G is the grocery subsidiary of H. Mom and Pop are willing to transfer the assets or stock of M & P in exchange for voting stock of H.

To accomplish these goals, H could cause G to acquire the stock of M & P in a parenthetical B reorganization. However, H may prefer to acquire the assets of M & P rather than the stock, possibly

---

55. Rev. Rul. 2001–25, 2001–12, C.B. 1291.

to avoid undisclosed liabilities of M & P. If so, H will cause G to acquire the assets of M & P for the stock of H in a parenthetical C reorganization and then drop down the assets so acquired into K Corp., a subsidiary of G. By following these steps, Mom and Pop will become shareholders of H, H will own G, and G will own the assets of M & P Corp. indirectly through its ownership of K Corp. Although the Supreme Court once ruled that such a transaction violates the continuity of proprietary interest doctrine because the assets become too far removed from Mom and Pop,[56] such asset drop-downs are now permitted by § 368(a)(2)(C). Indeed, under this provision the assets can be divided between G and its subsidiary should H so desire.[57]

More generally, reorganization status is not jeopardized by the acquiring corporation transferring to a subsidiary (or to a remote subsidiary) stock or assets acquired in the reorganization. Regs. § 1.368–2(k)(1). For example, in a reverse subsidiary merger under § 368(2)(2)(E), the acquiring corporation may transfer stock of the target corporation to a corporation controlled by the acquiring corporation, and that subsidiary may then retransfer the stock to a corporation which it controls, etc.

There is one interesting wrinkle to this ability of the acquiring corporation to drop assets or stock to controlled subsidiaries after an acquisitive reorganization. The statutory support for this flexibility is § 368(a)(2)(c), and in that provision this flexibility is explicitly confined to the A, B, C and G reorganizations, a list that notably excludes D reorganizations. Nonetheless, the Service has ruled that the benefit of § 368(a)(2)(C) extends to D reorganizations on the theory that "§ 368(a)(2)(C) is permissive and not exclusive or restrictive." Rev. Rul. 2002–85, 2002–2 C.B. 986. To be sure, it is hard to see a principled reason why a post-reorganization transfer of assets to a controlled subsidiary ought to disqualify an otherwise-valid D reorganization. But it seems pretty clear that is exactly what Congress intended by listing all of the reorganization patterns *other than* the D in § 368(a)(2)(C). Indeed, in the parenthetical language in § 368(a)(2)(A), Congress expressly provided that a transaction qualifying as both a C and a D reorganization *could* get the benefit of § 368(a)(2)(C); such language is unnecessary if both C and D reorganizations otherwise qualify under § 368(a)(2)(C).

---

56. See *Groman v. Commissioner,* 302 U.S. 82 (1937); *Helvering v. Bashford,* 302 U.S. 454 (1938).

57. See Rev. Rul. 64–73, 1964–1 C.B. 142. Do not confuse this ability to divide the target's assets between the acquiring corporation and its subsidiary with the *inability* in a B, C, or forward subsidiary reorganization to use voting stock of both corporations.

Recall that in a forward subsidiary merger the target corporation mergers into a controlled subsidiary of the acquiring corporation, so that after the transaction the acquiring has not directly acquired the stock or the assets of the target. The acquiring corporation might wish to rearrange its corporate structure by moving the stock of the controlled subsidiary to a lower tier in its corporate hierarchy, but will such a transfer invalidate the merger? Note that Regs. § 1.368–2(k)(1) only permits the transfer of stock or assets *acquired* in the reorganization; here, the acquiring corporation wishes to move the acquired assets indirectly by dropping down the stock of its controlled subsidiary, and that stock was not acquired in the reorganization. The Service now concedes that such a drop-down can be made tax-free.[58]

(f) Multi–Step Reorganizations. Suppose A Corp. makes a tender offer for the shares of T Corp. Under the terms of the offer, no transaction will occur unless a majority of the outstanding T Corp. shares are tendered, in which case A Corp. will acquire those shares in exchange for its own voting stock. If that first step is completed, A Corp. will then acquire the remaining shares of T Corp. in a squeeze-out merger using two-thirds of its voting stock and one-third cash as consideration. As a consequence, A Corp. will acquire the assets of T Corp. in exchange for about 83% voting stock and 17% cash. Should this two-step acquisition be taxed as a single-step C reorganization?

Several courts have been willing to treat such multi-step transactions as a unified, tax-free reorganization when the various steps are sufficiently interrelated to support application of the step-transaction doctrine under general tax principles.[59] In Revenue Ruling 2001–26,[60] the Service expressed its agreement with these cases. Note that the step-transaction doctrine will convert a multi-step acquisition into a tax-free reorganization only if the stepped-together transaction satisfies all of the technical requirements of a tax-free reorganization including the continuity of proprietary interest and continuity of business enterprise doctrines.[61]

Suppose A Corp. structures the acquisition of T Corp. in the following way. First, A Corp. creates a subsidiary corporation, X Corp., with cash and A Corp. voting stock. Second, X Corp. merges into T Corp., with T surviving. Under the terms of that merger, the

---

58. Rev. Rul. 2001–24, 2001–1 C.B. 1290.

59. *Seagram Corp. v. Commissioner,* 104 T.C. 75 (1995); *King Enterprises, Inc. v. United States,* 418 F.2d 511 (Ct. Cl.1969).

60. 2001–1 C.B. 1297.

61. For an excellent discussion of Revenue Ruling 2001–26, see Martin D. Ginsburg & Jack S. Levin, *Integrated Acquisitive Reorganizations,* 2001 Tax Notes 1909 (June 11, 2001).

T shareholders relinquish their T shares for the cash and A Corp. stock held by X Corp. while A Corp.'s stock of X is cancelled in exchange for common stock of T. Thus, after this step A Corp. owns all of the outstanding stock of T Corp., and the former shareholders of T Corp. own cash and stock of A Corp.

Third, T Corp. is liquidated into A Corp. pursuant to applicable state law (such a transaction of a controlled subsidiary into its parent is called an "upstream merger"). Thus, after this transaction the assets formerly held by T Corp. are held by A Corp., and the former shareholders of T Corp., to the extent they were not cashed out, are shareholders of the acquiring corporation (that is, are shareholders of A Corp.).

If each of these steps were treated as a distinct transaction, then step 1 would be an incorporation under § 351, step 2 would be either a taxable stock purchase (called a "qualified stock purchase" under § 338), or a forward subsidiary merger under § 368(a)(2)(E) (depending on the relative proportion of stock and cash), and step 3 would be a subsidiary liquidation under § 332. But assuming these steps are all are parts of a single, integrated transaction, how should they be characterized? The Service has ruled that they will be treated as a merger of T Corp. into A Corp. which therefore will constitute a good A reorganization so long as the various nonstatutory requirements of a reorganization are met.[62]

Reconsider this transaction but assume that A Corp. uses only cash to acquire T Corp. Now, the transaction cannot be recharacterized as an A reorganization because the continuity of proprietary interest requirement is not satisfied. Can, though, the taxpayer argue that the steps should nevertheless be stepped together to constitute not a tax-free reorganization but instead a direct purchase of T's assets, thereby giving A Corp. a cost basis in those assets? The Service ruled that such a recharacterization would represent an impermissible end-run around the detailed rules of § 388,[63] a statutory provision intended by Congress to be the exclusive mechanism by which a taxpayer can purchase stock and convert the transaction into a cost-basis purchase of the target's assets. Note that in the prior example when the steps were combined into a tax-free reorganization, the acquiring corporation ended up with a carryover basis in the acquired assets. Thus, the recharacterization was not inconsistent with the role of § 338.

As another example of the use of the step-transaction doctrine, assume P Corp. owns all the stock of two subsidiary corporations, S

---

62. Rev. Rul. 2001–46, 2001–2 C.B. 321. **63.** *Id.*

Corp. and T Corp. We know that a sale of all of the assets of T Corp. to S Corp., followed by a liquidation of T Corp., will be treated as a nondivisive D reorganization.[64] But what if P Corp. sells the stock of T to S (making T a wholly-owned subsidiary of S), followed by an immediate liquidation of T Corp.? If the sab is treated separately, it will be taxed under § 304 as the sale of stock between related corporations. But when combined with the liquidation, the effect of the transaction as a whole is that of a D reorganization, and the Service has ruled that this is how the transaction should be characterized.[65] The Service examined the legislative history of § 304 and concluded that Congress did not intend § 304 to override the reorganization provisions.

(g) "G" Reorganizations. Under prior law, a transfer of all or part of a corporation's assets to another corporation pursuant to a court-approved plan under the Bankruptcy Act could qualify for tax-free treatment under separate rules applicable to "insolvency reorganizations." In the Bankruptcy Tax Act of 1980, Congress ended the separate regime for debtor corporations in a title 11 (bankruptcy) case by adding a new category of tax-free corporate reorganization under section 368(a)(1): the G reorganization. Congress made this change in order to encourage and facilitate the rehabilitation of bankrupt debtor corporations. As a consequence, many prior law requirements for tax-free treatment were removed, parties were given additional flexibility in structuring the acquisition, and, most importantly, the acquiring corporation was permitted to succeed to the tax attributes of the acquired corporation (such as its net operating loss carryovers).

The G reorganization is the most flexible of the acquisitive tax-free reorganization provisions. It is a hybrid provision which borrows most of its characteristics from the other acquisitive reorganization provisions. It is similar to an "A" reorganization (a state law merger) in that it requires two corporations and the only limit on the nature of consideration used by the acquiring corporation is the judicial "continuity of proprietary interest" doctrine discussed at the beginning of this Chapter. However, state-law merger requirements need not be met. It is similar to a C reorganization in that it contemplates an acquisition of assets of one corporation by another corporation, but it does not require an exchange of assets solely (as relaxed by statute) for voting stock of the acquiring corporation. It is most like an acquisitive D reorganization, except a G reorganization does not require that the shareholders of the acquired corporation also be "in control" of the acquiring corporation.

---

64. See Chapter 10.02(d) supra.

65. Rev. Rul. 2004–83, 2004–2 C.B. 157.

A G reorganization is defined as (1) a transfer of assets (2) by one corporation to another corporation in a title 11 (bankruptcy) or similar case (3) followed by a distribution as described in § 354, § 355 or § 356 of the consideration received in the transaction. Each of these three requirements of the G reorganization is discussed below.

A G reorganization requires a transfer by a corporation of all or a part of its assets to another corporation, provided one of the corporations is in a bankruptcy (or similar case) and provided the transfer occurs pursuant to a plan of reorganization approved by the bankruptcy court. § 368(a)(3)(B). Thus, the transfer of stock of the debtor corporation to its creditors in satisfaction of their claims will not qualify as a G reorganization (although there may be no adverse tax consequences of such a transaction). Similarly, out-of-court transactions, Chapter 7 liquidating cases, and foreign reorganizations are ineligible.

For example, suppose Loss Corp. is hopelessly insolvent. Immediately prior to filing a bankruptcy petition, Loss Corp. agrees to transfer all of its assets to Public Corp. in exchange for Public Corp. common stock and Loss Co. will then distribute the stock received to its creditors in satisfaction of their claims against Loss Corp. This acquisition will not qualify as a G reorganization because it did not occur within a title 11 or similar case. Accordingly, the transaction will be tax-free only if it meets the standards of one of the other acquisitive reorganization provisions such as the A, C, or D.

As a second example, suppose Loss Corp. is in a Chapter 11 bankruptcy case. Loss Corp.'s plan of reorganization provides for a transfer of cash and certain non-operating assets to secured creditors and of all newly-authorized common stock to its unsecured creditors. All previously-authorized outstanding common stock is canceled. Loss Corp.'s plan will not qualify as a G reorganization because Loss Corp. has not transferred its assets to another corporation. Although not qualifying as a G reorganization, this transaction likely qualifies for tax-free treatment as a E recapitalization, a form of tax-free reorganization below.[66] See S. Rep. No. 96–1035, 96th Cong., 2d Sess. 36 (1980).

Distribution of stock or securities of the acquiring corporation in a transaction that qualifies under § 354 raises some difficult obstacles. Section 354(b) requires that "substantially all" the assets of the acquired corporation be transferred to the acquiring corporation. In the context of the C reorganization, the Service requires

---

66. See Section 10.05 *infra.*

(for advanced rulings) that at least 90% of the net assets and 70% of the gross assets be transferred in the reorganization.[67] Congress has indicated that the "substantially all" requirement be interpreted liberally in the context of the G reorganization in view of the underlying purpose of the provision to facilitate the rehabilitation of financially troubled corporations. Accordingly, "substantially all" the assets of the debtor corporation should be acquired even if the debtor sells assets to pay creditors or to rearrange its business affairs in order to obtain creditor approval of its plan of reorganization. S. Rep. No. 96–1035, 96th Cong., 2d Sess. 36–36 (1980). In private rulings, the Service has relaxed its definition of "substantially all" in the context of a G reorganization. See Ltr. Ruls. 8726055, 8521083.

In addition to the "substantially all" requirement, § 354(a) requires that stock or securities of the acquiring corporation be distributed to a holder of stock or securities of the acquired corporation. If holders of securities in the acquired corporation actually receive stock or securities (or if shareholders in the acquired corporation actually receive stock) in the acquiring corporation pursuant to the plan of reorganization, the transaction should qualify as a G reorganization even if the value of the stock or securities received represents a small percentage of the value of the total equity consideration given in the transaction. Thus, the threshold exchange requirement of § 354(a) should be satisfied if one security holder receives stock or securities (or if one shareholder receives stock) pursuant to the plan of reorganization. However, if (as is often the case in the typical corporate bankruptcy) all of the old stock of the debtor corporation is cancelled (because there is no equity left) and the acquiring corporation's stock is distributed to short-term creditors whose debt instruments do not rise to the dignity of a tax security, the threshold exchange requirement of § 354(a) will not be satisfied.

For example, suppose Loss Corp. is in a Chapter 11 bankruptcy case. Loss Corp.'s plan of reorganization provides for the transfer of "substantially all" its assets to Public Corp. in exchange for Public Corp. common stock with fair market value of $450 and cash of $550. The plan calls for the transfer of cash and certain non-operating assets to secured creditors and the distribution of all the Public Corp. common stock to Loss Corp.'s unsecured creditors. One of the unsecured creditors holds a 10–year bond, and assume that this bond is a "security" for tax purposes. The old Loss Corp. common stock is cancelled and the shareholders receive nothing under the plan. Because "substantially all" the assets were ac-

---

67. Rev. Proc. 77–37, 1977–2 C.B. 568.

quired by Public Corp. in exchange for an amount of common stock that should satisfy the "continuity of proprietary interest" doctrine, and because at least one Loss Corp. securityholder received stock pursuant to the plan, the transaction should qualify as a tax-free G reorganization.

The transaction in this example would not qualify as a G reorganization if all of Loss Corp.'s unsecured creditors held only short-term debt. One possible way of avoiding this technical trap in the statute is to convert the claims of the creditors into stock of the acquired debtor corporation prior to the date that the G reorganization is consummated, relying on *Helvering v. Alabama Asphaltic Limestone Co.*, 315 U.S. 179 (1942). In that case, the Supreme Court held that creditors of an insolvent corporation who received stock of a reorganized corporation had a "continuing interest" because, under the full priority rule of bankruptcy proceedings, they had "effective command over the disposition of the properties" of the old corporation.

However, in *Neville Coke & Chemical Co. v. Commissioner*, 148 F.2d 599 (3d Cir.1945), it was held that noteholders of a reorganized corporation who exchanged their notes for debentures and common stock could not claim nonrecognition of their gain under what is now § 354. The court relied on *Pinellas Ice & Cold Storage Co. v. Commissioner*[68] and *Le Tulle v. Scofield*[69] as establishing that notes received on an exchange do not evidence a continuing interest in the enterprise and are not "securities." It then held that the notes are equally deficient if given up in the exchange. The debtor was in financial difficulties at the time of the exchange, but the court was unwilling to find that the creditors already owned the entire equity, and in fact the old stockholders did participate in the exchange. If, however, the creditors of a distressed corporation in reorganization received stock or securities evidencing a proprietary interest in the enterprise, is it not probable that the claims they gave up, whatever their form, already represented in economic reality a proprietary interest in the assets?

In addition to the statutory requirements, a G reorganization must meet additional judicial requirements imposed on all tax-free corporate reorganizations. Principally, these include the "continuity of proprietary interest," "continuity of business enterprise" and "business purpose" requirements.[70] Finally, if a transaction qualifies as both a G reorganization and under one of the other reorgani-

---

68. 287 U.S. 462 (1933).

69. 308 U.S. 415 (1940).

70. See p. 219 *supra*.

zation provisions (or under § 332 or § 351), the transaction is treated as qualifying only as a G reorganization. § 368(a)(3)(C).

(h) The Status of Creditors in a Reorganization. Creditors will not necessarily participate in the reorganization exchange. For example, in a B reorganization, the creditors of the acquired corporation may simply ride through the reorganization, preserving intact their claims against their respective debtors.

Alternatively, the acquiring corporation may assume the transferor-corporation's liabilities, or take the properties subject to those liabilities, still without any exchange by the creditors. Ordinarily, this will not constitute "boot" to the transferee. § 357. Nor will creditors recognize gain or loss, since their claims have not been paid, retired, or exchanged. Moreover, § 368(a)(1)(C) states explicitly that the requirement that the acquisition be solely for the acquiring corporation's voting stock in a C reorganization is not breached by its assuming liabilities or taking property subject to liabilities.

On the other hand, there frequently will be an exchange. The creditors may surrender bonds, debentures, or notes of one corporation and receive stock or securities of another corporation. Even if an exchange of securities in the target corporation for stock or securities of the acquiring corporation is not part of the definition of a tax-free reorganization, the exchange nevertheless will qualify under § 354 because it falls within the definition of that section: an exchange of stock or securities of a party to a reorganization for stock or securities of another party to the reorganization, all in pursuance of the plan of reorganization. One difficulty that may arise, however, is that short-term notes (whether given up or received) may not qualify as "securities."

There may be other problems as well. If in conjunction with a B reorganization (stock for stock), the acquiring corporation issues bonds in exchange for bonds of the acquired corporation, will the transaction fall outside of § 368(a)(1)(B) on the ground that it is not "solely" for voting stock? If the stock-for-stock exchange qualifies, will the bondholders' exchange be "in pursuance of a plan of reorganization" under § 354(a)(1)? See Rev. Rul. 98–10, 1998–1 C.B. 1 (exchange of debt of the acquired corporation for stock of the acquiring corporation incident to B reorganization not taxable). Similarly in a C reorganization, what if the acquiring corporation issues its own evidences of indebtedness to creditors of the transferee corporation instead of merely assuming the liabilities? Should the transaction lose its status as a reorganization?

Whenever creditors of a corporation swap old debt for new—whether in the context of a reorganization (often a bankruptcy reorganization) or not—it must be determined whether the exchange is taxable to the creditors (possibly producing gain or loss) as well as to the corporation (possibly producing cancellation of indebtedness income). Consider the situation in which a corporation replaces its outstanding debt with new debt having different terms. For example, short-term, low-interest notes might be replaced with long-term, higher interest bonds. What are the tax consequences of such a debt swap?

Under Regs. § 1.1001–3, "a significant modification of a debt instrument . . . is deemed to result in an exchange of the original instrument." Accordingly, gain or loss can be recognized by the debt holder. If, for example, the value of the debt received exceeds the holder's adjusted basis in the debt surrendered, gain will be recognized on the exchange. This might be the case when the corporation's distress has been reflected in the market price of its notes so that current holders of those notes may have paid significantly less than face value. What constitutes a "significant modification" is contained in Regs. § 1.1001–3(e).

The transaction will also be taxable to the corporation, which raises the possibility of cancellation of indebtedness income to the corporation if it substitutes current low value debt for outstanding obligations initially issued for face value. Thus, if a corporation exchanges $1,100 face value bonds having current fair market value of $800 for each $1,000 short-term note outstanding, the corporation will recognize $200 of cancellation of indebtedness income on each exchange. Unless the exchange occurs while the corporation is insolvent or in a bankruptcy proceeding, the cancellation of indebtedness income will be taxable immediately. See §§ 61(a)(12) and 108(a). And if the insolvency exception applies, it is limited to the extent of the debtor corporation's insolvency. § 108(a)(3).

A corporation might also swap stock for debt. To the extent that the value of such stock is less than the issue price of the surrendered debt, once again the corporation will be faced with recognition of cancellation of indebtedness income except to the extent § 108 applies. And if application of § 108 to an insolvent or bankrupt corporation permits the corporation to exclude some or all of its cancellation of indebtedness income, the corporation will be forced to reduced its tax attributes (including its tax credits, NOL carryovers, and adjusted basis) as the tax "payment" for the exclusion. See § 108(b).

(i) A Retrospective on the Rules of § 368. Having looked at the various definitions in § 368, what general conclusions can we draw?

First, Congress seems to have agreed with the Supreme Court that the taxable sale of a corporation and a tax-free reorganization differ in the form of consideration received by shareholders of the transferor-corporation. This notion, the continuity of proprietary interest doctrine, informs much of the case and statutory law in this area. Permissible consideration is broadest in A reorganizations and in forward subsidiary mergers, for in these situations the only limitation is that imposed by the common law. At the opposite end of the spectrum are B reorganizations and reverse subsidiary mergers, for in these cases the only allowable consideration is voting stock. In between lies C reorganizations in which up to 20 percent boot may be allowable under § 368(a)(2)(B). The nondivisive D reorganization, because it requires that the shareholders of the transferor-corporation either *have* or *acquire* control of the transferee-corporation, does not easily fit anywhere into the pattern.

In addition, it should now be clear that the reorganization definitions are full of detail and complexity, detail and complexity that must be mastered by anyone involved in the transfer of corporate control. To be sure, two major principles run through the various forms of reorganization: continuity of proprietary interest and continuity of the business enterprise in modified corporate form. However, the implementation of these principles varies from provision to provision without rhyme or reason. The continuity of proprietary interest requirement, for example, is implemented differently in the A, B, C, D and reverse subsidiary reorganizations. Only the A and forward subsidiary reorganizations adopt the same approach to the continuing proprietary interest requirement, and what they adopt is the uncertainty and occasional irrationality of the common law in this area.

The American Law Institute adopted a series of proposals covering subchapter C. In particular, it proposed that any bulk transfer of assets from one corporation to another be treated as a tax-free reorganization if the corporate parties so elect. If not, gain or loss on the transfer is recognized and each party takes a fair market value basis in the property received. However, if the parties elect in favor of nonrecognition, then each party must use a carry-over basis in the assets received. By making reorganization status formally elective, these proposals eliminate the various inconsistent definitions now comprising § 368.

These proposals also eliminate the continuity of proprietary interest requirement. Regardless of the corporate-level election, a shareholder who exchanges stock for stock as part of a bulk transfer of corporate assets is given nonrecognition on the exchange and a carry-over basis in the assets so acquired. Shareholders whose interests are cashed-out, on the other hand, are fully taxed. Thus the problems posed by *Kass*, *McDonald's* and *Paulsen* are eliminated. To be sure, such an approach to corporate reorganizations will not eliminate all definitional questions. For example, the definition of a bulk transfer of assets necessarily will include some arbitrary lines. Nonetheless, such an approach would go a long way toward clearing the reorganization jungle.

10.03 Amalgamating Reorganizations: Taxation. In the absence of special statutory provisions, the various stock for stock and stock for asset exchanges forming the reorganization transactions would be taxable under the general provisions of the Code.[71] When, though, a transaction falls within § 368(a), a host of special provisions apply, most notably §§ 354, 356 and 358 at the shareholder-level and §§ 357, 361 and 362 at the corporate-level.

(a) Corporate–Level Taxation. In all reorganizations other than the B, there is a transfer of assets from one corporation to another. The taxation of the transferor-corporation is governed by § 361. For example, § 361 applies to the target corporation in a C reorganization when it transfers its assets in exchange for stock of the acquiring corporation.

Under §§ 361(a) and 361(b)(2), the transferor-corporation will never recognize loss on the exchange. In addition, under § 361(a), the transferor-corporation will not recognize gain on the exchange so long as it receives only stock and securities. Further, even if the transferor-corporation receives boot on the exchange, no gain will be recognized if the boot is distributed as part of the transaction. § 361(b)(1). Thus, the exchange will be a taxable event to the transferor-corporation only if it transfers appreciated property and receives in exchange some boot that is not then distributed as part of the reorganization.[72] Note that property transferred to a creditor is treated as distributed, § 361(b)(3), thereby further narrowing the possibility of recognition.

For example, suppose Target Corp. owns operating assets with adjusted basis of $950,000 and fair market value of $1,000,000. If Target Corp. transfers those assets to Acquiring Corp. in exchange for stock and securities of Acquiring in a C reorganization, Target

---

71. See *Marr v. United States*, 268 U.S. 536 (1925).

72. In a forward subsidiary merger under § 368(a)(2)(D), the acquiring corporation generally transfers stock of its parent to the target's shareholders, with such stock having been acquired from its parent in a § 351 transaction. In general, no gain or loss will be recognized to the acquiring corporation on this exchange *if* the stock of its parent was acquired as part of the plan of reorganization. See Regs. § 1.1032–2.

does not recognize any of the gain inherent in its assets. Further, if Target receives only $900,000 of stock and securities of Acquiring Corp. as well as $100,000 cash, Target will still be protected from recognition so long as Target distributes the cash (including a distribution to one or more of its creditors) as part of the reorganization. However, if Target fails to distribute the cash,[73] Target will recognize its gain on the exchange in an amount not exceeding the $100,000 boot. Here, that means Target will recognize gain of $50,000 because that is the entire gain realized by Target on the transaction.

When might the transferor-corporation fail to distribute boot received in the reorganization? In a C reorganization, the transferor-corporation is required to liquidate as part of the transaction absent special consent of the government. § 368(a)(2)(G). Similarly, a transferor-corporation is required to liquidate as part of a non-divisive D. § 354(b)(1)(B). Thus, a transferor-corporation rarely will retain boot received in the reorganization. However, under some circumstances the transferor-corporation will be treated as if it received boot when the transferee-corporation assumes liabilities of the transferor. See §§ 357(b), 357(c). Accordingly, a transferor-corporation in such circumstances will be forced to recognize gain if it transferred appreciated assets because it cannot avail itself of the opportunity in § 361(b)(1) to distribute the boot: liabilities assumed by the acquiring cannot be distributed. Note, though, that the liabilities-in-excess-of-basis rule of § 357(c) applies only to a D reorganization and not, for example, to an A or C. § 357(c)(1)(B).

The transferor-corporation's basis in the stock and securities received is equal to its basis in the property transferred, increased by any gain recognized on the exchange and decreased by any money received and by the fair market value of any property received. § 358(a)(1). That basis is allocated between the stock and securities in proportion to relative fair market values.[74] Noncash boot received takes a fair market value basis. § 358(a)(2). For computing the transferor-corporation's basis in the stock and securities received, assumption of its liabilities by another corporation as part of the reorganization is treated as cash received. § 358(d).

For example, reconsider the case in which Target Corp. exchanges assets with adjusted basis of $950,000 and fair market value of $1,000,000 to Acquiring Corp. in a C reorganization. Assume now that Target receives $900,000 worth of Acquiring's

---

73. Recall that Target Corp. must liquidate as part of the reorganization unless consent of the government is obtained. § 368(a)(2)(G)(ii).

74. See Regs. § 1.358–2.

stock, $60,000 cash, and Blackacre worth $40,000. Once again, if Target does not distribute the cash or Blackacre as part of the reorganization, Target will recognize a gain of $50,000 on the exchange. Under § 358(a)(1), Target will take a basis in the stock of Acquiring Corp. of $900,000, that being carry-over of $950,000 plus the gain recognized of $50,000 less the cash received of $60,000 and less the fair market value of Blackacre of $40,000. Target takes a basis in Blackacre equal to its fair market value, or $40,000. § 358(a)(2).

Reconsider this example but assume that Target distributes the cash as part of the reorganization. Now, Target recognizes only $40,000 on the exchange because that is the amount of boot (Blackacre) received but not distributed. Under § 358(a)(1), Target will take a basis in the Acquiring Corp. stock of $890,000, that being carry-over of $950,000 plus the gain recognized of $40,000 less the cash received of $60,000 and less the $40,000 fair market value of Blackacre. Thus, the $10,000 of Target's gain deferred on the exchange will reappear when Target sells the Acquiring stock. Note, though, that no gain will be recognized to Target if it distributes the Acquiring stock as part of the reorganization even though that stock has a basis below its fair market value. § 361(c). Target's basis in Blackacre again is equal to fair market value, or $40,000.

In most cases, the transferor-corporation will liquidate as part of the reorganization. The usual rules applicable to corporate liquidations do not apply in this context.[75] Instead, the transferor-corporation will recognize gain on the transaction to the extent it distributes appreciated property (other than stock and securities in the acquiring corporation). § 361(c)(1)–(4). Because property received in the reorganization by the transferor-corporation takes a fair market value basis in its hands, the only appreciated property available for distribution is property owned by the transferor-corporation prior to the transaction. For example, the transferor-corporation in a C reorganization need only transfer "substantially all" of its assets, and so when it liquidates, it will distribute any assets not transferred to the acquiring corporation.

Loss cannot be recognized by the transferor-corporation on the liquidating distribution. § 361(c)(1). The usual rule is that loss can be recognized on a liquidating distribution but not on a non-liquidating distribution.[76] No loss can be recognized by the transferor-corporation on its liquidating distribution because, in the context

---

75. See § 361(c)(4).

76. See §§ 336(a) (liquidating distributions), 311(a) (non-liquidating distributions).

of the overall reorganization, that distribution is best thought of as a nonliquidating distribution of the continuing entity.[77]

In contradistinction to the transferor-corporation, the transferee-corporation often may recognize gain or loss on the reorganization. No gain will be recognized by the transferee to the extent that it gives up only its own stock because of § 1032, a provision whose scope includes and exceeds the reorganization context. Section 1032, also applicable to a § 351 incorporation, provides that a corporation does not recognize gain or loss on the receipt of property in exchange for its own stock.

However, if the transferee-corporation uses boot as part of its consideration, gain or loss will be recognized if the boot is appreciated or loss property. For example, suppose that X Corp. transfers voting stock worth $90,000 and Blackacre worth $10,000 to T Corp. in a C reorganization. No reorganization provision protects X from recognizing gain or loss on this transfer of Blackacre. Accordingly, under the general rule of § 1001(a), X will be taxable on the gain, if any, realized on the transfer of Blackacre. Similarly, if X's adjusted basis in Blackacre exceeds Blackacre's fair market value, X will be entitled to claim a loss.

Suppose that X transfers its own securities to T Corp. instead of Blackacre. Does X recognize gain or loss on the exchange? No Code provision exempts from taxation that part of the transaction representing the exchange of securities for assets. However, recall that the acquisition of property by a taxpayer in exchange for the taxpayer's promise to pay later is treated as a purchase.[78] Thus, because a taxpayer is not, in general,[79] taxable on the purchase of property, X Corp. recognizes no gain because the receipt of assets in exchange for X Corp.'s securities is nothing but the purchase of those assets by X.

For example, suppose the transferee-corporation in a C reorganization transfers its own stock worth $900,000 and Blackacre worth $100,000 to the transferor-corporation in exchange for all of the transferor-corporation's assets. If the transferee-corporation's basis in Blackacre is $60,000, the transferee-corporation will recognize a gain of $40,000 on the exchange. The transferor-corporation will then take a fair market value basis of $100,000 in Blackacre. The transferee-corporation's basis in the property received, deter-

---

77. See § 311(b), discussed at Section 4.04 *supra* (no loss to distributing corporation allowed on nonliquidating distribution).

78. See *Crane v. Commissioner*, 331 U.S. 1 (1947).

79. One exception to this rule arises in connection with the repurchase by a taxpayer of the taxpayer's own debt instruments. See *United States v. Kirby Lumber Co.*, 284 U.S. 1 (1931).

mined under § 362(b), is carried over from the transferor-corporation, increased by any gain recognized by the transferor-corporation on the exchange. Consistent with treating the two corporations as a single entity after the reorganization, this basis rule ensures that asset appreciation will be taxed to the transferor-corporation or to the transferee-corporation but not to both.

(b) Shareholder–Level Taxation. Shareholder-level taxation is governed by §§ 354, 356 and 358. Under the general rule of § 354(a), no gain or loss is recognized by a shareholder exchanging stock or securities of one corporate "party" to the reorganization for stock or securities of another corporate "party" to the reorganization. Section § 368(b) defines "parties" for each type of reorganization as the corporations, *and only those corporations,* playing a role in the definition of the reorganization. For example, the parent of the acquiring corporation *is* a "party" to a parenthetical B reorganization but not to a nonparenthetical B. Similarly, there are only two corporate parties to a type A merger but three in a type A consolidation and the forward and reverse subsidiary mergers under §§ 368(a)(1)(D) and (E).

Section 354 specifically allows a shareholder to exchange securities as well as stock in a tax-free reorganization.[80] This is true even as to those reorganizations in which securities do not constitute allowable consideration at the corporate-level. For example, suppose that X Corp. acquires 80 percent of the assets of T Corp. in a C reorganization, and assume that 80 percent in this case constitutes "substantially all" of T's assets. The only allowable consideration in this transaction is voting stock of X; even the boot relaxation rule of § 368(a)(2)(B) would not help here.[81]

After the transfer of assets, T must liquidate, distributing the voting stock of X and its remaining assets to its shareholders. Those remaining assets might include previously acquired securities of X, and in such circumstances § 354 may be available to protect the shareholders from recognition of gain. The liquidating distribution of the target corporation might include securities of the acquiring corporation in an A reorganization or in a forward or reverse subsidiary merger, because in such reorganizations non-stock consideration can be used by the acquiring corporation.

80. Compare § 351 at Section 2.06(d) *supra* where securities do not constitute qualifying property. Note that stock warrants are treated as "securities" for purposes of § 356. Regs. § 1.354–1(e).

81. Under § 368(a)(2)(B), boot can be exchanged for assets only if 80% of the target corporation's assets are acquired for voting stock. Thus, when only 80% of the target's assets are acquired, there is no room for boot. See Section 10.02(c) *supra.*

Securities can even be exchanged as part of a B reorganization. For example, suppose A Corp. acquires all the outstanding stock of T Corp. in exchange for its own voting stock. As part of this one transaction, A Corp. also exchanges its own securities for the outstanding securities of T Corp. The stock portion of this transaction qualifies as a tax-free B reorganization, and because the exchange of the securities is a part of that reorganization, it is covered by § 354 even though the exchange of securities is not a part of the definition of the reorganization.[82]

While § 354(a) can apply to distributions of securities, it does not always do so. Under § 354(b), the receipt of securities is not tax-free to the extent that the principal (i.e., face) amount of the securities received by a shareholder exceeds the principal amount of the securities transferred. In particular, § 354(a) will offer no protection to the shareholder who transfers only stock and receives only securities.

The excess principal amount of any securities, and all other property received by the shareholder other than stock of a "party" to the reorganization, is taxable under § 356(a). Under that provision, receipt of such boot opens the door to recognition of gain in an amount not in excess of the value of the boot received. That is, and like the rule applicable to incorporations under § 351(b), like-kind exchanges under § 1031, involuntary conversions under § 1033, and a host of other transactions, a taxpayer receiving boot on the transaction recognizes the lesser of the gain realized on the transaction and the fair market value of the boot.[83]

In the context of a tax-free reorganization, a shareholder might give up or receive "nonqualified preferred stock" as that term is defined in § 351(g)(2). Recall that such stock is both preferred and limited; in particular, such stock does not participate in corporate growth to any significant extent.[84] In addition, such stock must either include a redemption feature making it only a short-term investment in the corporate enterprise or have a dividend rate tied to interest rates or some equivalent index making the stock little more than subordinated debt.

In general, if a shareholder gives up such nonqualified preferred stock for new, nonqualified preferred stock or for any other stock, the exchange is tax-free under § 354. However, if a share-

---

82. See, e.g., Rev. Rul. 98–10, 1998–1 C.B. 1.

83. This rule applies without change to the receipt of the excess principal amount of securities. See § 356(d)(2)(B). In particular, although it is an excess principal amount that triggers recogni-

tion, it is the fair market value of the excess principal amount that determines how much gain will be recognized. See Regs. § 1.356–3(b), especially example 4.

84. See Section 2.06(c) supra.

holder receives nonqualified preferred stock in exchange for stock (other than old nonqualified preferred stock), the exchange is fully taxable under § 1001(a). See § 354(a)(2)(C). In all events, though, even nonqualified preferred stock is treated as "stock" for determining whether the transaction qualifies as a reorganization, and even nonqualified preferred stock is treated as stock rather than as boot for determining the corporate-level tax consequences of the transaction.

Shareholder-level gain can be dividend or capital gain depending on the effect of the distribution to the shareholder. With qualified dividend income now taxed at the same rate as long-term capital gain, the character of the shareholder's recognized income becomes a relatively minor issue. Note in particular that regardless of the character of the income, it is the gain (rather than the gross amount received) that is taxable in either event. Thus, even if the shareholder recognizes dividend income, such income arises only after basis recovery.

Under § 356(a)(2), if the effect is that of a dividend, then the gain will be recognized as dividend income up to each share's allocable portion of earnings and profits. If not, the gain will be capital if the stock transferred was a capital asset in the hands of the shareholder. Even in a world in which dividends are taxed at the same rate as capital gain, § 356(a)(2) remains relevant: capital gain is better than dividend income because of the disabilities imposed on the recognition of capital losses. An individual taxpayer can offset capital capital gain by capital losses without limitation yet can offset ordinary income only up to a maximum of $3,000 per year; a corporate taxpayer cannot offset ordinary income by capital loss to any extent.[85] (Of course, a corporate taxpayer does not enjoy a preferential rate of taxation on capital gain or on qualified dividends.)

The courts have looked to the redemption rules of § 302 for guidance in determining the effect of receipt of boot under § 356. However, the courts divided over how the rules of § 302 should be incorporated into the § 356 analysis, some using a "before" test and some using an "after" one. The Supreme Court resolved the issue in *Commissioner v. Clark*,[86] in favor of the "after" test over the government's argument that the "before" test was more appropriate.

The "before" test was created in *Shimberg v. United States*.[87] In that case, the court held that an exchange has the effect of a

85. See §§ 165(f), 1211 and 1212.   **87.** 577 F.2d 283 (5th Cir.1978).
86. 489 U.S. 726 (1989).

dividend under § 356(a)(2) if "the distribution would have been taxed as a dividend if the distribution had been made prior to the reorganization or if no reorganization had occurred." Under this test, boot distributed as part of the reorganization is treated as if it had been distributed by the target corporation in a redemption prior to the reorganization. In this hypothetical redemption, each shareholder of the target corporation is treated as exchanging stock for the boot actually received in the reorganization. The rules of § 302 are then applied to this hypothetical redemption for determining the effect of the exchange on the shareholder.

For example, suppose the target corporation has 100 shares outstanding, owned 50 by B, 25 by C and 25 by D (all of whom are unrelated). Suppose further that, as part of the reorganization, B exchanges his shares for 500 shares of the acquiring corporation plus $5,000 while C and D each exchanges his shares for 250 shares and $2,500. Under the *Shimberg* test the exchange will have the effect of a dividend because the boot is received by the shareholders in proportion to their stock holdings and so cannot affect their relative interests in the target corporation. Accordingly, the shareholders will have dividend treatment to the extent of the earnings and profits of the target corporation.

The "after" test was fashioned in *Wright v. United States*.[88] As in *Shimberg,* the court in *Wright* was faced with shareholders of the target corporation who received boot in a reorganization. The court recharacterized the single reorganization into two transactions: (1) a reorganization in which hypothetical stock replaced the boot actually received by the shareholder; and (2) a redemption of this hypothetical stock in exchange for the boot actually received. The court then applied the redemption rules of § 302 to this hypothetical redemption.

The following example illustrates the strength of the *Wright* test and the weakness of the *Shimberg* test. Suppose that X Corp. merges into Y Corp. X has two shareholders, individuals P and Q. P and Q each owns half of the outstanding stock of X with a basis of $10,000 and a fair market value of $100,000. In the reorganization, P and Q each exchanges his stock of X for stock of Y worth $50,000 plus cash of $50,000. Assume that after the reorganization, P and Q each owns 1 percent of the outstanding stock of Y.

Under the *Shimberg* test, the effect of the exchange on P and Q is that of a dividend: it is pro rata, and had it occurred prior to the reorganization, it would have been subject to the distribution

---

88. 482 F.2d 600 (8th Cir.1973).

rules of § 301. Yet, the effect of the transaction in its entirety is to reduce substantially P's and Q's interest in the corporate venture.

Under the *Wright* test, we act as if P and Q had received only stock of Y in the reorganization. In this hypothetical redemption, P and Q would have received $100,000 in stock of Y, making them each almost 2 percent shareholders. Next, we assume that P and Q exchange the excess stock for the boot actually received. This exchange is a redemption in which P and Q go from 2 percent shareholders to 1 percent shareholders, and under the disproportionate distribution safe harbor of § 302(b)(2), the redemption would be taxed as an exchange. Accordingly, under the *Wright* test, the effect of the exchange is not that of a dividend, and P and Q will report their gain on the reorganization as capital gain.

In *Commissioner v. Clark*,[89] the Supreme Court adopted the *Wright* "after" test. The Supreme Court characterized the *Shimberg* "before" test as "sever[ing] the payment of boot from the context of the reorganization. . . . [Such an approach] is plainly inconsistent with the statute's direction that we look to the effect of the entire exchange." The Court also observed that the *Shimberg* test results in ordinary income treatment in most reorganizations, an improper effect of an "overly expansive reading of § 356(a)(2)."

While the Supreme Court was correct that the *Shimberg* "before" test usually is less advantageous to taxpayers than the *Wright* "after" test, there are situations in which this can be reversed. For example, suppose X Corp. merges into Y Corp. when each share of X Corp. and Y Corp. stock is worth $50, and each corporation is owned by individuals P, Q and R as follows:

Before Merger

	X Corp.	Y Corp.
P	50 (50%)	0 (0%)
Q	50 (50%)	90 (90%)
R	0 (0%)	10 (10%)
Total Shares	100	100

As a result of the merger, P receives $1,500 in cash and 20 shares of Y Corp. stock while Q receives $2,000 in cash and 10 shares of Y Corp. stock. Thus, after the merger Y Corp. has 130 shares outstanding, of which P owns 20, Q owns 100, and R owns 10.

89.   489 U.S. 726 (1989).

After Merger

	Y Corp.
P	20 (15.38%)
Q	100 (76.92%)
R	10 (7.69%)
Total Shares	130

Under the *Shimberg* "before" test, P and Q are treated as if they receive the boot in a redemption prior to the merger. As a result of this hypothetical redemption, P's interest in X Corp. increases from 50 percent (50 of 100 shares) to 66.7 percent (20 of 30 shares[90]). Q's interest, on the other hand, drops from 50 percent (50 of 100 shares) to 33.3 percent (10 of 30 shares). Thus, although P will have dividend income on the $1,500 boot (assuming adequate earnings and profits), Q will obtain exchange treatment on the $2,000 of boot under § 302(b)(2).

A very different result obtains under the *Wright* "after" test. Following *Wright,* we act as if P and Q each received only stock of Y Corp. in exchange for their shares of X Corp. (step 1), followed by a redemption of the shares hypothetically just received by P and Q (step 2). Because the shares of X Corp. and of Y Corp. are of equal value, P and Q would each receive 50 shares of Y Corp. stock in exchange for their 50 shares of X Corp. stock if each received only stock in the exchange. Thus, there would be 200 shares of Y Corp. outstanding, owned as follows:

After Hypothetical Exchange

	Y Corp.
P	50 (25%)
Q	140 (70%)
R	10 (5%)
Total Shares	200

In step 2, we treat 30 of P's shares and 40 of Q's shares as redeemed by Y Corp. Accordingly, P's interest drops from 25 percent (50 of 200 shares) to 15.38 percent (20 of 130 shares). Q's interest, on the other hand, increases from 70 percent (140 of 200 shares) to 76.92 percent (100 of 130 shares). Thus, P now qualifies for exchange treatment while Q recognizes dividend income.

The Service's refusal to follow *Wright*[91] was based in part on some unfortunate dicta in that opinion. If a distribution has the

---

90. Because each share of X Corp. stock is worth $50, the $1,500 boot corresponds to a redemption of 30 shares. Similarly, the $2,000 of boot received by Q corresponds to 40 shares of X Corp.

91. Rev. Rul. 75–83, 1975–1 C.B. 112, revoked by Rev. Rul. 93–61, 1993–30 C.B. 10, in light of the decision in *Commissioner v. Clark.*

effect of a dividend under § 356(a)(2), it must be determined whether there are sufficient earnings and profits to cover the distribution. The *Wright* court opined that the earnings and profits of only the acquiring corporation could be used to cover the distribution. The Service, unwilling to allow taxpayers to bail-out the earnings of the transferor corporation, refused to accept that dicta in *Wright*. Consistent with a "before" test, the court in *Shimberg* used the earnings and profits of the transferor corporation to characterize the distribution. One possibility apparently overlooked by the *Wright* and *Shimberg* courts is to use the earnings and profits of *both* corporations as is done in § 304.[92] The Supreme Court in *Clark* did not address this aspect of the § 356(a)(2) controversy. However, in deciding the *Clark* case the Tax Court[93] followed the *Wright* "after" approach and added:

> There is no reason why the redemption cannot be considered as having been made by one corporation with the consequences to be measured by the earnings and profits of another corporation.

Regardless of *how* the determination under § 356(a)(2) is made, note that the amount of income to a shareholder is limited to the shareholder's *gain* on the transaction. In general, corporate distributions not treated as exchanges are taxed as ordinary income to the full extent of the amount distributed without any basis recovery. If an exchange incident to a reorganization has the effect of a dividend, one would expect that the entire distribution would be ordinary income. Nevertheless, Congress persists in limiting § 356(a)(2) to gain, making § 356 an easy loophole for high-basis taxpayers.

For example, suppose that individual B owns all the outstanding stock of X Corp. and of Y Corp. Assume that Y Corp. has been quite profitable. How can B get his hands on Y Corp.'s income at a low tax cost? If Y makes a distribution it will be taxable under § 301. If B sells some X Corp. stock to Y Corp., § 304 will produce dividend treatment. Suppose instead that the two corporations merge in an A reorganization, and B exchanges his stock of X for stock of Y plus cash. If B realizes no gain on the transaction (because the X stock was unappreciated in B's hands), then the receipt of cash incident to the reorganization will be tax-free. Absent a reorganization or partial liquidation, there is no other way for a sole shareholder to remove funds from an on-going corporate venture without the imposition of tax.

---

92. See § 304(b)(2).

93. *Clark v. Commissioner*, 86 T.C. 138 (1986).

The basis of property received by shareholders in a reorganization is determined under § 358, the same section applicable to incorporations under § 351. Section 358 provides for an aggregate carry-over of basis increased by the amount of gain recognized, if any, by the shareholder. Boot received in the exchange is given a fair market value basis, with the remaining basis allocated to stock and securities received tax-free in proportion to relative fair market values. In effect, this rule ensures that § 354(a) provides deferral rather than exemption, with the amount of the deferred gain preserved in the basis of the stock and securities.

(c) A Note on "Securities". The continuity of proprietary interest, whether the judicial creature fashioned in the context of A reorganizations (and applicable to the forward subsidiary merger) or the statutory definitions found in the definitions of the B, C, non-divisive D, and reverse subsidiary mergers, requires the transfer of stock (sometimes voting stock) of the acquiring corporation to the shareholders of the acquired corporation. It is perhaps surprising then that the property which may be received tax-free in a reorganization includes not only stock but also securities, and this is true at both the corporate and shareholder levels. See §§ 361(a), 354(a)(1). But what is a "security"?

A security is a debt instrument of the issuing corporation, of course, but the term "security" does not encompass all debt instruments. In this context, a security is a debt instrument representing a continuing interest in the affairs of the issuing corporation. Other debt instruments—usually called notes rather than securities—resemble more closely the sale proceeds of the transferor's assets.

Until 1990, securities constituted qualified property (i.e., property that can be received tax-free) in an incorporation under § 351 as well as in a reorganization.[94] Accordingly, much of the judicial gloss on the term "security" developed in that context. Because courts treated the term "security" equivalently in these two areas, the case law developed under § 351 should still be good law in defining a security for the reorganization provisions.

A leading case on the definition of a security is *Camp Wolters Enterprises, Inc. v. Commissioner*,[95] where the Tax Court stated:

> The test as to whether notes are securities is not a mechanical determination of the time period of the note. Though time is an important factor, the controlling consideration is an over-all

---

94. There is a shareholder-level limitation that the principal amount of the securities received tax-free cannot exceed the principal amount of the securities given up. See § 354(a)(2)(A).

95. 22 T.C. 737, 751 (1954), aff'd, 230 F.2d 555 (5th Cir.1956).

evaluation of the nature of the debt, degree of participation and continuing interest compared with similarity of the note to a cash payment.

As *Camp Wolters* suggests, a note's maturity is probably the most important factor distinguishing a note from a security. In general, debt instruments with a five-year term or less will seldom qualify as securities while obligations with a term of ten years or more are likely to qualify.[96] As *Camp Wolters* also points out, maturity is not the only factor. A demand note might be a security if repayment is contingent on the performance of the corporation and the notes are subordinated to other debt instruments.[97]

Suppose Target Corp. issues debt instruments in 2004 with stated maturity of 2016, and assume these debt instruments are "securities" within the meaning of § 354. In 2014, Target Corp. merges into Acquiring Corp., with Acquiring Corp. surviving. As part of the merger, Acquiring Corp. issues new debt instrument to the former holders of the Target Corp. debt instruments having identical terms including a stated maturity date of 2016. While a debt instrument having a two-year term generally will not qualify as a "security," the Service has ruled that on these facts the new debt instruments will be treated as "securities" because they "represent a continuation of the security holder's investment in the Target Corporation in substantially the same form." Rev. Rul. 2004–78, 2004–2 C.B. 108. While not directly relevant to the continuity of proprietary interest doctrine, this ruling might suggest a further willingness to rethink the law as developed in *Robeling v. Commissioner*.[98]

At the corporate level in a reorganization, the distinction between a security and a mere note is unlikely to be important because the transferor-corporation receiving the debt instrument usually will distribute it, thereby precluding recognition of income.[99] At the shareholder level the distinction can be more important because receipt of boot (and a note is boot while a security may not be) forces the recognition of income. However, because gain from payment on a note can be reported on the installment method,[100] even here the distinction between a security and a note is largely irrelevant.[101]

96. For typical cases, compare *Nye v. Commissioner*, 50 T.C. 203 (1968) (ten-year note is a security) *with Bradshaw v. United States*, 683 F.2d 365 (Ct.Cl. 1982) (notes maturing annually for five years not securities).

97. See, e.g., *D'Angelo Associates v. Commissioner*, 70 T.C. 121 (1978).

98. 143 F.2d 810 (3d Cir.1944); see the discussion of *Paulson v. Commis-*

sioner, 469 U.S. 131 (1985), discussed in Chapter 10.02 supra.

99. See § 361(b)(1)(A).

100. See § 453(f)(6) (final flush language); Prop. Regs. § 1.453–1(f)(3)(ii).

101. One difference between receipt of a security and receipt of a note taxed

However, if the shareholder's gain is treated as a distribution under § 356(a)(2), then installment reporting is not permitted and notes will be treated like cash boot:[102] gain on the exchange, to the extent of the fair market value of the boot, will be recognized immediately. Thus, the importance of the *Clark* decision becomes magnified when short-term notes are in the picture.

10.04   Divisive Reorganizations

(a) Basic Requirements. In a divisive reorganization, one corporate enterprise is divided into two or more. A divisive reorganization can be used to divide one corporation into two so that warring shareholders can go their separate ways. A divisive reorganization also might be used to separate businesses that cannot, because of government regulations, be conducted by a single corporate entity.

A pro rata distribution by a parent corporation of the stock of a controlled subsidiary will effect a divisive reorganization in which shareholders of the parent corporation end up owning a brother/sister pair. For example, if Sub Corp. is a wholly-owned subsidiary of P Corp., a pro rata distribution of the Sub Corp. stock by P Corp. will change P and Sub Corp. from parent and subsidiary to two corporations owned by the same shareholders (i.e., a brother/sister pair). The same transaction can be effected by distributing the stock of the subsidiary in a pro rata redemption, with the only change being the number of shares of the parent corporation outstanding after the transaction. For historical reasons, the former transaction sometimes is called a "spin-off" while the latter is called a "split-off." A split-off often is not pro rata. For example, if P Corp. distributes the Sub Corp. stock to some shareholders in exchange for their P Corp. stock, the result is that some of the original P Corp. shareholders will continue to own P Corp. and some will own Sub Corp.

A divisive reorganization also might involve a § 351 incorporation as the first step. For example, if X Corp. owns two separate businesses, it might create a subsidiary corporation under § 351 by transferring one of the businesses to it. The subsidiary can then be

---

on the installment method lies in the shareholder's allocation of basis to the debt instrument. In addition, recognition of income on an installment obligation can precede receipt of payment under some circumstances, see § 453(e), while a shareholder who receives qualifying property in the form of a security will not recognize gain until principal payments received on the security exceed the shareholder's basis (or until the security is sold).

102. Note the "is not treated as a dividend" language at the end of § 453(f)(6).

spun-off (or split-off) as above. Alternatively, X Corp. could create two subsidiaries, Sub–1 and Sub–2. X would then transfer one business to Sub–1 and one to Sub–2, leaving X as a holding company. The complete liquidation of X would then result in a divisive reorganization, this time called a "split-up."

The different forms of a divisive reorganization share one common element: the potential for tax abuse. For example, consider X Corp. having substantial liquid assets (cash and marketable securities) as well as substantial earnings and profits. In order to bail out the cash and securities as capital gain, the shareholders of X might cause their corporation to spin-off the liquid assets. If this divisive transaction were tax-free, the shareholders could then sell off the new corporation's stock and thereby obtain the economic value of the liquid assets as capital gain. The shareholders would continue to hold X and its business assets, and when the purchasers of the new corporation liquidated it, the bail-out would be complete.[103]

To prevent this and similar abuses, the courts and Congress have limited tax-free divisive reorganizations to those meeting a variety of anti-abuse provisions. The statutory provisions are found in § 355, a section of the Code applicable to all divisive reorganizations. The Supreme Court has added to the statutory requirements the business purpose test, a test applicable to all reorganizations but having the most bite in the context of divisive reorganizations. This test grew out of one of the most famous tax cases ever, *Gregory v. Helvering*.[104]

The taxpayer in *Gregory* owned all the shares of United Mortgage Corp. United Mortgage in turn owned 1,000 shares of Monitor Securities Corp. To bail-out the Monitor shares as capital gain, the taxpayer caused United Mortgage to create a new corporation, the Averill Corp., by contributing the Monitor shares in exchange for shares of Averill. United Mortgage then distributed the stock of Averill to the taxpayer. Immediately thereafter, the Averill Corp. was liquidated, placing the Monitor shares in the taxpayers hands at capital gain rates.[105]

---

103. Observe that this liquidation may be tax-free at both corporate-and shareholder-levels if the securities are unappreciated.

104. 293 U.S. 465 (1935).

105. Under current law, any appreciation in the Monitor shares would be taxable to the Averill Corp. upon its liquidation. See § 336. At the time, though, the *General Utilities* doctrine allowed a distributing corporation to avoid recognizing gain on the distribution. Thus, the taxpayer in *Gregory* sought only a single, shareholder-level tax on the transaction even though the Monitor shares were appreciated.

The relevant statute in force at that time provided that a reorganization included "a transfer by a corporation of all or a part of its assets if immediately after the transferor or its stockholders or both are in control of the corporation to which the assets are transferred." Accordingly, the transaction met the literal language of the then-applicable divisive reorganization provision. Nonetheless, the Supreme Court held that a tax-free reorganization did not occur because "[t]he whole undertaking . . . was in fact an elaborate and devious form of conveyance masquerading as a corporate reorganization, and nothing else." As subsequently interpreted by Judge Learned Hand, the Supreme Court's opinion in *Gregory* stands for the proposition that "in construing words of a tax statute which describes commercial or industrial transactions we are to understand them to refer to transactions entered upon for commercial or industrial purposes and not to include transactions entered upon for no other motive but to escape taxation."[106]

The Supreme Court's condemnation of the *Gregory* transaction seems sound, but its focus on the tax-avoidance motive of the taxpayer may be misplaced. To be sure, the transaction in *Gregory* was motivated by tax avoidance, but so is the purchase of municipal bonds, the formation of many corporations, and many investments in real estate. All in all, if given a choice, taxpayers prefer lower taxes to higher taxes. What was most peculiar about the *Gregory* transaction was the creation and immediate destruction of the Averill Corp. A narrower holding in *Gregory* might have focused on the effect of the transaction: a division of United Mortgage did *not* occur because the Averill Corp. was liquidated immediately after the transaction. Regardless of the taxpayer's motive, the transaction did not accomplish that which Congress intended in the divisive reorganization statute.[107]

As applied to divisive reorganizations, the business purpose test requires that the transaction be motivated by some business

---

106. *Commissioner v. Transport Trading & Terminal Corp.,* 176 F.2d 570, 572 (2d Cir.1949). In Rev. Rul. 2003–52, 2003–1 C.B. 960, the owners of a farming corporation had two children, and one child wanted the corporation to emphasize the livestock business while the other wanted the corporation to emphasize the grain business. The Service ruled that a § 355 distribution had a valid corporate purpose because the distribution eliminated the business disagreement between the two future owners of the company and allowed each of the siblings to devote full-time effort to the business. The Service surprisingly was not troubled that the distribution also significantly furthered the estate planning objective of the current owners of the corporation.

107. See *Chisholm v. Commissioner,* 79 F.2d 14, 15 (2d Cir.1935) ("Had [the taxpayers in *Gregory*] really meant to conduct a business by means of the two reorganized companies, they would have escaped whatever other aim they may have had, whether to avoid taxes, or to regenerate the world.")

purpose of the corporate enterprise.[108] Such purposes include compliance with an antitrust order, resolution of a shareholder stalemate, and facilitation of a public offering.[109] Note that in all cases these are purposes germane to the conduct of the *corporation's* business. A shareholder's purpose is, in general, irrelevant. However, a shareholder's purpose may overlap a corporate purpose—resolution of a shareholder stalemate being one example—without tainting the corporate purpose.[110]

The regulations use the business purpose test to impose a best-fit requirement on § 355 transactions: a distribution will fail to qualify under § 355 if the business purpose underlying the transaction could be accomplished in a tax-free manner not involving the distribution of stock, unless the alternative transactions are impractical or unduly expensive. Regs. § 1.355–2(b)(3); see also Regs. § 1.355–2(b)(5) (examples 4 and 5).

These regulations also provide that a valid corporate purpose does not include the attempt to reduce federal taxes even if that reduction does not involve a bailout or other abuse to which § 355 is directed. Regs. § 1.355–2(b)(2). For example, a distribution made to facilitate an election under subchapter S does not qualify under § 355 because the purpose is unacceptable. Regs. § 1.355–2(b)(5) (example 6).

This aspect of the regulations should be subject to attack. Section 355 does not explicitly incorporate a business purpose test, so that the administrative or judicial imposition of such a test should be sustained only if the test furthers the underlying goal of the statute. Section 355 is an anti-bailout provision, not an anti-subchapter S provision. This aspect of the new regulations demonstrates the extent to which the non-statutory business purpose test has extended beyond its legitimate reach.

Having a business purpose will not guarantee tax-free treatment to the division, however, because § 355 imposes a series of additional hurdles.[111] The three statutory requirements imposed by

---

108. A transaction motivated neither by legitimate business concerns nor by tax-avoidance will not qualify as a tax-free reorganization. *Commissioner v. Wilson,* 353 F.2d 184 (9th Cir.1965).

109. See Regs. § 1.355–2(b)(5) (examples 1 and 2); Rev. Rul. 85–122, 1985–2 C.B. 118.

110. Regs. § 1.355–2(b)(2).

111. It is § 355 and not § 368 that defines the outer boundaries of the divisive reorganization because not all divisive reorganizations will fall within the definition of the D (or any other) reorganization. For example, the distribution by a parent corporation of the stock of an existing subsidiary may qualify for tax-free treatment under § 355 despite not being a "reorganization" in the § 368(a) sense. On the other hand, if assets are spun off by a transfer to a controlled corporation whose stock is then distributed, the division will fall within the definition of a D reorganiza-

§ 355 are the "device" restriction of § 355(a)(1)(B), the "active business" limitation of § 355(a)(1)(C), and the "distribution" requirement of § 355(a)(1)(D). The "device" restriction is the most ambitious, denying tax-free treatment under § 355 to any transaction "used principally as a device for the distribution of the earnings and profits of the distributing corporation or the controlled corporation [i.e., the corporation whose stock is distributed], or both." As the language in § 355(a)(1)(B) suggests, the "device" restriction addresses transactions, such as the one in *Gregory,* in which the taxpayers intend to sell either the distributing or the controlled corporation after the transaction.

The regulations under § 355 list three factors which constitute evidence of a "device."[112] First, the regulations say that a distribution which is pro rata or substantially pro rata bears close resemblance to a dividend and therefore presents the greatest opportunity for abuse. While it is hard to fault this reasoning, Congress seemingly rejected it: in § 355(a)(2)(A), we are told that application of § 355(a) should be determined "without regard to ... whether or not the distribution is pro rata." If a distribution being pro rata is treated as evidence of a "device," is § 355 being applied consistently with the mandate of § 355(a)(2)(A)?

The second factor treated as a "device" under the regulations is a post-distribution sale or exchange. The regulations further provide that if such a sale or exchange is negotiated prior to the distribution, the sale or exchange is substantial evidence of a "device." Given the second parenthetical in § 355(a)(1)(B), it is surprising that a pre-arranged sale or exchange is not treated under the regulations as conclusive evidence of a "device."

The third factor under the regulations indicating that the distribution is a device for the distribution of earnings and profits is the "nature, kind, amount and use" of the assets of the distributing and controlled corporations. The regulations recognize that spinning-off liquid assets or other assets not used in the distribution corporation's trade or business should not qualify for tax-free treatment. This aspect of the "device" limitation overlaps the active trade or business requirement, discussed *infra.*

The regulations also list factors indicating that a distribution is not a device for the distribution of earnings and profits[113] and, more strongly, describe distributions that ordinarily will not be treated as

tion. Note, though, that the definition of a divisive D reorganization references § 355, so that any corporate division— whether a D reorganization or not—

must satisfy the requirements of § 355 to obtain tax-free treatment.

112. Regs. § 1.355–2(d)(2).

113. See Regs. § 1.355–2(d)(3).

a "device."[114] For example, if neither the distributing corporation nor the controlled corporation have earnings and profits, the distribution will not be treated as a "device." This concession in the regulations certainly seems justified: no corporate distribution can bail-out earnings and profits if there are no earnings and profits to begin with. More generally, a distribution will not be considered a "device" if, in the absence of § 355, the distribution would not be taxable as a dividend to the distributees because it would qualify as an exchange under § 302(a) or § 303. Do not forget, however, that avoiding the "device" restriction of § 355(a)(1)(B) does not guarantee qualification under § 355: one must still face the active trade or business hurdle of § 355(a)(1)(C) as well as the distribution limitation in § 355(a)(1)(D).

The "active business" limitation of § 355(a)(1)(C) in many ways mirrors and overlaps the role of the device restriction. Under § 355(a)(1)(C), a division will not be tax-free unless the distributing corporation and the controlled corporation actively conduct trades or businesses after the transaction. This limitation on the scope of § 355 ensures that a corporation cannot spin-off liquid assets or passive investments as a prelude to a bail-out.

The "active business" provision of § 355(a)(1)(C) should remind you of the partial liquidation provision in § 302(b)(4).[115] You will recall that redemptions in partial liquidation of stock are given exchange treatment under §§ 302(b)(4) and 302(a). The theory behind preferential treatment for partial liquidations is that no bail-out occurs when a shareholder is forced to give up equity participation in the corporate enterprise as part of the transaction. This is consistent with the tax treatment of the sale of stock to third parties: a shareholder can "bail-out" the earnings and profits of a corporate business with impunity if the shareholder is willing to accept a reduced proprietary interest in the business.[116]

Consider the case of X Corp. engaged in manufacturing. Suppose X engages in the following transaction. First, X creates a new corporation, Y Corp., by transferring the land on which X's manufacturing plant is located. Second, X leases that land from Y at fair rent of $100,000 per year for 25 years. Third, X distributes the stock of Y to its shareholders pro rata. Should this distribution be tax-free under § 355?

In *Rafferty v. Commissioner*,[117] it was held that the holding of real estate for lease-back to the distributing corporation did not

---

114. Regs. § 1.355–2(d)(5).

115. See Section 5.02(d) *supra*.

116. The definition of "common stock" applicable to §§ 305 and 306 sim-ilarly reflects this interpretation of a bail-out.

117. 452 F.2d 767 (1st Cir.1971). See also Regs. § 1.355–3(b)(iv).

constitute an "active" trade or business. Accordingly, the distribution was not tax-free under § 355. Had the court held otherwise, the shareholders could receive the Y stock tax-free and then sell it, thereby recovering a substantial portion of their investment in X without diminishing their equity interests in the business.

A contrary result was reached in *King v. Commissioner*.[118] In that case, the court found significant that the real estate was fit for only a single use and was needed in the business conducted by the distributing corporation. That might have been relevant had not the real estate been leased back to the distributing corporation. In effect, what was spun-off was the right to receive lease payments. Lease payments often are a functional substitute for purchase payments made on an installment basis. Would the court in *King* have upheld the transaction if the distributing corporation had purchased the spun-off assets from the controlled corporation?

Leasing activities can constitute an "active" trade or business if the activity includes significant management or other services.[119] These services distinguish the activity from a mere passive investment. Note that the services must be conducted by employees of the corporation: hiring an independent contractor will not suffice.[120] If the services of an independent contractor could satisfy the active trade or business requirement, corporations could spin-off cash and then use the cash to pay independent contractors.

Cases like *Rafferty* and *King* can arise whenever an integrated business seeks to divide. For example, suppose X Corp. has engaged in the lumbering and milling business for several years. Can these two activities be separated tax-free under § 355? If all the lumbering output is sold to the mill, the answer is not obvious. Is an activity a "business" if there are no outside customers? Regs. § 1.355–3(c) (example 9) indicates such a horizontal division is permissible.

The active trade or business requirement plainly requires the conduct of two active trades or business after the division, but does it require two before as well? In *Coady v. Commissioner*,[121] a corporation engaged in heavy construction settled a dispute between its two shareholders by dividing itself in half. A subsidiary corporation was formed with part of the corporation's equipment, cash and a construction contract. The stock of the subsidiary was

118. 458 F.2d 245 (6th Cir.1972).

119. Regs. § 1.355–3(b)(2)(iv)(B); see also Rev. Rul. 79–394, 1979–2 C.B. 141.

120. Rev. Rul. 86–125, 1986–2 C.B. 57.

121. 33 T.C. 771 (1960), aff'd, 289 F.2d 490 (6th Cir.1961); accord, *United States v. Marett*, 325 F.2d 28 (5th Cir. 1963).

then distributed in complete redemption of one of the shareholder's stock. Although the Service challenged this division, it was sustained by the court. Such vertical divisions are now explicitly permitted by the regulations.[122]

The active business requirement will be satisfied only by businesses actively conducted for the prior five years. This rule ensures that a corporation will not be able to bail-out earnings and profits by purchasing an active trade or business and then spinning it off. For example, just as X Corp. cannot spin-off its liquid assets tax-free under § 355, so too X will fail to qualify under § 355 if it uses its liquid assets to purchase a business and then distributes this new business within 5 years.

On the other hand, a business may be acquired during the 5 year period in a tax-free transaction without violating the rule. Because tax-free transactions represent changes in form not significant enough to justify taxation, acquisition of a business in a tax-free transaction signifies that the corporation actually conducted the business prior to the acquisition, albeit in another form. Examples of permissible tax-free transactions include incorporations under § 351, subsidiary liquidations under § 337, and tax-free reorganizations as defined in § 368.

A corporation cannot use a newly created trade or business to satisfy the active trade or business requirement, but there is no prohibition on expanding an existing business during the five years prior to the § 355 distribution. See, for example, examples 7 and 8 of Regs. 1.355–3(c), in which expansions of existing business explicitly are permitted. But the line between the expansion of a business and the creation of a new business can be hard to find. For example, exploiting newly-discovered oil on land historically used for a ranching business is the creation of a new trade or business. Regs. § 1.355–2(c) (example 3). However, the expansion of a brick-and-mortar shoe store onto the web is a mere expansion of an existing trade or business rather than the creation of a new trade or business. Rev. Rul. 2003–38, 2003–1 C.B. 811.

Note that the "active business" requirement applies to the distributing corporation as well as to the controlled corporation. Were the rule otherwise, the active business requirement could be avoided by transferring everything *other than* liquid assets or passive investment to the controlled corporation. Sale of the stock of the distributing corporation would complete the bailout. There is thus a symmetry in § 355 as to the distributing corporation and the controlled corporation. You should not think of the distributing

---

122. Regs. § 1.355–3(c) (example 4).

corporation as the original corporation or of the controlled corporation as the new corporation. Rather, both corporations should be considered as parts of the old corporation.

Note that for determining whether the distributing corporation is engaged in the active conduct of a trade or business, the activities of the corporation and all of its controlled subsidiaries are aggregated. § 355(b)(3). This allows the activities constituting the trade or business to be divided among multiple corporations and still satisfy the active trade or business requirement. Indeed, there is no requirement that any part of the trade or business be conducted by the distributing corporation itself. Note also that the same aggregation rule applies for determining whether the controlled corporation is engaged in the active trade or business immediately after the distribution.

Suppose A Corp. acquires the assets of T Corp. in a taxable transaction, and assume that S Corp. is and has been a wholly-owned subsidiary of T Corp. for more than 5 years. Will a distribution by A of the S Corp. stock qualify under § 355 if made within 5 years of the acquisition of T Corp. by A Corp.? No, regardless of the length of time S Corp. has been actively conducting a trade or business. § 355(b)(2)(D)(i); see Rev. Rul. 89–37.[123] This rule ensures that A cannot spin off a business conducted in a subsidiary corporation more easily than it can spin off a business conducted internally.

Note that while the active trade or business requirement requires that the assets of each corporation include an active trade or business, it imposes no limitation on any other assets held by either corporation. So, for example, the controlled corporation might include a trade or business worth $100,000 as well as investment assets worth $1,000,000. If ownership of this controlled corporation is distributed in a § 355 distribution, a sale of the distributed stock by the shareholders will in effect bail-out substantial investment assets at the minor cost of losing control of a small active business.

Congress determined that some cash rich divisive reorganizations should not be tax-free and enacted § 355(g) to eliminate them. Under § 355(g)(1), a distribution will not qualify under § 355 if two-thirds or more of the assets of the distributing corporation or of the controlled corporation consist of investment assets as specified in § 355(g)(2)(B) *and* any person holds a 50% or greater interest in either corporation immediately after the distribution (an interest that was not held immediately prior to the distribution).

---

123. 1989–1 C.B. 107.

The specific type of cash rich division targeted by Congress was the situation where a minority shareholder of the distributing corporation essentially was redeemed out of the enterprise with investment assets. Such a distribution should be taxable to the distributing corporation and to the distributee, but (until § 355(g) was enacted) bundling a modest active trade or business and the investment assets into a new corporation would convert the distribution into a fully tax-free transaction.

Reconsider the "device" limitation of § 355(a)(1)(B) in light of the "active business" restriction. The "device" restriction speaks to pre-arranged sales. As we have seen, though, the active business limitation ensures that disposition of either corporation will result in a reduced interest of the corporate enterprise. Why should pre-arranged sales be condemned if the active business requirement has been met?

The regulations indicate that a "device" exists when the transaction has the potential for withdrawal of earnings and profits without implicating the usual distribution rule, namely § 301. They further provide that pro rata distributions, although allowable under § 355,[124] present the greatest opportunity for abuse. However, the factors cited by the regulations as relevant to the "device" inquiry—the nature and use of the assets transferred, whether either corporation ends up with a new trade or business or liquid assets—are adequately addressed by the active business limitation.

What role should the "device" language play? Consider the case of X Corp. which has conducted two distinct businesses for more than 5 years. The spin-off of one of X's businesses under § 355 ordinarily should present no problem, but what if the earnings of one of the businesses has been reinvested in the other business during the last 5 years? If the division is allowed, disposition of one business will effect a bail-out of the earnings and profits of the other business. Such a transaction might be vulnerable to challenge under the active business limitation,[125] but the "device" language seems more appropriate.

The last restriction imposed by § 355 is the "distribution" requirement of § 355(a)(1)(D). That section requires the distributing corporation to distribute all of the stock of the controlled corporation that it owns or distribute control and establish that retention of the remainder "was not in pursuance of a plan having as one of its principal purposes the avoidance of Federal income

---

124. See § 355(a)(2)(A).　　　　**125.** See, e.g., Rev. Rul. 59–400, 1959–2 C.B. 784.

tax." The concern to which § 355(a)(1)(D) speaks is illustrated by the following example.

X Corp. owns all the outstanding stock, both common and preferred, of Y Corp. X distributes all the common stock of Y but retains the preferred. If the shareholders subsequently dispose of their stock of X, they will bail-out some of the earnings and profits of Y.[126] To prevent this, the distribution requirement of § 355(a)(1)(D) mandates a complete division between the two companies.

(b) Taxation of Successful and Failed Divisions. If a corporate division meets all the tests of § 355, then the distribution of stock and securities of the controlled corporation will be tax-free to both the shareholders and to the corporation. The corporation is protected from recognition of gain by § 311(b)(1)(A), limiting recognition to distributions "to which subpart A applies." The shareholder is protected by § 355(a). Note, however, that a shareholder who receives securities with principal amount in excess of principal amount of any securities turned in will be taxed, just as under § 354. In addition, if a corporation distributes boot in addition to the stock and securities, gain (but not loss) can be recognized on the boot. §§ 355(c), 361(c).

A shareholder receiving boot in a § 355 *distribution*, whether excess securities or other property, is taxed under § 356(b). This provision taxes the receipt of boot as a distribution of property under § 301. It is thus less favorable than § 356(a), which applies to boot received in amalgamating reorganizations and to § 355 *exchanges.* You will recall that recognition under § 356(a) is limited to a shareholder's realized gain on the transaction.[127]

If a transaction fails to qualify under § 355, how will it be taxed?[128] If the transaction is a failed pro rata spin-off, then presumably each shareholder will be taxed under § 301 on the stock received. However, if the transaction is structured as a split-off, then presumably the redemption rules of § 302 will be applied. Consider, though, the following split-up.

X Corp. operates two businesses. It transfers one of the businesses to newly-formed Y Corp. and one to newly-formed Z Corp.,

126. This is a "bail-out" because the shareholders will receive a price for their X stock representing in part the value of the Y preferred stock owned by X. When that Y stock is subsequently redeemed, the bail-out will be complete: funds will have come out of corporate solution and the shareholders will have been taxed at capital gains rates without surrendering a significant interest in X Corp. See Chapter 6 *supra.*

127. See Section 10.03(b) *supra.*

128. If the failed divisive reorganization contains within it a valid § 351 incorporation, that part of the transaction will remain tax-free under § 351.

and then X completely liquidates. If this transaction fails to qualify under § 355, is it taxed as a complete liquidation? Indeed, can it be taxed as a complete liquidation even if it does qualify under § 355? Note that if the distribution by X includes substantial boot, and if the shareholders of X have a high basis in their X stock, then taxation as a complete liquidation may actually be preferable to taxation under §§ 355 and 356(b).[129] Nevertheless, if taxation under § 355 is available, taxation as a complete liquidation is not. See § 336(c).

(c) Divisive Reorganizations and Transfers of Control. Congress has in two complex subsections of § 355 tried to ensure that tax-free divisions cannot be used to shield transaction that have the effect of a sale of a corporate business. These provisions, § 355(d) and § 355(e), each provide that what would otherwise be a tax-free distribution under § 355 becomes taxable *to the distributing corporation.* Neither provision, though, seeks to tax the distributee-shareholders. Thus, these provisions do not so much limit the reach of § 355 as limit its effect, and each provision is triggered (albeit in different ways) by a transfer of control of the distributing or of the controlled corporation.

(i) Pre–Distribution Transfers of Control. If one person by purchase acquires 50% or more (by vote or value) of the stock of the distributing corporation or of the controlled corporation within 5 years of the distribution, then gain on the distribution is taxable to the distributing corporation. § 355(d)(1)-(2). For purposes of this section, special attribution rules apply, see § 355(d)(7), and "purchase" is defined to include any taxable acquisition as well as some tax-free incorporations, see § 355(d)(5).

Consider the following example. P Corp. owns operating assets with fair market value of $300,000 and all the stock of Sub Corp. with adjusted basis of $100,000 and fair market value of $150,000. Acquiring Corp. wishes to purchase the business operated by Sub Corp., and to do so it purchases for fair market value of $150,000 one-third of the outstanding stock of P Corp. The stock purchased by Acquiring Corp. is then redeemed by P Corp. in exchange for all the stock of Sub Corp., and were this transaction tax-free to P Corp. under § 355(c), it would in effect have permitted the sale of Sub Corp. to Acquiring Corp. without the imposition of a corporate-level tax.

---

129. Of course, if the corporation's assets have substantially appreciated, taxation as a complete liquidation will entail recognition of gain at the corporate-level under § 336(a).

However, because of § 355(d), the distribution is taxable to P Corp., forcing P to recognize $50,000 of gain. This taxation is imposed because Acquiring Corp. ends up owning 50% or more of Sub Corp., and that stock interest either was purchased directly (here, it was not) or was received as a distribution on stock that was itself purchased (as was the case here). Accordingly, the stock of Sub Corp. is a "disqualified distribution" under § 355(d)(1), the distributed shares of Sub Corp. therefore no longer are treated as "qualified property" and so the distribution of those appreciated shares is taxable to P Corp. under § 355(c)(2).

It is worth observing that there is no obvious tax abuse to which § 355(d) speaks because transactions described in § 355(d) represent a mere change in corporate ownership without any change in corporate asset basis. That is, distributions taxed under § 355(d) consist only of financial assets (stock and securities of the controlled corporation), and so never remove appreciated real assets from corporate solution nor increase the basis of real assets remaining within corporate solution. Since one corporation can purchase the stock of another corporation without the imposition of a corporate-level tax (and, of course, without a corporate-level step-up in basis), it is unclear why the same result should not hold true when the purchaser wishes to buy only a single division within a corporate structure. But the operation of § 355(d) clearly prevents it.

(ii) Post–Distribution Loss of Control. Recall that the "device" language of § 355(a)(1)(B) condemns distributions otherwise described in § 355(a) if there is a pre-arranged transfer of stock following the distribution. While this "device" language seems absolute on its face,[130] lawyers argued that some pre-arranged stock transfers might nevertheless pass muster. The *Morris Trust*[131] case involved a divisive reorganization followed by an A (amalgamating) reorganization. In *Morris Trust*, a state bank spun-off its insurance business prior to merging with a national bank. Because a national bank may not, in general, conduct an insurance business, the division was a necessary condition to the merger. After the merger, shareholders of the state bank owned the insurance business but only a minority interest in the merged national bank—control of assets formerly used by the state bank, in other words, was transferred to the shareholders of the acquiring national bank.

---

130. However, note that while the distributing corporation must distribute at least 80% control of the controlled corporation, then shareholders need end up with only 50% control, see § 368(a)(2)(H), so that the shareholders can, as part of the overall transaction, transfer a significant portion of the distributed stock to others.

131. *Commissioner v. Morris Trust,* 367 F.2d 794 (4th Cir.1966).

The Commissioner attacked the tax-free status of the spin-off as a device. The thrust of the challenge was that the shareholders did not have "control" of the distributing corporation immediately after the transaction. The court, however, found nothing in the statute requiring the shareholders to control the distributing corporation immediately after the transaction. Such a requirement, the court held, applied only to the controlled corporation (i.e., to the corporation whose stock is distributed as part of the transaction).

The court's analysis of the statute, at least in one regard, was deficient. The statute requires that shareholders of the distributing corporation be "in control" of the controlled corporation immediately after the distribution. While there is no statement that they must also be in control of the distributing corporation, this absence of statutory language is easy to explain: the shareholders of the distributing corporation, as a group, are *always* "in control" of the distributing corporation immediately after the transaction. After all, they are the shareholders.

What caused the problem in *Morris Trust* was that the shareholders relinquished control of the distributing corporation immediately after the transaction. In other words, they "sold or exchanged" some of their stock immediately afterward, precisely the conduct condemned by the device language of § 355(a)(1)(B). The court in *Morris Trust* completely overlooked the symmetries of § 355, thinking that a bail-out could occur only by disposition of stock of the controlled corporation. Yet, as we have seen, the distributing corporation and the controlled corporation play equal roles in § 355.

The issue posed by *Morris Trust* that the court should have focused on was whether a pre-arranged disposition is condemned by the device language of § 355(a)(1)(B) when the disposition occurs as part of a *tax-free* transaction. Such a disposition does not bail-out any earnings and profits because the shareholders continue to hold stock, though stock of a new corporation. On the other hand, the transaction in *Morris Trust* does seem to have failed the literal language of the "device" requirement because there was a pre-arranged disposition of shares of the distributing corporation.

The effect of the transaction in *Morris Trust* was to give control of part of the corporate enterprise to new shareholders. Does the statute permit such a result? The transaction in *Morris Trust* could have been accomplished an alternate way: the state bank/insurance company could have transferred its banking business to the national bank in exchange for a minority interest in the national bank, and then that stock could have been distributed to the state bank's shareholders. However, had this route been taken the transaction would have been taxable at two levels: (1) at the corporate level because the transfer by the state bank/insurance company fails the control test applicable to § 351 transactions; and (2) at the shareholder level because the distribution fails the control test applicable to § 355 distributions.

Consider first the corporate level taxation. While the transfer from one corporation to another corporation of appreciated assets does not represent a bail-out of earnings and profits (because the transferred assets remain in corporate solution), such a transfer generally is a taxable event under the general rule of § 1001(a): when appreciated assets are sold or exchanged by a corporate or noncorporate taxpayer, gain is realized and usually recognized.

To be sure, the various acquisitive reorganization provisions permit the transfer of assets between corporations without the imposition of a corporate level tax. But Congress has limited those provisions to the transfer of substantially all of the transferor-corporation's assets. In *Morris Trust*, the banking business was transferred but the insurance business was retained, and assuming the insurance business was not insubstantial, the transaction should therefore fail to qualify for tax-free reorganization treatment at the corporate level.[132]

Consider next the shareholder level tax. Some of the pre-transaction value in the state bank/insurance company shares was converted into shares of the national bank. In general, the realization doctrine subjects to taxation appreciation in assets when converted into a new form, and from that perspective the transaction should also have been taxable at the shareholder level. However, the change in form was not considerable: stock has been converted into other stock, and the new stock continues ownership in a previously-owned business (the state banking business). Thus, Congress might well postpone the shareholder level tax until disposition of the new shares.

In the actual *Morris Trust* case, the court held for the taxpayer, and that holding was codified and expanded in the current regulations. Now, regulations permit a pre-arranged disposition of shares of the distributing or the controlled corporation without triggering the "device" language of § 355(a)(1)(B) so long as this disposition is part of a tax-free reorganization.[133] In addition, even

---

132. See Helvering v. Elkhorn Coal Co., 95 F.2d 732 (4th Cir.1937).

133. Regs. § 1.355–2(d)(iii)(E); see also Rev. Rul. 2003–79, 2003–2 C.B. 80, in which the Service ruled that a § 355 distribution could be followed by a C reorganization in which the assets of the controlled corporation are acquired by an unrelated corporation and then the controlled corporation liquidates. Sadly, in that ruling the Service reaffirmed that if the assets of the distributing cor-

taxable dispositions will not necessarily be treated as a bail-out: taxable dispositions of less than 20 percent of the corporation's stock are, under these regulations, substantial but not conclusive evidence of a "device." However, Congress ultimately determined that the *Morris Trust* case represents an abuse of § 355, and in § 355(e) that perceived abuse is attacked in a peculiar and complex way.

Section 355(e) was enacted in 1997 for two principle reasons: first, because Congress believed "[i]n cases in which it is intended that new shareholders will acquire ownership of a business in connection with a spin off, the transaction more closely resembles a corporate level disposition of the portion of the business that is acquired." Second, rejecting the asymmetries in *Morris Trust*, Congress "believe[d] that the differences in treatment of certain transactions following a spin-off, depending upon whether the distributing or controlled corporation engages in the transaction, should be minimized."

Consider the following: B Corp., a state-chartered bank, has owned for many years all the stock of I Corp., an insurance company. The stock of I Corp. is distributed to the shareholders of B Corp., and then B changes its charter to that of a national bank and raises new funds through a public offering. Assume that the spin-off of I Corp. was a necessary first-step in the public offering because national banks cannot own insurance companies.

Assuming the active trade or business requirement of § 355(a)(1)(C) is met, the distribution by B of the I Corp. stock should satisfy all the requirements of § 355(a)(1). Indeed, the device language of § 355(a)(1)(C) should not be implicated because no stock of the distributing corporation (i.e., B) and no stock of the controlled corporation (i.e., I) is sold or exchanged as part of the transaction. However, if the post-distribution public offering is sufficiently large, the distribution by B Corp. of the I Corp. stock will be taxable at the corporate level (though it will remain tax-free at the shareholder level) under § 355(e).

Section 355(e) is triggered if an otherwise tax-free spin-off under § 355 is part of a plan for one or more persons to acquire 50% or more control (by vote or value) of the distributing corporation or of the controlled corporation.[134] In the example above, if the

---

poration (rather than the assets of the controlled corporation) had been acquired, the post-distribution acquisition would not have qualified as a C reorganization under *Elkhorn Coal*.

134. Any transfer of control occurring less than two years before or after the spin-off presumptively is part of such a plan. § 355(e)(2)(B). Transfers taking place outside that 4–year window

public offering results in new shareholders acquiring 50% or more of the vote or value of B Corp. (see § 355(f)(4)(A) incorporating § 355(d)(4)), gain (but not loss) will be recognized to B on the spin-off as if B sold the I Corp. stock for its fair market value. And note that the same taxation would result if new shareholders acquired 50% or more control of I Corp. rather than of B Corp.

The legislative history of § 355(e) makes clear that no adjustment should be made to the basis of any corporate assets as a result of this taxation. This makes little sense and has the result of imposing a triple tax on corporate earnings: once under § 355(e) on the distribution by the distributing corporation of the stock of the controlled corporation, a second time at the corporate level when the controlled corporation sells the appreciated assets or otherwise earns income from them, and a third time when the shareholders sell or exchange the distributed stock of the controlled corporation. One would expect that the controlled corporation would get a step-up in the basis of its assets if the distributing corporation is taxed under § 355(e), just as would occur if the assets had simply been sold in a taxable transaction. Indeed, such a basis step-up is mandated by statute in a similar context under § 338.[135] Nonetheless, the effect of § 355(e) apparently is to demand an eventual extra corporate level tax as the price for obtaining shareholder level deferral (under § 355(a)) on the transaction.

Not all transfers of control will trigger taxation under § 355(e). If the new shareholders acquiring control of the distributing or of the controlled corporation already had control of the other corporation, taxation under § 355(e) is avoided. See § 355(e)(3)(A)(iv). And, of course, the actual distribution under § 355(a) works a transfer of control (from the distributing corporation to its shareholders), but that inevitable transfer of control is irrelevant under § 355(e)(3)(A)(ii).

While § 355(e) is triggered by the transfer of corporate control, certain asset acquisitions are treated as control transfers. Under § 355(e)(3)(B), tax-free asset acquisitions (such as a tax-free merger or C reorganization) are equated to stock transfers for purposes of § 355(e). Note that both taxable and tax-free stock transfers can trigger § 355(e) but only tax-free asset transfers can have that effect. This rule makes sense because § 355(e) imposes a corporate-level tax on the transaction, and if the assets were transferred in a

receive no presumption for or against taxation under § 355(e), so such cases will be decided based on the usual burden of proof rules (generally favoring the government) as well as on all the

facts and circumstances of the particular case.

135. See § 338(h)(1).

taxable transaction, the corporate-level tax has already been incurred.

This discussion should make clear the § 355(e) is both more and less than a congressional rejection of the *Morris Trust* case. *Morris Trust* held that a tax-free transfer of control of the distributing corporation is not a "device" within the meaning of § 355(a)(1)(C), and that holding remains good law. On the other hand, taxation at the corporate level under § 355(e) is triggered if post-distribution control of the distributing corporation or of the controlled corporation is transferred in any manner. Thus, this rule applies to tax-free acquisitions (including tax-free asset transfers as occurred in *Morris Trust*) and to taxable transactions. Note, though, that nothing in § 355(e) limits the device language in § 355(a)(1)(C) so that a pre-arranged taxable transfer of control might invalidate the entire transaction under § 355(a)(1)(C), thereby subjecting the transaction to taxation at both the corporate and individual levels.

Because § 355(e) subjects the distributing corporation to taxation on any appreciation in the assets of the controlled corporation, at least one asymmetry remains. Suppose P Corp. owns two businesses, a toy business with assets having adjusted basis of $500,000 and fair market value of $900,000 and a software business with assets having adjusted basis and fair market value of $900,000. If P Corp. wishes to divide these two business under § 355 and then transfer control of one of the two to new investors, it can do so without paying any toll under § 355(e) by transferring the assets of the software business to a newly-formed corporation and then distributing the stock of the newly-formed corporation to its shareholders under § 355. To be sure, when control of either business is relinquished, § 355(e) will be implicated, but because the software assets were unappreciated, no taxation results. Had P Corp. instead spun-off the assets of the toy business, § 355(e) would have forced P to recognize a gain on the spin-off of $400,000.

(d) Alternatives to § 355. Congress has tried to ensure that all divisive transactions run the gauntlet of § 355 if they are to be tax-free. For example, the transferor-corporation in a C or a non-divisive D reorganization must liquidate as part of the transaction, thereby guaranteeing that only the transferee-corporation will survive the reorganization and carry-on the corporate business. Taxpayers, though, have sought to avoid the restrictions of § 355 by shoe-horning divisive transactions into other Code sections. For example, suppose that Subco is the wholly-owned subsidiary of P Corp. If Subco distributes shares of its own stock to the P shareholders for some of the P Corp. stock, the effect of the transaction

is to convert the parent/subsidiary pair into a brother/sister pair (albeit with cross-ownership between brother and sister). How should the exchange of Subco stock for P Corp. stock be taxed?

Formally, the transaction looks to be an exchange at the shareholder-level, taxable under § 1001(a). To Subco on the other hand, it is simply a distribution of its own stock for property, a tax-free event under § 1032(a). Accordingly, the transaction will produce little or no tax liability if the P Corp. shareholders have a high stock basis in their P Corp. shares.

Because Subco is distributing its own stock, the transaction does not fall under § 355 even though the transaction does have a divisive impact. The Commissioner has sought to tax such transactions under § 304(a)(2), and under that provision the distribution of property can be taxed as ordinary income to the distributees.

However, § 304(a)(2) only applies to the distribution of "property," and "property" for purposes of § 304 does not include stock of the distributing corporation. § 317(a). The Service takes the position that P Corp. should be treated as the distributing corporation in the transaction, but the courts have refused to read § 304(a)(2) that way.[136] Yet, if Subco (or P Corp.) owns only liquid assets, the distribution opens the door for a possible bail-out.

For example, suppose P Corp. has substantial earnings and profits as well as considerable cash. P creates Subco by contributing the cash to Subco in exchange for Subco common stock. This transaction is tax-free to P under § 351 and to Subco under § 1032. Subsequently, the P shareholders transfer some of their P Corp. common stock to Subco in exchange for Subco preferred stock of equal value. To maximize the bail-out, the P Corp. stock given up should be worth exactly as much as the cash now held by Subco. Since the Subco stock is not "property" for § 304(a)(2), this exchange is taxable to the P shareholders under § 1001(a), giving them a recovery of basis and then capital gain. In addition, because the issuance of the Subco preferred stock is fully taxable to the P shareholders (albeit as capital gain), this preferred stock is not § 306 stock.

The P shareholders can then sell the newly acquired Subco preferred shares to outside investors who will then have those shares redeemed, or the P shareholders can have those shares redeemed directly from them. Once the Subco preferred stock is redeemed, the bail-out is complete: no gain will be recognized on the redemption (or on the pre-redemption sale to outside investors)

---

136. *Bhada v. Commissioner,* 89 T.C. 959 (1987), aff'd sub nom. *Caama-* *no v. Commissioner,* 879 F.2d 156 (5th Cir.1989).

because the P shareholders' bases in the preferred stock are equal to their fair market value. Thus, the value of the cash will be removed from corporate solution at a tax cost of only capital gain.

10.05　One–Party Reorganizations. In § 368(a)(1)(E) and (F), Congress has defined two different one-party reorganizations. An E reorganization is a recapitalization in which a single corporation rearranges its financial structure. For example, as part of a recapitalization a corporation might create a new class of stock, replace outstanding debt instruments with preferred stock, or alter the relationship between common and preferred stockholders. In each case some or all of the shareholders will turn in their old stock and securities and receive in exchange new stock and securities. If the transaction qualifies as an E reorganization, the transaction can be tax-free.

The second type of one-party reorganization is an F reincorporation. As the language of § 368(a)(1)(F) indicates, reincorporations involve the change of a single corporation's state of incorporation or similar attribute. Although the reincorporation provision once played a substantial role in the reorganization drama, recent statutory changes to § 368(a)(1)(F) have reduced its importance.

The most important use of the recapitalization technique is to allow older management of a closely held corporation to make room for the next generation. Consider the case of X Corp. having a single class of common stock outstanding, held equally by three sisters. These sisters formed the company many years ago and watched it prosper. They would like to pass control on to their daughters while preserving a steady income stream for life. The daughters are eager to run the company, but they lack sufficient assets to buy it outright.

In such circumstances, a preferred stock recapitalization will accomplish the goals of both generations. X Corp. will recapitalize, issuing preferred stock to the founding sisters with aggregate par value equal to the current value of the company. As part of the recapitalization, the daughters will contribute a small amount of cash in exchange for common stock.

Because the par value of the preferred stock equals the total value of the company, the fair market value of the common stock is almost nil. Thus, the founders of the company have not lost any part of their investment. However, if the preferred stock is limited to par value on liquidation, then all future growth will inure to the benefit of the new generation. In addition, the preferred stock can provide a stable form of income for the founding sisters in the form of annual dividends.

Just as not all statutory mergers qualify as A reorganizations, so too not all rearrangements of a corporation's capital structure qualify as recapitalizations. In *Bazley v. Commissioner*,[137] a corporation recapitalized by causing each shareholder to turn in his shares and receive in exchange five new shares plus some securities. The taxpayer characterized the exchange as a tax-free reorganization while the Commissioner characterized it as a taxable distribution of the securities.

The Supreme Court had no difficulty in agreeing with the Commissioner. This case had considerably more impact before the enactment of § 354(a)(2) because that section treats excess securities received in a reorganization as boot. Had § 354(a)(2) been in force at the time of *Bazley,* the taxpayer would have been required to recognize gain on the transaction even if it had qualified as an E reorganization. Nonetheless, taxation of a reorganization under § 354(a)(2) is not the same as taxation of a transaction failing to qualify as a statutory reorganization, especially in light of section § 453(f)(6).

Under § 453(f)(6), securities received in a reorganization and taxed as boot qualify, in some circumstances, for recognition under the installment method. Under the installment method, gain is recognized only as proceeds on the obligations are received or if the installment obligation is sold. In the case of securities received in a reorganization, this allows a taxpayer to defer recognition of gain until the securities are sold or called by the corporation.

The benefit of § 453(f)(6) is unavailable to readily tradable securities.[138] In addition, it cannot apply to securities received in a reorganization unless any gain recognized is taxable under § 356(a)(1), that is, if the gain does not have the effect of a dividend. Whether boot received in a reorganization has the effect of a dividend is determined by application of the "after" test under *Commissioner v. Clark*.[139]

The continuing importance of *Bazley* is that securities received under § 301 never qualify for the installment method. Thus, if the transaction fails to qualify as a recapitalization or other statutory reorganization, securities received in the transaction will be taxable when received. Stock exchanged as part of the transaction, on the other hand, under some circumstances will still be received tax-free.[140]

137. 331 U.S. 737 (1947).
138. See § 453(f)(4).
139. See Section 10.03(b) *supra.*

140. See § 1036 (tax-free exchange of common for common or preferred for preferred).

The taxation of securities received thus can be (1) tax-free under § 354(a)(1) to the extent of securities turned in, (2) taxable (not in an amount in excess of gain realized) and reported on the installment method, or (3) taxable immediately.[141] All three methods will produce different tax results for the recipient shareholder. In particular, the basis consequences to the shareholder are different under § 354 and § 453(f).[142]

Recall that "nonqualified preferred stock" as defined in § 351(g)(2) generally is not treated as stock if received by a shareholder as part of a corporate reorganization.[143] However, this taint for preferred, nonparticipating stock is removed in the case of recapitalizations of family-owned corporations, see § 354(a)(2)(C)(i), an important exception for elderly taxpayers hoping to pass on control of a family business without the imposition of substantial estate and gift tax.

Reincorporations under § 368(a)(1)(F) once included the amalgamation of several corporations owned by the same shareholders.[144] However, the Tax Equity and Fiscal Responsibility Act of 1982 added the words "of one corporation" to § 368(a)(1)(F), thereby ending the use of the F reorganization to join multiple corporations.

The legislative history of this amendment to § 368(a)(1)(F) makes clear that Congress did not intend to remove the following kinds of transactions from the scope of the F reorganization. X Corp. desires to reincorporate in a new state. Accordingly, New X Corp. is formed in the new state. X then transfers all of its assets to New X in exchange for all New X's stock, and then X completely liquidates. This simple reincorporation technically involves two corporations (X and New X), but only one *active* corporation. The legislative history of the 1982 act indicates that F reorganizations can involve multiple corporations so long as only one is active.

---

141. If, as in *Bazley,* the transaction fails to qualify for reorganization treatment, then receipt of the securities may be taxed under § 301 and, if there are sufficient earnings and profits, will be taxed as ordinary income equal to the fair market value of the securities received.

142. Under § 358, basis is divided between the stock and securities received tax-free in proportion to relative fair market values. § 358(b). Under §§ 356 and 453(f), the boot securities are allocated a fair market value basis,

see § 358(a)(2), with a consequent reduction in the shareholder's stock basis, see § 358(a)(1)(A)(i). Of course, the shareholder's basis in the securities will not equal fair market value until the installment gain is recognized. See generally Prop. Regs. § 1.453–1(f)(2).

143. See Section 2.06(c) *supra.*

144. E.g., *Reef Corp. v. Commissioner,* 368 F.2d 125 (5th Cir.1966); *Davant v. Commissioner,* 366 F.2d 874 (5th Cir. 1966).

Because the A, B, C and nondivisive D reorganizations specifically cover multi-party amalgamating reorganizations, you might wonder why taxpayers have tried so hard to fall within the confines of the F reorganization. The answer is that the rules historically governing the carry-over of tax attributes such as net operating losses were much more favorable to the single party reorganizations (recapitalizations and reincorporations) than to the multi-party reorganizations. The carryover of tax attributes incidental to corporate reorganization is discussed in the next Chapter.

A multi-step transaction, if it results in the assets of one corporation remaining in corporate solution in the hands of a nominally different corporation, may qualify as an F reorganization. For example, suppose X Corp. conducts two businesses and wishes to separate each business from the liabilities of the other. This can be accomplished in a variety of ways. For example, one business could be dropped into a wholly-owned subsidiary or disregarded entity. Similarly, X Corp. could become a holding company by dropping each business into a new subsidiary.

But what if one of the businesses includes real estate subject to potential environmental clean-up costs that can be imposed on the owner of the property *or on an prior owner*. Now, transferring the real estate to a subsidiary will not shield X Corp's other assets from the remediation liability because that liability can be imposed directly on X Corp. as a prior owner of the real estate.[145] A divisive reorganization will do the trick but satisfaction of the various § 355 requirements might be impossible.

Consider the following transaction. X Corp. creates NewCo and transfers its non-real estate business to NewCo. NewCo then forms Y–LLC, a wholly-owned limited liability company that is treated as a disregarded entity for tax purposes. X Corp. then merges into Y–LLC under applicable state law, with Y–LLC the survivor. After these steps, NewCo owns the non-real estate assets directly and owns the real estate assets indirectly through its ownership of Y–LLC.

---

145. Note that retaining the real estate in X Corp. and dropping the other business in a subsidiary entity will not work because ownership of the subsidiary is an asset X Corp. and so potential subject to the liabilities of X Corp.

CHAPTER 11. COMBINING TAX ATTRIBUTES

11.01 Introduction. In transactions covered by §§ 332, 351, 355, and 368, the Code has specific provisions relating to the carryover of basis with respect to property transferred or stock exchanged in such transactions. Thus, § 358 provides, generally speaking, for a transfer of the adjusted basis of exchanging shareholders to the new stock or securities acquired by them. Similarly, § 362 provides that property acquired by a corporation in connection with a § 351 transaction or in connection with a reorganization normally will have the same basis as the property had in the hands of the transferor. See also § 1223 relating to the holding period of property received in connection with such transactions and § 168(i)(7) for a step-in-the-shoes rule applicable to depreciation.

However, corporations have a great many more tax attributes than basis and holding periods of assets. Different corporations may have different accounting methods, methods of depreciation with respect to property, earnings and profits accounts, foreign tax credits, and net operating loss carryovers. Consistent with the philosophy of the nonrecognition provisions such as §§ 351, 355, and the transactions to which § 368 applies, these tax attributes should remain undisturbed after such transactions. One would also expect similar rules to apply in the case of those special mergers consisting of liquidations of controlled subsidiaries into their parents to which §§ 332, 337, and 334(b) apply.

For example, if two corporations merge, one would expect that after the merger, in calculating whether distributions were made out of earnings and profits, one would look to the combined earnings and profits of the two corporations. Generally speaking, § 381 (providing for carryover of tax attributes in certain tax-free exchanges) and other provisions of the Code carry out such expected results.

On the other hand, it should also be noted that where a corporation sells all of its assets, the purchaser does not acquire the selling corporation's tax attributes because the selling corporation remains in existence. If a selling corporation liquidates, its tax attributes disappear. Similarly, when a corporation makes an election under § 338 to be treated as if it sold its assets to itself, the former corporation's tax attributes disappear.[1]

This simplified discussion ignores the problems created over many decades by what some call the "trafficking" in corporations having substantial net operating losses and other desirable tax attributes (for example, high-basis low-value assets). Individuals having business deductions in excess of income can carry such losses back or forward as prescribed by § 172 but cannot readily sell these tax benefits to others. Where such net operating loss carryovers are lodged in a corporate entity, however, sale of the loss is no more difficult than the sale of the stock of the corporation— provided that the tax attributes are not reduced or eliminated by the transfer of the stock. As described below, Congress and the Treasury have actively resisted perceived "trafficking" in loss corporations.

11.02   Section 381. Section 381 provides for the carryover of tax attributes from a transferor corporation to an acquiring corporation in certain transactions. The transactions covered are (1) a liquidation of a controlled subsidiary and (2) type A, C, or F tax-free reorganizations as well as certain nondivisive D reorganizations and G reorganizations involving bankruptcy. Note that in a § 368(a)(1)(B) stock-for-stock reorganization, there is no need for the rules of § 381 since the corporate existence of the acquired company continues even though there is an exchange at the shareholder level. The same holds true for § 368(a)(1)(E) recapitalizations. In other words, § 381 deals, as its opening sentence states, with "the acquisition of assets of a corporation by another corporation."

The attributes that are inherited in a qualified transaction are subject to the operating rules of § 381(b). Section 381(b)(3) provides that the acquiring corporation may not carry back a post-acquisition net operating loss or net capital loss to a pre-acquisition year of the transferor. Here the rules impinge not on the carryover of the transferor's attributes to the transferee but instead block the use by the transferee of its own losses against income of a transferor corporation for a year prior to the merger.

Section 381(c) lists numerous tax attributes of the transferor that carry over to the transferee. Of these, the most prominent one that will be discussed in greater detail below is the net operating loss carryover of § 381(c)(1). Note that while loss carryovers are transferred to the acquiring company, they can be used only against future income of the transferee. Other important inherited attrib-

---

1.   For a discussion of § 338, see Section 9.03 *supra*.

utes include the transferor's earnings and profits. § 381(c)(2). Under § 381(c)(2)(A) the earnings and profits or deficit in earnings and profits of the transferor carry over to the transferee, but under § 381(c)(2)(B) an inherited deficit in earnings and profits may be applied only against the transferee's post-transfer earnings and profits and not against the transferee's accumulated earnings and profits.

11.03 Section 382. Suppose in year 1 of its existence, X Corp. operates at a $100 loss (i.e., deductions exceed income by $100). In year 2, X Corp. produces $100 of income. Overall, X Corp. has $0 of income, and its tax consequences should reflect that. Strict adherence to the annual accounting concept would prevent X Corp. from offsetting income in year 2 with the loss in year 1. In fact, X Corp. is permitted to carry forward the year 1 loss to offset the income earned in year 2. § 172. Similarly, if X Corp. had earned $100 of income in year 1 and had suffered a $100 loss in year 2, the year 2 loss could be carried back to offset the year 1 income (i.e., X Corp. would file an amended return for year 1). Under § 172(b), a corporation can generally carry a loss back 2 years and forward 20 years if necessary, using up the loss in the earliest years in which there is sufficient income to absorb the loss.

Now suppose that X Corp. has a $100 loss in year 1 and that Y Corp. has $100 of income in year 1. If X Corp. merges into Y Corp. with the X Corp. shareholders receiving Y Corp. stock, should Y Corp. be able to use the $100 loss to offset the $100 of income? After all, if X Corp. could carry its losses back and forward, why should it not be permitted to carry its losses sideways to offset Y Corp.'s income? However, there may be some concern that the merger of X into Y Corp. is solely motivated by the presence of the net operating losses. For example, suppose that X Corp.'s assets at the time of the merger are worth $0. Even so, Y Corp., if it pays taxes at a 35 percent rate, may be willing to exchange up to $35 of Y Corp. stock for the X Corp. stock in the merger if the use of the X Corp. net operating loss will save $35 in taxes that Y Corp. would otherwise pay on its $100 of income.

While it is by no means clear that such a tax-motivated purchase is inefficient, Congress has since 1954 wrestled with the perceived problem of "trafficking" in net operating losses. On one hand, the carryover provisions perform an averaging function that allows corporations to overcome the limits of our annual accounting system. On the other hand, where NOLs are used to offset totally unrelated income (such as the acquisition of a corporation solely to obtain its NOLs), perhaps no legitimate averaging function should be performed.

Section 382 adopts the following approach to the perceived trafficking problem. After a substantial ownership change, the earnings which can be offset by a net operating loss are limited, but the amount of the net operating loss that can be used by the acquiring corporation is not directly limited. The limitation-on-earnings approach is intended to approximate the results that would occur if a loss corporation's assets were combined with those of a profitable corporation in a partnership. In such a case, only the loss corporation's share of the partnership's income could be offset by the corporation's NOL carryforward.[2] Generally, the loss corporation's share of the partnership's income is limited to earnings generated by the assets contributed by the loss corporation. Section 382(f) prescribes an objective rate of return (the federal long-term tax-exempt rate) on the value of the corporation's net equity. The annual limitation, then, is the product of the prescribed rate and the value of the loss corporation's equity immediately before a specified ownership change. § 382(b).

For example, suppose that X Corp., a calendar year taxpayer, has $1 million of net operating loss carryforwards. On January 1 of year 1, all of the stock of X Corp. is sold in a transaction that triggers § 382. On that date, the value of X Corp.'s stock was $500,000 and the applicable rate of return was 10 percent. In year 1 (and for each year thereafter), X Corp. could offset $50,000 (10 percent of $500,000) of income with the NOL carryforward. The same limitation would apply if X Corp. were merged into another corporation if there has been an ownership change as defined in § 382(g). To the extent that X Corp. does not earn enough in year 1 to absorb the $50,000 amount, the excess loss is carried forward to year 2 and is added to the $50,000 NOL limitation allowed in that year. § 382(b)(2).

It is peculiar that the limitation of § 382 applies to the sale of stock of a loss corporation: after the sale, the only income sheltered by the corporation's losses is produced by the assets of the loss corporation itself. Thus, there is no obvious trafficking from a stock sale, even one that results in a transfer of control. Perhaps Congress feared that the loss corporation will join the consolidated group of the purchaser (if the purchaser is a corporation) or appreciated assets will be contributed to the loss corporation after the stock sale, but one would think that the loss limitation of § 382

---

2. See § 704(c).

could be triggered by these events following a stock sale rather than by the sale alone.

The § 382 limitation, although somewhat artificially determined, applies notwithstanding the actual performance of a loss company. For example, suppose that all of the stock of L Corp., a loss corporation, is sold by B to P in a transaction that triggers § 382. After the acquisition, the amount of income that can be offset by the pre-acquisition NOLs is determined under § 382 (i.e., value of L Corp. multiplied by the federal long-term tax-exempt tax rate). This limitation applies even if L Corp. after the acquisition produces more income than the § 382 limitation deems produced. Conversely, if L Corp. is merged into P Corp. in a transaction that triggers § 382, P Corp. can offset income as determined under § 382 even though the assets of the former L Corp. do not in fact produce that amount of income. Note that using the federal long-term tax-exempt rate as a proxy for the actual return on the assets may produce too large or too small a deduction. However, once the § 382 limitation is determined, it is used every year until the pre-change NOLs are used up.

(a) *Ownership Changes.* Section 382 is triggered by an "ownership change." An ownership change occurs when the stock of a loss corporation which is owned by one or more 5 percent shareholders increases by more then 50 percentage points[3] as a result of an "owner shift" or an "equity structure shift." § 382(g). A series of unrelated transactions occurring during a 3 year period may be aggregated to constitute an ownership change. §§ 382(g), (i).

An owner shift occurs when there is a greater than 50 percentage point change in stock ownership by 5 percent shareholders. For purposes of the 5 percent rule, all non–5 percent shareholders are aggregated as a single 5 percent shareholder. To illustrate, assume that Y Corp. is publicly traded and held by shareholders none of whom own greater than 5 percent. Random trading among less than 5 percent shareholders does not create an owner shift because the aggregation of all non–5 percent shareholders owns 100 percent before and after each trade. However, if B and C each buy one half of the Y Corp. stock from the previous shareholders, an owner shift occurs because B and C have gone from holding 0 percent to 100 percent.

Similarly, if Y Corp. were a closely held corporation owned by B and C, and Y Corp. made a public offering of 51 percent of its stock, then an owner shift would occur because the group of non–5

---

3. An ownership change occurs when there is a 50 percentage point change, not a 50 percent change. For example, if X owns 30 percent of Y Corp., X must end up with 81 percent, not 45 percent of Y Corp. to trigger § 382.

percent shareholders will go from holding 0 percent to 51 percent of Y Corp.

An "equity structure shift" generally includes any tax free reorganization except a divisive D, an F, or a G reorganization. § 382(g)(3). A more than 50 percent equity shift occurs when after the reorganization the percentage of stock held by one or more of the new loss corporation's 5 percent shareholders is at least 50 percentage points higher than the percentage of the old loss corporation's stock held by them during the testing period.[4]

Suppose that X Corp., a loss corporation, merges into Y Corp. Neither corporation has any 5 percent shareholders. In the merger, the former X Corp. shareholders get 49 percent of the Y Corp. stock. A more than 50 percent equity shift occurred because the Y Corp. shareholders (aggregated as a single 5 percent shareholder) go from 0 percent to 51 percent shareholders of the new loss corporation.[5]

The test period used to determine if an ownership change has occurred is the three year period preceding an owner shift or equity structure shift.[6] Several unrelated transactions during the test period may constitute an ownership change. To determine if an ownership change has occurred, it is necessary to measure the difference between a 5 percent shareholder's highest and lowest percentage ownership during the test period.

(b) Constructive Ownership. For purposes of § 382, it is only the stock of individuals that is used to determine ownership changes. Under § 318(*l*)(3), the constructive ownership rules apply in determining owner shifts and equity structure changes. Stock owned by entities is deemed owned by the shareholders, partners or beneficiaries of those entities in proportion to their interests.

(c) Preferred Stock. Certain preferred stock is not counted in determining ownership changes.[7] Under § 1504(a)(4), stock that is nonvoting, is limited and preferred as to dividends, does not participate in corporate growth, has redemption and liquidation rights not exceeding the issue price, and is not convertible is not included as "stock." The label of the stock (common or preferred) is not

---

4. The old loss corporation is the one with NOLs before the reorganization; the new loss corporation is the one entitle to use the NOLs after the reorganization. § 382(k).

5. If X Corp. shareholders received at least 50 percent of the Y Corp. stock

there § 382 would not have been triggered.

6. § 382(i)(1). After one ownership change occurs, the next test period begins the day after that ownership change.

7. § 382(k)(6).

determinative, and the Secretary has broad discretion in deciding which stock is counted.

(d) Options. Stock of a loss corporation that is subject to an option is treated as acquired by the option holder for purposes of determining whether *that holder* has participated an ownership change. Therefore, some options may be considered as exercised while others are ignored. For example, suppose B owns all 100 currently outstanding share of X Corp., and has an option to purchase 100 additional X Corp. shares. B sells C 35 shares and grants C an option to buy B's remaining 65 shares. To test if the sale triggered a § 382 ownership change, only C's option is deemed exercised. Therefore, C goes from a 0 percent to a 100 percent shareholder, and triggers the § 382 limitation.

(e) Continuity of Business. Under § 382(c), a loss corporation's NOL carryforwards are disallowed for the two years following the ownership change unless the new loss corporation either (1) continues the old loss corporation's historic business or (2) uses a significant portion of the old loss corporation's assets in a business. This continuity requirement is designed to distinguish acquisitions motivated by NOLs from those motivated by a desire to obtain assets or a business.[8]

(f) Corporate Value. Recall that the § 382 limitation is computed by multiplying the value of the loss corporation's assets by the by the federal long-term tax-exempt rate. A corporation's value equals the value of its stock. Because the ability to use NOLs increases as the value of the loss corporation increases, there is an incentive for the loss corporation's shareholders to increase corporate value by contributing property to the corporation prior to an ownership change. Section 382(*l*)(1) is an "anti-stuffing" rule which disregards the value of contributions made within two years of the ownership change for purposes of determining the value of a corporation's value. The anti-stuffing rule does not apply if the contribution adds to the corporation's trade or business.

Congress was also concerned that a loss corporation's value might be inflated by investment assets held to generate income to be offset by the corporation's business NOLs. Section 382(*l*)(4) provides that if at least one third of a loss corporation's assets are nonbusiness assets, the value of the corporation, for purposes of § 382, does not include the nonbusiness assets (reduced by any attributable indebtedness). Stock of a 50 percent or more owned subsidiary is not a nonbusiness asset. With such a subsidiary,

---

8. See *Alprosa Watch Corp. v. Commissioner,* 11 T.C. 240 (1948) (shareholder purchased stock of loss corporation, sold assets to original shareholders, and infused corporation with new business).

§ 382(*l*)(4)(E) uses a look through rule that attributes ownership of a percentage of the subsidiary's assets to the parent.

An insolvent corporation may have a value of $0, and, therefore, be entitled to no NOL deductions after an ownership change. Section 382(*l*)(5) provides a special rule that does not limit the use of NOLs for corporations involved in bankruptcy or similar proceedings if at least 50 percent of the loss corporation's stock immediately after the change is owned by former shareholders and certain long term creditors. However, if a second ownership change occurs within two years of the initial change, the § 382 limitation is reduced to zero. Other provisions prevent a purchaser who acquires a corporation immediately before bankruptcy from using NOLs without limitations.

(g) Built-in Gain and Built-in Losses. The income that can be offset by NOLs includes expected future income from operations and gain inherent in the loss corporation's appreciated assets. Under § 382(h)(1)(A) a loss corporation with "unrealized net built-in gain" may increase its § 382 limitation by the "recognized built-in" gain for any tax year within the five year recognition period. A "net realized built-in gain" is the amount by which the value of the corporation's assets exceeds the aggregate bases immediately before an ownership change. A "recognized built-in gain" is any gain recognized on disposition of an asset during the recognition period if the taxpayer establishes that the asset was held by the loss corporation before the change and the gain occurred before the change date. Recognized built-in gain cannot exceed the net unrealized built-in gain reduced by the recognized built-in gains for prior years in the recognition period.

The pre-change loss whose deductibility is limited by § 382 includes NOL carryforwards arising prior to the change year, the allocable portion of a corporation's NOLs for the year in which the change occurs, and certain built-in losses and deductions. §§ 382(d), (h)(1)(B). Just as a corporation with NOLs may be attractive, acquisition of a corporation with built in losses may be equally desirable. Under § 382(h)(1)(B), if a loss corporation has net unrealized built-in loss, any recognized built-in loss during the five year recognition period is deemed a pre-change loss, and is subject to the § 382 limitation.

11.04 Section 383. Pursuant to § 383(a) the Secretary may promulgate regulations to limit capital loss carryforwards under § 1212 to the taxable income of the loss corporation not exceeding the § 382 limitation. Any capital loss carryforward used in a post-change year will reduce the § 382 limitation that is applied to pre-change losses. Similar rules apply to excess credits (e.g., the alternative minimum tax credit under § 53 and the foreign tax credit under § 901) and passive activities losses.

11.05   Section 384. Section 382 does not inhibit a loss corporation from acquiring a profitable corporation if there is no ownership change with respect to the loss corporation. In this situation, there is no trafficking in losses; rather the loss corporation seeks to improve its economic performance through the acquisition. Accordingly, suppose that L Corp., a loss corporation owned by B, acquires P Corp., a profitable corporation owned by C, for cash, and that L Corp. and P Corp. report tax liability on a consolidated return. The ability of L Corp. to use its pre-acquisition NOLs to offset P Corp.'s post-acquisition income is not inhibited by § 382. The same is true if P Corp. merged into L Corp., as long as no ownership change in L Corp. takes place.

But suppose P Corp. is a "burnt-out" tax shelter—an entity that has produced depreciation deductions for its owners and which now has a large built-in gain because the bases of its assets have been adjusted downwards under § 1016 while the property's fair market value has not decreased correspondingly. For example, suppose after generating depreciation deductions, P Corp. has depreciable assets with an aggregate basis of $100,000 and a fair market value of $900,000, subject to a $800,000 mortgage liability. If P Corp. sells the assets, the taxes on the $800,000 gain exceed the $100,000 of cash that P Corp. can expect to receive on an arm's-length sale.

Suppose that the stock of P Corp. is acquired by L Corp. and they file a consolidated return or that P Corp. merges into L Corp. In the absence of a remedial provision, L Corp.'s pre-existing NOLs can be used to offset gain generated by the post-acquisition sale of the acquired assets. L Corp. may be happy to pay $100,000 in cash to acquire the appreciated assets. C, the ultimate seller of the tax shelter, may be happy to receive any cash or other property for C's interest in the burnt-out shelter. But Congress was unhappy with this technique of "laundering" the built-in gain from the sale of assets with pre-existing NOLs.

Section 384 applies if one corporation acquires control of another corporation and either corporation is a gain corporation (i.e., a corporation with net unrealized built-in gain at the time of acquisition). Control is defined as stock representing at least 80 percent of vote and value of the acquired corporation. § 384(c)(5). Section 384 also applies to an asset acquisition if the acquisition qualifies as a tax-free A, C or acquisitive D reorganization. If both the acquiring and the acquired corporations were part of the same control group under § 1563 (using a 50 percent ownership test) during the previous 5–year period (or the term of a corporation's existence if shorter), § 384 will not apply. § 384(b).

If § 384 is applicable, the provision denies the use of any "pre-acquisition loss" of a loss corporation (but not the gain corporation) to offset any "recognized built-in gain" of the gain corporation during the 5–year recognition period. § 384(a). In the examples above, L Corp.'s NOLs cannot be used to offset gain recognized on the sale of P Corp.'s appreciated assets. The term "pre-acquisition loss" includes NOLs and net unrealized built-in losses that are recognized during a 5–year recognition period. § 384(c)(3)(A). The term "recognized built-in gain" refers to any gain on the disposition of an asset during a 5–year recognition period except to the extent that it can be established that the asset was not held by the gain corporation on the acquisition date. § 384(c)(1)(A).

There is overlap between §§ 382 and 384 in some cases while in other cases one or neither of the provisions will apply. Suppose that B owns all of the stock of L Corp., a company with NOLs, and C owns all of the stock of P Corp., a company with built-in gains. If L Corp. purchases all of the stock of P Corp. and they file a consolidated return, § 382 will not prevent the use of L Corp.'s losses against P Corp.'s future income because there is no ownership change for L Corp. However, § 384 will prevent the use of the NOLs to offset any built-in gains recognized by P Corp. during the 5–year recognition period.

If instead, L Corp. merges into P Corp. and C ends up with more than 50 percent or more of the surviving corporation, § 382 will limit the use of L Corp.'s NOLs and § 384 will also apply to limit any NOLs allowable under § 382 which would otherwise be used to offset any of P Corp.'s recognized built-in gains. If P Corp. had no built-in gains prior to the merger, then only § 382 would apply to limit the use of the NOLs.

Suppose L Corp. and P Corp., which are unrelated, form a joint venture partnership, LP, which attempts to allocate income under the partnership agreement disproportionately to L Corp. As a technical matter, there has been no triggering event for purposes of §§ 382 or 384. Nevertheless, Congress has given the Service authority to apply these loss limitation principles in abuse situations. §§ 382(m)(3), 384(f)(1).

11.06　Section 269. Section 269, which covers both asset and stock acquisitions, applies when an acquirer possesses a "bad" state of mind. Under § 269(a) a deduction for an NOL carryover will be disallowed if the control of a corporation or its assets was acquired for the principal purpose of avoiding tax by securing a deduction. There are two requirements for § 269: (1) an acquisition; and (2) a tax avoidance motive. Section 269 may limit deductions otherwise allowed by §§ 382–384.[9]

Section 269 applies not only when NOL carryovers are acquired by a profitable company, but also when the benefits of an NOL carryover are acquired by a loss corporation acquiring a profitable business.[10] The acquisition test is triggered by either of the following: (1) any person(s) acquiring sufficient stock to hold at least 50 percent of the total combined voting power or total value of all shares (§ 269(a)(1)); or (2) a corporation acquiring property of another corporation with a carryover basis (§ 269(a)(2)). Section 269(a)(2) disallows NOL carryovers resulting from a corporate reorganization with an improper purpose involving unrelated corporations. If an acquired corporation is controlled directly or indirectly by an acquiring corporation or its shareholders immediately before the acquisition, § 269 does not apply. Therefore, a merger between commonly controlled corporations will not result in the loss of NOL carryovers.

While the term "evasion or avoidance of tax" is not defined, it is not limited to fraud. Obtaining an NOL carryover that the acquirer would not otherwise enjoy results in tax avoidance. However, tax avoidance must be the "principal purpose" and, therefore, exceed any other purpose in importance. If nontax motives outweigh tax avoidance motives, then § 269 will not apply.[11] Section 382 is triggered by objective criteria, § 269 by subjective criteria. Section 269 may disallow an NOL carryover even when § 382 does not.

Recall that in the liquidation of a subsidiary, the parent recognizes no gain and inherits the subsidiary's basis in its assets. Under § 381(a)(1), a parent also succeeds to the tax attributes of its liquidated subsidiary. Under § 269(b)(1) deductions and other tax attributes that would otherwise be acquired may be disallowed if: (1) there is a qualified stock purchase; (2) a § 338 election is not made; (3) the acquired corporation is liquidated pursuant to a plan adopted within two years of acquisition; and (4) the principal purpose of the liquidation is tax avoidance.

---

9. See Regs. § 1.269–7.

10. See *Commissioner v. British Motor Car Distributors*, 278 F.2d 392 (9th Cir.1960) (NOL deductions disallowed when new owners acquired stock of a loss corporation and contributed new as-

sets that changed the corporation's business and made it profitable).

11. See *U.S. Shelter Corp. v. United States*, 13 Cl.Ct. 606 (1987).

11.07   Affiliated Corporations. In principle, every corporation reports its income and deductions separately from other corporations. The consolidated return provisions offer an opportunity for taxpayers to ignore this principle where instead of operating several businesses in one corporation, several corporations are used. The use of multiple corporations might be the result of internal growth (i.e., new corporations formed via § 351), purchase or reorganization (i.e., a subsidiary acquisition through a B reorganization).

Why would individuals choose to operate a business or businesses through multiple corporations rather than through a single corporation? There may be a host of reasons—including both tax and nontax reasons. Some of the nontax reasons for maintaining, acquiring, or forming multiple corporations include: (1) minimizing potential tort liability; (2) regulatory restraints or benefits of combining businesses within a single corporation; (3) avoiding state law complications; (4) the existence of favorable, nontransferable contractual arrangements; (5) alleviation of labor problems; and (6) the existence of corporate goodwill.

Some of the tax advantages associated with multiple corporations include: (1) the availability of differing accounting methods, taxable years, and other elections; (2) reallocation of income to avoid progressive tax rates; (3) the availability of multiple tax benefits, such as the accumulated earnings tax credit (although this benefit is substantially limited by § 1561 which applies most corporate dollar limitations to members of a controlled group); (4) more favorable disposition of unwanted assets (e.g., through a tax-free spin-off); and (5) greater flexibility with regard to earnings and profits and shareholder distributions.

Notwithstanding the tax advantages that sometimes attend multiple corporations, affiliated groups of corporations often find it desirable to file as though they constitute a single corporation. Under §§ 1501–1504, affiliated groups of corporations are given a privilege of making a single consolidated tax return that allows them to be treated as a single corporation for certain tax purposes. Only affiliated corporations with a common parent corporation may make the election. Thus, if B, an individual, owns the stock of X Corp. and Y Corp., the two corporations may not file a consolidated return. If, though, B owns the stock of H Corp. which owns the stock of X Corp. and Y Corp., then X Corp., Y Corp. and H Corp. can file a consolidated return.

Once the election is made for a taxable year, the corporations must continue to file on a consolidated basis unless the Commissioner consents to a termination or the common parent corporation is no longer in existence. Pursuant to a broad statutory grant

(§ 1502), the Treasury has promulgated detailed Regulations that often provide, for corporations filing consolidated returns, different rules than those that normally apply under the Code.[12] These Regulations effectively constitute the law of consolidated returns. Under § 1501, a group electing to file a consolidated return consents to these Regulations.

(a) Eligibility for Filing. A consolidated return may be filed by an "affiliated group" of corporations. Under § 1504, that term means certain "includible" corporations linked through specified stock ownership requirements. Most corporations are "includible," with certain exceptions such as tax exempt corporations, life insurance companies, foreign corporations, regulated investment companies, and S corporations. The stock ownership provision of § 1504 requires one or more chains of includible corporations connected to a common parent such that: (a) stock with at least 80 percent of the voting power of all classes of stock and at least 80 percent of the value of each includible corporation must be owned directly by one or more of the other includible corporations; and (b) the common parent must also directly meet the 80 percent tests with respect to at least one of the other includible corporations. Note that the direct ownership requirement rules out corporations owned by an individual or group of individuals or by a nonincludible corporation. If a consolidated return election is made by an affiliated group, all includible corporations in the group must file a consolidated return.

Under the stock ownership rules of § 1504(a), "stock" does not include certain nonvoting preferred stock (usually called "plain vanilla" preferred stock). § 1504(a)(4). Accordingly, such stock is often used by members of an affiliated group to raise outside equity capital without destroying the right to file a consolidated return. Under § 1504(a)(5), options are generally ignored in determining eligibility unless not treating the option as exercised would result in substantial federal tax savings and it is reasonably certain that the option will be exercised. Regs. § 1.1504–4.

(b) Election to File a Consolidated Return and Other Accounting Considerations. A consolidated return may be filed only if all affiliated corporations consent on the first consolidated return. Regs. § 1.1502–75(b). Once an election is made, the affiliated group must continue to file on a consolidated basis unless the Commissioner grants permission to discontinue for "good cause." Regs.

---

12. The extent to which the consolidated return regulations may specify rules other than those that apply to unaffiliated corporations is a hotly contested issue. In *Rite Aid v. United States*, 255 F.3d 1357 (Fed.Cir.2001), the Federal Circuit invalidated a portion of Regs. § 1.1502–20, holding that the consolidated return regulations can deviate from the normal rules of the Code only to solve a problem created by the filing of a consolidated return.

§ 1.1502–75(c)(1). The taxable year for a consolidated return is based on the common parent's annual accounting period. In general, the subsidiaries must adopt the parent's period. Regs. § 1.1502–76(a)(1). However, the subsidiaries are not required to adopt the accounting method of the common parent. Instead, each member of the group employs the method that would be used if it were filing a separate return. Regs. § 1.1502–17(a). Each member of an affiliated group is severally liable for the group's consolidated tax liability. Regs. § 1.1502–6.

(c) *Computation of a Consolidated Return: In General.* The basic concept underlying the treatment of a consolidated return is that the affiliated group is in effect a single taxable entity, notwithstanding the existence of multiple corporations. As such, the tax liability ought to be based on dealings with "outsiders" rather than dealings within the group. With this "single taxpayer" approach in mind, consider the basic computational features.

The tax liability of an affiliated group filing a consolidated return is based on "consolidated taxable income." To determine the consolidated taxable income, the separate taxable income (or loss) of each group member is determined separately (subject to special rules relating to intercompany transactions and distributions, accounting methods, etc.). Regs. § 1.1502–12. These separate incomes are then combined. In addition, each member's capital gains and losses, charitable contributions, § 1231 transactions, and net operating losses are aggregated for purposes of applying the various statutory limitations. Regs. § 1.1502–11. The pre-credit consolidated tax liability is then computed in accordance with §§ 11, 541, 531, 1201, etc., on the consolidated taxable income. Finally, any consolidated alternative minimum tax credit, general business credit, or foreign tax credit is subtracted. Regs. § 1.1502–2.

(d) *Computation of a Consolidated Return: Intercompany Transactions.* One of the most significant aspects of the consolidated return regulations is the treatment of intercompany transactions. These transactions include sales of property, payments of interest and rent, contributions of property, and similar activities between members of the consolidated group.

The treatment under the regulations of intercompany transactions is based upon two principles: matching and acceleration. The matching principle generally treats transactions between members of a consolidated group as if they were divisions of a single corporation. As a result, the tax consequences of an intercompany transaction generally will be deferred until one of the members deals with an outsider. For example, if Sister Corp. sells an asset to Brother Corp., recognition of gain or loss on that transaction generally will be deferred until Brother resells the asset to some non-member of the group. Regs. § 1.1502–13(c)(7)(iv)(example 1).In this way the tax consequences of the intercompany transaction "match" in time the tax consequences of the sale to the outsider. In addition, the tax consequences of an intercompany transaction generally must match the tax consequences of a corresponding transaction in terms of character as well.

For example, assume that the asset sold by Sister Corp. to Brother Corp. is depreciable by Brother Corp. Brother Corp. is permitted to use its cost basis in the asset for computing subsequent depreciation, but as Brother Corp. benefits from any cost basis in excess of Sister's adjusted basis in the property at the time of sale, Sister Corp. must recognize a portion of the gain that went unrecognized when the sale was made. Regs. § 1.1502–13(c)(7)(iv)(example 4). Indeed, because the depreciation deductions to Brother Corp. can offset ordinary income, the matching principle requires that the income recognized to Sister Corp. also be ordinary, see Regs. § 1.1502–13(c)(4)(i), a result generally in accordance with sales of depreciable property between related parties, see §§ 1239 and 707(b)(2).

If property is sold from Sister Corp. to Brother Corp. and then resold by Brother Corp. outside the group on an installment basis, the matching principle requires that Sister Corp. recognize any gain on the intercompany sale as collection on the installment note is made by Brother Corp. Regs. § 1502–13(c)(7)(iv)(example 5). The matching principle also ensures that if Sister Corp. or Brother Corp. is a dealer in the property sold, installment reporting is not available to Brother Corp. or to Sister Corp. on this transaction.

The acceleration principle backstops the matching principle by providing that in appropriate circumstances the tax consequences of an intercompany transaction will be recognized before any transaction with an outsider. See Regs. § 1.1502–13(d). For example, if in the example above Brother Corp. ceases to be a member of the consolidated group (because, for example, a significant portion of its stock is acquired by some nonmember), Sister Corp.'s gain or loss on the sale, not previously taken into account, will be triggered. Regs. § 1.1502–13(d)(1)(ii)(A)(1). In general, the acceleration principle requires that gain or loss not yet taken into account on an intercompany transaction be recognized when matching is no longer possible.

Because the consolidated return regulations provide their own recognition and nonrecognition rules for intercompany transactions, they also provide that many of the Code's more general provisions do not apply in the consolidated context. Thus, there are no § 1031 exchanges between members of a consolidated group, Regs. § 1.1502–80(f), and section 304 does not apply to sales between consolidated corporations, § 1.1502–80(b). On the other hand, many anti-abuse provisions continue to apply to intercompany transactions including §§ 269. 482, and 1091. Regs. § 1.1502–13(a)(4).

(e) Computation of a Consolidated Return: Intercompany Distributions. Consistent with the theme that an affiliated group is a single taxable entity, dividend distributions between members of the group are excluded from the computation of consolidated taxable income. Regs. § 1.1502–13(f)(2)(ii). The "investment basis adjustment" rules generally require that the parent's basis in the common stock of a subsidiary be reduced by the amount of intercompany dividend distributions, Regs. § 1.1502–32. The theory behind this downward adjustment in basis is similar to that underlying the treatment of S corporations.[13] Because the parent's stock basis is adjusted upwards when a subsidiary earns income, the distribution from that subsidiary must decrease the basis. Distributions of property are governed by rules similar to those in §§ 301 and 311 except that both gains and losses recognized by the distributing corporation are governed by the intercompany transaction rules discussed above. Regs. § 1.1502–13(f)(2)(iii). Distributions in liquidation are treated under the normal liquidation rules.[14] Regs. §§ 1.1502–13(f)(5), 1.1502–80(a).

(f) Investment Basis Accounts and Excess Loss Accounts. In accordance with the single taxable entity concept, the consolidated return regulations attempt to avoid a duplicate recognition of investment gain (or loss) by a parent corporation that is attributable to earnings of a subsidiary (or losses) that have already been accounted for on the consolidated return.[15] The "investment basis adjustment" (IBA) provisions of Regs. § 1.1502–32 require a parent to make annual adjustments to its basis in the stock of the subsidiaries. The result is a fluctuating stock basis. In general, basis is adjusted for the "modified taxable income" of the subsidiary. In this context, "modified taxable income" is composed of four items: (1) the subsidiary's taxable income or loss (with some timing limitations on loss); (2) tax-exempt income broadly defined (and so including, for example, dividends received to the extent offset by a dividends-received deduction); (3) noncapitalizable, nondeductible

13. See Chapter 13 *infra.*

14. See Chapter 8 *supra.*

15. See *Charles Ilfeld Co. v. Hernandez*, 292 U.S. 62 (1934), where the Court prevented a consolidated group from claiming a double deduction by offsetting the parent's income with subsidiary losses and then attempting to claim a loss on the sale of the subsidiary stock.

items (such as payments of illegal bribes and kickbacks as well as
expiring loss carryovers); and (4) the fair market value of property
distributed by the subsidiary to the parent. Regs. § 1.1502–
32(b)(2)-(3). The regulations set forth with particularity whether
the additions and subtractions from basis apply to common or
preferred (if any) stock.

In other contexts, we have encountered basis adjustments, see,
e.g., § 301(c)(2) and § 1367, but in these contexts basis cannot be
reduced below zero. However, the IBA rules do permit a negative
basis for the parent's stock in the subsidiary. This negative basis is
described in Regs. §§ 1.1502–32(a)(3)(ii), 1.1502–19(a)(2), as an
"excess loss account" (ELA). The account will create income in the
hands of the parent upon the occurrence of certain specified events.
Regs. § 1.1502–19(c). For example, assume that P has a stock basis
of $30 in the stock of S, its subsidiary, and that P and S file a
consolidated return. If S suffers a loss of $50 which is fully used to
offset some of the group's consolidated taxable income, the ELA
account would be $20. If P later sells the S stock for $20, a $40 gain
must be recognized—the $20 sales proceeds plus the $20 ELA. The
tax returns reporting $50 of loss deductions and $40 of gain will
correspond to the economic result to P of its investment in S—$30
paid for the stock, less $20 received on the sale.

(g) Limitations on Consolidated Reporting. Congress and the
Treasury have perceived a danger of consolidated reporting when a
loss corporation is acquired in order to apply its net operating loss
deductions (or other favorable tax attributes) against income of
profitable affiliated group members. The problem here is the same
as that raised in a reorganization or purchase context under §§ 381
and 382. Indeed, where applicable, those provisions govern the
treatment of affiliated group members. Members of a consolidated
group are treated as a single entity (i.e., as if the group's subsidiaries were unincorporated). Reg. § 1.1502–91(a)(1). See generally
Reg. § 1.1502–91 to–99.

The regulations describe the parent change method which
focuses on ownership changes with respect to a loss group's common parent stock. Regs. § 1.1502–92T(b)(1). For example, suppose
that B owns all of the stock of P Corp. which files a consolidated
return with its 80 percent owned subsidiary, Subco. Individual C
owns the other 20 percent of Subco. During year 1, the P Corp.
group incurs a $200 consolidated NOL, attributable entirely to
Subco. In year 2, B sells 60 percent of P Corp. to D, an unrelated
individual. C retains the 20 percent minority interest in Subco.
Because the consolidated group is treated as a single entity for
purposes of § 382, the sale of stock from B to D triggers § 382 (i.e.,

D's ownership in the P Corp. group has gone from 0 percent to 60 percent) even though D's ownership in Subco would not trigger § 382 (i.e., after the purchase D owns 60 percent x 80 percent, or 48 percent of Subco). Under § 382, the P Corp. group's use of Subco's NOL will be limited. The Regulations also provide special rules applicable to new members entering a loss group and leaving the loss group. Regs. §§ 1.1502–94 (entering members), 1.1502–95 (departing members).

In calculating the § 382 limitation, the value of the stock of each member of the loss group (other than stock owned directly or indirectly by another member) is multiplied by the federal long-term tax-exempt rate. For example, suppose that B owns all of the stock of P Corp. which owns 80 percent of the stock of L Corp. C, who is unrelated to B, owns the other 20 percent of L Corp. P Corp. and L Corp. file a consolidated return. P Corp.'s stock has a value of $1,000 (excluding the value of P's stock in L Corp.) and L Corp.'s stock has a value of $100. L Corp. has a NOL of $600 incurred while a member of the P Corp. group. B sells 100 percent of the P Corp. stock to C. The sale is an ownership change for the P Corp. group, triggering § 382. The consolidated § 382 limitation is the product of the long-term tax-exempt tax rate and $1100, the sum of P Corp.'s $1,000 value and the $100 value of the L Corp.'s assets. If the long-term tax-exempt rate is 10 percent, then the P Corp. group can offset up to $110 of consolidated taxable income each year with L Corp.'s NOL.

The other rules that apply under § 382 generally apply in the consolidated group context to the entire group. For example the ability to use an NOL is increased if a loss group has a net unrealized built-in gain that is recognized during the five-year recognition period. Reg. § 1.1502–93(c). Also, the business continuity requirement of § 382 is applied to the group as a whole. Reg. § 1.1502–93(d).

While § 382 does apply to consolidated groups, the regulations also impose an additional limitation on the ability of the NOLs of one member to be used by the group as a whole to offset consolidated taxable income. This limitation is known as the "separate return limitation year," or SRLY. Reg. § 1.1502–1(f). Generally, pre-affiliation losses cannot be utilized to offset post-affiliation consolidated taxable income, except to the extent that the new member of the group contributes to the consolidated income. Regs. § 1.1502–21(c). A SRLY member's contribution to consolidated taxable income is determined on a cumulative basis over the period during which the SRLY member is a member of the consolidated group. Also, the SRLY limitation can be applied on a subgroup basis to SRLY members who were previously affiliated in another group and who continue to be affiliated in the new group. Similar rules exist for other tax attributes. See Regs. §§ 1.1502–4(f) (foreign tax credit carryovers), 1.1502–22(c) (capital loss carryovers).

The SRLY rule may appear to duplicate the § 382 limitation, but there are situations where § 382 does not apply although the SRLY rule does. In addition, the reach of the SRLY rule is substantially limited by the overlap rule, see Regs. §§ 1.1502–15(g), 1.1502–21(g). Under the overlap rule, the SRLY limitations do not apply if a member joins the group in a transaction that causes § 382 to apply or within six months of such a transaction.

For example, suppose that B, an individual, and P Corp. each owns 50 percent of L Corp. stock. L Corp. has NOLs. If P Corp. purchases an additional 30 percent of the L Corp. stock from B, no ownership change has occurred under § 382 because no shareholder of P Corp. has increased ownership in L Corp. by more than 50 percentage points. However, even though § 382 does not limit the use of L Corp.'s losses by the P Corp. group if it files a consolidated return, the SRLY rule limits the use of L Corp.'s pre-consolidation NOL by the P Corp. group. Under Reg. § 1.1502–21(c), the deduction of the SRLY loss by the P Corp. group is limited to the taxable income of the member with the SRLY loss (i.e., L Corp.). In some cases where the acquired corporation with a SRLY loss is part of a group of related corporations, the taxable income of this SRLY subgroup can be offset by the SRLY loss. Reg. § 1.1502–21(c)(2).

Or suppose that a profitable corporation acquires another corporation, not because it has any net operating losses, but rather because it has a large debt that is about to become worthless. Or perhaps the corporation to be acquired has assets that it is about to sell at a loss. Section 382 discourages the acquisition of a corporation with such "built-in" losses. While the SRLY rules can apply to the acquisition of a corporation having such built-in losses, see Regs. § 1.1502–15, they in fact will not be triggered if § 382(h) applies to the acquisition.

CHAPTER 12. PENALTY PROVISIONS

12.01 Introduction. The organizing feature of Subchapter C is that corporate earnings from operations be taxed twice—once when the corporation earns them and once again when they are distributed. Historically, it has been Congress's intention that both taxes should be at ordinary income rates. Whether these guiding principles are sound is explored in Chapter 1. In this Chapter, the focus is on Code provisions enacted to protect this double tax regime.

It is not true that Congress intended that all corporate earnings be taxed twice at ordinary income rates. For example, a corporation might earn income that is taxed at ordinary income rates, but rather than distributing those earnings as a dividend to its shareholders, the corporation might accumulate the income, thereby increasing the fair market value of its stock. The shareholders could then turn that appreciation into cash by selling this stock, having the corporation redeem the stock or liquidating the corporation. All three of these possibilities might allow the shareholders effectively to receive the corporate earnings at capital gains rate. Avoiding or deferring the shareholder-level tax or turning ordinary income into capital gain is a strategy taxpayers have historically pursued.

Suppose instead that the corporation has not yet recognized a gain because it has not yet sold its appreciated inventory. If it sells the inventory and distributes the proceeds, the corporation will be taxed at ordinary income rates on the sale, and the shareholders will have ordinary income on the distribution. If instead a shareholder sells the stock of the corporation which has appreciated in value to reflect the corporation's appreciated inventory, the shareholder would normally recognize a capital gain in the absence of any remedial provisions.

Having envisioned that Subchapter C permits circumvention of the double tax system, Congress has enacted various penalty provisions intended to raise the cost of avoiding a corporate or shareholder-level tax. The accumulated earnings tax and personal holding company tax are levied on the corporation in addition to normal corporate taxes (e.g., under §§ 11 and 55) to prod the corporation into making distributions that will be taxed as dividends. The collapsible corporations provision exacts its penalty by converting what would otherwise be a shareholder's capital gain into ordinary income.

304

12.02 Accumulated Earnings Tax: Overview. Historically, corporate tax rates have been lower than individual rates. This differential led some high bracket individuals to incorporate their businesses in order to accumulate the earnings at the corporate-level until such time as the individual was in a lower tax bracket. Even when the top individual rates are lower than the top corporate rates, accumulation remains a useful strategy. Once a corporation has earned income and paid the appropriate taxes, the decision whether to distribute or accumulate is not based solely on any differential between the corporate and individual rates. Instead, the decision is based partly on the differential between the tax rate on ordinary income and the rate on capital gains and partly on the advantages from deferral.

If a corporation earns $100 after its taxes, the decision whether to distribute is influenced in part by the potential for deferral. By not distributing, the corporation can invest the $100 earning a return that will be taxed once at the corporate level. While it is true that there may be a shareholder-level tax on the eventual distribution, meanwhile the corporation is earning income on dollars that would otherwise have been paid in taxes. If instead the corporation distributes the $100, the shareholders will have $100 minus the shareholder-level tax to invest.

Historically what has made this deferral troublesome is the ability of shareholders to defer distributions until the shareholders are in lower tax brackets. Or shareholders might be able to convert ordinary income into capital gain. Moreover, as long as our tax system allows a step-up in basis of assets at death under § 1014, there will be an incentive for taxpayers to defer taxes with a consequent loss to the Treasury. Suppose a taxpayer holds stock with a basis of $30 and a fair market value of $100 due to $70 of corporate earnings. Upon death, the taxpayer's estate or beneficiary can either sell the stock or have the corporation redeem the stock without recognizing gain since both the basis and fair market value of the stock will be $100.

The accumulated earnings tax is a penalty intended to encourage distributions to shareholders. The tax is triggered by an accumulation of earnings beyond the reasonable needs of the business. If there are excess earnings, the base of the accumulated earnings tax is the corporation's "accumulated taxable income" for the year. Notice that *accumulated* earnings provide an evidentiary foundation for imposition of the tax. But once it is determined that the tax applies, the tax base is *current* earnings available for distribution— accumulated taxable income.

Section 535 defines "accumulated taxable income" as taxable income minus a dividends-paid deduction and a specified accumulated earnings credit. Taxable income is modified to reflect more accurately dividend-paying capacity. Once the tax base is determined, § 531 imposes a tax at the highest individual rate.

Historically, many tax observers (but not the Service) believed that the accumulated earnings tax could not apply to publicly held corporations since there would be difficulty in ascertaining the tax avoidance motive where no individual or group had effective control. However, Congress sided with the Service by enacting § 532(c) which provides for application of the accumulated earnings tax regardless of the number of shareholders.[1]

12.03 Accumulated Earnings Tax: Unreasonable Accumulations. Section 532(a) imposes the accumulated earnings tax on corporations that accumulate income with a subjective tax avoidance motive. Section 533 presumes the improper motive if there is an accumulation "beyond the reasonable needs of the business"—a more objective standard. Theoretically, it would be possible for a corporation with an improper motive to be subject to the accumulated earnings tax even though in fact the corporation did not accumulate earnings in excess of the reasonable needs of the business. Conversely, a corporation that accumulates beyond the reasonable needs of the business should not be subject to the tax if there is no improper motive for the accumulation.

The regulations contain a list of factors to be considered in determining whether the tax avoidance motive is present, including: (a) dealings between the corporation and its shareholders, including loans or expenditures for the shareholders' personal benefit; (b) investments in assets not connected to the corporation's business; and (c) the corporation's dividend history. These factors do not control but are evidentiary. Thus, a corporation might not be subject to § 531 even though it has a poor dividend record.

If a tax avoidance motive is present, how strong must it be to activate the accumulated earnings tax provisions? In *United States v. Donruss Co.*,[2] the government argued that the taxpayer must establish that tax avoidance was not "one of the purposes" for accumulating earnings. The taxpayer argued that it must prevail if tax avoidance was not the "dominant, controlling, or impelling"

---

1. See *Technalysis Corp. v. Commissioner*, 101 T.C. 397 (1993) (court noted that widely held corporations can be subject to accumulated earnings tax if tax avoidance purpose exists; Technalysis had 1,500 shareholders and 30 percent of its stock was held by five members of the board of directors).

2. 393 U.S. 297 (1969).

reason for the accumulation. The Court resolved the case in favor of the government. *Donruss* does not address how much purpose is enough. Do the accumulated earnings tax provisions apply if the taxpayer has a 1 percent tax avoidance motive and a 99 percent business motive?

Notwithstanding the subjective standard contained in § 532, it is the more objective "reasonable needs of the business" test in § 533 that is generally dispositive. While no statutory definition exists, § 537(a)(1) provides that reasonable needs includes the "reasonably anticipated needs of the business." The regulations identify five nonexclusive grounds that may justify an accumulation.[3]

The first two grounds embrace a bona fide expansion of the business or the acquisition of a new business. Either of these reasons is a common justification for accumulation. The two major concerns pertaining to this justification are the relationship between the accumulation and the expansion, and the definition of what constitutes "the business." The more attenuated the relationship between the accumulation and the expansion, the more likely it is that the Service will charge an unreasonable accumulation. Concrete plans for expansion are helpful but not controlling. If the accumulations were reasonable when made, a subsequent abandonment of plans will not cause liability.

Determining what is the business of the corporation is no easy matter. The regulations provide that the business includes "any line of business which [the corporation] may undertake."[4] The "any line of business" language appears to support even a radical change in the nature of a corporation's business. Suppose a corporation engaged in manufacturing designer clothes in Beverly Hills accumulates earnings to acquire a meatpacking plant in Chicago? So long as the corporation is accumulating earnings to expand "the business" rather than to make "an investment," the regulation should protect the taxpayer.

A third ground justifying accumulation is the retirement of bona fide business indebtedness. The tension here is between debt held by non-shareholders and debt held by shareholders. Accumulating earnings to retire the former is a reasonable business need. Debt held by shareholders—particularly if held pro rata—is more suspect. Generally, accumulation of earnings for the purpose of later redeeming shareholders' stock is not permitted.[5] To allow

3. Regs. § 1.537–2(b).

4. Regs. § 1.537–3(a).

5. If a corporation can show that the redemption will further the corporation's business, the accumulation may

accumulation for debt retirement but not for stock redemption is a factor favoring capitalization with debt rather than equity.

The fourth ground listed in the regulations is assuring a fund of liquid assets to finance operations of a business during its typical operating cycle. In *Bardahl Manufacturing Corp. v. Commissioner*,[6] the court created a statistical formula for determining the anticipated working capital needs of a business during an operating cycle. The formula serves as a guideline only. The operating cycle is the period of time required to convert cash into inventory, inventory into accounts receivable, and accounts receivable into cash. For example, if the period from purchase of inventory to receipt of cash for the goods sold is three months, the working capital needs are 25 percent of total annual operating costs and costs of goods sold.

The fifth ground is accumulation for investments or loans to suppliers or customers in order to maintain the business of the corporation. These types of investments are considered by the regulations to be integral to the taxpayer's trade or business.[7]

In addition to the listed reasons for accumulations, accumulations can be justified for a host of other business reasons including the need to fund a pension plan, reasonable self-insurance against casualties or litigation liability and reserves to meet a threatened strike.

Even if a taxpayer can establish reasonable needs of the business, one might argue that accumulated earnings could be distributed to shareholders and then reinvested in the corporation. The Supreme Court in *Helvering v. Chicago Stock Yards Co.*,[8] considered a one-man corporation that accumulated earnings to pay off certain obligations of its subsidiaries. The Court suggested that the taxpayer could distribute the earnings to the shareholder who would either reinvest the earnings or discharge the liabilities directly. Applied rigorously, this reasoning would make virtually all accumulations unreasonable if the shareholders' after-tax proceeds would be sufficient to meet corporate needs.

12.04 Accumulated Earnings Tax: Matching Earnings and Reasonable Needs. Even if the reasonable needs of a business can be accurately quantified, determining what corporate

---

be justifiable. Thus, accumulation to redeem the stock of a dissenting minority shareholder may be reasonable. See also *Hughes, Inc. v. Commissioner*, 90 T.C. 1 (1988) (accumulation to redeem stock to prevent a takeover was reasonable).

6. 24 T.C.M. 1030 (1965) and 25 T.C.M. 935 (1966).

7. See *Corn Products Refining Co. v. Commissioner*, 350 U.S. 46 (1955). But see *Arkansas Best Corp. v. Commissioner*, 485 U.S. 212 (1988).

8. 318 U.S. 693 (1943).

assets are available to meet those needs is not always clear. That determination must be made in order to determine if for the year or years in question the taxpayer is unreasonably accumulating earnings. Suppose X Corp. has accumulated earnings and profits of $1 million, its reasonable needs for the year in question require $600,000, and its current earnings and profits, which are not distributed, are $500,000. Just because the accumulated earnings exceed the needs of the business does not mean that the current earnings are being unreasonably accumulated. For example, if the accumulated earnings have all been reinvested in productive corporate assets, there may be no earnings available other than the current earnings to meet the reasonable needs of the business.[9]

On the other hand, if the accumulated earnings have been retained or reinvested in assets unrelated to the corporation's business then the current accumulation might be unreasonable. Thus, if X Corp. invested the $1 million of accumulated earnings and profits in marketable securities, those securities would serve as evidence that current accumulations were unnecessary. Suppose instead that X Corp. invested $900,000 of its accumulated earnings in needed machinery and equipment and $100,000 in marketable securities which have appreciated in value to $600,000. In evaluating whether the current $500,000 accumulation is reasonable, should the securities be valued at cost or fair market value? If the former, then the current accumulation would be reasonable to meet the corporation's $600,000 needs. If the latter, then the current accumulation would be unreasonable since the securities could be sold to meet the corporation's needs. In *Ivan Allen Co. v. United States*,[10] the Supreme Court held that the fair market value was the appropriate measure despite the taxpayer's argument that the realization doctrine mandated valuation of the securities at cost.[11]

12.05 Accumulated Earnings Tax: Burden of Proof. Initially the burden of proof is on the taxpayer to prove that earnings have not been accumulated with a tax avoidance motive. Section 534 allows the taxpayer to shift the burden of proof to the government in proceedings before the Tax Court.[12] Summarily stated, the provision places the burden of proof on the government unless it notifies the corporation before the notice of deficiency is sent. Even then, the burden shifts back to the government if the taxpayer

---

9. It is important to keep in mind that the earnings and profits account is not the equivalent of cash-on-hand.

10. 422 U.S. 617 (1975).

11. The Court did not force the taxpayer to be taxed on unrealized gain, but instead used the unrealized gain as evidence of an unreasonable accumulation.

12. Why should the shift in burden only apply in Tax Court proceedings?

submits a statement setting forth with specificity the grounds on which it will rely.[13]

12.06　Accumulated Earnings Tax: Computation of the Accumulated Earnings Tax. The accumulated earnings tax is imposed on accumulated taxable income which is defined in § 535 to be taxable income with specified adjustments minus a dividends-received deduction and an accumulated earnings credit. The adjustments to taxable income are intended to measure more accurately dividend-paying capacity. Many of the adjustments are similar to or the same as those made in computing earnings and profits. Thus, taxable income is reduced by nondeductible expenses that nevertheless diminish dividend paying capacity such as accrued corporate income taxes, disallowed charitable deductions, and disallowed capital losses under § 1211. Conversely, some items that are deductible in computing taxable income are added back in determining accumulated taxable income since the items do not diminish the ability to pay dividends. These items include the net operating loss deduction, capital loss carryovers and the dividends-received deduction.

Once the adjustments have been made, § 535 allows the taxpayer to take a dividends-paid deduction since the tax base is aimed at *undistributed* corporate earnings. The dividends paid deduction is permitted for dividends actually paid during the taxable year and for consent dividends. §§ 561–565. A consent dividend is a dividend that is not actually distributed. Instead the shareholders agree to treat a portion of the corporation's earnings as if they were distributed and then contributed by the shareholders back to the corporation. The consent dividend procedure allows a corporation to avoid the accumulated earnings tax without actually making a distribution (as long as the shareholders report dividend income). § 565.

The final step in computing accumulated taxable income is the determination of the accumulated earnings credit. Congress created the credit to permit a small corporation to accumulate some earnings and profits without subjecting itself to accumulated earnings tax liability. Under § 535(c)(2) a corporation may accumulate up to $250,000 of earnings and profits without risk of the accumulated earnings tax.[14] The $250,000 amount is a cumulative and not a

---

13. The Tax Court will rule in advance on the sufficiency of the taxpayer's response.

14. For corporations whose "principal function ... is the performance of services in the field of health, law, engineering, architecture, accounting, actuarial science, performing arts, or con-

sulting" the credit is restricted to $150,000. It is not clear why these service corporations should receive a smaller credit than a corporation with investment income that has virtually no business activities.

yearly amount. Amounts accumulated in excess of $250,000 are still permitted if the corporation can show that the accumulation is necessary to meet the reasonable needs of the business.

Once the accumulated taxable income is determined § 531 applies a tax at the highest individual rate. The accumulated earnings tax is not a self-assessing tax. A taxpayer becomes liable for the tax only after notification by the Service rather than when the taxpayer's return is filed. In light of this fact, interest has historically been charged only from the date the Service demands payment rather than the date the return was originally due to be filed. Since 1986, interest accrues from the date the return was originally due to be filed. § 6601. It somehow seems odd that interest can accrue before a liability arises.

12.07 Personal Holding Company Tax: Overview. Enacted in 1934, the personal holding company provisions were aimed at corporations controlled by a limited number of shareholders who use the corporate form to avoid higher individual tax rates. Congress felt that the accumulated earnings tax provisions were inadequate to address the problem in part because it is often difficult to show the subjective forbidden purpose. The personal holding company provisions are more objective.

Examples of the perceived misuse of the corporate form include the incorporated portfolio, personal service corporations and incorporated personal assets. If corporate rates are lower than individual rates, there is an incentive for an individual to organize a corporation to hold investment assets so that the interest, dividends and other portfolio income would be taxed at the lower rates.[15] The same shifting of income can apply to personal services. An actor, athlete or any other worker might organize a corporation and agree to work for it at a modest salary. The corporation would then hire itself out to those desiring the service at the fair market value of the services. The difference between the fair market value received and salary paid would be taxed at the lower corporate rates. The third device involved the transfer of a personal asset such as a yacht or country estate to a corporation which would then rent the asset back to the shareholder. The intention here is that the corporation could use the depreciation and other related deductions to offset not only the rental income but other corporate income.

To determine if a corporation's income is personal holding company income requires two tests—a stock ownership test and an income test. Under the stock ownership test, the tax applies to

15. The individual could cause the corporation to distribute the income at a time when the individual is in a lower bracket.

closely held corporations if more than 50 percent in value of the stock is owned directly or indirectly through attribution by five or fewer individuals. The income test is satisfied if at least 60 percent of "adjusted ordinary gross income" is "personal holding company income." § 542.

If the personal holding company provisions apply, there is a tax at the highest individual rate. Since the purpose of the provision is to force distributions, a corporation can avoid the tax through a deficiency dividend mechanism. § 547.

12.08   Personal Holding Company Tax: Stock Ownership Test. The purpose of the stock ownership test is to ensure that the personal holding company tax falls only on those corporations most likely to be manipulated by their shareholders for nonbusiness purposes. The behavior that Congress was concerned about is more likely to occur in closely-held corporations where a handful of shareholders determine corporate behavior. The test is satisfied if at any time during the last half of the taxable year, more than 50 percent in value of the corporation's stock is owned directly or indirectly by or for not more than 5 individuals. § 542(a)(2). Note that if there are fewer than 10 shareholders, the stock ownership test is automatically satisfied.

The attribution rules apply in determining stock ownership. But note that the rules under § 544 differ somewhat from those in § 318. For example, there is attribution among siblings under § 544. These attribution rules prevent a holding company from escaping the personal holding company tax by imposing an operating company between the holding company and the individual owner or by spreading ownership among many family members.

12.09   Personal Holding Company Tax: Income Test. Since almost all closely-held corporations will satisfy the stock ownership test, it is the income test that has taken on the most importance in the personal holding company area. Congress did not intend for the personal holding company tax to apply to every corporation with the "tainted" personal holding company income. It is only where the personal holding company income is a significant part of the corporation's operating income that the tax might apply. The income test is satisfied if at least 60 percent of the corporation's "adjusted ordinary gross income" for the year is personal holding company income.

(a) Adjusted Ordinary Gross Income. In computing adjusted ordinary gross income, ordinary gross income is first determined by excluding from gross income gains from the sale or disposition of

capital assets and assets used in the trade or business. § 543(b)(1). These items are excluded to provide a better picture of the corporation's "every day" operating income. Further adjustments are made to reflect some high-gross/low-net income activities. Since the personal holding company tax applies only if personal holding company income (the numerator) equals or exceeds 60 percent of adjusted ordinary gross income (the denominator), there is an incentive for taxpayers to increase the denominator (adjusted ordinary gross income) of the fraction. Operating high gross income activities that produce little or no net income is a means of increasing the denominator.

For example, rental and royalty activities can produce high gross income but low net income once depreciation, interest and property taxes are taken into account. Accordingly, only the net income from rents and mineral royalties enters the adjusted ordinary gross income calculation.

Note that a corporation can still swell the denominator by operating a high-gross/low-net business. Suppose X Corp. has $60,000 of personal holding company income and adjusted ordinary gross income of $80,000. By operating a business that produces $21,000 of ordinary income but has $21,000 of deductions, the corporation will avoid satisfying the income test.[16]

Note also that a corporation with a high cost of goods sold might find itself unwittingly a candidate for personal holding company taxation if it has even a small quantity of personal holding company income since its gross income and hence its adjusted ordinary gross income will be quite small.[17]

(b) Personal Holding Company Income. Section 543(a) attempts to distinguish the "tainted" personal holding company income from "legitimate" operating income. The provision is aimed at income from passive sources. Accordingly the following items may qualify as personal holding company income: dividends, interest, royalties, annuities and rents. In keeping with the original intention to discourage personal service corporations, amounts received under personal service contracts may be personal holding company income. To discourage the incorporation of personal assets, amounts received from certain shareholders for the use of corporate property are personal holding company income.

---

16. The corporation will have personal holding company income of $60,000 and adjusted ordinary gross income of $101,000.

17. See Regs. § 1.61–3(a) which defines gross income from a manufacturing business as total sales less the cost of goods sold.

Of all the passive income sources, perhaps the most troubling are royalties and rents. Royalties generally include periodic receipts from licenses to use various kinds of intangible property such as patents, trademarks and franchises.[18] Sometimes it is difficult to distinguish a license which generates a royalty from an outright sale on the installment method which is not classified as personal holding company income or from rental payments which are subject to the special requirements of § 543(a)(2).[19] A second problem is that some royalties may be generated by active business operations. For example, a corporation that actively developed and licensed computer software prior to 1986 was subject to the personal holding company provisions on the royalty income. The Tax Reform Act of 1986 amended §§ 543(a)(1)(C) and 543(b) to provide that such royalties do not constitute personal holding company income if earned by an active business. To qualify, the recipient must: (1) be actively engaged in the trade or business of developing software; (2) derive at least 50 percent of its income from such software; (3) incur substantial trade or business expenses; and (4) distribute to its shareholders most of its passive income other than the royalties.

Rental income like royalty income can be generated both passively and actively. Section 543(a)(2) makes the distinction with a bright line test based on the percentage of adjusted ordinary gross income that is from rental income. If adjusted income from rents[20] constitutes 50 percent or more of a corporation's adjusted ordinary gross income, the rental income is not personal holding company income.[21] Therefore, a corporation engaged primarily in rental activities can escape personal holding company status. Note that the provision makes no effort to determine the amount of corporate involvement in the rental activities. A corporation with rental income that comprises 40 percent of its adjusted ordinary gross income must treat the rental income as personal holding company income to be added to any other personal holding company income even though the corporation, through its employees, actively participated in the rental activity.[22] Even if the 50 percent test is satisfied, rental income will constitute personal holding company

---

18. Mineral, oil and gas royalties are addressed separately. § 543(a)(3).

19. See, e.g., *Dothan Coca–Cola Bottling Co. v. United States,* 745 F.2d 1400 (11th Cir.1984).

20. Defined in § 543(b)(3), the term essentially means net rental income.

21. A similar test is applied to royalties from copyrights as well as mineral,

oil, and gas royalties. § 543(a)(4) (copyrights), § 543(a)(3) (mineral, oil and gas royalties).

22. See, e.g., *Eller v. Commissioner,* 77 T.C. 934 (1981) (income from operation of commercial shopping center and mobile home park was personal holding company income despite level of services).

income if a corporation having substantial nonrent personal holding company income fails to distribute it to its shareholders.[23]

Not all rents are addressed by § 543(a)(2). Compensation for the use of corporate property by a shareholder owning 25 percent or more stock is automatically personal holding company income. § 543(a)(6). This provision reaches all payments for incorporated personal assets such as yachts and summer estates. Moreover, any deductions in excess of the rent cannot be used to offset other personal holding company income in determining undistributed personal holding company income, the base on which the tax is applied.[24]

Note also that if § 543(a)(6) applies, it applies to all assets rented by 25 percent shareholders—even nonpersonal, business assets. For example, if a 25 percent shareholder rents a hotel from a corporation that satisfies the stock ownership test and the shareholder operates that asset, the rent received by the corporation will constitute personal holding company income.[25] Section 543(a)(6) softens this result by applying only if the corporation has personal holding company income—other than rent—in excess of 10 percent of its adjusted ordinary gross income.[26] Note then that it may still be possible to incorporate personal assets without personal holding company tax implications if a corporation does not exceed the 10 percent threshold.

Enacted in part to discourage the use of the corporate form by entertainers and other providers of services, § 543(a)(7) along with § 269A are weapons available to the Service. Section 269A provides the Commissioner with power to reallocate income from a corporation to the individual actually performing the services. Section 543(a)(7) respects the corporation as an entity but treats the personal services income as personal holding company income if the individual who is to perform the services is designated or can be designated by some person other than the corporation and the designated person owns directly or indirectly 25 percent or more by value of the corporation's stock. If there is merely an expectation on the part of the payor that a particular shareholder will perform

---

23. Section 543(a)(2)(B) provides that dividends paid must equal or exceed the amount (if any) by which the non-rent personal holding company income exceeds 10 percent of adjusted ordinary gross income.

24. Section 545(b)(6) will not limit the deductions if the rent paid by the shareholder is reasonable and other conditions are met.

25. See, e.g., *Hatfried, Inc. v. Commissioner,* 162 F.2d 628 (3d Cir.1947).

26. Amounts received from 25 percent or greater shareholders are excluded from this calculation.

the services but no designation, the income is not personal holding company income.[27]

12.10   Personal Holding Company Tax: Computation. If a corporation satisfies both the stock ownership and income tests, § 541 imposes a tax at the highest individual rate on undistributed personal holding company income. Section 545 defines undistributed personal holding company income as taxable income adjusted to reflect the corporation's net economic gain for the year. The adjustments are similar to those made in determining accumulated taxable income for purposes of the accumulated earnings tax. Thus, federal taxes are deducted, the dividends-received deduction is eliminated, and charitable deduction restrictions are eased. Net capital gains are deducted thereby allowing corporations to accumulate long-term capital gains. § 545(b).

Once these adjustments are made, the corporation is permitted a dividends-paid deduction in accordance with § 561. The deduction is the sum of actual dividends paid during the year,[28] consent dividends and the dividend carryover. The consent dividend mechanism in § 565 allows shareholders to agree to treat a specified portion of the corporation's earnings and profits as a dividend even in the absence of an actual distribution. The procedure enables a corporation wishing to avoid the personal holding company tax to do so without making an actual distribution. The amount of the consent dividend is treated as though the corporation made a distribution followed by a contribution to capital by receiving shareholders. The dividend carryover under § 564 is the excess of dividends paid during the two preceding years over the corporation's taxable income for those years.

Dividends paid in property will qualify for a deduction. Under Regs. § 1.562–1(a), the deduction is limited to the property's adjusted basis at the time of distribution. In *Fulman v. United States*,[29] the regulation was upheld, but in light of the substantial repeal of *General Utilities*[30] in § 311(b) the regulation would cause strange results. A corporation might make a distribution of appreciated property that would increase its taxable income (and therefore its undistributed personal holding company income) by the difference between the property's fair market value and its adjusted basis. Yet, the undistributed personal holding company income

---

27. See, e.g., Rev. Rul. 75–67, 1975–1 C.B. 169 (no personal holding company income for doctor's personal service corporation).

28. Dividends paid within the first two and one-half months of the follow-

ing year also can be deducted to a limited extent. § 563(c).

29. 434 U.S. 528 (1978).

30. See discussion at Section 4.04 *supra*.

would be decreased only by the property's adjusted basis. It would be bizarre if a distribution of property could increase personal holding company liability.

Once the corporation's personal holding company tax liability has been determined, it can mitigate or eliminate the liability through the dividend deficiency procedure. § 547. This procedure allows a corporation to make a dividend distribution to shareholders once the Service has determined that there is personal holding company liability. However, the deficiency dividend procedure does not diminish the liability for interest or penalties.

CHAPTER 13. S CORPORATIONS

13.01 Introduction. We have already looked at C corporations, corporations that are treated as taxpayers independent of their shareholders. Some corporations, though, called S corporations, file an informational return but do not (with some exceptions) pay income taxes.[1] Instead, an S corporation's items of income and deduction are passed-thru to its shareholders who report these items directly on their individual income tax returns.

Subchapter C of the Internal Revenue Code,[2] §§ 301–385, provides most of the provisions governing the taxation of *all* corporations, C corporations and S corporations alike. Subchapter S, §§ 1361–1379, adds those provisions specially applicable to S corporations. One important aspect of the taxation of S corporations is the coordination of the rules in these two subchapters. Indeed, § 1371(a)(1) provides: "Except as otherwise provided in this title, and except to the extent inconsistent with this subchapter, subchapter C shall apply to an S corporation and its shareholders." Accordingly, in this Chapter we will examine sections in both subchapters C and S, but when examining a provision in subchapter C, our emphasis will be on its application to S corporations.

There are two basic models upon which pass-thru taxation can be designed: the entity model and the aggregate model. Under a pure entity model, the entity computes its taxable income without reference to any tax attributes of its beneficial owners. That is, the entity's basis in its assets is independent of any asset basis of its shareholders or partners, the entity has a taxable year and method of accounting independent of the taxable years and accounting methods of its owners, etc. Once the entity's taxable income or loss is computed, it is passed-thru to its owners.

Under a pure aggregate model, the entity has no tax attributes of its own and does not compute a taxable income. Instead, the entity is treated as no more than an aggregate of its owners, so that, for example, it has no independent basis in its assets but instead uses the aggregate of its owners' bases. Thus, a separate depreciation schedule must be maintained for each owner's interest in each entity asset, each owner may have a distinct holding period

---

1. The terms C corporation and S corporation are defined in § 1361(a).

2. More accurately, subchapter C (corporate distributions and adjust-

ments) of Chapter 1 (normal taxes and surtaxes) of Subtitle A (income taxes) of the Internal Revenue Code of 1986, as amended.

for each asset, etc. While a pure aggregate approach to pass-thru taxation is possible, in practice it would be very cumbersome to implement.[3]

13.02 Qualification and Election. For a corporation to be taxed as an S corporation, it must be a "small business corporation" as defined in § 1361(b) and it must file an election pursuant to § 1362(a). Despite the name, the definition of a small business corporation is not based in any way on the size of the corporation's business. "Small" in this context refers to the number of shareholders: a "small business corporation" under § 1361(b) cannot have more than 100 shareholders.[4] Other requirements are: (1) the corporation must be domestic; (2) all shareholders must be individuals or estates, certain qualifying trusts, see § 1361(c)(2), pension, profit-sharing or stock bonus plans qualifying under § 401, or charitable organizations, see § 1361(c)(7), (3) no nonresident alien may be a shareholder; and (4) the corporation may have only one class of stock outstanding. In addition, the corporation must not be an insurance or financial company, or be any one of several other special types of corporations. See § 1361(b)(2).

If a corporation satisfies these requirements, it may file an election to be taxed as an S corporation. Every shareholder must consent to this election, § 1362(a)(2), although once made, the election need not be ratified by new shareholders who acquire stock after the election is filed. Because the effect of an S corporation election is to pass-thru and tax shareholders on the corporation's income, requiring unanimous shareholder consent eliminates any possible argument that taxing a shareholder on the corporation's income violates the Constitution.

If an S corporation election is filed during the first 2½ months of the corporation's taxable year, the election can be effective for the current year. If the election is filed after more than 2½ months into the current taxable year, it automatically becomes effective for

---

3. The taxation of S corporations is close to a pure entity model. For those familiar with the taxation of partnerships, this means: (1) there is no corporate analog to § 752; (2) distributions of property from a corporation to a shareholder are generally taxable to the entity (and through it, to its shareholders), and contributions to a corporation can be taxable depending on the ownership interests of the contributing shareholders; (3) there are no optional basis adjustments akin to §§ 734(b) and 743(b); (4)

there is no provision equivalent to § 704(c); and (5) the flexibility for which partnership taxation is most noted is absent from subchapter S because there are no special allocations of corporate-level income and deductions. Thus, subchapter S is very different from subchapter K.

4. Note that all the members of a family are treated as a single shareholder for this purpose. § 1361(c)(1).

the subsequent year. § 1362(b).[5] Once filed, an election continues until it is revoked or the corporation ceases to be a "small business corporation."[6]

An S corporation may file a revocation of its election so long as shareholders holding more than one-half of its shares agree. § 1362(d)(1). Note that this does *not* require consent by a majority of the shareholders: if, for example, one shareholder owns 51 of the 100 outstanding shares of the corporation, then that shareholder alone has the ability to terminate the S corporation election and the remaining shareholders have no say in the matter. The revocation may specify a prospective date, although like the election itself, a revocation can be effective for the current taxable year if filed within the first 2½ months of the year.

An S corporation election will be terminated without regard to its shareholders' desires if the corporation fails to satisfy the requirements of a small business corporation. For example, if one shareholder sells her shares to several others, the total number of shareholders may exceed 100, immediately terminating the S corporation election. Similarly, a shareholder could sell her stock to an impermissible trust or to a nonresident alien, and again the S corporation election would be terminated.

It might be the case that the corporation accidentally terminates its S corporation election under § 1362(d)(2). If the corporation can convince the Internal Revenue Service that the termination was inadvertent, S corporation status can be restored without legal interruption.[7] However, the Service may require of the corporation and of its shareholders any adjustments the Service deems appropriate.

Note that the provisions governing the S corporation election plainly contemplate the possibility that a corporation will spend part of its existence as a C corporation and part as an S corporation. We will initially consider only those corporations electing to be taxed as S corporations throughout their existence; the taxation of an S corporation having a C corporation history is substantially more complex. For example, such S corporations can terminate their S corporation election by having too much passive income.[8]

---

5. However, an election filed more than 2½ months after the start of a taxable year can still be effective for that year if "reasonable cause" for the delay can be shown. See § 1362(b)(5); Rev. Proc. 2000–5, 2000–1 I.R.B. 158. In this context, "reasonable cause" likely will be found if the statutory deadline was not missed by design.

6. Once an S corporation's subchapter S election terminates, the corporation is prohibited from filing a new election for 5 taxable year years. § 1362(g).

7. See § 1362(f).

8. See § 1362(d)(3).

We will examine the issues arising from the transition from C corporation to S corporation (and from S corporation to C corporation) in Section 13.11 *infra*.

13.03 One Class of Stock. Every system of pass-thru taxation needs a mechanism for allocating the entity's income and loss among its owners.[9] The "one class of stock" requirement in § 1361(b)(1)(D) is the mechanism for allocating income among owners of an S corporation. Because an S corporation can have only a single class of stock, the corporation's income and loss can be allocated in proportion to stock ownership. Were there two or more classes of stock outstanding, each shareholder's proportionate ownership of the corporation would be difficult to define.

After much debate, regulations were issued interpreting the "one class of stock" limitation in § 1361(b)(1)(D). These regulations provide that a corporation is not treated as having more than one class of stock if "all outstanding shares of stock [of the corporation] confer identical rights to distribution and liquidation proceeds."[10] In particular, different shares may have different voting rights without violating the one class of stock requirement.[11]

Especially in closely-held corporations, shareholders often sign agreements restricting their rights to transfer their stock. For example, an employee may be required to sell her stock to another shareholder or back to the corporation if she terminates her employment. Sale and redemption agreements triggered by death, bankruptcy and divorce also are common. If a shareholder signs such an agreement, do the restrictions transform the shareholder's stock into a second, impermissible class of stock?

In general, the answer is no. Under the regulations, "[t]he determination of whether all outstanding shares of stock confer identical rights to distribution and liquidation proceeds is made based on the corporate charter, ... applicable state law, and binding agreements relating to distribution and liquidation proceeds."[12] The regulations specifically provide that these "governing instruments" do not include buy-sell agreements, agreements re-

---

9. In the partnership context, that mechanism is § 704. Most partnership income can be allocated among the partners as they see fit, subject only to the "substantial economic effect" test of § 704(b). However, to protect assignment of income concerns, partnership gain and loss arising from a variation between property basis and fair market value at the time of contribution must be allocated to the contributing partner

pursuant to § 704(c). As you may know, much of the flexibility and complexity of subchapter K has its origins in these two provisions.

10. Regs. § 1.1361–1(*l*)(2)(i).

11. This provision is found not only in the regulations but also in the statute. § 1361(c)(4).

12. Regs. § 1.1361–1(*l*)(2)(i).

stricting the transferability of shares, and similar arrangements unless (1) a principal purpose of the agreement is to circumvent the one class of stock requirement and (2) the agreement establishes a purchase price that, at the time the agreement is entered into, is significantly in excess of or significantly below the fair market value of the stock.[13] Further, bona fide agreements to redeem or purchase shares at death, divorce, disability or termination of employment are disregarded without further showing.[14]

The regulations offer several examples applying these rules. For example, suppose an S corporation enters into an agreement providing that distributions to its shareholders will be made in such proportions as to ensure that each shareholder will receive the same amount after taking into account state tax burdens. Thus, shareholders residing in Texas (which imposes no state income tax) will receive $100 per share, while shareholders in Georgia (which imposes a state income tax of as much as 8%) receive $108.70 per share.[15]

In this example, the corporation will be treated as having *more than* one class of stock outstanding because a binding agreement relating to distribution proceeds is a "governing instrument" and this governing instrument alters distribution rights such that those rights are not identical among all outstanding shares. An opposite result would be reached if the corporation declared equal distributions but then withheld differing amounts in accordance with differing state withholding laws: in this latter circumstance, the amounts withheld would constitute constructive distributions so that the total actual plus constructive dividend amount would be equal for all shareholders.[16]

As a second example, suppose an S corporation distributes 50% of its taxable income within 3 months of the close of its taxable year, and suppose further that this distribution must be made in the same proportion as the corporation's taxable income is reported. If individual A owned all 100 outstanding shares of the corporation at the beginning of the corporation's taxable year and sold 50 of those shares half way through the year to individual B, the distribution would be made 75% to A and 25% to B.

---

13. Regs. § 1.1361–1(*l*)(2)(iii)(A). These regulations further provide that agreements providing for the purchase or redemption of stock at book value or at a price between book value and fair market value will not be considered as establishing a price significantly in excess of or below the fair market value of the stock.

14. Regs. § 1.1361–1(*l*)(2)(iii)(B).

15. An 8% tax imposed on $108.70 equals $8.70, so the after-tax amount equals $100.00

16. Compare examples (6) and (7) of Regs. § 1.1361–1(*l*)(2)(v).

Does this arrangement create a second class of stock? Note that the corporate distribution is *not* made in proportion to stock ownership *as of the date of the distribution.* Although one might think that the outstanding shares do not have identical rights with respect to distributions and therefore constitute more than a single class of stock, the regulations specifically permit distributions to be made in proportion to varying stock ownership during the year so long as such distributions are made "within a reasonable time after the close of the taxable year in which the varying interests occur."[17]

You know that shareholder investment in the form of debt often offers tax advantages over investment in the form of equity. For example, periodic returns on debt (i.e., interest) are deductible to the corporation while periodic returns on equity (i.e., dividends) are not. Similarly, payments in retirement of corporate debt qualify for exchange treatment (i.e., recovery of basis followed by capital gain) while payments in retirement of corporate equity must pass the hurdles of § 302(b) to avoid taxation as dividends.

Ever seeking to protect the federal fisc, the Commissioner often asserts that shareholder debt should be reclassified (and taxed) as equity. In the context of subchapter S, the usual advantages of debt over equity disappear. Nonetheless, the Commissioner might seek to reclassify nominal debt as equity so as to challenge the very validity of the corporation's subchapter S election: if nominal debt is reclassified as equity, might it not be treated as a second class of stock which then terminates the S corporation election?

One important aspect of the regulations is that a corporate instrument not nominally classified as equity (i.e., debt, call options, and other financial instruments) will not violate the one class of stock requirement unless (1) the instrument is reclassified as equity under general principles of tax law, and (2) a principal purpose of issuing the instrument is to circumvent the rights to distribution or liquidation conferred on the corporation's outstanding shares by the governing instruments or to circumvent the limitation on eligible shareholders. Further, debt instruments owned only by the corporation's shareholders in proportion to their stock holdings (and for that reason likely to be reclassified as equity) are not treated as a second class of stock under these regulations. As a corollary, no debt held by the sole owner of an S corporation can violate the one class of stock rule.[18]

---

17. Regs. § 1.1361–1(*l*)(2)(iv).   **18.** Regs. § 1.1361–1(*l*)(4)(ii)(B)(2).

Even corporate debt failing these standards can still avoid being classified as a second class of stock if it is a written unconditional promise to pay a sum certain on demand or on a specific due date if (1) the interest due on the debt is not contingent on the corporation's profits, the payment of dividends, or the borrower's discretion; (2) the debt is not convertible into corporate equity; and (3) the debt is held only by an individual (other than a nonresident alien) or a trust or estate allowed to be a shareholder of an S corporation under § 1361(c)(2).[19] This safe harbor for "straight debt" is available even to debt subordinated to other debt of the corporation.[20] Finally, this safe harbor is available to indebtedness held by "a person which is actively and regularly engaged in the business of lending money"; that is, "straight debt" can be held by financial institutions even though financial institutions are not eligible to be shareholders of an S corporation.

13.04 Formation. There are no special rules governing the formation of an S corporation. Accordingly, we look to the general rules of subchapter C—§ 351 and related provisions—for the applicable rules.[21]

13.05 Pass–Thru of Corporate Income and Deduction. An S corporation is not a taxpayer.[22] Like a partnership, an S corporation computes its taxable income and then passes that income through to its owners. Here, those owners are its shareholders, and each shareholder reports a proportion of the corporation's income based on the shareholder's relative ownership of the corporation's outstanding shares. For example, if shareholder X owns 15 of the 100 outstanding shares of S Corp.'s outstanding stock, then X reports 15% of S Corp.'s taxable income or loss. If a shareholder's percentage of stock ownership changes during the year, the corporation's income is allocated ratably to each day of the year and then passed-thru to each shareholder in proportion to the shareholder's ownership interest on each day. § 1377(a).

The character of items of income and deduction recognized by the corporation and passed-thru to its shareholders is preserved. For example, capital gain recognized by the corporation will be reported as capital gain by the shareholders, and charitable contributions made by the corporation will be treated as charitable deductions of the shareholders.[23]

---

19. Regs. § 1.1361–1(*l*)(5)(i).

20. Regs. § 1.1361–1(*l*)(5)(ii).

21. See Chapter 2 *supra*.

22. An S corporation with a C corporation history can be a taxpayer. See Section 13.11 *infra*.

23. See § 1366(a)–(b).

The allocation of corporate income among the shareholders in proportion to stock ownership is mandatory and cannot be varied. In the partnership context, items of income and deduction can be allocated among the partners almost any way they desire, limited only by the requirement that allocations have "substantial economic effect." This flexibility is wholly missing from subchapter S. In fact, the rule that corporate income be apportioned according to stock interests does not give way even in the face of assignment of income concerns.

For example, suppose individuals A and B form S Corp., with A contributing cash of $10,000 and B contributing inventory with adjusted basis of $6,000 and fair market value of $10,000. Each receives 50 shares of S Corp. stock, so that when the inventory is sold, each will report half of the $4,000 gain realized on the sale. In the partnership arena and consonant with assignment of income concerns, pre-contribution appreciation in the contributed assets must be allocated to the contributing partner under § 704(c). Thus, in the partnership context B would be taxable on the entire gain of $4,000. In subchapter S, however, the gain is allocated between A and B in proportion to relative stock ownership.

Recognition of pass-thru income by a shareholder must increase outside (i.e., stock) basis so that the income will not be taxed twice. Similarly, recognition of pass-thru loss must decrease outside basis so that loss will not be recognized twice. This is in fact the case under § 1367(a) including treating tax-exempt income like taxable income and non-deductible, non-capitalizable expenses such as illegal bribes and kickbacks like deductions.

Of course, realized but unrecognized corporate level income should not pass-thru to an S corporation's shareholders. Rather, the income should be taken into account only when it ultimately is recognized by the corporation. For example, if an S corporation exchanges Blackacre for Whiteacre in a transaction qualifying for nonrecognition under § 1031 as a like-kind exchange, the shareholders should not increase their stock bases by any unrealized appreciation in Blackacre. Because that unrealized appreciation is carried over at the corporate level into Whiteacre, no shareholder level basis adjustment is yet appropriate.

When an S corporation recognizes income from the cancellation of indebtedness that qualifies for exclusion under § 108, the propriety of a shareholder level basis adjustment is problematic. Under § 108(d)(7), the basic nonrecognition rule of § 108(a) is applied at the corporate level as is the reduction of tax attributes rule of § 108(b). However, suspended pass-thru corporate losses (that is, losses suspended at the shareholder level by the basis limitation of

§ 1366(d)) are treated as corporate level tax attributes for applying § 108(b).

Consider the case of an S corporation that borrows $1,000,000 and then spends those borrowed proceeds in some deductible way. Because the corporate level borrowing did not increase shareholder stock basis, the corporate level $1,000,000 deduction cannot be claimed by the shareholders but instead is suspended. If the lender then forgives repayment of the loan and the corporation's income from cancellation of indebtedness is excludible by reason of the insolvency exception in § 108(a)(1)(B), should the shareholders be permitted to increase their stock basis by the excluded income, thereby unsuspending the prior deductions? In *Gitlitz v. Commissioner*,[24] the Supreme Court held that the prior deductions are in fact unsuspended. This result gives the benefit of the insolvency exception in § 108(a)(1)(B) to the shareholders of an insolvent S corporation, shareholders who may well be solvent in their own right. Congress reversed the holding of *Gitlitz* by amending § 108(d)(7) to deny a step-up in basis to S corporation shareholders for their share of the corporation's cancellation of indebtedness excluded by § 108.

The *Gitlitz* case represented the Supreme Court's attempt to apply in a consistent way a number of complex (and arguably inconsistent) statutory provisions. It is most notable for its emphasis on a plain reading of the statute in lieu of a detailed examination of the purposes underlying a particular code section and the legislative history behind it. Given the complexity of the code sections involved in *Gitlitz*, it is hard to criticize the Court's conclusion. But as part of its analysis the Court asserted that the shareholders of an S Corporation must increase their stock basis for their share of taxable, tax-exempt, *and tax-deferred* corporate level income. As to taxable and tax-exempt income, the Court plainly is correct. But as to tax-deferred income (such as the realized but unrecognized gain in a tax-free like-kind exchange), the Court's statement makes no sense and simply cannot be right; presumably this *Gitlitz* dicta will be ignored by future courts.

An S corporation's items of income and deduction are passed-thru to its shareholders on the last day of the corporation's taxable year. § 1366(a)(1). Accordingly, shareholders whose taxable years do not coincide with that of the corporation will enjoy some deferral, with the greatest deferral enjoyed by those shareholders whose taxable years end just prior to the close of the corporation's taxable year.

24. 531 U.S. 206 (2001).

Furthermore, under § 1378, an S corporation is not free to choose its taxable year. Unless the S corporation can convince the Service that it has a sufficient business purpose to justify some other taxable year, an S corporation must use the calendar year as its taxable year.[25] While this rule eliminates deferral opportunities for calendar year taxpayers, it mandates deferral for fiscal-year taxpayers beyond that enjoyed by most taxpayers. Of course, because shareholders of S corporations must be individuals[26] and individuals invariably are calendar-year taxpayers, restricting S corporation's use of fiscal years should present little real opportunity for deferral.

Pass-thru of corporate loss is limited to a shareholder's outside basis. § 1366(d). However, in this situation outside basis includes not only the shareholder's stock basis but also her basis in certain corporate debt. While the limitation of § 1366(d) operates much like § 704(d) limiting the pass-thru of partnership loss to the partner's outside basis, the § 1366(d) concept of debt basis makes the S corporation limitation considerably more complex.

13.06 Shareholder Debt and Equity Basis; Loss Limitations.

(a) Debt and Equity Basis. An S corporation shareholder can only claim his share of the corporation's pass-thru deduction to the extent of his basis in the corporation. § 1366(d). However, in this context basis includes not only the shareholder's equity basis but also his debt basis in his corporate investment. To better understand the loss limitation rule applicable to S corporation shareholders, we must first look closely at the basis consequences of a loan.

Suppose Debtor borrows $100 from Lender. To Lender, the loan is an asset. As with any asset, we can sensibly ask what the owner's basis in the asset is. Basis, of course, is the amount of cash the asset holder can receive in exchange for the asset without recognizing gain. See § 1001(a). Here, Lender can receive the $100 principle amount of the debt back from Debtor without recognizing income. Accordingly, Lender's basis in the debt must be $100. Indeed, if Lender receives less than $100 back from Debtor, Lender will be entitled to claim a deduction for a bad debt. See § 166(a)(2),

---

25. An S corporation can elect to use a fiscal year ending September 30 or later, see § 444, offering the potential of as much as three months of deferral to its shareholders. However, an S corporation making such an election is required to make a cash deposit with the govern-ment equal to the anticipated deferral, see § 7519, effectively eliminating any tax arbitrage benefit from making the § 444 election.

26. With some exceptions, see § 1361(c)(2)–(3).

a result fully consistent with ascribing a $100 basis to Lender's debt.

When Debtor uses the borrowed proceeds to purchase property, Debtor will take a cost basis in the property acquired. Thus, the effect of the loan is to give $100 of basis to both Lender and to Debtor; for Lender, basis is in the right to repayment; for Debtor, basis is in the borrowed proceeds or in property acquired with those proceeds. A borrowing transaction thus produces a doubling of total basis.[27]

For determining the extent to which pass-thru losses may be claimed on an S corporation shareholder's individual return, the shareholder may use both her equity and debt basis to absorb such losses. Equity basis is nothing but stock basis. Debt basis in this context means the shareholder's basis, if any, in loans she has made to the corporation. That is, debt basis refers to basis enjoyed by the shareholder not in her capacity as shareholder but rather in her capacity as lender. Of course, if the shareholder has made no loans to the corporation, debt basis will be zero.

Because debt basis may be absorbed by pass-thru loss, if an S corporation shareholder lends funds to the S corporation and then sells the note, the shareholder may recognize income on the sale even if the third party pays less than face value for the note. That is, the rule of § 1366(d) does not create additional basis for the lender-shareholder but only permits the lender-shareholder to shift basis from the note to the shareholder's interest in the venture.

We know that pass-thru of corporate income must increase outside basis: outside basis adjustments arising from the pass-thru of income and deduction are the linchpin of pass-thru taxation. Because there are two distinct outside bases per shareholder (one equity and one debt), we must determine how pass-thru of corporate income affects each. Subchapter S provides a simple ordering rule: if pass-thru losses have been absorbed by debt basis, subsequent pass-thru income will increase debt basis before equity basis until the debt basis has been fully restored.

For example, suppose individual A forms S Corp. by contributing $10,000 in exchange for 100 shares of S Corp. stock. In addition, A loans $40,000 to S Corp., and assume the loan is

27. More accurately, no doubling of basis occurs because Debtor has a negative basis in the debt itself. That is, Debtor will have to repay the principal amount of the debt without receiving a deduction for the expenditure. Debtor sometimes is said to have a $100 "sisab" (backward basis) in the repayment obligation to make clear that Debtor's tax relationship to the loan transaction is the inverse of Lender's relationship. For the remainder of this discussion, we will ignore Debtor's inverse basis (sisab) in the loan.

respected for tax purposes (i.e., the loan is not treated as equity). If the corporation distributes $15,000 to A, A must report $5,000 of income because the amount of the distribution exceeds A's stock basis by that amount. Of course, A will reduce her stock basis to zero.

Suppose that the corporation invests its remaining cash of $35,000 in some activity, and suppose further that this activity produces a loss of $5,000 the following year. Although A's stock basis is zero, this $5,000 may pass-thru to A because it can be absorbed by A's debt basis. That is, A will report the $5,000 loss on her individual return and will reduce her debt basis to $35,000.

If the corporation recognizes $8,000 of income the following year, that income will pass-thru to A and will increase outside basis. Because debt basis is restored before equity basis, the first $5,000 of pass-thru income increases A's debt basis from its current value of $35,000 back to its initial value of $40,000. § 1367(b)(2)(B). The remaining $3,000 of basis increase is applied to A's stock, increasing its basis from zero to $3,000. Any future pass-thru of income will increase A's stock basis *only* unless A's debt basis subsequently is reduced: debt basis can never be increased under § 1367(b)(2)(B) beyond its original value.[28]

Basis can be increased by contributing additional amounts to the corporation. Amounts that are contributed to capital, exchanged for additional stock or loaned to the corporation will increase a shareholder's basis in the stock or, in the case of a loan, the basis in corporate debt. There may be a risk though in contributing money to a corporation experiencing losses in order to pass-through the losses. To contribute $50,000 in order to pass-through $50,000 of losses (which will save less than $50,000 in actual taxes) may not be wise if the shareholder stands to lose the investment because the corporation performs poorly.

Suppose instead of buying additional stock for cash a shareholder exchanges a $50,000 note for the stock. Does the shareholder take a $50,000 basis in the stock, which would permit the shareholder an additional $50,000 of pass-thru loss, or is the basis $0? Some courts have upheld[29] the Service's position that the shareholder's basis in the stock does not reflect the note.[30] This position seems directly contrary to the Supreme Court's decision in *Crane* that the cost of property includes borrowed proceeds.[31] When a

---

28. See Regs. § 1.1367–2(c)(1).

29. See *Alderman v. Commissioner*, 55 T.C. 662 (1971).

30. See Rev. Rul. 81–187, 1981–2 C.B. 167.

31. *Crane v. Commissioner*, 331 U.S. 1 (1947).

taxpayer acquires real estate with a purchase money mortgage, the fair market value of the note given to the seller is included in basis.[32] Why should the purchase of stock be treated any differently?

While the Tax Court has upheld the Service's "$0 basis" position when a shareholder contributes his own note to the corporation, two Courts of Appeal have disagreed.[33] Although differing in their reasoning, each court concluded that a shareholder should be given basis for the fair market value of the shareholder's own note contributed to the corporation, at least when the note bears fair interest and the note represents a bona fide indebtedness of the contributing shareholder. However, one court made clear that its conclusion did not extend to the contribution of a shareholder's note to an S corporation,[34] a peculiar reservation given that the same provisions–§§ 351, 357, and 358–apply in the C and S contexts.

Suppose that instead of lending money directly to the corporation, a shareholder guarantees a $50,000 loan obtained by the corporation. Can the shareholder claim a debt basis of $50,000 which can then be used to absorb the S corporation's losses? It is often the case that lenders will insist that shareholders co-sign notes on loans made to closely-held corporations. Allowing each shareholder to claim a debt basis for the full amount of the loan or even a pro rata portion of the loan might be to allow shareholders loss deductions for amounts they might never have to lose if the lender looks to the principal-corporation for payment or if the guarantor-shareholder has a right of indemnification against the principal-corporation. On the other hand, if the shareholder is the principal or a principal debtor, then it might be appropriate to claim a debt basis as if the lender had loaned the money to the shareholder who re-loaned it to the S corporation.

Typically, courts will use a two-step process to resolve these surety/principal debtor situations.[35] First, under applicable state law a court will determine if the shareholder is a principal debtor. To the extent the debtor has a right of indemnification, it is not a principal. If the shareholder is a principal debtor, then the shareholder can claim a basis in the debt for purposes of absorbing losses incurred by the S corporation. If the shareholder is determined not

32. See, e.g., *Mayerson v. Commissioner,* 47 T.C. 340 (1966).

33. *Peracchi v. Commissioner,* 143 F.3d 487 (9th Cir.1998); *Lessinger v. Commissioner,* 872 F.2d 519 (2d Cir. 1989).

34. *Peracchi,* 143 F.3d at 494 n.16.

35. See, e.g., *Harrington v. United States,* 605 F.Supp. 53 (D.Del.1985).

to be a principal on the note, then the second step of the process gives the shareholder a debt basis only to the extent a shareholder actually makes payments on the note.

However, some courts have focused more on the economic reality surrounding the loan. If in fact the lender looks to the shareholder as the principal and the borrowing S corporation is thinly capitalized, perhaps the principal's right of indemnification against the corporation is virtually worthless.[36] In such a case, perhaps it is appropriate to allow the shareholder a basis in the debt which can be used to offset S corporation losses.[37] Or should the shareholder be bound by the legal ramifications of signing the note as a guarantor rather than a principal?

In *Estate of Leavitt v. Commissioner*,[38] a bank made a loan to an S corporation that was guaranteed by the shareholders. At the time of the loan, the corporation's liabilities exceeded its assets and the corporation was unable to meet its cash flow requirements. The loan was issued by the bank only because of the financial strength of the shareholders. When the S corporation experienced further losses, each shareholder sought to deduct his proportionate share of the loss to the extent of his basis in the stock and debt of the corporation, increased by the amount of the loan.[39] The court rejected each taxpayer's position that under general debt-equity principles, the shareholders should be viewed as borrowing the money and advancing it to the corporation (either as a debt or stock investment). In ruling against the shareholders, the court emphasized the shareholders' inconsistent behavior in claiming to be the principal debtor but at the same time not reporting interest and principal payments made by the corporation as constructive distributions.[40]

There is much to the argument that a guarantor should receive debt basis as if the bank made a loan to the shareholder followed by

36. Similarly, if a corporation is wholly-owned, should the sole shareholder's right of indemnification deprive him of a basis in the debtor? Or is it a meaningless right since the shareholder will bear the burden of repayment by decreasing the worth of his corporation? Perhaps the indemnification right does have significance where it might allow the shareholder to recover corporate assets that might otherwise be used to satisfy the claims of others against the corporation.

37. See, e.g., *Selfe v. United States*, 778 F.2d 769 (11th Cir.1985).

38. 875 F.2d 420 (4th Cir.1989).

39. It is not clear whether each shareholder increased basis by the full amount of the loan because the guarantees were unlimited or by a pro rata portion of amount loaned.

40. *Old Colony Trust Co. v. Commissioner*, 279 U.S. 716 (1929). The court assumed that a constructive distribution would be taxable to the shareholders. However, a shareholder of an S corporation receiving a constructive dividend would reduce stock basis before reporting any income. § 1368.

a loan to the S corporation. Ultimately, a guarantor is "on the line" for payment to the lender if the corporation fails to pay. That is, the test used to justify a debt basis when a shareholder makes an actual loan to the corporation could be: if the corporation defaults, will the shareholder bear the risk of loss. Should the result be different where the shareholder has made the same promise to a bank but has not advanced the proceeds? Under *Crane v. Commissioner*,[41] the Supreme Court established that basis consequences are the same to a taxpayer whether property is acquired with borrowed funds or through an actual cash outlay. Arguably, the fact that the S corporation shareholder has not made an immediate economic outlay should be irrelevant. Whether the corporation is thinly capitalized should also be irrelevant. The central question is who bears the economic risk in the event of the corporation's default. To the extent a shareholder bears the risk of loss (i.e., the bank will look to the shareholder-guarantor), a shareholder should have a basis that will allow the shareholder to claim a pro rata portion of the S corporation's loss deductions.[42]

On the other hand, in the case of a shareholder who actually makes a loan to an S corporation, there is an asset: the corporation's note that has basis in the hands of a shareholder. In the case of a shareholder who is a guarantor, there is no note to which basis can attach. Accordingly, in the absence of a major revision of subchapter S, it may be appropriate to deny a guarantor a basis for purposes of using loss deductions unless actual payment on the note is made. And in any event that is where the law now is.

(b) At–Risk Rules and Passive Loss Limitations. Concerned that taxpayers sometimes generate "artificial" deductions, Congress has enacted an arsenal of provisions to impose "better" accounting for tax purposes. Two of the more important provisions are the at-risk rules and the passive loss rules, both of which apply to taxpayers in their capacity as S shareholders.

Shareholders of an S corporation are subject to the at-risk rules of § 465 which limit losses from specified activities passed-thru from the corporation to the amount a shareholder has at risk with respect to the activity. A shareholder's amount at risk is equal to the amount of personal funds plus the adjusted basis of unencumbered property committed to the enterprise.[43] If a shareholder borrows funds and provides them for use by the corporation in an activity, the shareholder is at risk only to the extent the sharehold-

---

41. 331 U.S. 1 (1947).

42. To the extent a shareholder reduces his debt basis in taking corporate-level loss deductions, the shareholder should recognize income when the corporation pays off the loan.

43. See § 465(b)(1).

er is personally liable for repayment. If a shareholder contributes encumbered property to the S corporation, the shareholder is considered at risk for an amount equal to the basis of the asset minus any encumbrance for which the shareholder is not personally liable.[44] If the S corporation borrows money for an activity, the shareholders cannot increase their personal at-risk amount unless they are personally liable without any right of indemnification.

In an effort to discourage tax-motivated investments, Congress has attempted to limit losses from passive business activities to offsetting income from those activities rather than offsetting income from active businesses or portfolio income (e.g., interest, dividends). This layer of loss limitations applies after other limitations specified in the Code.

For example, suppose S Corp. is engaged in a publishing business, but shareholder B does not "materially participate" in the business.[45] B has a stock basis of $7,000 and a debt basis of $5,000. In year 1, S Corp. suffers a $10,000 loss. Under the subchapter S provisions, B can offset other income with the loss to the extent of B's investment in the corporation—his stock and debt bases. Accordingly, B would reduce the stock basis from $7,000 to $0 and the basis in the debt from $5,000 to $2,000. Having jumped the loss limitation hurdle of § 1366(d), B must then confront the passive loss limitation of § 469. The $10,000 loss can only be deducted to the extent B has at least $10,000 of income from passive activities. B will not be able to offset earned income or portfolio income with the loss. If B has insufficient passive income to offset, the deduction will be suspended. § 469(b). Note that the bases of B's investment in S Corp. decrease regardless of whether § 469 permits the deduction.

Section 469(c)(2) defines rental activity as passive notwithstanding the level of a shareholder's participation in the activity. An S corporation engaged in renting thus will be subject to the passive loss limitation. But if a taxpayer "actively participates"—a standard that is less stringent than material participation in a rental real estate activity, losses from the activity can be used to offset up to $25,000 of non-passive income.[46] Active participation might include activities such as approving new tenants, deciding on rental terms and approving expenditures.

---

44. Prop. Regs. § 1.465–24.

45. See § 469(h) and especially Regs. § 1.469–5(T).

46. See § 469(i). However, the $25,000 amount is reduced by 50 per-cent of the amount by which the taxpayer's adjusted gross income exceeds $100,000. § 469(i)(3).

(c) Pre–Contribution Appreciation and Related Problems. While the one class of stock rule ensures that an S corporation's income and loss will be allocated among its shareholder's in proportion to ownership interests, it plays havoc with assignment of income concerns. For example, suppose individuals X and Y form XY Corp., an S corporation, with X contributing cash of $10,000 and Y contributing Blackacre with fair market value of $10,000 and adjusted basis of $6,000. If each shareholder receives 10 shares of XY stock in exchange for the contribution, they will each report one-half of the corporation's earnings. Accordingly, if the corporation's only taxable activity is a sale of Blackacre for its current value of $10,000, each shareholder will report $2,000 of income on her individual return and will increase outside basis by the same amount. By contributing Blackacre to the corporation in anticipation of sale, Y is able to shift half of the tax to X.[47]

Assume that the corporation invests its $20,000 in Whiteacre, and that when Whiteacre increases in value to $30,000, Y sells her shares of stock to Z. Because Z is acquiring one-half of a corporation now worth $30,000, presumably Z will pay $15,000 for the shares sold by Y. If Whiteacre is subsequently sold, half of the gain will be includible to Z even though no corporate asset has appreciated since Z bought-in to the enterprise. The sale of shares from Y to Z did not so much work a shift of income as a doubling: Y was taxed implicitly on her share of the increase in value of Whiteacre when she sold her stock to Z, and Z is taxed again on that increase in value when Whiteacre is sold to a third party and the gain is passed-thru to the shareholders. Of course, this income will adjust Z's stock basis upward from $15,000 to $20,000, so Z will enjoy an offsetting loss should she sell her stock immediately thereafter. But because Y's share of gain from Whiteacre is taxed to Z upon disposition of the property by the corporation and the offsetting loss is deferred until Z sells her shares, Z loses the time value of money on that taxable gain.[48]

13.07 Family Ownership and Section 1366(e). Suppose Mother forms S Corp., an S corporation, by contributing cash of $10,000 in exchange for 100 shares. As the corporation begins to turn a profit, Mother gives some or all of the shares to her children. Because the corporation's income is taxed to its shareholders, the effect of the stock transfer is to shift some or all of the corpora-

---

47. In the partnership context, Y would be taxable on the full $4,000 of gain under § 704(c).

48. In the partnership context, this timing problem could be avoided by the partnership filing an election under § 754 so that Z's purchase of Y's interest in the venture would trigger an optional basis adjustment under § 743(b).

tion's income from Mother to her children. Does this run afoul of the assignment of income doctrine?

In general, the answer is no. Recall that income from property can be shifted by a transfer of the income-producing property.[49] The corporation's profit is just one form of income from property, and transfer of the stock is the transfer of the income-producing property. Transfer of the corporation's stock is, in general, no more abusive than a transfer of the initial $10,000 cash.

But what if the corporation's profit is derived in part from Mother's labor? For example, suppose that S Corp. is in the business of accounting, and it provides accounting services to its customer by hiring Mother, a public accountant. If Mother is paid only a small salary for her efforts, much of the value of Mother's services will be reported as corporate profit and will be passed-thru and taxed to the children.

In such circumstances, the Commissioner may reallocate some of the corporation's income back to Mother to more accurately reflect her contribution to the enterprise. § 1366(e). Indeed, if Mother has transferred all of her shares so that she is no longer a shareholder, the Commissioner may tax some of the corporation's profit directly to Mother to approximate a fair salary for her services. Section 1366(e) broadly authorizes the Commissioner to reallocate income if one member of a family is undercompensated for services or the use of capital used by an S corporation owned in whole or in part by other family members.[50]

13.08 Nonliquidating Distributions. In general, a distribution of appreciated property by an S corporation is taxed to the corporation as if it sold the property to a third-party for fair market value. That is, the corporation is taxed on the appreciation in the property at the time of distribution. § 311(a)–(b)(1). This corporate gain, like all corporate income, is then passed-thru to the corporation's shareholders at the close of the taxable year. Note, though, that no loss can be recognized on a nonliquidating distribution, and so any loss realized on such a distribution is gone forever.

The distribution can also produce gain to the distributee-shareholder, but only if the value of the distributed property exceeds the shareholder's stock basis. § 1368(b). Note that only equity basis can absorb distributions—in this context, a shareholder's debt basis is irrelevant. Consistent with this rule, the distribu-

---

49. See, e.g., *Blair v. Commissioner*, 300 U.S. 5 (1937).

50. This section is similar to, but far broader than, § 704(e)(2), a section targeted at family partnerships.

tee reduces stock basis by the value of the property distributed[51] and takes a fair market value basis in any property distributed. If the S Corporation has subchapter C earnings and profits (from a previous year in which it was not an S corporation), the shareholder-level treatment of the distribution is more complex, but we will defer that complexity until later.[52]

Because a distribution of appreciated property will produce gain to the corporation, gain that will pass-thru to the shareholders and will increase their stock bases, one might reasonably ask whether any such basis increase is available to reduce gain recognized by the distributee. For example, suppose individual X owns 50% of the outstanding stock of S Corp. with an adjusted basis of $10,000 in that stock. What are the tax consequences to X if S Corp. distributes Blackacre to X when Blackacre is worth $12,000 and has an adjusted basis to S Corp. of $8,000?

One might conclude that X recognizes $2,000 on the distribution as distributee (because the value ($12,000) of Blackacre exceeds X's $10,000 stock basis by $2,000) and is taxed on an additional $2,000 of corporate-level income (because S Corp. is taxed on the $4,000 appreciation in Blackacre, and X's share of that appreciation is $2,000). However, might it not be the case that X recognizes the $2,000 of pass-thru income *first*, so that X's stock basis is adjusted upwards by $2,000 before computing the tax consequences of the distribution to X as distributee? If true, X's stock basis of $12,000 can fully absorb the $12,000 fair market value of Blackacre, so that by this reasoning X recognizes no income beyond the $2,000 passed-thru from the corporation.

This ordering is supported by § 1368(d)(1) which provides that taxation of a distributee "shall be applied by taking into account (to the extent proper) . . . the adjustments to the basis of the [distributee] shareholder's stock described in § 1367." On the other hand, we know from § 1366(a) that corporate-level items are passed-thru to the shareholders on the last day of the corporation's taxable year. Since the corporate-level gain recognized on the distribution of property therefore is passed-thru on the last day of the corporation's taxable year, application of § 1368(d)(1) seems to imply that the shareholder-level tax consequences of a distribution are not determined until the close of the corporation's taxable year.

51. If the distributee recognizes income on the distribution because his stock basis is insufficient to absorb the full amount of the distribution, stock basis is reduced only by so much of the value of the property as was not recognized as income, § 1367(a)(2)(A), thereby reducing stock basis to (but not below) zero.

52. See Section 13.11 *infra*.

The regulations make clear, as indicated above, that the shareholder-level tax consequences of a distribution cannot be determined until the close of the corporation's tax year. As a consequence, all taxable activities of the corporation can affect the shareholder's tax treatment of a mid-year distribution. Consider the following example taken from these regulations:[53]

A, an individual, owns all 10 outstanding shares of S Corp. with adjusted basis of $1 per share. S Corp. is a calendar-year S corporation. On March 1, S makes a distribution of $38 in cash to A. For the entire year, S has net taxable income of $24. As a result of the distribution, A recognizes $4 of income computed as follows: income on the distribution equals the excess of the amount distributed [$38] over the sum of A's prior stock basis [$10] + pass-thru income from the current taxable year [$24]. Of course, A's stock basis must be reduced to zero as well. § 1367(a)(2)(A).[54]

Reconsider the example above but assume that the distribution consists of property having an adjusted basis to the corporation of $10 and a fair market value of $38. Now, the distribution will not result in any recognition to A because A's year-end stock basis, after adjustment for pass-thru income and loss, is $62,[55] and that amount is sufficient to absorb the entire $38 value of the distribution. A's stock basis will end up at $24, reflecting an increase of $52 for pass-thru income and a decrease of $38 for the distribution. See § 1367(a)(1)(A), (2)(A).

As indicated above, we treat the pass-thru of corporate-level income as occurring prior to the determination of the tax consequences attendant upon a corporate distribution. The basis impact of corporate-level deductions, though, are determined only *after* the tax consequences of distributions are computed. This rule (income before distribution, losses after) minimizes the likelihood that a corporation distribution will be taxable to the distributee-shareholder.

For example, suppose individual B owns 10 of the outstanding 100 shares of X Corp., an S corporation, with adjusted basis of $50 per share. Suppose further that B has a debt basis of $350. How will B be taxed if B receives a distribution of $250 with respect to his stock and the corporation has a net loss of $5,000 for the year?

---

53. Regs. § 1.1368–3 (ex. 1).

54. This treatment is very different from that of subchapter K. Under § 731(a), a distribution of cash to a partner is taxable to the partner to the extent the amount of cash distributed exceeds the partner's *pre-distribution* outside basis. In subchapter S, we use the shareholder's *year-end* outside (i.e., stock) basis.

55. Prior stock basis of $10 + pass-thru income of ($24 + $28), for a total of $62.

If both income and deductions were passed-thru prior to computing the tax consequences of the distribution, we would first pass-thru the corporation's loss. Of the $5,000 loss, one-tenth of $500 is allocable to B, and so B would claim a pass-thru deduction of $500 on his individual return and reduce his stock basis to $0 under § 1367(a)(2)(B). Because B's stock basis would now be $0, the distribution (received at anytime during the taxable year) would force B to recognize income of $250.

But the ordering rule of § 1368(d)(1) is reversed for deductions so that the tax consequences of the distribution are determined before the pass-thru loss. Thus, the distribution is tax-free under § 1368(d)(1) and B reduces his stock basis to $250. Then, the $500 loss is passed-thru to B, with half of the loss absorbed by B's stock basis and half absorbed by B's debt basis. That is, by treating the pass-thru loss as coming *after* the distribution, B can use his equity basis to absorb the distribution and then have his debt basis absorb the pass-thru loss.

Does the ordering rule of § 1368(d)(1) apply *item-by-item* or only on a *net* basis. For example, suppose an S corporation has $100 of income and $150 of loss for a taxable year in which it makes a distribution to a shareholder. Does the shareholder first increase her basis by $100, then determine the tax consequences of the distribution, and only thereafter reduce basis for the $150 of loss, or is the income and loss netted to a single loss of $50 so that the shareholder never increases basis but only determines the tax consequences of the distribution and then reduces basis for the net loss of $50? The answer turns on whether the items of income and deduction are "nonseparately computed" items within the meaning of § 1366(a)(2). An S corporation's nonseparately computed items of income and deduction are netted together to form a single item of income or deduction; if that net figure is income, then it increases the distributee's basis immediately before the distribution while if it is a net deduction it is taken into account immediately after the distribution. Separately stated items are passed through without any netting so that separately stated income items increase stock basis immediately before the distribution while separately stated deductions are taken into account immediately after the distribution. See Regs. § 1.1368–3 (example 2). Thus, the ordering rule of § 1368(d)(1) applies on both a net basis (as to nonseparately computed items) and on an item-by-item basis (as to separately computed items). In general, separately computed items are those having a distinct character (such as capital gains) that must be preserved as they pass through the corporation to the shareholders' individual tax returns.

13.09 Dispositions of Shares and Liquidating Distributions.

(a) Disposition of Stock Not in Redemption. The disposition of stock in an S corporation is taxed just like the disposition of stock in a C corporation. That is, gain or loss is recognized on each share based on the difference between the amount realized as compared with the shareholder's adjusted basis in the stock. § 1001. However, disposition of stock in an S corporation is more complex than disposition of stock in a C corporation because (1) the disposition affects the pass-thru of corporate-level tax items, (2) the disposition can affect the taxation of distributions made to the selling shareholder, and (3) distributions as well as pass-thru of corporate level items of income and deduction affect stock basis, so that a shareholder who sells stock of an S corporation cannot determine the amount of gain or loss on the sale until the close of the corporation's taxable year.

Disposition of shares in an S corporation will affect taxation of the corporate-level items because such items are passed-thru in proportion to relative stock ownership on a day-by-day basis. § 1377(a)(1). For example, suppose individual A owns 50 of the 100 outstanding shares of S Corp., an S corporation using the calendar year as its taxable year. On June 30, A sells 25 of those shares to individual B. If the corporation has net taxable income for the year of $2,000, A must report $750 on her individual return: $500 for six months ownership of 50% of S Corp. and $250 for six months ownership of 25% of S Corp.[56]

Suppose that A had sold all 50 of her shares in S Corp. on June 30. Now, A reports only $500 of S Corp.'s income, that being half the income for half the year. Note that it does not matter *when* S Corp. earned the income. Thus, A reports the same $500 whether S Corp. earned $1,000 in each half year or if S Corp. lost $1,000 in the first six months and then earned $3,000 in the last six months. Because corporate tax items are ratably allocated to each day of the corporation's taxable year, it does not matter when during the year the corporation accrued or received any particular item.

A shareholder who sells her entire interest in an S corporation during the middle of the corporation's taxable year might prefer that her share of the corporation's tax items not depend on corporate activities occurring after the shareholder terminates her interest in the activity. If the selling shareholder and buying sharehold-

---

56. For ease of computation, we assume that June 30 is exactly one-half of the year.

ers agree, they may elect to treat the corporation's taxable year as ending on the date of sale, with a new taxable year beginning on the following day. § 1377(a)(2). If such an election is filed, the outgoing shareholder will be taxable on her share of corporate activities occurring only on or prior to the day she terminates her interest in the S corporation. Similarly, the incoming shareholder will be taxable on her share of corporate activities occurring after the sale.

Disposition of some or all of a shareholder's stock in an S corporation also affects the taxation of distributions made to the selling shareholder prior to the sale of the stock. Recall that distributions of cash or property are tax-free to the distributee-shareholder to the extent that the amount of the distribution does not exceed the distributee-shareholder's stock basis. § 1368(b)(1). Recall also that it is the shareholder's stock basis as of the close of the corporation's taxable year which is used in this comparison, so that the shareholder's stock basis is adjusted for pass-thru items of income and deduction.

If a shareholder sells some or all of her shares during the taxable year, § 1367(a) adjustments to the basis of the transferred shares for pass-thru items of income as well as the downward basis adjustments for all prior distributions are effective immediately prior to the stock transfer.[57] To understand what this means, assume that individual A owns 40 of the 100 outstanding shares of S Corp., an S corporation using the calendar year as its taxable year. As of January 1, A owns these 40 shares with an adjusted basis of $10 per share. On June 30, A sells 15 of her 40 shares to individual C for $15 per share. During the entire calendar year, S Corp. earns $200.

To compute A's gain on the sale of the 15 shares, we must know A's adjusted basis in those shares. We begin with A's adjusted basis of $10 per share as of the beginning of the calendar year. We then increase that adjusted basis for A's share of the corporation's income. Treating June 30 as the mid-point of the year, $100 of the corporation's gain is allocated to the period from January 1 through June 30 and the remaining $100 is allocated to July 1 through December 31. Accordingly, each of the 100 outstanding shares is allocated $1 for the first half of the year, so that A's stock basis as of June 30 is increased to $11 per share. Thus, the sale of 15 shares for $15 per share yields a taxable gain of $4 per share, or $60 total gain. In addition, A must report $65 of pass-thru income for the year.

57. Regs. § 1.1367–1(d)(1).

Add now to this example the additional fact that A received a distribution of $80 sometime during the first half of the year. Now, we must adjust the basis of the transferred shares not only for the pass-thru income allocable to the pre-transfer period but also for the distribution. The tax effect of the $80 distribution is to reduce A's stock basis by $80 total, or $2 per share. Accordingly, A's adjusted basis in the shares as of the date of sale is now $9,[58] producing a taxable gain of $6 per share or $90 total. Individual A still reports pass-thru income of $65 on her individual return.

(b) Redemptions of Stock. The role played by § 302 in the context of S corporations is very different from its role in the context of C corporations. Individuals owning shares of stock in a C corporation generally seek exchange treatment when shares are redeemed because recovery of basis followed by capital gain usually is more favorable to them than dividend income. If, though, the redeeming corporation is an S corporation, distribution treatment is generally more favorable: while exchange treatment still produces recovery of basis followed by capital gain, only the basis in the shares redeemed is available to offset the amount of the distribution. Dividends from an S corporation, on the other hand, can be absorbed by a shareholder's entire stock basis.[59]

For example, suppose individual B owns 40 of the 100 outstanding shares of X Corp., an S corporation. If X Corp. redeems 20 of B's shares for $100 per share when B has an adjusted basis of $80 per share, exchange treatment will cause B to recognize a gain of $20 per share times 20 shares, or $400 total. On the other hand, if the redemption is taxed as a distribution, the entire amount distributed of $2,000 can be absorbed by B's stock basis of $3,200, so B will recognize no gain on the distribution. Of course, B's adjusted basis in his remaining 20 shares will be only $60 per share; had the transaction been taxed to B as an exchange, his adjusted basis in the remaining shares would stay at $80 per share. Thus, distribution treatment reduces the gain that B must recognize currently but at the cost of stock basis.

The effect of a redemption on the redeeming corporation does not turn on application of § 302—that section governs only the shareholder's taxation. To the corporation, a distribution in redemption of stock is simply a distribution, so that the corporation will be taxed on any gain (but not loss) in the distributed property.

58. This $9 per share adjusted basis is computed as follows: initial basis of $10 plus pass-thru income of $1 less distribution of $2 equals $9.

59. Because of the dividends-received deduction available to corporate shareholders, see § 243, redemptions from an S corporation are in some ways like dividends from a C corporation to corporate shareholders.

Of course, any gain so recognized will be passed-thru to the shareholders in proportion to their stock interests on a day-by-day basis.

(c) Liquidating Distributions. When a corporation liquidates— that is, when it distributes all of its assets to its shareholders in exchange for all of its outstanding shares—the transaction technically is a distribution in redemption of stock. However, liquidating distributions are not taxed to the shareholders under § 302 or to the distributing corporation under § 311; rather, the special provisions of §§ 331, 334(a), and 336 apply.

Consider first the corporation. Recall that nonliquidating distributions of appreciated property produce recognition of income to the distributing corporation as if the property had been sold to a third party. This taxation continues in the context of liquidating distributions, but now loss can be recognized as well. § 336(a). However, the recognition of corporate-level loss is considerably limited by the rules of § 336(d), discussed more fully in the context of C corporations.[60] As always, corporate-level recognition of gain or loss will be includible by the shareholders, § 1366, and will increase or decrease their stock basis, 1367(a).

At the shareholder level, the transaction is treated as an exchange of the stock for the distributed assets. § 331(a). As a result, gain or loss (generally capital gain or loss) can be recognized on the transaction. Often, though, the basis adjustment rules of § 1367(a) will work so that each shareholder's stock basis precisely equals the value of assets received in the distribution. In any event, the shareholder takes a fair market value basis in the distributed assets. § 334(a).

(d) Sales of Stock to a Corporate Purchaser. Suppose P Corp., a C corporation, is interested in acquiring the business conducted by T Corp., an S corporation. The acquisition can be structured either as a purchase of the assets of T Corp. followed by a liquidation of T Corp. or as the purchase of the stock of T Corp. Will these two essentially identical transaction produce identical tax results?

If P Corp. purchases the assets directly, P Corp. will acquire a cost basis in the assets. T Corp. will recognize gain and loss on the sale, with the character and amount of gain and loss dependent on T Corp.'s adjusted basis in each asset and the character of each asset in the hands of T Corp. This gain and loss will pass-thru to the shareholders of T Corp., and they will adjust their stock basis accordingly. If T Corp. then distributes the cash proceeds to the shareholders in a complete liquidation, gain or loss will be recog-

---

60. See Section 8.02(b) *supra.*

nized to the shareholders to the extent the amount of cash distributes is greater or less than their stock basis as adjusted for the sale of assets.

If P Corp. purchases the stock of T Corp. from the shareholders, the shareholders will recognize the same gain or loss as in the prior transaction, taking into account both the pass-thru gain or loss from the sale of the assets and the gain or loss from recognized on the liquidating distribution of cash. Indeed, the only difference should be in the character of that gain or loss because in the first transaction some of the gain or loss arises from disposition of the corporation's assets while in the second transaction all of the gain or loss arises from the sale of the stock.

While the shareholder-level taxation of the two transactions is similar, the corporate-level tax consequences are very different: a purchase by P Corp. of the shares of X Corp. denies P Corp. a cost-basis in the assets.[61] To be sure, P Corp. can avoid this low-basis by purchasing the assets directly, but for a variety of business reasons acquisition of the stock may be more advantageous. For example, the assets of T Corp. might include favorable leases that cannot be transferred or the assets of T Corp. might be encumbered by indebtedness that includes a due-on-sale provision.

Regulations promulgated under § 338(h)(10) respond to this problem by permitting the shareholders of an S corporation to elect to treat the sale of their stock as the sale of the corporation's assets followed by a liquidation of the corporation.[62] That is, it permits a transaction cast in the second form described above to be taxed as if it had been cast in the first form. This offers significant tax advantages to the corporate purchaser, and presumably such a purchaser will be willing to pay more for the stock if such an election is made.

A § 338(h)(10) election can be filed by the selling shareholders only if a corporate purchaser makes a "qualified stock purchase" of the S corporation's stock. In this context, a "qualified stock purchase" means the acquisition of 80 per cent or more of the S corporation's stock in a transaction fully taxable to the selling shareholders. See §§ 338(d)(3), 338(h)(3). If a valid § 338(h)(10) election is made, the stock acquisition is treated as an asset acquisition for all purposes. Regs. § 1.338(h)(10)–1(d)(9). In partic-

---

61. In addition, T Corp.'s election to be taxed as an S corporation terminates because the corporation now has an impermissible shareholder. See §§ 1361(b)(1)(B); 1362(d)(2). As a result, the former S corporation becomes a C corporation; the consequences of such a transitions are discussed more fully below. See Section 13.11 *infra.*

62. See Regs. § 1.338(h)(10)–1, especially Regs. § 1.338(h)(10)–1(e) (example 10).

ular, if the S corporation was once a C corporation, the transaction can trigger application of the tax on built-in gains under § 1374.[63] The regulations also permit the shareholders to report their gain on the installment method if the they sold their stock for an installment obligation of the purchaser. Regs. § 1.338(h)(10)–1(d)(8).

13.10   Qualified Subchapter S Subsidiaries

An S corporation can own 100% of the stock of a "qualified subchapter S subsidiary," defined in § 1361(b)(3)(B) to mean a corporation that otherwise is eligible to be an S corporation but whose stock is owned by an electing S corporation. If the S corporation elects for its subsidiary to be treated as a qualified subchapter S subsidiary (sometimes called a "Q–Sub"), then for tax purposes the Q–Sub loses its independent status; instead, all of its assets are treated as owned directly by its parent S corporation. § 1361(b)(3)(A). For this reason, a Q–Sub is referred to as a "disregarded entity" or a "tax nothing."

Note the difference in the stock ownership of an S corporation and a Q–Sub: while the shareholders of an S corporation generally must consist exclusively of noncorporate individuals, the only permissible shareholder of a Q–Sub is an S Corporation. However, if the actual shareholder of a Q–Sub is a disregarded entity, we look through that entity to its parent for tax purposes. Thus, S Corp., an S corporation, can own 100% of the outstanding shares each of Daughter Corp. and Son Corp., two Q–Subs, and then Daughter and Son can each own one-half of the outstanding shares of GrandChild Corp., yet another Q–Sub. In this way, Q–Subs can be used to form complex corporate structures.

For example, suppose an S corporation has two risky businesses as well as substantial investment assets. If the business and investment assets are held by a single corporation, the investment assets are potentially available to creditors of the risky businesses. If, though, the risky businesses are each placed in a separate Q–Sub, the investment assets are protected from the claims of the risky businesses and each of the risky businesses is protected from the other.

Suppose S Corp. runs two businesses, risky business and secure business. The shareholders of S Corp. would like to insulate the assets of secure business from those of risky business. However, the assets of risky business are encumbered by loans that do not permit transfer of the risky business assets until the loan is fully repaid.

63.   See Section 13.11(a)(2) *infra.*

How can the shareholders of the S corporation accomplish their purpose?

Transfer of the assets of secure business to a Q–Sub will not work because that will leave the assets of secure business (in the form of the Q–Sub stock) at risk. Transfer of the assets of the risky business would work but cannot be accomplished under the terms of the loan agreement. However, the shareholders of S Corp. can form a new S corporation and then transfer their stock of the existing S corporation to the newly formed corporation. Thus, the operating corporation becomes the subsidiary, and a Q–Sub election is immediately filed. Finally, the assets of secure business are transferred to the Q–Sub's parent (that is, to the newly-formed S corporation) in a state-law dividend. For tax purpose, though, this final step is ignored because the Q–Sub's assets are treated as owned directly by its S corporation parent. Thus, the state law dividend is a non-transaction for tax purposes and has the non-tax effect of protecting the assets of secure business from the risks associated with risky business. For a wealth of planning opportunities using Q–Subs, see Michael S. Lux & Scot A. McLean, The IRS Clears the Air on S Corporation Subsidiaries—Proposed Regulations Under Code Sec. 1361(b)(3), J. Passthrough Entities July–August 1998, at 29.

While an election to be taxed as an S corporation will not be effective until the corporation's next taxable year unless filed within the first 2½ months of the corporation's taxable year, § 1362(b), a Q–Sub has more flexibility: an election can be made at any time, and it can be effective immediately. Regs. § 1.1361–3(a)(2)-(3). Indeed, if shareholders of an existing C corporation wish to elect S corporation in the middle of the year, they can transfer their C corporation stock to an S corporation and then cause the (now subsidiary) C corporation to become a Q–Sub. See the example in Regs. § 1.1361–3(a)(4). Of course, if the S corporation is formed solely for this purpose, the Commissioner might challenge the transaction under § 269 or the general business purpose doctrine. See Regs. § 1.1361–4(a)(2).

The S corporation parent of a Q–Sub can revoke the Q–Sub election at any time. Regs. § 1.1361–3(b)(1). It also can revoke the election up to 2½ months retroactively. Regs. § 1.1361–3(b)(2). This retroactive revocation has no counterpart for the S corporation parent.

A Q–Sub election will be terminated if the corporation ceases to be an eligible entity. § 1361(b)(3)(C). This has a parallel for the S corporation parent. § 1362(d)(2). Indeed, if the S corporation parent ceases to be an S corporation, the Q–Sub will immediately loses its status as a Q–Sub. See § 1361(b)(3)(B)(i). Perhaps more importantly, the Q–Sub will lose its status as a Q–Sub if a single share of its stock is transferred from the parent S corporation to any person or entity including a transfer of less than 100% of the Q–Sub stock to another S corporation. *Id.* In all cases, the effect of a termination is to cause the assets owned by the former Q–Sub to be treated as if transferred to a new corporation in exchange for its stock. § 1361(b)(3)(C).

If an existing C corporation elects to be treated as a Q–Sub, the C corporation is treated as distributing all of its assets to its S corporation parent in a liquidating distribution. In general, this deemed distribution will be tax-free to both the (deemed liquidating) C corporation as well as to its S corporation parent under §§ 332 and 337. Regs. § 1.1361–4(a)(2). However, the regulations add that "[t]he tax treatment of the liquidation or of a larger transaction that includes the liquidation will be determined under the Internal Revenue Code and general principles of tax law, including the step-transaction doctrine." *Id.* For example, if control of the C corporation is obtained by the S corporation in a transaction that otherwise qualifies as a "B" or a "D" reorganization, the transaction will taxed under the reorganization provisions and not as a simple § 332 liquidation. See Regs. § 1.1361–4(a)(2)(ii) (examples 2–3).

13.11   Transition Issues.

(a) From C Corporation to S Corporation. An existing C corporation can elect S corporation status so long as it satisfies the requirements set forth in § 1361(b) relating to maximum number of shareholders (75), maximum number of classes of shares outstanding (1), etc. As discussed above,[64] an election under § 1362 will be effective for the corporation's next taxable year unless the corporation wishes the election to be effective for its current taxable year and the election is filed within the first two and one-half months of the year. Once the election becomes effective, the corporation becomes subject to the provisions of subchapter S and is taxed as described previously. However, because the corporation has a C corporation history, it is subject also to some special subchapter S rules.

1. SHAREHOLDER TAXATION OF DISTRIBUTIONS. In general, profits earned by a C corporation are taxed twice, once when earned by the corporation and a second time when distributed to the corporation's shareholders. However, not all distributions from a C corporation

---

64. See Section 13.02 *supra.*

to its shareholders are taxable dividends: distributions exceeding the corporation's earnings are treated as a return of the shareholder's capital to the extent of the shareholder's stock basis, with any excess taxed as gain from the sale or exchange of shares of stock.[65] Every C corporation must maintain an "earnings and profits" account, and distributions will be taxed as dividends only to the extent of this account.

When an existing C corporation having a positive earnings and profits account elects S corporation status, there is the potential for tax avoidance. Distributions of post-election earnings should be passed-thru tax-free to the shareholder-distributees but distributions out of the corporation's pre-election earnings and profits account should be taxable as dividends under subchapter C's regime. Section 1368(c) adopts a pro-taxpayer rule: distributions are, in general, assumed to be out of post-election earnings to the extent of such earnings; only after all post-election earnings have been exhausted are distributions treated as coming from pre-election earnings and profits. To keep track of the corporation's post-election earnings, the statute defines an "accumulated adjustments" account (often called the "AAA" account, or simply the "triple A") which must be maintained by each S corporation having a positive C corporation earnings and profits account.[66] This AAA account reflects, with one modification, the corporation's post-election undistributed earnings.

Recall that distributions of S corporations having no C corporation history are taxed to the distributee-shareholders under § 1368(b). Under this provision, the distribution is tax-free to the extent of the shareholder's stock basis, with any excess taxed as gain from the sale or exchange of shares. This same provision applies to S corporations having a C corporation history only if the corporation has no C corporation earnings and profits. As discussed above, if the corporation has positive C corporation earnings and profits, distributions are taxed to its shareholder-distributees under § 1368(c).

Look closely at the three tiers of § 1368(c). Tier 1, § 1368(c)(1), provides that distributions to the extent of the corporation's accumulated adjustments account are taxed under § 1368(b); that is, such distributions are taxed like all distributions made by S corporations lacking C corporation earnings and profits. Tier 2, § 1368(c)(2), provides that distributions in excess of a corporation's accumulated adjustments account are taxed as dividends to the extent of the corporation's C corporation earnings and

---

65. See § 301(c).   **66.** See § 1368(e)(1).

profits account. Tier 3, § 1368(c)(3), applicable to distributions to the extent they exceed *both* the corporation's accumulated adjustments account *and* the corporation's earnings and profits account, provides precisely the same rule as tier 1, namely taxation under § 1368(b) as if the distribution had been made by a corporation having no earnings and profits.

Consider the following example. X Corp. files an S corporation election effective January 1, 2004. As of that date, X Corp. has C corporation earnings and profits of $10,000. All outstanding shares of X Corp. are owned by individual J with aggregate stock basis of $12,000. During 2004, X Corp. recognizes $6,000 of taxable income and makes distributions totaling $30,000.

First, the $6,000 of post-election earnings pass-thru to shareholder J and increase her stock basis to $18,000. Second, of the $30,000 distributed to J, $6,000 is received tax-free under §§ 1368(c)(1) and 1368(b), reducing J's stock basis back to $12,000. Of the remaining $24,000 distributed to J, $10,000 is taxed as a dividend under § 1368(c)(2), reducing X Corp.'s earnings and profits to $0 and leaving J's stock basis at $12,000. The remaining $14,000 is taxed under §§ 1368(c)(3) and 1368(b), so that $12,000 is received tax-free and $2,000 is taxed as gain from the sale or exchange of J's shares, with J's stock basis reduced to $0.

If X Corp. should recognize, say, $2,000 of income in 2005, it can then distribute up to that amount tax-free under § 1368(c)(1) because recognition of income increases the corporation's accumulated adjustments account. Indeed, if X Corp. earns $2,000 in 2005 and distributes less than $2,000 in that year, X Corp.'s accumulated adjustments account will remain positive and can absorb distributions in subsequent years.

An S corporation's accumulated adjustments account can be reduced below zero by corporate losses. For example, suppose Y Corp. has earnings and profits of $10,000 and accumulated adjustments of $7,000. If the corporation distributes $5,000, that amount is treated as a distribution of pass-thru income under § 1368(c)(1) and reduces Y Corp.'s accumulated adjustment account down to $2,000. If the corporation recognizes a taxable loss of $5,000 in the next year, the accumulated adjustments account is reduced to negative $3,000, so that any distribution during this year will be taxed as a dividend to the extent of the corporation's $10,000 earnings and profits. Further, if the corporation earns only $1,000 in the following year, the accumulated adjustments account remains negative (i.e., negative $2,000), so again tier 1 is unavailable to shelter distributions. That is, if the corporation distributes $1,000 during that year, the full $1,000 will be taxed as a dividend.

Even though the corporation distributes no more than it earns during the year, the distribution will be taxable to its shareholder-distributees.

Recall that tax-exempt income of an S corporation increases its shareholders' stock bases so that tax exempt income will not be taxable when distributed or upon disposition of the shares. Despite this, tax-exempt income does *not* increase an S corporation's accumulated adjustments account. To understand what this means, consider the following example.

Z Corp. files an S corporation election effective January 1, 2004. As of that date, Z Corp. has earnings and profits of $5,000. All of the outstanding shares of Z Corp. are owned by individual M with aggregate adjusted basis of $12,000. During 2004, Z Corp. recognizes no taxable income or loss but receives tax-exempt income of $1,000. In addition, Z Corp. distributes $500 to M.

Under § 1367(a)(1)(A), the tax-exempt income increases M's stock basis to $13,000. However, the tax-exempt income does not increase Z Corp.'s accumulated adjustments account, so that account remains at $0. Thus, the entire distribution is taxed under § 1368(c)(2) (i.e., under tier 2) as a dividend to Z and reduces the corporation's earnings and profits account to $4,500. M's stock basis remains at $13,000.

Do not conclude from this example that the tax-exempt income received by the corporation will be taxed as a dividend to M. It will not be: all post-election income of the corporation will be received by M tax-free under the pass-thru/basis adjustment mechanism of §§ 1367(a)(2)(A) and 1368(b)(1). When a corporation has both pre-election earnings and profits as well as post-election income, an ordering rule must be used to determine if distributions are deemed to come first out of the pre-or post-election accounts. Section 1368(c) provides that ordering rule.

Recall that the effect of the three tiers in § 1368(c) is to provide that distributions are assumed to come first out of the accumulated adjustments account and only after that account is exhausted out of pre-election earnings and profits. Because post-election tax-exempt income does not go into the corporation's accumulated adjustments account, distributions will be deemed to come out of pre-election earnings and profits before they are assumed to come out of post-election tax-exempt income. Distributions out of post-election tax-exempt income still come out tax-free to the shareholders but under tier 3 rather than under tier 1 as does post-election taxable income. That is, distributions out of post-election tax-exempt income get the same treatment to the shareholders as does post-election taxable income, but such distributions are deemed to be made *last*, after the accumulated adjustments account and the earnings and profits account are depleted. Because post-election tax-exempt income does not increase the corporation's earnings and profits account, its distribution will not result in additional dividend income.

If the shareholders of an S corporation having C corporation earnings and profits desire, the ordering rule of § 1368(c)(1)-(2) can be reversed, so that distributions are assumed to come out of earnings and profits before the accumulated adjustments account. This election can be made on an annual basis and requires the consent of all shareholders receiving a distribution during the year. § 1368(e)(3). Because the effect of such an election is to accelerate dividend income to the shareholders, it rarely is made. However, certain disabilities sometimes are imposed on an S corporation that has C corporation earnings and profits, and these disabilities can be avoided by distributing out the corporation's earnings and profits.

2.   CORPORATE-LEVEL TAX ON BUILT-IN GAINS. Suppose a C corporation owns substantially appreciated property. If this corporation sells the property and then distributes the proceeds, two taxes will be owed: one on the corporate-level gain and a second on the shareholder-level dividend. If the corporation sells the property and then files an S corporation election, both taxes are still incurred: the first as a C corporation and the second upon eventual distribution because of § 1368(c)(2). But suppose the corporation files an S corporation election before selling the property. So long as the election is effective *prior to* sale of the property, the corporation's gain will not increase its C corporation earnings and profits account because the gain will be recognized *after* the corporation's earnings and profits account is closed by the election.

To inhibit corporations from electing S corporation status only to avoid the double tax on appreciated property, Congress enacted § 1374. This section, applicable during the first 10 years of the corporation's S corporation existence,[67] imposes an annual tax equal to the corporation's "net recognized built-in gain" for the year multiplied by the highest corporate income tax rate (currently 35%). This tax can be understood only by working though the definitions in § 1374(d).

Look first at § 1374(d)(1). A corporation's "net unrealized built-in gain" equals the excess of the fair market value over the adjusted basis of all corporate assets–including zero-basis intangibles such as goodwill and customer lists–owned by the corporation

---

67. See § 1374(d)(7).

when its S corporation election becomes effective. "Net unrealized built-in gain" is thus fixed in amount once the election becomes effective and need not be recomputed each year.

As the corporation sells or exchanges the assets it held when its S corporation election became effective, its built-in unrealized gains and losses becomes realized and recognized. Built-in gains and losses will also be recognized as a cash-basis S corporation collects on its accounts receivable and makes payments on its accounts payable. During each of the corporation's first 10 taxable years as an S corporation, we compute the excess, if any, of its recognized built-in gains for the year over its recognized built-in losses, and this excess is called its "net recognized built-in gain." As you might expect, post-election appreciation does not contribute to the computation of "built-in gain,"[68] and post-election reduction in value does not add to "built-in loss."[69] These amounts, adjusted for certain items of income and loss, are then netted to form the corporation's "net recognized built-in gain" for the year.

The § 1374 tax is then imposed on this amount, subject to the limitation that if the corporation's total taxable income for the year is less than its "net recognized built-in gain" for the year, the tax is imposed only on the corporation's total taxable income. This limitation should come into play only if the corporation recognizes a net loss for the year, excluding recognition of its built-in gains and losses. However, if this limitation applies, the amount of the corporation's "net recognized built-in gains" which escape the § 1374 tax is carried forward to the next year.[70] Thus, all of the corporation's built-in unrealized gain should eventually be subject to the § 1374 tax unless the corporation holds property for more than 10 years after its S corporation election becomes effective or has net losses for the same period. Note that an S corporation can also reduce its liability under § 1374 if it has net operating loss carryforwards from its years as a C corporation: such NOLs can be claimed against the § 1374 tax on built-in gains. § 1374(b)(2).

If an S corporation is subject to the § 1374 tax on built-in gains, the amount of the tax so imposed is treated as a loss of the corporation for the year in which the tax is imposed. § 1366(f)(2). As a result, the amount of the tax is passed-thru to the corporation's shareholders like any other corporate loss, with the character of the loss determined by reference to the built-in gains upon which the § 1374 tax was imposed.

---

68. See § 1374(d)(3).

69. See § 1374(d)(4).

70. See § 1374(d)(2)(B).

3. RECAPTURE of LIFO Benefits. Many taxpayers find it advantageous to account for inventory on a last-in, first-out (LIFO) basis, an accounting convention generally permitted by the Code. See generally § 472. However, upon the conversion of a C corporation using LIFO status to an S corporation, an immediate tax is imposed on the net benefit obtained by using LIFO accounting as compared with the more conservative first-in, first out (FIFO) accounting. § 1363(d)(1). While this additional tax can be paid over four years, § 1363(d)(2), the tax burden it imposes can be so large as to eliminate the conversion as a viable opportunity.

4. DISABILITIES ASSOCIATED WITH PASSIVE INVESTMENT INCOME. Consider the case of a C corporation having substantial earnings and profits when its S corporation election becomes effective. Because of the ordering rule of § 1368(c), the shareholder-level tax on those earnings will be deferred until all post-election taxable income has been distributed. Congress apparently feels this deferral is inappropriate if the corporation amounts to no more than an incorporated pocketbook: if the corporation invests too much of its funds in passive investment income, it will be subject to a special corporate level tax and can even lose its status as an S corporation. Note, though, that these passive investment income rules apply only to S corporations having C corporation earnings and profits so that they can be avoided by distributing out the earnings and profits before or after the election is effective. Of course, if the earnings are not fully distributed before the S corporation election becomes effective, the disabilities imposed on excess passive investment income can be applicable until the earnings and profits are fully removed. To expedite distributions of its earnings and profits, an S corporation can elect under § 1368(e)(3) to treat its distributions as coming first out of its earnings and profits rather than out of its accumulated adjustments account.

i. Corporate Tax on Excessive Passive Income. Section 1375 imposes a tax on an S corporation having C corporation earnings and profits if its "net passive income" exceeds 25% of its gross receipts for the year. The definition of "net passive income" is in §§ 1375(b)(2)–(3) and 1362(d)(3)(D) and includes, in general, the corporation's gross receipts from royalties, rents, dividends, interest, annuities as well as gains from the dispositions of capital assets less any deductions properly allocable to these items. "Excess net passive income" is then defined by reference to a complicated formula in § 1375(b)(1).

Consider the following example. Z Corp. is an S corporation having C corporation earnings and profits. During the current taxable year, the corporation has passive income of $50,000, deductions attributable to passive income of $10,000, and total taxable gross receipts of $100,000. (Assuming the corporation has no other deductions, its taxable income thus equals $90,000, although we do not need to know the corporation's taxable income to compute the tax under § 1375.)

Under § 1375(b)(1)(A), we have:

$$\frac{\text{excess net passive income}}{\text{net passive income}} \;=\; \frac{\text{excess passive income}}{\text{passive income}}$$

where "passive income" and "net passive income" have already been defined and "excess passive income" (a term not used in the Code) means the extent to which the corporation's passive income exceeds 25% of the corporation's gross receipts. Here, passive income equals $50,000, net passive income equals $50,000 minus $10,000, or $40,000, and excess passive income equals $50,000 minus 25% of $100,000, or $25,000. Accordingly, we have:

$$\frac{\text{excess net passive income}}{\$40,000} \;=\; \frac{\$25,000}{\$50,000}$$

Therefore, the "excess net passive income" in this example equals $40,000 times one-half, or $20,000. The tax under § 1375 is then imposed on this amount at the highest corporate income tax rate (currently 35%), for a total tax of $7,000.[71]

Unlike the § 1374 tax on built-in gains, this tax is not imposed unless the corporation has positive C corporation earnings and profits. Suppose the shareholders of an S corporation believe their corporation lacks earnings and profits and so they allow the corporation to invest most or all of its funds in passive-income producing assets. Suppose the IRS then audits the corporation with respect to a taxable year prior to the effective date of the corporation's subchapter S election. If this audit should yield so much as one dollar of additional corporate income for that earlier year, the shareholders will discover their corporation is now subject to the § 1375 tax. To be sure, had they known of the additional subchapter C earnings, they would have distributed them out of the corporation. But not knowing of these earnings until much later, they now find themselves trapped.

Section 1375(d) responds to the unfairness of this situation. If the shareholders cause the corporation to distribute out the unan-

---

71. The corporation's excess net passive income under § 1375 cannot exceed the corporation's taxable income, § 1375(b)(1)(B), although for this purpose the corporation's taxable income is computed without allowance for any net operating loss deduction under § 172 and the deductions in §§ 241–250 (excluding the deduction in § 248 for organizational expenditures).

ticipated C corporation earnings and profits within a "reasonable" time after the unanticipated earnings and profits are discovered, the government can waive the § 1375 tax. Of course, if the corporation has a positive accumulated adjustments account, an election under § 1368(e)(3) may be necessary and the shareholders' prior determination that the corporation lacked C corporation earnings and profits must have been made in good faith. If the § 1375 tax is not waived, it reduces the amount of the corporation's passive investment income passed-thru to the corporation's shareholders. § 1366(f)(3).

ii. Forced Termination of S Corporation Status. While the corporate-level tax imposed by § 1375 on excessive passive investment income received by S corporations having subchapter C earnings and profits should encourage S corporations with minor amounts of earnings and profits to distribute out their earnings and profits or reduce their receipt of passive investment income, those corporations willing to pay the § 1375 tax face an even greater burden. Under § 1362(d)(3), if an S corporation having subchapter C earnings and profits has passive investment income exceeding 25% of its gross receipts for three consecutive years, the corporation's election as an S corporation is terminated. As with § 1375, "passive investment income" is defined to mean gross receipts from "royalties, rents, dividends, interest, annuities, and sales and exchanges of stock and securities," § 1362(d)(3)(D)(i), with some exceptions, see § 1362(d)(3)(D)(ii)–(iv).

Because the forced termination in § 1362(d)(3) is so easy to avoid, it rarely is operational. However, because its impact is so severe, one should be certain to avoid it. As with the corporate-level tax in § 1375, the forced termination under § 1362(d)(3) applies only to corporations having C corporation earnings and profits. Accordingly, S corporations lacking a C corporation past can simply ignore § 1362(d)(3), and S corporations having a C corporation past can render § 1362(d)(3) inapplicable by electing under § 1368(e)(3) to treat its distributions as coming first out of its C corporation earnings and profits.

4. No Carryover from C Year to S Year. If a C corporation incurs capital losses in excess of its capital gains, the excess may not be deducted but instead is carried back or forward to a taxable year or years in which excess capital gains are recognized. §§ 1211(a), 1212(a). Similarly, if a C corporation incurs operating deductions in excess of taxable income, the excess is carried backward or forward as a net operating loss deduction. See § 172. However, in no event may an excess capital loss, a net operating loss, or any other carryover, be carried from a year in which a

corporation is a C corporation to a year in which the corporation is an S corporation. § 1371(b)(1). Note that no carryover of any kind can originate in any year when the corporation is an S corporation. § 1371(b)(2). As a result, there are no carryovers from S years to C years *or* from S years to other S years. Unused corporate losses may be available for shareholder use under § 1366(d)(3).

(b) From S Corporation to C Corporation. A corporation's status as an S corporation can terminate by revocation under § 1362(d)(1), by the corporation failing to meet the standards of § 1361(b), see § 1362(d)(2), or by receipt of excessive passive investment income if the corporation has C corporation earnings and profits, see § 1362(d)(3). Regardless of the method of termination, the results are the same: if the termination is effective on a date other than the last day of the corporation's taxable year, the taxable year is divided into two short taxable years.[72] The first short taxable year ends on the day preceding the date of termination of the S corporation's election, § 1362(e)(1)(A), and the second short taxable year begins on the following day, § 1362(e)(1)(B). By this mechanism there is no taxable year during which the corporation is sometimes an S corporation and sometimes a C corporation. The two short years together are sometimes referred to as the "S termination year." § 1362(e)(4).

Recall that when a corporation having subchapter C earnings and profits becomes an S corporation, distributions out of pre-S corporation earnings and profits are taxed as dividends while distributions out of post-S corporation earnings are taxed as a return of basis. See § 1368(c). When an S election terminates, a similar issue arises because distribution of pre-termination earnings should be taxed as basis recovery while post-termination distributions should be taxed as dividends. Unfortunately, the rule is not so simple.

Under § 1371(e)(1), post-termination cash distributions will be treated as made out of pre-termination S corporation earnings to the extent of the corporation's accumulated adjustments account. All other distributions will be taxed under § 301, the provision generally applicable to distributions from C corporation. However, an important limitation on § 1371(e)(1) is that its benefits extend only to cash distributions made during the corporation's "post-termination transition period," and that usually extends one year from the effective date of the corporation's termination of its S

---

72. A termination under § 1362(d)(3) for excessive passive investment income necessarily is effective on the first day of the corporation's taxable years. § 1362(d)(3)(A)(ii). Terminations under § 1362(d)(1) by revocation and under § 1362(d)(2) by ceasing to be a small business corporation can be effective on any day of the corporation's taxable year. See §§ 1362(d)(1)(C), 1362(d)(2)(B).

corporation status. See § 1377(b). Distributions made after the close of the post-termination transition period will be subject to § 301 even if the corporation's accumulated adjustments account has not been fully depleted, so that if the corporation has (or generates) sufficient earnings and profits, the eventual distribution of profits made during the corporation's S period will nevertheless be taxed under subchapter C's regime.

Note that post-termination gains and losses will not affect the corporation's accumulated adjustments account. In addition, post-termination distributions of property (i.e., of anything other than cash) are taxed under § 301 even though the property may have been acquired or may have appreciated while the corporation was an S corporation. Accordingly, if a corporation is contemplating changing from an S corporation to a C corporation, the early disposition of appreciated property may be warranted if sale of the property in the near future is anticipated.

Finally, recall that tax-exempt income of an S corporation does not add to its accumulated adjustments account. § 1368(e)(1)(A). In the context of a transition from a C corporation to an S corporation, this peculiarity affects the order in which corporate distributions are deemed to be out of C corporation earnings and profits or out of S corporation earnings. When the transition is the other way, though, the exclusion of tax-exempt income from the corporation's accumulated adjustments account has a more dramatic impact: post-termination distribution of the tax-exempt income will always be taxed under subchapter C's § 301. This arises because the relief offered by § 1371(e)(1) to post-termination distributions of S earnings extends only to the extent of the corporation's accumulated adjustments account. Because tax-exempt income does not go into the accumulated adjustments account, its distributions are unprotected by § 1371(e)(1).

While the transition from S to C status brings little tax relief, there is one positive aspect. If the corporation had a prior C history, and if there is a surviving net operating loss from that earlier C period, it can be used by the corporation in its reincarnation as a C corporation. While § 1371(b)(1) prohibits carryovers from C years to S years, there is no prohibition on carryovers from C years to C years, even if several S years are sandwiched in between. However, those S years count for determining if the carryover has expired. § 1371(b)(3).

While S corporation losses generally pass-thru to the shareholders, § 1366(d)(1) limits the pass-thru to the extent of a shareholder's stock and debt basis. If a corporation's status as an S corporation terminates, any losses suspended by application of § 1366(d)(1) can be claimed by the affected shareholders in the following year only, subject to the limitation that such losses cannot exceed their stock basis then. § 1366(d)(3). Of course, any losses so claimed must reduce stock basis, § 1366(d)(3)(C), just as they would were subchapter S applicable in full, see § 1367(a)(2)(B).

TABLE OF CASES

References are to Pages.

359

TABLE OF CASES
References are to Pages.

TABLE OF CASES
References are to Pages.

*